JESUS THE SPIRIT BAPTIZER

Jesus the Spirit Baptizer

Christology in Light of Pentecost

FRANK D. MACCHIA

WILLIAM B. EERDMANS PUBLISHING COMPANY
GRAND RAPIDS, MICHIGAN

Wm. B. Eerdmans Publishing Co.
4035 Park East Court SE, Grand Rapids, Michigan 49546
www.eerdmans.com

27 26 25 24 23 22 21 20 19 18   1 2 3 4 5 6 7 8 9 10

ISBN 978-0-8028-7389-7

Library of Congress Cataloging-in-Publication Data

Names: Macchia, Frank D., 1952– author.
Title: Jesus the Spirit baptizer : Christology in light of Pentecost / Frank D. Macchia.
Description: Grand Rapids : Eerdmans Publishing Co., 2018. |
    Includes bibliographical references and index.
Identifiers: LCCN 2018020961 | ISBN 9780802873897 (hardcover : alk. paper)
Subjects: LCSH: Pentecost. | Jesus Christ—Person and offices. | Holy Spirit.
Classification: LCC BT123 .M1515 2018 | DDC 232—dc23
    LC record available at https://lccn.loc.gov/2018020961

In memory of my Doktorvater, *Jan Milič Lochman (1922–2004),*
for whom the Christus fundamentum *was vital to*
the entire Christian witness in the world

Contents

Preface

Writing a Christology with Pentecost at the horizon has at least implicitly been a goal of mine ever since I became convinced, nearly fifteen years ago, that Spirit baptism was the root metaphor in the New Testament for the entire Christian witness to Jesus Christ as Lord. I vividly recall that, while writing my book *Baptized in the Spirit: A Global Pentecostal Theology* (Zondervan, 2006) during 2004–2005, I found myself fundamentally disagreeing with Wolfhart Pannenberg's near exclusive focus on Jesus's resurrection as the culminating point of his identity and mission. It occurred to me that Jesus's impartation of his risen life—and not merely the risen life per se—was the culminating act of his victorious life, and it was most clearly indicative of his essential unity with the Father and with the leading of the Spirit in fulfilling the Father's cause in the world. But at that point I had not developed my criticism of Pannenberg's method fully enough to state it clearly. It was not until my next major study, *Justified in the Spirit: Creation, Redemption, and the Triune God* (Eerdmans, 2010), that I began to focus more explicitly on my interest in the Christ of Pentecost. The chapter on the atonement in that second book suggests how we might view the crucifixion and resurrection of Christ in the light of Pentecost. It was during my work, shortly thereafter, on the concluding fragment of Karl Barth's *Church Dogmatics* (IV/4) that I fully realized that Christ's entire mission may be viewed as a baptism in fire (culminating in the crucifixion) and a baptism in the Spirit (culminating in the resurrection)—not two separate baptisms, mind you, but one in Spirit-and-fire for our redemption.

Pentecost is the culminating event of Christ's identity and mission, because he is to baptize in the Spirit and fire, as John the Baptist announced. Christ is baptized in the Spirit and fire so that he can similarly baptize all flesh. The difference is that his fire was the alienation of sin and death, while those taken up in his Spirit baptism, incorporated into him, experience only the sanctifying fire of the Spirit's renewal. While other theologians, such as James D. G. Dunn, Walter Kasper, and Edward Schillebeeckx, have suggested viewing Pentecost as the culminating point of Christ's identity and mission, my desire has been to write an entire Christology developing that point. The result is this present volume. I offer it as part of a larger conversation, of which I feel privileged to be a part.

FRANK D. MACCHIA

Acknowledgments

I wish to offer heartfelt gratitude to my wonderful wife, Verena, who stood by me throughout this project, offering support and wisdom. I cannot adequately express my life with her in words. As for my colleagues, many have stimulated my thinking on Christology over the years. Gratitude belongs especially to Amos Yong (Fuller Theological Seminary) and Dale Irvin (New York Theological Seminary). I also wish to thank Vanguard University for the much-needed sabbatical that allowed me the time to write this book, and especially to the Religion Department for supporting it. Southeastern University in Lakeland, Florida, and the Barth Center at Princeton Theological Seminary granted me valuable opportunities to offer insights from my research during public lectures that I offered in both locations. I finally wish to thank Eerdmans for believing in this project and for sharing my enthusiasm for it from the beginning. May Christ be glorified in what I write about him in the pages that follow.

Introduction

"He received it as man, he poured it out as God."

—Augustine, *De Trinitate* 15.46

"God has raised this Jesus to life, and we are all witnesses of it. Exalted to the right hand of God, he has received from the Father the promised Holy Spirit and has poured out what you now see and hear. For David did not ascend to heaven, and yet he said:

> "'The Lord said to my Lord:
> "Sit at my right hand
> until I make your enemies
> a footstool for your feet."'

"Therefore, let all Israel be assured of this: God has made this Jesus, whom you crucified, both Lord and Messiah."

—Acts 2:32–36

The above text tells us that Jesus, on the Day of Pentecost, as the anointed Messiah and exalted Lord, poured out the Holy Spirit from his heavenly Father. According to the previous chapter in Acts, Jesus did this to "baptize" others in the Spirit in order to empower the Christian movement toward the fulfillment of God's cause in the world (Acts 1:5–8): "For John baptized with water, but in a few days you will be baptized with the Holy Spirit . . . and you will be my witnesses" (1:5, 8).[1] Indeed, all four Gospels feature John

1. Scripture quotations are taken from the New International Version unless otherwise noted.

the Baptist, Jesus's chief forerunner, as announcing that Christ will baptize others "in the Holy Spirit and fire" (Matt. 3:11; Mark 1:8; Luke 3:16; John 1:33). It is interesting to note that Luke does not mention the baptism in "fire" in Acts 1:5. Could this be because Christ had already borne the fire of condemnation and death for them (the baptism of his death in Luke 12:50)? He endured this fire on the cross so that he, raised and exalted, could fulfill his mission by baptizing them in the Spirit of life and holiness. Through this Spirit baptism, humanity fulfills its destiny "to glorify God and enjoy him forever"[2] as vessels of God's Spirit and in union with the Spirit-anointed Son, Jesus Christ our Lord.

In pouring forth the Spirit, Christ also fulfills his destiny to be our Lord and elder brother. The exalted Christ's bestowal of the Spirit at Pentecost is the culminating point of Christ's mission on earth and is thus a valuable lens through which to view the chief questions of Christology—and to answer them: "Who is Jesus Christ in relation to God? Is he truly divine? Who is Christ in relation to humanity? Is he truly human? How do we understand his work and his ongoing significance in the light of his identity? In the above text, Christ is exalted as "Lord and Messiah" in order to pour forth the Spirit upon all flesh. The exalted Messiah, who has received the Spirit, is also the Lord who pours forth the Spirit to all flesh. What does this act tell us about Christ's person and work?

In his commentary on the above passage, St. Augustine claims that Christ showed his humanity by receiving the Holy Spirit on our behalf, and he showed his deity by pouring forth the Spirit upon us:

> How then can he who gives the Spirit not be God? Indeed how much must he who gives God be God? None of his disciples ever gave the Holy Spirit; they prayed that he might come upon those on whom they laid hands. . . . He received it as man, he poured it out as God.[3]

Augustine thus uses Pentecost to answer the central questions of Christology in a new light. Rather than using Augustine's terms concerning Christ and the Spirit—"received it as a man" and "poured it out as God"—one could speak of Christ, in line with John the Baptist, as the one who will be baptized in the Spirit in order to baptize others in the Spirit. John foresaw

---

2. Quoting the Westminster Catechism.

3. Augustine, *De Trinitate* 15.46, trans. Edmund Hill (Hyde Park, NY: New City Press, 1991).

the coming of a messiah who would mediate a "river" of the Spirit into which he would "baptize" others unto restoration or judgment (depending on how people responded). John the Baptist witnessed to the Spirit's descent on Christ, and he heard the Father's declaration that Christ is the beloved and favored Son (Matt. 3:16–17; Mark 1:10–11; Luke 3:22; John 1:33). Jesus was himself being baptized in the Spirit in order to baptize others in the Spirit, implicitly in union with him and his cause in the world. This event of Christ's Spirit baptism at the Jordan River harks back to Jesus's conception by the Spirit as the holy Son of God in Mary's womb (Luke 1:35), and within the broader context of the New Testament, it looks ahead to the declaration of Christ's sonship through his resurrection by the Spirit from the dead (Rom. 1:4). It is from this victory over sin and death that the Spirit-baptized Messiah can baptize others in the Spirit at Pentecost (imparting the Spirit of life and holiness to them as Lord). Indeed, in bearing the Spirit for us, Christ also endured our baptism in fire on the cross so that, by rising victoriously from the dead, he could open the path to the Spirit for us—the path of union with him and of communion with the Father. In union with him, the fire baptism becomes a sanctifying force because of his victory over sin and death. In him we are joined to the Spirit, and in the Spirit we are joined to him. "And if anyone does not have the Spirit of Christ, they do not belong to Christ" (Rom. 8:9). Joined to him in the Spirit, we are also joined to his mission in the world.

Augustine's remark that Jesus received the Spirit as human but poured out the Spirit as God is an important point of departure for us; but, at the very outset, it requires some qualification. We are not to take from Augustine the notion that one can separate the two natures of Christ, divine and human, strictly along the line of the reception and impartation of the Spirit. All that Jesus did, he did as the divine-human Christ, one person in two distinct but inseparable natures. Furthermore, Christ's reception of the Spirit is not only indicative of his humanity. As I will have occasion to note below, the Son enjoyed the communion of the Spirit precisely as divine and from all eternity. In this light, Christ's reception of the Spirit in his lifetime revealed his divine life as well as his human life.[4] Second, Christ's impartation of the Spirit did not merely involve his deity: though it was indeed a divine act—for, as Augustine says, only God can impart God—it was also carried out through Christ's faithful and exalted human-

---

4. See Thomas Weinandy, *The Father's Spirit of Sonship: Reconceiving the Trinity* (Eugene, OR: Wipf and Stock, 2011).

ity. That is, Jesus did not simply bear the Spirit as something external to his embodied life so that he could then pass this Spirit on to us; rather, Christ bore the Spirit as a transformative reality that shaped his embodied life as well as the Spirit's ongoing work in history. The Spirit is now the "Spirit of Christ," with the final goal of shaping people into Christ's faithful and exalted image. And Christ is now the elder brother ("firstborn son") of the new creation, who is joined to him by the Spirit (Col. 1:15). In imparting the Spirit, he imparts himself to us as the Son, granting us access to his heavenly Father and to his Father's cause in the world. At Pentecost, Jesus's Spirit-baptized humanity becomes the sacrament or word in which we are united to Christ, and in him we share in God and God's mission in the world.

Hence, we should qualify the Augustine quote to say that Jesus bore the Spirit *and* imparted the Spirit to others as Jesus Christ our Lord, divine and human. But Augustine still had a valid point: we can make the case that Christ's baptism in the Spirit and fire focuses chiefly (though not exclusively) on his taking on human flesh for us, and his impartation of the Spirit to others draws attention chiefly (though not exclusively) to his divine lordship. Christ did indeed receive the Spirit as flesh in order to impart that Spirit as the sovereign Lord of life. With some qualifications, this statement can function as the key insight of a Christology that honors Jesus's incarnation as both the divine Son (Logos Christology) *and* Jesus as conceived and anointed in his human life by the Spirit (Spirit Christology).

The significance of the outpouring of the Spirit in the above quotation from Acts 2:32–36 is the fact that Christ's mission on earth is not complete until that moment when he opens his Spirit-baptized life to creation by fulfilling the Father's promise to impart the Spirit to all flesh. "I am going to send you what my Father has promised" (Luke 24:49). Christ does not fulfill the human obligation to glorify God only by offering his obedient life on the cross for us and then rising up vindicated and sanctified in the Spirit. Though pivotal, the events of crucifixion and resurrection are set in the Gospel narratives (and beyond) within a larger history of Christ's journey in the Spirit to redeem and renew humanity. He must give of himself to the Father's cause in the world by fulfilling the Father's promise to creation to pour forth the Spirit of life to all flesh (Acts 2:17–21; Joel 2:28–32). Luke ends his Gospel narrative with Christ's announcement that he will do precisely this (Luke 24:49), and he begins his Acts narrative with a striking description of his act of doing so. This is no mere addendum to Christ's mission, nor is it an entirely new act in the drama of the messianic mission; it is the beginning of Act Two, but it is also the *culmination* of Act One. This Spirit's outpouring is a christological act (and as such a triune act), one that John the Baptist tells us is key to the *messianic mission.*

This event of baptizing others in the Spirit reveals Jesus's unity with God, for it is in this act that Christ imparts the Spirit in unity with the Father and does so in a way that also reveals his essential unity with the Spirit. Jesus's unity with God must be displayed in relation to both the Father *and* the Spirit, for the Spirit is also divine. Why doesn't the resurrection of Jesus by the Spirit reveal this? It actually does—in part. This unity is most fully revealed (for now), however, at the point where God self-imparts to creation in such a way as to take the creation into the divine embrace, not just representatively—ultimately in the cross and the resurrection—but actually at the point of the impartation of the Spirit to all flesh. This is because the Son's mission includes his self-giving to the Father and the Spirit's cause in the world. This mission is thus not yet fulfilled through his act of representing us in his journey to the cross and resurrection, but also as he extends himself to us at Pentecost. God is the self-imparting God who overflows the barriers of sin and death so as to take humanity into the divine embrace. Christ shows himself to be essentially one with this God at Pentecost. Likewise, Christ's unity with humanity is not only shown at the resurrection, where the faithful Son who descended into human alienation at the cross was vindicated and exalted by the Spirit. Christ's unity with us is also shown at Pentecost, where he binds us by this same Spirit to his embodied life and destiny out of love for us. Isn't his very humanity that is given to us at the cross and vindicated in the resurrection fully revealed when he actually binds *others* to himself, to his faithful and exalted embodied life? Christ is indeed the Spirit Baptizer. It is what he came to be, what he is, and what he will be fully revealed when he returns: the Christ of the new Creation, in union with him by the Spirit and in glory to the heavenly Father.

The story of Christ is thus ongoing. Acts 1:1 characterizes the Gospel of Luke as depicting all that Christ "began to do and to teach." In the text from Acts 2 quoted above, Christ's pouring forth of the Spirit thus reaches for the time when the Father makes Christ's enemies a footstool for his feet (2:35). But for now, the culminating point of Christ's work and self-disclosure occurs here, where Christ reigns as Lord and, as the Lord of life, imparts his Spirit to a fallen and dying world. Pentecost as the decisive disclosure of Christ's identity is also the experiential beginning for those called to follow him. This is where we first encounter Christ: where we confess him as Lord by the Spirit to the Father's glory (1 Cor. 12:3; Phil. 2:11). He calls us to himself and unites us to him by baptizing us in the Spirit. It is for this purpose that he joined himself to flesh and went to the cross. Into him, "we were all baptized by one Spirit so as to form one body—whether Jews or Gentiles, slave or free—and we were all given the one Spirit to drink" (1 Cor. 12:13). The effects of this incorporation into Christ and into his body of believers are felt throughout life as we continue to "drink" of the Spirit and partake of Christ in dramatic moments of Spirit filling, sanctification, communion, worship, and witness, leading all the way to mortal existence being "swallowed up by life" at the resurrection (2 Cor. 5:4). This is the eschatological horizon of our baptism in the Spirit, our ultimate participation in Christ and the love of the Father. The church is born and has its ongoing life in the outpouring of the Spirit and in union with Christ the Spirit Baptizer. The church can do Christology only because Christ, on that fateful Day of Pentecost, imparted himself to creation in this way. Christ's identity as the Spirit Baptizer joins him in his very identity to an ever-increasing diversity of brothers and sisters. But his ongoing identity is faithful fundamentally to his sojourn on earth as the one baptized in the Spirit and fire on our behalf. This is how he continues to give himself to us in a diversity of ways. It may be said of Peter's sermon quoted above in Acts 2:32–36, "In bringing the story of Jesus to the time of Jesus' pouring out the Spirit, Peter has not only revealed the complete source of the audience's existence, but also the final revelations of who this Jesus is who brought this experience about."[5]

The purpose of this book is to view all of the events of Christ's life and mission through the lens of their fulfillment at Pentecost. Each event will be recognized for its own unique and forceful contribution to the story of Jesus; but Pentecost, as the culmination of the story, will be granted a privileged place as the horizon toward which the story's trajectory is directed. The basic plan is as follows. The book has three parts, with two major chapters in each part. Part 1 will deal with the task of Christology: Chapter 1 with Christological method and Chapter 2 with additional challenges that needed to be overcome in pursuing the task of Christology historically. Part 2 will then explore Christ's incarnation (Chapter 3) and anointing at the Jordan River (Chapter 4). Part 3 finally covers the climactic moments of his death and resurrection (Chapter 5) and Pentecost as the place from which we look

---

5. John J. Killgallen, "A Rhetorical and Source-Traditions Study of Acts 2.33," *Biblica* (January 1, 1996): 196.

with hope for his return (Chapter 6). Though I will proceed chronologically from incarnation to Pentecost, I will seek throughout to understand each step through the lens of what Christ does at Pentecost. It is there that he, the last Adam and the Lord of life (1 Cor. 15:45), opens himself to creation as the mediator of the Spirit from the Father. Every step we take in this Christology will honor that event.

PART 1

The Task of Christology

CHAPTER 1

Christological Method

"Christ is the starting point and measure of all Christological statements."

—Wolfhart Pannenberg, *Systematic Theology*, volume 2

As I noted in the introduction, the chief question of Christology is the identity of Jesus Christ. Who is Christ in relation to God? Is he one with God? What do we mean when we say that? Who is he in relation to humanity? Is he authentically human? And what does it mean to say *that*? What does all of this mean for us—and for our destiny? The attempt to answer such enormously important questions must follow a disciplined path of discovery. The specific question of this chapter is about how we might fruitfully proceed along this path. What should our approach be? That is the specific question of *christological* method. On a personal level, we first encounter Christ through the word of the gospel as it is given to us through some aspect of the life of the church. The church is the social base of our encounter with Christ; the revelation of Christ in the church's life is the place where we naturally begin our personal quest for the meaning of Christ. We are awakened to Christ as Lord by the Spirit through the word, and are incorporated into him by faith under the sign of water baptism (1 Cor. 12:13); and together we seek, through various core practices—such as preaching, the Lord's Supper, worship, fellowship, and mission—to discern his identity and way in the world. The social base of the church is particularized by varying social and historical contexts in which churches live and have their being; but it is also united by one faith and one baptism, the one Lord into whom we are all incorporated by the Spirit (Eph. 4:1–6). The Christ who encounters us is the Christ self-imparted to us at Pentecost, the Christ who opens space in himself for this increasingly diverse body.

All of this implies that our personal encounter with Christ in the world has its anchor in something deeper than our shared experience. The Spirit Baptizer at Pentecost has his own history that he opens to us, indeed, that he has opened to us from the beginning of that history. How he gives of himself to us now—and how we faithfully discern that in the Spirit—will be guided by that history. Here I refer not only to the basis of that history in Old Testament Scripture, leading up to Christ's coming into the world, but specifically to the events of Christ's mission on earth: incarnation; anointing at the Jordan River; life ministry; death, resurrection and ascension; and the pouring forth of the Spirit on the Day of Pentecost. In this chapter I want to emphasize that Pentecost is the *culminating event* of that history. Christ imparts the Father's love and himself as Lord and elder brother of the new humanity by pouring forth the Spirit on all flesh on the Day of Pentecost (Acts 2:33-36). Thus Pentecost locates Christ's mission most clearly within the larger mission of the triune God. At this event, he most clearly reveals the objective basis of Christology; simultaneously, he opens up our shared personal life in him. I wish to propose here that Pentecost be viewed as the *focal point* of christological method.

Of course, all the events of Christ's life and work are crucial to understanding his identity. But the point of fulfillment still arguably has a privileged place in our understanding of the whole. This issue, however, must be handled with care. I agree with Karl Barth that the events of scriptural revelation are a "bird in flight" (I would add that they are sent by the Father and carried by the wind of the Spirit).[1] Surely this insight applies to the events of Christ's life and mission. It is thus impossible to capture this bird through human thought, which means that it is also difficult to focus this question of Christ's identity so overwhelmingly on one event in the story that the others are not granted their own unique force and significance. However, John the Baptist, Christ's chief forerunner according to all four Gospels and Acts, implicitly points to Pentecost (where the bird has landed, so to speak) as especially significant to an understanding of Christ's identity and mission. He witnessed the Spirit's descent on Christ at his baptism, and he knew that Christ would be the one to "baptize" people in the Spirit. Spirit baptism is John the Baptist's shorthand description of Christ's messianic

---

1. Karl Barth, *Evangelical Theology: An Introduction* (Grand Rapids: Eerdmans, 1992), 9–10.

mission (Matt. 3:11–12; Luke 3:16; Mark 1:8; John 1:33; Acts 1:5). Christ will bear the fire of judgment in order to impart the Spirit as a sanctifying rather than destructive force to us all.

A Christology from Below

The dominant tendency in the early centuries of the Christian era was not to focus on Pentecost (which is what I will propose). The classical Christology of the creeds concentrated instead on the incarnation, where the divine Word (Logos), or Son of the Father, became flesh for our salvation (Luke 1:35; John 1:14). The christological method that focuses on the incarnation is thus metaphorically called a *Christology from above*. Because of its focus in the church's early centuries on the divine Word (Logos) of the Father coming down into flesh (John 1:14), it is also called a "Logos Christology." Though it is to be appreciated for its insights, however, the classical christological method "from above" is potentially problematic. A concentration on the incarnation as the point of departure in discerning Christ's identity runs the risk of assuming that Christ's divine and human "natures" were to be viewed as parallel realities, abstract from each other and joined together by the divine initiative. This assumption has led to two problems. First, a separate analysis of divine and human natures that were defined each in abstraction from the other led to an overemphasis on their opposition. God was thought to be unchanging and immune to suffering, while human nature changes and suffers. These assumptions are not to be dismissed out of hand; indeed, such differences between the Creator and the creation do exist. They help us see the depth of divine love and the beauty of the paradox involved in this infinite love revealed in human weakness. But the paradox tells us something about this divine love (its excessive reach) and something about this humanity (fulfilled in its reception by the grace of this reach). In other words, without this mutually illuminating insight into what incarnation actually tells us about "deity" and about "humanity," a one-sided concentration on abstract differences between them can lead to the tendency to uphold the incarnation only by lessening the full deity or the full humanity—as though one can only touch the other if one is compromised in the process. As we will see, some will attempt to maintain the integrity of both natures by keeping them separate, even during the incarnation itself.

For example, in the fourth century, Arius could not imagine the true God as coming into flesh or suffering on a cross, so he felt compelled to regard Christ as less than fully divine (called subordinationism because Christ is essentially subordinated to the Father). Not long afterwards, Apollinaris could conceive of the incarnation only by lessening Christ's humanity, denying that Christ had a soul (others, who were defenders of Christ's deity, did the same). Earlier, the Gnostics even denied that Christ was human. For them, Christ only appeared to be human (a heresy called "docetism").[2] Does preserving Christ's humanity mean lessening his deity, or does preserving his deity lessen his humanity? The problem here is not the use of "natures" in discussing Christ: rather, the problem is discussing these natures as separate things that can be defined apart from each other as a prelude to discussing them in union through incarnation. God is not an object that can be defined apart from the divine self-disclosure as the principle of freedom and redemption for all of reality! Any true definition of the incarnation is only possible from the vantage point of the incarnation itself, from the vantage point of the *entire span* of Jesus's life in the flesh. It is only from this revelation that we can know what deity and humanity are. Barth wrote of God that the "meaning of his deity . . . cannot be gathered from any notion of supreme, absolute, non-worldly being. It has to be learned from what took place in Jesus Christ."[3] The deity revealed in the incarnation is a deity that is divine precisely in *taking on flesh and going to the cross* so as to impart life to dying humanity. A humanity that is revealed in the incarnation is a humanity that is human precisely by being *incarnated by the Son so as to be exalted by the Spirit* in communion with God.

The second problem of assuming that Christ's divine and human "natures" are to be viewed as parallel realities is that the "Christology from above" tended to concentrate almost exclusively on the relationship of the Son to the heavenly Father. What about the relationship of Jesus to the Holy Spirit? As I have noted, the Holy Spirit is divine, too. If Jesus is fully divine, he is one in essence with both the Father and the Spirit. The Spirit was involved in the incarnation (Luke 1:35); the divine Son takes on flesh *by the Spirit*. This fact opens the incarnation to a history that leads to the Jordan River and to the Spirit's anointing of Jesus there for a far-reaching purpose. The divine Son will bear the Spirit in order to do what only the divine Son could do,

2. Docetism comes from the term *dokein,* which means "to appear."

3. Karl Barth, *Church Dogmatics,* IV/1: *The Doctrine of Reconciliation,* ed. G. W. Bromiley and T. F. Torrance (Edinburgh: T & T Clark, 1956), 177. I am grateful to Christophe Chalamet for drawing my attention to this quote in "No Timelessness in God: On Differing Interpretations of Karl Barth's Theology of Eternity, Time and Election," *Zeitschrift für dialektische Theologie,* Supplement Series 4 (January 1, 2010): 34.

namely, die in our place and conquer death through resurrection, so as to impart the Spirit to all flesh at Pentecost. At Pentecost the heavenly Father imparts the Spirit to all flesh through the mediation of the faithful Son. As divine, the Son can impart the Spirit; as human, the Son does this through the sacrament of his faithful and glorified (vindicated) flesh. A Christology from above that focuses on the incarnation is correct to emphasize the issue of Christ's divine and human identity; there is a place for focusing on this great event of incarnation. But the question of Christ's essential unity with the Father must include the Son's essential unity with the Spirit, who is also essential to the Father's cause in the world—the Father's promise to the world. This fact makes it impossible to understand the incarnation without the lens of Jesus's history in bearing and imparting the Spirit on behalf of the Father. Incarnation has an *eschatological* horizon and purpose. Adoptionism, which saw Jesus as only a Spirit-anointed man (and not divine in nature), betrays this history, this eschatological horizon, for only a divine Son can impart the Spirit he bears to all flesh. The incarnation is thus important as an anchor to Jesus's anointing at the Jordan. But the *importance of the Spirit to Christ's identity* makes it impossible to understand the incarnation apart from Pentecost.

Therefore, the Christology from above required qualification in the light of Jesus's actual history as man of the Spirit devoted to the Father's cause in the world. Starting especially with *The Quest of the Historical Jesus*, Albert Schweitzer's 1906 classic, two developments in the modern era came together to suggest a way forward toward appreciating this history.[4] The first was the new modern emphasis on the historical Jesus, an attempt to understand Jesus as having a life that is human in every way, especially as set within his own Jewish context, an emphasis that Schweitzer took from Hermann Reimarus. Schweitzer, in fact, made Reimarus a leading figure in his book (15–26). This methodological trend was necessary. But in celebrating it, Schweitzer assumed that it would devastate the Christological dogma of the incarnation as affirmed in the creeds. He noted that early modern quests for the historical Jesus would provide the historian with a break from classical Christology, which, caught up as it was with the incarnation, "cut off the last possibility of a return to the historical Jesus." For Schweitzer, therefore, "dogma had first to be shattered before people could once more go out in quest of the historical Jesus." In fact, the Jesus of history would become "an ally in the struggle against the tyranny of dogma" (5).

---

4. Albert Schweitzer, *The Quest of the Historical Jesus* (Minneapolis: Fortress, 2001), 14–26. Hereafter, page references to this work appear in parentheses within the text.

However, the effort to provide objective portraits of Jesus was easier said than done. Schweitzer notes that each epoch of attempts to re-create the true historical Jesus "found its own thoughts in Jesus; that was, indeed, the only way in which it could make him live." Indeed, "each individual created Jesus in accordance with his own character" (6). The role of personal bias, however, did not doom historical investigation into the life of the man Jesus. Schweitzer's book is filled with appreciation for the insights that were discovered about Jesus's human life in the context of his Jewish setting. But Schweitzer had no illusions about the difficulty involved in separating one's historical reconstruction from one's own "dogmatic" assumptions about the results of this historical inquiry, even if they would be different from the dogma of the incarnation emphasized in the classical creeds of the church.

The second modern development that suggested a new way forward for the christological method was the rise in the attention paid to eschatology for understanding Jesus's identity and mission. Schweitzer praised Reimarus here once again: "If old Reimarus were to come back again," Schweitzer says, "he might confidently give himself out to be the latest of the moderns, for his work rests upon a recognition of the exclusive importance of eschatology" (10). But it was Johannes Weiss who would best capture this emphasis. Jesus emerged in this modern research as an apocalyptic prophet who awaited the coming kingdom of God to earth. Armed with this insight, Schweitzer responded to various efforts at writing portraits of the historical Jesus by noting that they typically neglected Jesus's role as an end-time prophet who lived for the inauguration of God's kingdom. Taking note of Jesus's eschatological expectation also served to contextualize him, bringing to grander fulfillment Reimarus's early concentration on Jesus's ancient Jewish context. Schweitzer closed his discussion with William Wrede, whom he criticized for neglecting eschatology in his understanding of the historical Jesus. Interestingly, Schweitzer himself viewed Jesus's eschatological hopes as having been permanently crushed at the time of his crucifixion, though Schweitzer regarded Jesus's courage as laudable (303–14).

In reading Schweitzer's famous book, one is struck with the impression that the future of Christology lies in a renewed appreciation for the historical Jesus, especially his typically Jewish apocalyptic devotion to the future reign of his heavenly Father over the world. But if, as Schweitzer believed, Jesus's eschatological hopes were crushed at his crucifixion, what really was the cash value of his devotion to the kingdom of his heavenly Father? If Jesus's entire identity is caught up in devotion to the Father's coming reign—and this expectation is dashed against the rock of the crucifixion—what is left of Jesus's identity? What is left of Christology? Not much.

But what if Jesus's kingdom expectation was not ultimately crushed? What if, as the gospel tells us, it led to resurrection and to his vindication as indispensable to the victory of God over sin and death? What would *that* imply concerning Christ's identity? This is the prominent question that preoccupied Wolfhart Pannenberg in his classic *Jesus—God and Man*.[5] Though not written predominantly with Schweitzer's challenge in mind, this book answers Schweitzer in a way that arguably does justice to both classical dogma and the historical Jesus. Pannenberg agrees that Jesus viewed his entire life and mission as given over to the coming reign of the Father, but he follows the witness of the New Testament in believing that this expectation was vindicated at the resurrection with some very fruitful results for Christological method.

It would be helpful, as we unpack Pannenberg's method, to begin with his recognition that research on the subject of the historical Jesus had shrouded Jesus's self-understanding during his lifetime in a certain amount of ambiguity. After the release of Schweitzer's classic study, historical-Jesus research took a skeptical turn, especially in Germany, which became apparent by the mid-twentieth century in the work of Rudolf Bultmann. Bultmann helpfully sought to understand the Gospels from the vantage point of the proclamation of the churches that contextualized their writing. But this contextualization of the Gospels raised the question of how much of what they tell us is reflective of what Jesus actually said and did. Moreover, a certain ambiguity as to what Jesus knew about his own identity and mission was also taken for granted in the context of historical skepticism. But Bultmann was not significantly concerned about such problems, since for him Jesus's legacy was to be found precisely in the proclamation of the churches that originally formed the substance of the Gospels and of the entire New Testament. For Bultmann, the early proclamation of the churches reflected in the New Testament was how Jesus "rises" from historical obscurity to speak to us in subsequent generations. How much of this proclamation actually goes back to the historical Jesus is not the crucial question, especially since historical investigation—as uncertain as it is—can never be an adequate foundation for how he continues to speak to us through the proclamation of the gospel. Of the relative failure of older attempts to objectively capture the historical Jesus, Bultmann says:

---

5. Wolfhart Pannenberg, *Jesus—God and Man* (Philadelphia: Westminster, 1978).

Historical research can never lead to any result which could serve as a basis for faith, *for all its results have only relative validity.* How widely the pictures of Jesus presented by liberal theologians differ from one another! How uncertain is all knowledge of the "historical Jesus"! Is he really within the scope of our knowledge? Here research ends with a large question mark—and here it *ought* to end.[6]

It is not that, for Bultmann, we cannot know anything reliable about the historical Jesus. There were several general lines of inquiry that were reasonably certain for him. Especially in the light of Schweitzer's work, Bultmann was convinced that earlier efforts to write a biography of Jesus that captured his unique "personality" were doomed to failure; what matters is Christ's address to us in the proclamation: "The decisive thing is his person (not his personality), *here* and *now*, the event, the commission, the summons."[7] The crucial point for Bultmann is that Christ in the flesh is the Word of the Father and lives on in the Christian proclamation as received by faith.[8]

Pannenberg inherited an element of skepticism about what could be established historically about Jesus—skepticism, I should add, that has more recently been balanced to a significant degree by great gains in historical scholarship on Jesus by giants in the field such as Raymond Brown, James D. G. Dunn, and N. T. Wright.[9] Still, the New Testament gives us an incomplete picture of Jesus's actual historical life and personality. Ambiguity in terms of the historical picture of Jesus remains. There are tensions within the Gospels that must be recognized. However, this ambiguity does not prevent us from responding to the diversity of the New Testament witness to

6. Rudolf Bultmann, *Faith and Understanding*, vol. 1 (New York: Harper and Row, 1966), 30.

7. Bultmann, *Faith and Understanding*, 1:284.

8. A helpful, sympathetic treatment of Bultmann may be found in James F. Kay, *Christus Praesens: A Reconsideration of Rudolf Bultmann's Christology* (Grand Rapids: Eerdmans, 1994).

9. Note, e.g., Raymond Brown, *The Birth of the Messiah: A Commentary on the Infancy Narratives of Matthew and Luke* (New Haven, CT: Yale University Press, 1999); Raymond Brown, *The Death of the Messiah: From Gethsemane to the Grave*, 2 vols. (New Haven, CT: Anchor Bible Edition, 1994); James D. G. Dunn, *Jesus and the Spirit: A Study of the Religious and Charismatic Experience of Jesus and the First Christians as Reflected in the New Testament* (Grand Rapids: Eerdmans, 1997); Dunn, *Christology in the Making: A New Testament Inquiry into the Origins of the Doctrine of the Incarnation*, 2nd ed. (Grand Rapids: Eerdmans, 1996); N. T. Wright, *Jesus and the Victory of God*, vol. 2 of *Christian Origins and the Question of God* (Minneapolis: Fortress, 1997); see also N. T. Wright, *The Resurrection of the Son of God*, vol. 3 of *Christian Origins and the Question of God* (Minneapolis: Fortress, 2003).

Jesus in faith, for faith is not dependent on absolute historical certainty. Bultmann overplays this point. But the element of ambiguity about the historical Jesus cannot be denied and can even be viewed as an opportunity for humble dialogue. Robert Jenson concludes that "we must carry our working picture of Jesus with a certain tentativeness—which is a theological good thing."[10] At any rate, there are lines of inquiry into the historical Jesus that have obviously been fruitful. What understandably seemed fairly certain to Pannenberg (and others) was that Jesus was wholly given over throughout his life to the coming reign of his Father. This much could be argued, even in the midst of historical skepticism.

So we are left with Schweitzer's challenge to whether or not Jesus's life of devotion to the coming reign of God was vindicated and confirmed as valid. Here is where Schweitzer stops short. But it is precisely here that Pannenberg boldly moves forward to discover the very core of Christ's identity in the vindication of his eschatological expectation. How does he do that? The kingdom of God did not, of course, visibly come to the earth, at least not in the way expected at the time of Jesus's life and mission on earth. In fact, Jesus was crucified as a blasphemer. The astounding witness of the New Testament, however, is that the blasphemers were shown to be those who crucified Jesus. God overturned the verdict of the crucifixion by raising Jesus from the dead *by the Spirit* and vindicating Christ as the faithful Son, "who through the Spirit of holiness was appointed the Son of God in power by his resurrection from the dead: Jesus Christ our Lord" (Rom. 1:4). The kingdom of God anticipated by Jesus's proclamation and life ministry did indeed come, but fundamentally in his *resurrection from the dead*, where his sonship was revealed by the Spirit. Since his entire identity was tied to his devotion to the coming reign of his Father, his resurrection not only vindicates but fully discloses that identity. The entire sojourn of Christ, from the incarnation to the cross, is thus to be interpreted in anticipation of Christ's resurrection. This is the central point of Pannenberg's christological method.

From the beginning, Pannenberg was convinced that Bultmann had missed an important point here. The early proclamation of Jesus is not itself the chief eschatological event that vindicates Jesus as being relevant to subsequent generations, as Bultmann implies. That event was the resurrection.[11]

---

10. Robert W. Jenson, "Identity, Jesus, and Exegesis," in *Seeking the Identity of Jesus: A Pilgrimage*, ed. Beverly Roberts Gaventa and Richard B. Hays (Grand Rapids: Eerdmans, 2006), 51.

11. Pannenberg, *Jesus—God and Man*, 24–25.

Pannenberg implicitly took from Barth the idea that the resurrection is in itself the eschatological proclamation of Christ as the good news for creation, the event that bears the weight of all proclamation in the church. Thus, for Barth, "there has never been a tradition about Jesus Christ which was not shaped by the reference back from His resurrection and ascension."[12] For Pannenberg, it was also the resurrection that confirmed and verified signs throughout Jesus's life that he was indispensable to the coming reign of his Father. Indeed, it seemed to Pannenberg that, at the very least, a case could be made that Jesus was eschatologically oriented and gave himself over to his heavenly Father and to the Father's coming reign. A good case could even be made that Jesus assumed unique authority in proclaiming and acting in favor of the coming reign of God, even to the point of implying his indispensability to its arrival. Whatever else could—justifiably or not—be said about the historical Jesus, at least this much was arguable. So the resurrection vindicates all of this and confirms that the man Jesus is indispensable to the reign of the Father, and thus indispensable to the divine life and cause in the world. In the resurrection, Jesus is shown to be not only human but essentially one with the Father's coming reign, which Pannenberg takes to mean essentially one with the Father, implying that Christ is fully divine.

Is Jesus's identity as divine and human determined by the resurrection? Let us unpack this point of departure more specifically. First, Pannenberg emphasizes that Jesus spent his entire life relating to his Father, "not directly to 'the Logos' as the second Person of the Trinity, but to the heavenly Father."[13] Precisely as human, Jesus gave himself over completely to the Father's coming reign in the world. This *devotion to the Father's reign* determined Jesus at the very core of his being. Second, Christ shows throughout his life that he considered his life as indispensable to the coming reign of the Father. Not only was the Father's coming reign determinative of Christ's being, but Christ considered himself indispensable to the Father's coming reign.

Third, for Pannenberg, God's reign has to do with God's lordship and is thus essential to God's very being. God is sovereign; God is Lord. God's reign is thus not just something God *does*; it is what God *is*. "The Deity of God is his rule."[14] If Christ is *determined* at his essence by the Father's com-

12. Karl Barth, *Church Dogmatics*, IV/2: *The Doctrine of Reconciliation*, trans. G. W. Bromiley (Edinburgh: T & T Clark, 1958), 136.

13. Pannenberg, *Jesus—God and Man*, 334.

14. Wolfhart Pannenberg, *Theology and the Kingdom of God* (Philadelphia: Westminster John Knox, 1969), 55. Hereafter, page references to this work appear in parentheses within the text.

ing reign, Christ is determined at his essence by the Father's very being, as God. Also, if Christ is *indispensable* to the Father's coming reign, he is also indispensable to the Father's very being as God. Christ is shown by this to be one in essence with the Father *as God*. For Pannenberg, the resurrection of Jesus is the place where his lifelong unity with the Father's coming reign as Lord is confirmed and fully revealed. At the resurrection, therefore, Jesus is shown to have always been one in essence with the Father. How else can it be? One cannot "become" in time essentially one with the Father if one were not always so. Still, this unity was eschatologically confirmed at the resurrection and is to be regarded as valid beforehand—at the incarnation—in *anticipation* of that event.

Fourth, Jesus's unity with the Father's reign or essence thus implies *indirectly*, for Pannenberg, Jesus's unity of person with the eternal Son of the Father. It is not true that Jesus spent his life pointing to the eternal Son and saying, "I am he." Rather, it is true that, by implying an essential unity with the reign or lordship of the Father, and by having that unity confirmed in the resurrection, Jesus showed himself by way of *implication* to have the same relationship with the Father that is shared by the eternal Son of the Father. Since there cannot be two sons who are essentially one with the Father (for the eternal Son of the Father is the "one and only" [John 1:18; 3:16]), Jesus is also shown at the resurrection to be, and to always have been, *the* one and only eternal Son of the Father (Rom. 1:4)! Pannenberg used Hegel to define personhood as a mode of existence characterized by self-giving love (339–41). So, the unity of person or identity between Jesus as human and the eternal Son is clear precisely at the point of Jesus's all-consuming love for the Father and devotion to the Father's coming reign. It has always been the eternal Son's person or mode of existence to be so completely given over in love and devotion to the lordship of the Father (335–36). By having this same relationship to the Father as the eternal Son has always had, Jesus is shown— by way of *implication*—to be united in person with the eternal Son (345).

Fifth, in focusing on the resurrection as the decisive event of unity between Jesus and God, Pannenberg relied on what may be called an "eschatological ontology" that envisioned the future destiny of all things as actually determining their nature from the very beginning. For Pannenberg, in a very real sense the future determines the past. This is true not only for the life of Jesus with respect to his resurrection but also, analogously, for all of reality. Only the final revelation of God's lordship over creation at the new creation will disclose the true meaning of history and the origins of nature itself. All revelation in history is dependent on that final revelation for its content. "God's revelation in history . . . has the form of an anticipation of the definitive manifestation of his eternal and omnipotent deity in the event of the consummation of all time and history."[15] Christ's resurrection is the revelation in history of that end and, as such, what determines the meaning of all that leads up to it and follows from it. For Pannenberg, the risen Christ interprets all of history, all of creation. The eschatological revelation of God at the point of the consummation of God's reign in the world—as revealed in Christ's resurrection—is, in fact, "indissolubly linked" to every other article of faith. That which anticipates the resurrection includes not only the events of Jesus's life (including his incarnation) but also, further back, creation itself. At the consummation of God's kingdom in the new creation, "God will finally be shown to be its Creator."[16] In a sense, God actualizes Godself as Creator and Lord in the fulfillment of God's kingdom in the world through Jesus Christ. Not only are we already ontologically what we shall become at the fulfillment of God's kingdom, so is God.[17] Christologically, this means that Christ's identity was established at the resurrection, but this event determined who he was from the beginning. Rather than the resurrection being the consequence of the incarnation, the incarnation is in a sense the consequence of the resurrection! Since the resurrection shows that Jesus was throughout his life indispensable to the reign and very essence of the Father as Lord, it also shows that Jesus was the incarnation of the Word of the Father in flesh. The resurrection reveals the truth of the incarnation, and the incarnation anticipates the truth of the resurrection.

Pannenberg calls his point of departure at the resurrection a Christology "from below," because the focus on the resurrection opens space for Jesus's lifelong devotion to the Father in all of its historical particularity to be revelatory of Christ's identity. Pannenberg does indeed end up at the place where the incarnation begins (Jesus's essential unity with the Father and with humanity), but this truth is understood "from below" or through Christ's entire sojourn from the incarnation to the resurrection. This is not to say that Jesus's identity as both divine and human is something that simply evolves, as if it comes into being in degrees. But we must bear in mind that this unity is indeed mediated by Jesus's human devotion, by his entire human life of total self-giving to the Father's coming reign. Pannenberg thus

15. Wolfhart Pannenberg, *Systematic Theology*, 3 vols. (Grand Rapids: Eerdmans, 1991–98), 3:531.

16. Pannenberg, *Systematic Theology*, 3:540.

17. Pannenberg, *Systematic Theology*, 2:389-96.

speaks of "the relation of Jesus to the Father and his self-subordination to the Father, which is the condition of the manifestation of the Son in him."[18] Indeed, precisely "in and because of this dedication to the Father, Jesus is identical with the person of the Son."[19] Pannenberg could even write that Christ is led personally throughout his sojourn "deeper and deeper into this identity of his person as the Son of the Father."[20] For Pannenberg, however, the question of how conscious Jesus was of his identity as the eternal Son is beside the major point of Christology, since it is the divine decision at the resurrection that is the decisive event of verification. In short, for Pannenberg, the *resurrection is the meeting place* between a Christology from below and a Christology from above.

Pannenberg offers us a provocative way of taking with utmost seriousness both the history of Jesus's human devotion to the loving reign of the Father and his identity as the Word, or Son of the Father become flesh, helping to heal the breach between historical Jesus research and dogmatic Christology. He emphasizes the fact that what gets verified at the resurrection is the only way we have of making sense of dogmatic Christology. We should not begin Christology with metaphysical assumptions imported into the incarnation from someplace outside of what is revealed in Jesus's sojourn to the resurrection. Pannenberg insists that a christological method from above that neglects Jesus's human history is closed to us, for "one would have to stand in the position of God himself in order to follow the way of God's Son into the world."[21] His attention to Christ's resurrection as the place where God verifies Jesus as the Son of the heavenly Father opens space for the history of Jesus's human sojourn on earth to play a vital role in his exaltation without settling for an adoptionism that denies Jesus's deity. What it means to talk about the unity of Jesus with God is not just assumed from the beginning of any christological discussion; it is discerned in Jesus's life-long self-giving to the lordship of the Father as vindicated and verified in the resurrection. Moreover, Pannenberg allows us to regard Jesus's path as an entirely human path and then to recognize how he was revealed at the resurrection to have also been the divine Son all along. Brilliant.

Pannenberg does not intend to say that classical Christology totally neglects the history of Jesus's devotion to the Father from below, though

---

18. Pannenberg, *Systematic Theology*, 3:387.
19. Pannenberg, *Jesus—God and Man*, 339.
20. Pannenberg, *Systematic Theology*, 3:389.
21. Pannenberg, *Jesus—God and Man*, 35.

it arguably neglects the truly human nature of that history to some extent. Nor does he intend to say that a Christology from below could stand alone, even if it is our point of departure. Walter Kasper's warning is certainly to be accepted: "A Christology purely 'from below' is therefore condemned to failure. Jesus himself understands himself 'from above' in his whole human existence."[22] Though Christ is throughout his life devoted to the coming reign of the Father, he is also aware that he has come from the Father to do the Father's will. This insight is present very strongly in the Gospel of John (e.g., John 7:29), but it is also found in the synoptic Gospels. Simon Gathercole has shown that the numerous "I have come to . . ." statements of Jesus that dot the landscape of all four Gospels (e.g., Matt. 5:17) imply that Christ came "from above," or from the heavenly Father to earth.[23] Pannenberg's methodology is not thereby nullified, since he used his christological method "from below" to address the chief question of the Christology from above, namely, Christ's unity of essence with the Father and unity of person as divine and human.

Still, legitimate questions can be raised. Pannenberg's idea that the future determines the present can be one-sided. It is important to emphasize that, though created beings may be said to be essentially what they will become, what they will become arises also from what they are becoming amid a wide range of possibilities in every present moment leading up to that culmination. Hence, analogies drawn from nature to explain the retroactive causality of the resurrection would need to grant equal weight to a causality that moves from the past toward the future (the arrow of time). Pannenberg helps us understand how the resurrection determines retroactively all that precedes these events. However, since creation was made for the resurrection, one cannot ignore that there is a teleological reach in the direction of these decisive points of confirmation as well. We need to emphasize that, just as the incarnation anticipates the resurrection, the resurrection also fulfills the incarnation. What God is proved to be in the final time of fulfillment cannot reveal an internal change in God if God's eternal immutability is to have any meaning. As Karl Rahner points out, God can *become* something wonderful *in something else*, but in doing so remains who God always is in Godself.[24]

In addition, the question that needs to be pressed is whether or not

---

22. Walter Kasper, *Jesus the Christ* (Kent, UK: Burns and Oates, 1976), 247.

23. Simon J. Gathercole, *The Pre-existent Son: Recovering the Christologies of Matthew, Mark, and Luke* (Grand Rapids: Eerdmans, 2006).

24. Karl Rahner, *Foundations of Christian Faith* (New York: Crossroad, 1982), 220.

Pannenberg's Christology from below includes an adequate theology of the incarnation. The doctrine of the incarnation will be the focus of this book's chapter 3. The question here is whether or not shifting the determinative center from the incarnation to the resurrection has removed any real notion of the eternal Son's assuming flesh upon his conception in Mary's womb.[25] The concept of eschatological anticipation requires unpacking. Does it include genuine incarnation? Pannenberg does refer to a "personal union" of the eternal Son and the embodied life of Jesus, and it is precisely through this union that God "unites himself to us."[26] For Pannenberg, there is also an "identification" of the eternal Son and Jesus in Jesus's lifelong self-giving to the Father: "The person of Jesus Christ is identical with the eternal Son."[27] Pannenberg rejects a metaphysical discussion of Christ's natures (divine and human) that treats them as separate entities in need of union. But he does regard Jesus's conception by the Spirit in Mary's womb as anticipating the resurrection, implying already a genuine identification of Jesus as the eternal Son of the Father. There do seem to be the makings here of an authentic notion of incarnation as anticipating the confirmation of Jesus's unity with God that was given at the climactic moments of his mission. This point requires further development, for a strong doctrine of the unity of person in Jesus as the eternal Son is required if Jesus is to be viewed as absolutely essential or indispensable to the Father's coming reign or cause in the world. There can be no independence of Christ's human life from that.

More to the point of my own methodological focus on Pentecost, I especially want to deal with the adequacy of describing the resurrection as the decisive moment in which Jesus is confirmed as the divine-human Son of the Father. The incarnation by the Spirit of God anticipates the resurrection only with the simultaneous anticipation of Jesus's reception of the Spirit at the Jordan. Jesus "rose" from Mary's womb, conceived by the Spirit (Luke 1:35), *and* from the waters of the Jordan River, anointed by the Spirit in order to *impart life to others* (Luke 3:22)—in order to foreshadow his later rising up from the dead to decisively impart the Spirit to all flesh. Why this rising? Paul says that Jesus rose from the dead as the last Adam who is the "life-giving spirit" (1 Cor. 15:45). The resurrection has as its immediate goal Jesus's

---

25. Roger Olson, in his early evaluation of Pannenberg's Christology, doubted that Pannenberg has an incarnation doctrine. Roger Olson, "The Self-Realization of God: Hegelian Elements in Pannenberg's Christology," *Perspectives in Religious Studies* 13, no. 3 (Fall 1986): 207–33.

26. Pannenberg, *Jesus—God and Man*, 386–87.

27. Pannenberg, *Jesus—God and Man*, 389.

bestowal of Easter life onto all flesh by imparting the Holy Spirit from the heavenly Father. Jesus's reception of the Spirit at the Jordan anticipates the risen Christ, but only because he receives the Spirit at the Jordan to baptize others in the Spirit.

In imparting the Spirit to others, Christ indwells them and incorporates them into his risen life in fulfillment of the Father's will. Christ's unity of essence with the Father and the Spirit is thus verified at the resurrection but only as fulfilled at Pentecost, where the risen Christ opens his life to the world. He rises for this purpose: he is the Spirit Baptizer. It is at Pentecost that Jesus is finally shown to be indispensable to the self-impartation of the triune God to creation. Pentecost shows his unity of essence with the Father and the Father's cause in the world. The Spirit is the promise of the Father to the world (Luke 24:49). Pentecost also shows his unity of person with the eternal Son, who bears the Spirit to mediate the Spirit to others. And it shows his essential unity with the Spirit, who proceeds from the Father through the Son in order to renew creation in the Son's image. To revise Pannenberg's argument, I wish to note that Jesus is one with the Father's lordship by pouring out the Spirit of life on a dying creation: "I will put breath in you, and you will come to life. Then you will know that I am the Lord" (Ezek. 37:6). Since the Father's and the Spirit's lordship is essential to who they are as God, Christ's indispensable unity with that lordship in pouring forth the Spirit shows him to be essentially one with the Father and the Spirit, and, by implication, to be one in person with the Son, who reigns as the Lord of life.

Walter Kasper has shown that the resurrection needs Pentecost because the resurrection itself is God's overabundant love "surpassing itself and emptying itself," not only beyond the bounds of sin and death but also of time and place.[28] For Kasper, Jesus is filled to overflowing with the Spirit so that he could bestow that Spirit on all flesh as the image of the love that the Spirit is to give to all flesh on behalf of the Father (252–59). Jesus breaks the bonds of sin and death in order to give of himself decisively to all flesh precisely by joining with the Father in pouring forth the Spirit at Pentecost. Since Jesus is conceived by the Spirit as the embodiment of the Son in flesh, his mediating that Spirit involves mediating his life to us. In that act of mediation, Christ shows himself to be essentially one with the Father as the source of divine love and the Spirit as the eschatological freedom and reach of that love in the world. As the embodied image of that faithful love, Jesus also shows himself

---

28. Kasper, *Jesus the Christ*, 190. Hereafter, page references to this work appear in parentheses within the text.

to be one in person with the eternal Word of the Father who was eternally earmarked as the mediator of the Spirit from the Father. As Kasper notes, Jesus is the "goal and measure" of the Spirit's work, and the Spirit grants that work its eschatological and universal reach (252–56). The cosmic Christ mediates salvation to all of creation through the eschatologically free Spirit. "A Christology in a pneumatological perspective is therefore what best enables us to combine both the uniqueness and the universality of Jesus Christ" (267–68). This mutual working of Son and Spirit in unity with the Father's cause in the world reaches its climax at Pentecost.

Therefore, I wish to propose that Pentecost is the decisive confirmation of Jesus's divine-human identity—rather than the resurrection alone. As Kasper implies, Christ's resurrection does not just confirm the signs from his life of his unity with the Father. As the consequence of Christ's Spirit conception and Spirit-filling, his resurrection is an overflow of the Spirit that is poured out beyond Christ at Pentecost. Out of him flow rivers of living water (John 7:38). It is through his pouring forth of the Spirit via his crucified and risen humanity that the Father's promise of excessive love was poured out on the world. "See what great love the Father has lavished on us, that we should be called children of God" (1 John 3:1). Pentecost fulfills Christ's entire journey, from the incarnation to the resurrection. Christ was always meant to overflow so that he could *take others into union* with himself. This is what has always defined his person, namely, self-giving love. His entire journey, from his incarnation to his crucifixion and resurrection, creates the means by which he incorporates all flesh into his life in the Spirit, his life with the Father. Mediating a river of the Spirit for others on behalf of the Father reveals Christ's very identity and mission.[29]

Noteworthy here is Edward Schillebeeckx's statement concerning Christ: "As Son in union with the Father he is at the same time the principle of the Holy Spirit."[30] Christ's unity with the Father is confirmed at the event in which his unity with the Spirit is equally clear. This event is not only Christ's resurrection but also Pentecost, because the Spirit raises Christ on behalf of the Father in order to bring all flesh into the divine embrace. When we view it through the lens of this event, we realize that Christ's unity with the Father involves the Father's cause in the world, the Father's promise of the Spirit

---

29. See Brian O. McDermott, "Roman Catholic Christology: Two Recurrent Themes," *Theological Studies* 41, no. 2 (June 1980): 349–67.

30. Edward Schillebeeckx, *Christ the Sacrament of the Encounter with God* (Kansas City, MO: Sheed and Ward, 1963), 43.

that the Son was always to fulfill as vital to his own self-giving to the world: "I am going to send you what the Father promised" (Luke 24:49). We can look at Pentecost as the fulfillment of the resurrection and note that Christ's personhood is not only self-giving love directed to the Father on behalf of humanity, but is also "unbounded" self-giving love poured out onto all flesh from the Father and through the Spirit.[31] God is shown to be the self-imparting God who incorporates all flesh into the triune life. With respect to Pentecost, we can ask this: If personhood is realized in such self-giving love, then Jesus's devotion to the Father must also be combined from the beginning with a devotion to the eschatological reach of the Spirit's leading and outpouring, which is the Father's love promised to the world. In fact, seen through the lens of Pentecost, all three persons of the Godhead would be defined this way. "God can prove himself to be that self-communicating love in the history of Jesus Christ only if he *is* this love in itself."[32] The Father loves, the Son is the embodiment of that love, and the Spirit is the perfection of that love poured out in eschatological freedom so that the Son may incorporate others into divine communion and mission.

The Focus on Pentecost

The eschatological reach of Christ's lordship throughout creation through the Spirit's outpouring thus fulfills the revelation of Christ's identity: Christ's identity is revealed when he self-imparts to creation in a way that takes others in. "God alone is the fount and Lord of life (cf. 1 Sam. 2:6; Job 12:9–10; Deut. 32:39; Ps. 104:29, etc.)."[33] This is why, Dimitru Staniloae has observed, "it was only at Pentecost that the apostles fully recognized Christ as God."[34] St. Augustine likewise says, in commenting on Christ's impartation of the Spirit at Pentecost (Acts 2:33–36): "Indeed, how much must he who gives God be God![35] Furthermore, it also becomes clear at Pentecost that Christ reveals quintessential humanity precisely in imaging divine love in

---

31. See Kasper, *Jesus the Christ*, 246.

32. Kasper, *Jesus the Christ*, 183.

33. Kasper, *Jesus the Christ*, 261.

34. Dimitru Staniloae, "Trinitarian Relations and the Life of the Church," in *Theology and the Church* (Crestwood, NY: St. Vladimir's Seminary Press, 1980), 24; quoted in Eugene F. Rogers, *After the Spirit: A Constructive Pneumatology from Resources outside the West* (Grand Rapids: Eerdmans, 2005), 68.

35. Augustine, *De Trinitate* 15.46.

a way that can receive others. The union of the divine Son and the flesh he assumes is clearest when Christ, at Pentecost, imparts the Spirit via the sacrament of his faithful humanity in order to conform humanity to his image. Here he is fully disclosed most decisively as true deity and true humanity. Christ pours forth the Spirit from the fullness of his faithful and exalted flesh in order to be the firstborn over the creation (Col. 1:15), our elder brother (Rom. 8:39), and head of his body (1 Cor. 12). As I will seek to explain below, Pannenberg's focus on the resurrection as the decisive point of verification for Christ's divine and human identity is not entirely wrong—only incomplete.

Enormously helpful is Jürgen Moltmann's focus on Pentecost as the place where Christ shifts from being the bearer to the imparter of the Spirit (from the Christ of the Spirit to the Spirit of Christ). He noted that this transition is a Trinitarian act initiated by the Father.[36] As such, it is an objective act of divine self-giving. Pannenberg was hesitant to locate the culmination of Jesus's messianic mission at Pentecost due to the tendency of Protestant liberalism to base Christology on the experience or consciousness of Christ in the church. The nineteenth-century progenitor of theological liberalism, Friedrich Schleiermacher, helpfully began his Christology with the point that "the peculiar dignity of the Redeemer can be measured only by his total activity as resting upon that dignity, while this activity can be seen in its completeness only in the corporate life he founded."[37] In other words, the total activity of Christ that reveals the dignity of his person culminates in the founding of our life together as a people corporately conscious of Christ. In discerning the dignity of Christ's person, we thus have to ask who he has to be in himself in order to be who he is to us in our consciousness of him. Schleiermacher does not limit the basis of Christology to our shared God consciousness. He bases Jesus's dignity as Redeemer on his "total activity," which involved the entire span of his life. On the other hand, for Schleiermacher, this activity can only be seen in its completeness "in the corporate life he founded," or in our consciousness of God mediated by him. In the end, who he *is* "depends on the fact that living receptivity for His influence is *already* present, and *continues* to be present" in us.[38] This is where Schleiermacher's helpful method went too far.

36. Jürgen Moltmann, *The Spirit of Life: A Universal Affirmation* (Minneapolis: Fortress, 1992), 58–70.

37. Friedrich Schleiermacher, *The Christian Faith* (Philadelphia: Fortress, 1976), 377.

38. Schleiermacher, *Christian Faith*, 371.

It is correct to base our understanding of Christ's unique dignity on Christ's total activity as fulfilled at Pentecost, including his incorporation of us into himself as our elder brother and Lord. Our quest to discover who Christ is begins with that confession of Christ as the Lord who was given authority in order to impart life to others (John 17:2). But the basis of our discovery cannot be our shared experience or consciousness of Christ, even if our understanding of this is expanded beyond the internal life of religious consciousness to include communal and contextual considerations. Pentecost in the light of Jesus's sojourn that led up to it must rather be the basis of how we practice our diversely shared experiences of Christ. Those experiences, though significant for appreciating the diversity of the cloak that Christ now wears, are determined by—and accountable to—Christ's objective self-giving to us from his own history, a history that culminates for now at Pentecost. Schleiermacher's brilliance was in including Christ's founding of his church in his total activity as Redeemer, so that Pentecost must be the key to what forms the basis of our judgments about Christ's identity. Schleiermacher's shortcoming was in extending that basis to include the corporate experience of Christ in the church to the point where that experience is granted climactic and determinative significance.

Understandably, Pannenberg sought to correct Schleiermacher by making the objective event of the resurrection rather than our corporate experience of Christ the *basis* of our discernment of Christ's ongoing significance to history. But Pannenberg did not proceed far enough in his understanding of the objective basis for discernment. He stopped short of including the event that functioned as the purpose of the victory of the resurrection. Christ broke through the barriers of sin and death in the resurrection in order to make way for the Spirit, to make way for his eschatological significance as the Christ of his body and of the new creation. Pentecost thus has *objective significance* as the climactic event that forms the basis of christological dogma. It is not merely a symbol of the subjective rise of faith in Christ by way of the Spirit. Pentecost thus belongs first to Christ's own history of self-giving that led up to and climaxed in that event *before* it belongs to our corporate life and experience. As a person, Christ is self-determining and self-revealing. The basis of our discernment of that self-disclosure is not our corporate experiences but rather the story of Christ's self-giving that climaxes at Pentecost in his self-giving to us.

In tracing the steps to Pentecost in the biblical witness, it becomes clear that Pentecost cannot be constructed from the raw materials of our self-determined religious experiences or practices. This fact protects Pentecost from simply functioning as a symbol of our self-serving understandings of spiritual fulfillment. Pentecost is not a triumphant event in the commonsense understanding of that term. The first Pentecost is not celebrated through self-aggrandizing and self-serving practices. Instead, the practices of celebration that characterized the first Pentecost were shaped by the story of Christ's sojourn to the cross and—*from there*—to resurrection and Pentecost. Pentecostal practices arose in this light as a proclamation of God's generous self-giving to the world, the self-sacrificial and generous sharing of sustenance with those in need, a baptism into his death and a rising again into his self-giving love, the breaking of bread in memory of a life broken for the world and poured out for the world, a fellowship that is merciful and just, and a witness that proclaims Christ and extends divine mercy and justice to the world (Acts 2).[39] The meaning of the Pentecost event and the practices that arise from that event are not to be drawn primarily from our experiences, but from Christ and the canonical witness to his story of self-giving. The background of that Pentecost event is thus not simply Christ's exaltation but also his humiliation, not only his baptism in the renewing Spirit but also his baptism in fire on behalf of those who are lost, broken, and dying. In fact, Christ's Spirit baptism and his baptism in fire were mutually illuminating. He was exalted in the Spirit as the one who took his share in humans' captivity to sin and death so that they could be free. Pentecost is bound to the story that leads up to it, *bound* but not *closed* (not closed precisely because it is bound to his story of self-giving). Pentecost is open to an ever-expanding eschatological fulfillment because it is bound to the story of Jesus, to the one who joined himself to others, not only representatively, but also actually by way of the Spirit poured forth from the Father through him.

Given the importance of the events of Jesus's life that led up to Pentecost, our focus on Pentecost, on the Spirit Baptizer, cannot represent a lack of appreciation for the fact that Christology is complex. When one looks at Christology, one finds several key events: the conception and birth of Jesus; his baptism and reception of the Holy Spirit at the Jordan River; his life ministry and sojourn to Jerusalem; his crucifixion, resurrection, and exaltation; his bestowal of the Holy Spirit on behalf of the heavenly Father; his ongoing role as Lord, prophet, and high priest; and the final new creation after his return. John the Baptist had a shorthand way of summarizing this journey: he who bears the Spirit will baptize in the Spirit (Matt. 3:11; Mark 1:8; Luke 3:16; John 1:33). As the climactic event of Christ's self-giving to

---

39. I am grateful to Michael Welker for personally drawing this point to my attention.

all of creation, Pentecost gives us the *Christus preasens* (Christ present to faith) and grants us a foretaste of the Christ who will appear at the *parousia*. The Christ whom John the Revelator saw in blazing glory in the midst of his churches in the first chapter of Revelation was the hope of the world, the one who will return to reign forever with his heavenly Father. He bears the wounds of his fire baptism as he shines forth the light of God as the one baptized and exalted in the Spirit; he shines his light to other lamps so that they can reflect it. This Lord who has bound his crucified and risen life to the church and to the entire creation is the one who is responsible in Revelation for transforming the wounded creation into the dwelling place of God: "Look! God's dwelling place is now among the people, and he will dwell with them. They will be his people, and God himself will be with them and be their God" (Rev. 21:3). Thus Pentecost is a fitting place to concentrate Christological method. This event is at the intersection of *memory* and *hope*.

The classical creeds of the Christian church did not summarize Christ's overall identity and mission with a concentration on Pentecost, though the church fathers implied the importance of this horizon on occasion. There were contextual reasons for the neglect. As I will show in the following chapter, the metaphysical challenges facing Christology in the early centuries directed attention to the doctrine of the incarnation. But one sees a different emphasis in the pages of the New Testament canon. There one finds highlighted John the Baptist's shorthand reference to the anointed Christ as the one who will baptize in the Spirit and fire. Informing John's reference to Christ as the Spirit Baptizer is the Old Testament promise of the coming reign of God (Matt. 3:2), which was intimately connected in ancient Judaism to the coming of God (Isa. 40:3; 43:4–5), including the coming of God's Spirit (Joel 2:28–29). This is why John the Baptist is said to prepare the way for the coming of God, precisely by preparing the way for Christ (Isa. 40:3; Mark 1:1–3), and why John knew that Jesus was the chosen one when the Spirit descended on him (John 1:33). Christ is the chosen one because he is bringing the Spirit with him, and with the Spirit will come the final time of judgment and renewal.

John's messianic expectation was thus forged from his expectation of the coming Spirit. That was fitting because the term "Christ," or "Messiah," meant anointed one. All four accounts of Christ's baptism highlight his reception of the Spirit from the Father—and the Father's concomitant announcement that Christ is the beloved Son (Matt. 3:16; Mark 1:8; Luke 3:22; John 1:33). And Jesus quotes from Isaiah 61:1–2 in his inaugural address at the start of his messianic ministry, a text that uplifts his anointing by the Spirit:

32

"The Spirit of the Lord is on me,
    because he has anointed me
    to proclaim good news to the poor.
He has sent me to proclaim freedom for the prisoners
    and recovery of sight for the blind,
to set the oppressed free,
to proclaim the year of the Lord's favor." (Luke 4:18–19)

Strikingly absent from Luke's account of Jesus's quoting from Isaiah 61:1–2 is the phrase at the end of Isaiah 61:2: ". . . and the day of vengeance of our God." The text quoted by Jesus ends with "to proclaim the year of the Lord's favor." Proclaiming the day of God's vengeance is left out in the Luke passage. Christ the Messiah will bear this fire himself so that he will be able, through the victory of his resurrection, to pour forth the sanctifying and renewing Spirit to all flesh.

There is no question that messianic expectation in the New Testament is significantly shaped around this expectation that Jesus bears the Spirit to fulfill the Father's cause in the world, the cause of renewing all things in the Son's image by bestowing the Spirit to all flesh. This is the promise of the Father that Jesus came to fulfill (Luke 24:49). Pentecost is thus a fitting point of concentration for a messianic Christology. Those who have researched the relatively late rise of messianic expectation in Judaism know that the church's reading of Old Testament texts messianically pointed to a horizon of meaning that to some extent went beyond the original intent and setting of the ancient texts that they used.[40] The kings were considered to be anointed by the Spirit; but not all rulers measured up to their calling. In Psalm 2:2, Yahweh and the anointed one work against hostile kings and rulers. In the eighth century BCE, the hope of a royal messianism began to develop in response to wicked and inept kings that seemed to dim the glory of the Davidic line.[41] Even David and the faithful kings did not qualify as the fulfillment of the world kingdom expected in texts like Psalm 2.[42] From the Hasmonean Dynasty of the second century

---

40. See Joachim Becker, *Messianic Expectation in the Old Testament* (Philadelphia: Fortress, 1980); see also Michael F. Bird, *Are You the One Who Is to Come? The Historical Jesus and the Messianic Question* (Grand Rapids: Baker Academic, 2009).

41. Brown, *Death of the Messiah*, 1:474.

42. Tremper Longman III, "The Messiah: Explorations in the Law and the Writings," in *The Messiah in the Old and New Testaments*, ed. Stanley E. Porter (Grand Rapids: Eerdmans, 2007), 20.

BCE, ideas surrounding a coming messianic deliverer deepened in the Israelite imagination.[43] Not all Jews expected a messiah, and there were different ideas among those who did when it came to the specifics of his identity and reign.[44] However, there were common themes. They tended to expect a coming king, priest, and conqueror.[45] Popular was the hope that there would be "an inbreaking of the power of Yahweh that would revive the dynasty and ensure its permanence by raising up a worthy successor to David."[46] John the Baptist announced the coming of the anointed one with the help of texts that foretold the coming of the Spirit. John uniquely stressed that the Messiah will not only arrive in the power of the Spirit, but will *mediate the Spirit's work* in the world. Using his baptisms in the Jordan River as a metaphor, John imagines that the Christ will occasion a mighty river of the Spirit into which he will submerge all unto judgment and renewal. However, there was a rub for the early Christians. Craig Evans says that the "rub for early Christians—and it was a big rub—was the crucifixion of Jesus."[47] Messianic expectation among the followers of Jesus had to be adjusted to accommodate this shocking turn of events. John the Baptist's concept of a baptism in fire will provide a framework for Jesus's own understanding of his coming death (Luke 12:50).

John's creative metaphor took on richer meaning in the light of the crucifixion, resurrection, and Pentecost. The Christ will end up bearing the fire of judgment so as to rise in the Spirit as the one who mediates the Spirit to all flesh, and, with the Spirit, the benefits and challenges of his faithful sonship. The baptism of fire is transformed through union with Christ from an alienating into a sanctifying force. In the New Testament, the Messiah is shown to be Lord over all and indeed reigns over all precisely by renewing all things in the Spirit of life. Though more complex than John the Baptist could have imagined, he presented us with an overarching picture of Christ's identity and mission that leads christological method to Pentecost as the climactic event this side of eternity. This was vital to John's task—as Christ's chief and immediate forerunner.

Walter Kasper thus notes that Christ's messianic identity and universal lordship were originally shaped within the framework of the expansively

43. Bird, *Are You the One?*, 32–36.

44. Brown, *Death of the Messiah*, 1:474.

45. Longman, "The Messiah," 30.

46. Longman, "The Messiah," 47.

47. Craig A. Evans, "The Messiah in the Old and New Testaments: A Response," in Porter, ed., *The Messiah in the Old and New Testaments*, 233.

eschatological promise of the Spirit (e.g., Joel 2:28–32).[48] Pannenberg recognizes that Jewish expectation of eschatological resurrection did not depend on the resurrection of only one individual to inaugurate the new creation. Yet Christianity, from the beginning, identified Jesus's resurrection in precisely this way.[49] Pannenberg does not pause to explore this fact except to say that the resurrection shows Jesus to be essential to the coming of God's reign to earth. Pentecost, however, grants us insight into the larger reason for the cosmic significance granted Jesus's resurrection. The risen Christ is known as the final Adam, precisely as the "life-giving spirit." "So it is written: 'The first man Adam became a living being; the last Adam, a life-giving spirit'" (1 Cor. 15:45). The outpouring of the Spirit on all flesh through the crucified and risen Christ provided the interpretive lens through which Jesus's resurrection was understood as a universal reality, the inauguration of the new humanity. Pentecost is the context in which the risen Christ is understood to be Messiah as the Lord over all. It is in the Spirit that we come to recognize the risen Christ as Lord over the new creation (1 Cor. 12:3). Thomas's confession before the risen Christ, "My Lord and my God" (John 20:28), thus anticipates Pentecost. The Word of the Father was said to have created all things (cf. John 1:1–5) and thus has universal significance as well. But Pentecost clarifies and elaborates on that significance. The eschatological Spirit that anointed Christ and raised him up from the dead will anoint all flesh in him and raise them up in his image. The resurrection of the crucified Christ is thus clearly and decisively discerned as gospel (good news) through the lens of Pentecost.

Pentecost, the place of our incorporation into Christ, is indeed the place where our confession of Jesus as Messiah and Lord begins (Acts 2:36; 1 Cor. 12:3). As Larry Hurtado has shown, it was the encounter with the risen and exalted Christ as Lord from the moment of the church's birth (Pentecost) that caused the church to assume that Christ was essentially divine. In making this point, Hurtado rightly opposes the earlier assumption of Wilhelm Bousset that the church's belief in Christ's identification with God evolved gradually as the church moved from its monotheistic Jewish beginnings to its appeals to Gentile, Hellenistic audiences that were polytheistic. Bousset does point correctly to Gentile polytheism and gradations of the divine reality as opening up the possibility of various degrees of deity in the divine life, making it possible for there to be semidivine beings connecting the tran-

---

48. Kasper, *Jesus the Christ*, 264–67.
49. Pannenberg, *Systematic Theology*, 2:350.

scendent deity with the creaturely world. However, Bousset wrongly views this development as the reason for the divine attributions applied to Christ behind the rise of the New Testament witness. The idea of semidivine beings was to pose serious problems for Christology later on. As we will note, this idea can be said to have influenced Justin Martyr in the second century and beyond. But one cannot trace this back to Paul and other New Testament witnesses, as Hurtado correctly points out.[50]

This is not to say that the Greek devotion to demigods was not an ancient idea or that it did not influence ancient Judaism. In challenging Bousset's method, however, Hurtado notes that the Judaism of the New Testament authors was uncompromisingly monotheistic. This observation makes it all the more interesting that the earliest christological texts, such as Philippians 2:4–11, give every indication of being a recognition of Christ's full deity among his original followers, precisely among those who were uncompromisingly monotheistic! Jesus is given the highest name and is confessed in worship as Lord, a practice only directed toward God in ancient Judaism (Phil. 2:11).[51] So this deity attributed to Christ did not arise as a result of polytheistic influence but rather as a result of Christ's indispensable role in the redemption wrought by God from the cross to Pentecost. Only God can save and reign as Lord. If Jesus is essential or indispensable to salvation and to the inauguration of God's reign in the world, Jesus is essential to the divine life and may be identified as divine in the full sense of what that term implies. N. T. Wright has bolstered Hurtado's insight by noting that Jesus fulfilled the early Jewish expectation that God would visit the earth to redeem humanity. Jesus's fulfillment of this expectation convinced his early Jewish followers of his divine identity.[52] But, as Hurtado has shown, these early Jewish followers of Jesus did not abandon their monotheism in the process. They merely arrived at a "variant form" of monotheism that opened up room for including Jesus Christ within it.[53] Remarkably, they did not abandon their monotheism in the process. This decision opened the door for the later expressions of Trinitarian faith.

It is important to add, however, that the Spirit's divine identity was not a mere afterthought of late-fourth-century Christian theologians. The Spirit's identification with God was already assumed within ancient Judaism.

---

50. Larry W. Hurtado, *Lord Jesus Christ: Devotion to Jesus in Earliest Christianity* (Grand Rapids: Eerdmans, 2003), 1–26.

51. Hurtado, *Lord Jesus Christ*, 19–52.

52. Wright, *Jesus and the Victory of God*, esp. 615–23.

53. Hurtado, *Lord Jesus Christ*, 50.

Lloyd R. Neve notes that the Spirit is viewed in the Old Testament as God's breath, the medium of God's presence and work in the world.[54] When the authors of the New Testament adjusted the life of the one God to make space for Jesus as indispensable to that life, they had the Spirit in mind in one sense: they had this in mind because Jesus, in his resurrection and at Pentecost, imparts himself to the world by imparting the Spirit. This entire "early high Christology" trend is convincing, especially as it may be adjusted in the light of Jesus's role as the Spirit Baptizer.

This methodological concentration on the Christ of Pentecost as the Spirit Baptizer locates the incarnation within a trajectory that leads to the start of the Spirit's economy. The conclusion of the messianic mission is precisely the beginning of the Spirit's mission. This overlap is foreshadowed in the Spirit's involvement throughout Jesus's life, from the incarnation to the resurrection (e.g., Luke 1:35; 3:22; Heb. 9:14; Rom. 1:4). The incarnation anticipates Pentecost. More precisely, the incarnation anticipates the entire cluster of final messianic acts from the crucifixion to Pentecost. Though Karl Barth was fond of saying that the incarnation contains within itself the entire story of Jesus, he was also careful to note that the meaning of this event is to be filled in by a larger series of events. Barth helpfully retells the larger story of Christ within the framework of Jesus's baptism in the "Holy Spirit and fire." The baptism in fire is the "baptism" of Christ's death, his plunge into divine judgment or the consequences of alienation from God (Mark 10:39). One may connect this to what Barth says about the Son of God's humiliation, which spans the journey from the incarnation to the cross. For Barth, the baptism in the restorative Spirit is by implication the exaltation of the Son of man. These two (humiliation and exaltation) are not sequential for Barth; rather, they are simultaneous and mutually defining. The Son of man is exalted (implicitly, baptized in the Spirit) precisely by going through the humiliation of his identification with sinners in the journey from the incarnation to the cross (baptized in fire), which includes Jesus's identification with repentant sinners at his baptism under John.[55]

In Barth's Christology, there is a line drawn between Christ's identity *in himself* as the reconciliation between God and humanity (attained in the journey from the incarnation to the cross) and Christ as present to faith

54. Lloyd R. Neve, *The Spirit of God in the Old Testament* (Cleveland, TN: CPT Press, 2011), 1–4, 41.

55. Karl Barth, *Church Dogmatics*, IV/4: *The Doctrine of Reconciliation*, trans. G. W. Bromiley (Edinburgh: T & T Clark, 1969), 30–31.

through the resurrection. In service to this bifurcation, Barth located the overcoming of Jesus's baptism in fire at the cross. The resurrection was then said to reveal or declare this victory, and Pentecost then becomes the place where we, by faith, have our history joined to Christ's. Barth was correct to make a clear distinction between Christ in himself and Christ as present to us. Indeed, we should avoid Schleiermacher's basing of Christology in part on our consciousness of Christ. But Barth failed to adequately recognize that this difference is to be focused on the line between the *Spirit-baptized* and the *Spirit Baptizer*. Had Barth followed that line of distinction as of chief significance, he would have highlighted Pentecost as the most decisive point of transition from the "in himself" to the "present to us." After all, Pentecost is not just the point of our access to Christ by faith; it is also objective as an event of divine self-giving. Had Barth focused on Pentecost as the transition from Christ's historic journey for us to Christ's presence to history and beyond, he would also have had a more adequate basis for viewing the "in himself" as itself fulfilled precisely in the "present to us," in the sense that this is an objective event of self-giving and incorporation through the impartation of the Spirit. The cross and the resurrection are both pivotal in their own way in the movement from the Spirit-baptized to the Spirit Baptizer. But it is to be emphasized that Christ's impartation of the Spirit and incorporation of the other into the divine life and mission is the place where the pivot most decisively occurs between the *in himself* and the *present to us*, in which the "present to us" is both fulfilled and defined by the "in himself." After all, Jesus is in himself the Spirit Baptizer, the one who incorporates the other into the divine life.

James D. G. Dunn proposed that Pentecost is indeed the culmination of Jesus's messianic mission. Pentecost does not merely depict our access by faith to a mission fulfilled at the cross and made available to history in the resurrection; rather, for Dunn, Pentecost is the ultimate culmination, or *telos*, of Jesus's entire mission as the Messiah. Dunn writes in no uncertain terms: "The climax and purposed end of Jesus' ministry is not the cross and the resurrection, but the ascension and Pentecost."[56] I have learned much from Dunn about Jesus as baptized in the Spirit and fire so as to baptize others in the Spirit. Unfortunately, later in his otherwise enormously insightful *Christology in the Making*, he does not develop these points. Of course, his concentration in that book is on the issue of the incarnation; but he does

---

56. James D. G. Dunn, *Baptism in the Holy Spirit*, Studies in Biblical Theology, 2nd series 15 (London: SCM Press, 1970), 44.

not follow through on his seminal work on Spirit baptism to develop the doctrine of the incarnation in the light of Pentecost. In his later work Dunn does note that the Jesus of the New Testament is the "Lord of the Spirit," who "began to share in God's prerogative as the giver of the Spirit."[57] But that is as far as he goes. This point requires much further development as the horizon in the New Testament for the incarnation. If inclusive of Christ's impartation of the Spirit, a Spirit Christology need not preclude a Trinitarian theology supportive of Christ's full deity, as a number of theologians have shown, notably Walter Kasper, Ralph Del Colle, Eugene Rogers, Myk Habets, and Leopoldo A. Sanchez.[58] All of these theologians have pointed to the importance of Jesus's role as bearer and mediator of the Spirit in a way that does not preclude his deity but rather supports it. Only God can impart life.

The Christ of Pentecost and Soteriology

Methodologically, it is beyond question that Christology has always been done with some notion of salvation and of human need hovering in the background. The role that such notions should play in Christology has become an important methodological issue. What is the relationship between Christology and soteriology, and how can *Pentecost enrich and expand our understanding* of this relationship? "Our task is to understand the concrete Gospel in the light of this person," writes Karl Barth concerning Christ.[59] Christ as Spirit Baptizer is well suited as a place from which to understand the rich relationship between Christology and this gospel of salvation. Pentecost brings Christ's saving work to creation, revealing his fundamental unity with God and humanity precisely at the place where God takes humanity into the divine life and communion as the self-imparting God, not just representatively but actually. After all, the Christ is not just the Christ at his anointing, but also at his Spirit baptizing. He is anointed in his journey *from incarnation to resurrection* in order to be the Spirit Baptizer! As Messiah

---

57. Dunn, *Christology in the Making*, 142.

58. Kasper, *Jesus the Christ*; Ralph Del Colle, *Christ and the Spirit: Spirit-Christology in Trinitarian Perspective* (New York: Oxford University Press, 1994); Rogers, *After the Spirit*; Myk Habets, *The Anointed Son: A Trinitarian Spirit Christology*, Princeton Theological Monograph Series (Eugene, OR: Wipf and Stock, 2010); Leopoldo A. Sanchez, *Receiver, Bearer, and Giver of God's Spirit: Jesus' Life in the Spirit as a Lens for Theology and Life* (Eugene, OR: Pickwick, 2015).

59. Karl Barth, *Church Dogmatics*, II/2: *The Doctrine of God*, trans. G. W. Bromiley et al. (Edinburgh: T & T Clark, 1978), 73.

and Lord he receives the Spirit to mediate the Spirit (Acts 2:33–36). This is how his lordship is actualized as an eschatological and cosmic reality. There is thus no way to detach Christology from soteriology—or ecclesiology, for that matter—if Pentecost is the focal point.

Though inseparable and mutually illuminating, a certain priority of place must be given to Christology in its relationship to soteriology. It is especially important for a Christology of Pentecost to note that Christology is to be viewed as determinative for soteriology. Though a biblical understanding of anthropology and soteriology will enhance Christological discussion, Christology must play the decisive role in determining their relationship. Christ is the focal point of fulfillment for the biblical witness. It is particularly true that we cannot simply construct our Christology from our own self-made understandings of human need and salvation. All during this discussion we have been dwelling on the problem involved in basing Christology on our perceived experience of Christ. The figure of Christ would become nothing more than a corporate experience constructed by church practices. Christ ends up being whatever we make him out to be in the life and needs of the church. Paul Tillich's assumption that "Christology is a function of soteriology" thus goes too far.[60] Soteriology would then lack an adequate foundation in the person of Christ, for Christ is more than a symbol of human salvation or community.[61] Not only is his self-offering anchored in his own Spirit-baptized life and journey, the significance of his person as offered to creation through the eschatological Spirit far exceeds what we experience him to be as Savior and Lord within our limited contexts and capacities. There are indeed clear directions from the liberating story of Jesus that guide christological discernment today. For example, Jesus is clearly shown to be on the side of a generous offering of grace so that others might repent and receive. He sides with the oppressed and the outcasts of society, while still opening communion to those who repent from among the oppressors. Justice is not retaliation but a reconciling communion that gives rise to communities governed by mercy and mutual regard. Christ at no point sides with the dark powers; his authority is solely on the side of liberation and healing. He gives himself entirely to the Father's cause in the world by following the leading of the Spirit in giving of his life for the redemption and renewal of humanity. These directions in the hands of

60. Paul Tillich, *Systematic Theology*, vol. 2 (Chicago: University of Chicago Press, 1957), 250.

61. Pannenberg, *Jesus—God and Man*, 48.

the Spirit are global and expansively eschatological, always creatively and challengingly renewing even our noblest yearnings for the new humanity shaped in Christ's image. Through the Spirit, Christ is drawing us toward an eschatological conformity to his sonship. The Spirit Baptizer as presented to us in the biblical witness must be the enduring anchor for our experience of Christ in the church and beyond.[62] "Soteriology must follow fundamentally from Christology, not vice versa."[63]

Yet, though Christology has priority to soteriology methodologically, the two are still inseparable and tend to exercise a mutual influence on each other in our thinking, and will continue to do so, whether we realize it or not, for better or for worse. It is natural for Christology to be discussed in close connection to soteriology. We come to know the significance of Christ for us through what he does to save us. And we come to know Christ precisely at Pentecost as the one who took up our sorrows to be our life-giver, our elder sibling and Lord, the head of his body, and the firstborn over the entire new creation. The sixteenth-century Reformer Philipp Melanchthon put it this way: *Hoc est Christum cognoscere, beneficia eius cognoscere* ("To know Christ is to know his benefits"). How can we broach the question of Christ's identity except through what we know of his work and benefits—both objectively and subjectively?[64] Note what Barth says: "How could a theology which does not know the freedom of God's grace, which does not know the mystery of His way, which does not know the fear of God as the beginning of wisdom, how can such a theology call itself a theology of revelation and faith?"[65] The stakes are high, for the expansive richness of Christ implies an equally expansive and rich soteriology. As an ancient sermon expresses this: "Brethren, we ought so to think of Jesus Christ as of God, as of the judge of living and dead. And we ought not to belittle our salvation; for when we belittle him, we expect also to receive little."[66] However, not only will a belittling of Christ belittle salvation in him, the inverse is also true: a *truncated soteriology* can

---

62. This is the major point of Kevin Vanhoozer, *The Drama of Doctrine: A Canonical Linguistic Approach to Christian Doctrine* (Louisville: Westminster John Knox, 2005).

63. Pannenberg, *Jesus—God and Man*, 48.

64. A point made by Luke Timothy Johnson in *Living Jesus: Learning the Heart of the Gospel* (New York: Harper Collins, 1999).

65. Karl Barth, *Church Dogmatics*, I/1: *The Doctrine of the Word of God*, trans. G. W. Bromiley (Edinburgh: T & T Clark, 1975), 422.

66. 2 *Clement* 1.1–2; quoted in Jaroslav Pelikan, *The Emergence of the Catholic Tradition: The Christian Tradition; A History of the Development of Doctrine* (Chicago: University of Chicago Press, 1971), 1:173.

also limit our Christology. So it behooves us to be aware of this problem and to think about our soteriological assumptions in order to open up adequate space for the directions of Christology suggested by Christ's full sojourn from the incarnation to Pentecost. To that point, the Christ of Pentecost suggests an understanding of salvation that is incorporative, participatory, eschatological, and transformative.

The history of soteriology may be viewed as a struggle to reach for such Pentecostal holism. Problematically, the ancient heresy of Gnosticism considered creation to be too evil to be redeemed. The Gnostics even refused to identify the Creator as the Father of Jesus Christ, and they denigrated the Old Testament. Salvation for them was only for the immaterial soul. In response to this threat, theologians of the second and third centuries sought to lift up the Old Testament and to grant our God-given capacity to respond to God's grace an important role to play in salvation. They responded favorably to the Old Testament's emphasis on obeying the law of God as a vital consequence of grace. They connected Christology to what may be called a "graced synergy," or cooperation with divine grace in the direction of spiritual progress. In protest to a Gnostic neglect of the Old Testament themes of creation and law, the apostolic fathers emphasized moral progress and the divinely given creaturely capacities to obey.[67] Similarly, Origen avoided fatalistic doctrines of the Gnostics and the Stoics by highlighting our capacity to respond favorably to the Spirit or grace of God. He was convinced that Valentinus's notion of an unchangeable and predestined human nature (both good and evil) cannot account for the role of the human will in converting to righteousness or in leaving a righteous path for unrighteousness.[68]

This understanding of salvation as cooperation with God can be problematic itself, since grace is not something external to us—not something with which we could cooperate. There can be no cooperation except from grace itself. Any notion of cooperation with grace can thus imply an illusion of human autonomy with respect to God, as though we have inherent in us an ability to cooperate with grace as something external to us, as a mere aid in our own self-generated progress. To avoid this illusion, we must emphasize that cooperation with God takes place only *within* grace, *within* God. In the light of Pentecost, this means cooperation within Christ's self-

---

67. Thomas F. Torrance, *The Doctrine of Grace in the Apostolic Fathers* (Grand Rapids: Eerdmans, 1959), 138–41.

68. See Thomas P. Scheck, *Origen and the History of Justification: The Legacy of Origen's Commentary on Romans* (Notre Dame, IN: University of Notre Dame Press, 2008), 20–30.

offering to us in the Spirit, the goal of which is union with Christ. Salvation in the light of Pentecost is thus fundamentally *incorporative, participatory,* and *transformative.* There is no human cooperation with God apart from this. Indeed, Origen does imply that graced cooperation with God does not occur *between* God and autonomous human agents, but rather *in* God, participating in grace or in the very life of God. For Origen, this partaking of God through Christ leads to *deification.* He writes of the human mind that the *"nous* which is purified is lifted above all material realities so as to have a clear vision of God, and it is deified by its vision."[69]

Such a participatory understanding of salvation as deification and *theōsis* (or a transformation in God toward greater union with God) was indeed present in the soteriology of the West, but even more so in the East, especially in the early centuries of the Alexandrian tradition. Early Alexandrian theologians Clement, Origen, and Athanasius "elevated the soteriological theory of *theosis* to new heights."[70] The Cappadocians also favored *theōsis* due to Gregory of Nazianzus's reading of Origen and Gregory's desire to be faithful to Athanasius. Athanasius saw Christ as the means whereby God self-imparts to flesh so that all flesh can partake of God: "God became man so that man might become God."[71] Gregory expanded on this statement as follows: "And since, then, God is made man, so man is perfected as God, and that is my glory."[72] Of course, none of this means that we should blur the line between God and the human soul. Deification is our partaking of God and our being transformed into God's likeness. We never become divine in some unqualified sense. Nevertheless, this soteriology emphasized the transformation of the human self into the divine image of Christ.[73]

Since salvation as *theōsis* dispels the myth of human autonomy, it was important for the Alexandrians to speak of Christ's sojourn on earth in a way that avoids describing his human life as independent of his identity as the divine Son. So the Alexandrians emphasized the unity of natures in the one person of Christ and interpreted his progress in the Spirit in order to

---

69. Origen, *Commentary on John* 3.27; quoted in J. A. McGuckin, "The Strategic Adaptation of Deification," in *Partakers of the Divine Nature: The History and Development of Deification in the Christian Traditions*, ed. Michael J. Christensen and Jeffrey A. Wittung (Grand Rapids: Baker Academic, 2006), 101.

70. McGuckin, "Strategic Adaptation of Deification," 97.

71. Quoted in McGuckin, "Strategic Adaptation of Deification," 101.

72. Gregory of Nazianzus, *Carmina Dogmatica* 10.5–9; quoted in McGuckin, "Strategic Adaptation of Deification," 101.

73. McGuckin, "Strategic Adaptation of Deification," 104.

avoid any hint of a human Christ who cooperates with his divine self toward an independent human progress. Of course, there is a distinction of natures to be acknowledged, for Christ is the man of the Spirit and is, precisely as such, identical with the eternal Son. A case can be made that the eternal Son from all of eternity was generated from the Father via the Spirit and loved the Father through the Spirit. Therefore, Christ shows himself to be identical in person to the eternal Son precisely as the man who bears the Spirit to impart the Spirit in devotion to the Father and the Father's cause in the world. His humanity is destined to share in the glory of the Son in order to be the sacrament of the Spirit to all flesh. But there is no cooperation between Jesus and the eternal Son, as though Jesus is somehow autonomous in his human identity. The Christ of Pentecost thus demands an unqualified unity of person in Christ, for Christ bears the Spirit to impart the Spirit *as Lord*. Douglas Fairbairn notes that the "idea that God gives us himself through Christ and the Holy Spirit virtually demands a strongly unitive Christology, in which the personal subject of Christ is the Logos himself."[74] The Alexandrian tradition was thus *implicitly faithful* to the Christ of Pentecost.

Fairbairn notes, however, that the christological tradition of Antioch, Syria, was in danger of advocating the illusion of human autonomy and anchored this in Christology. This tradition ran the risk of viewing Christ as progressing in the Spirit as an autonomous agent cooperating with the divine Son who was incarnate within him. Such a danger would imply a dual subject in which the humanity of Christ "cooperates" with the divine Logos in order to attain moral progress. As Fairbairn has shown, this is the heresy that the Chalcedonian Definition sought in part to correct in the fifth century. Fairbairn says that, regarding the tension between the Antiochene and Alexandrian traditions, "there was a question whether grace consisted of Christ giving the Christian power, aid, and assistance in reaching that perfect human condition or whether God gave the believer participation in his own immortality and incorruption."[75] The latter—Alexandrian—tradition was most consistent with the Christ who bears the Spirit precisely so as to impart the Spirit as Lord. Though one cannot understand deification through incarnation in a way that denies essential human capacities in Christ, neither can we envision "cooperation with grace" between the natures in Christ, which creates the illusion of total human autonomy, either in the person of Christ

---

74. Douglas Fairbairn, *Grace and Christology in the Early Church*, Oxford Early Christian Studies (Oxford: Oxford University Press, 2003), 69.

75. Fairbairn, *Grace and Christology*, 14.

or analogously in our relationship with God. I will take up this issue more thoroughly in the chapter on the incarnation.

Here I only wish to note that the influence of soteriology on Christology was indeed profound. And it did not end with the debates of the fifth century. It was opened afresh throughout the history of Christology. For example, the Protestant Reformers raised the issue of the christological foundation of justification by faith. An evangelical Christology that emphasizes justification by faith can limit Christology, unless couched within union with Christ and participation in Christ through the gift of the Spirit.[76] Within the older context of existential theology, for example, the close link between Christology and the doctrine of justification by faith tended to dissolve the significance of Jesus into the word of acquittal that comforts believers gripped by guilt and anxiety. Rudolf Bultmann was famously criticized for regarding the resurrection as having no objective basis in history apart from this word of acquittal and for neglecting the cosmic significance of salvation. Bultmann did indeed write in moving terms of how, through this word, the sinner is encouraged to depend entirely on the grace of God in all things, casting aside all forms of humanly contrived security and opening up in radical ways to unforeseen possibilities. Bultmann's existentially relevant Christ is indeed compelling, as far as it goes. But within this narrow Bultmannian framework, one is left wondering whether in the end Christ ends up being nothing more than a symbol of human enlightenment concerning one's dependence on God in an uncertain world. As I noted above, to avoid collapsing Christ into the existentially relevant word of acquittal by God, Barth drew attention to Jesus's very person as the reconciliation between God and humanity. There is no justification by faith without the "proclamation" of the Christ incarnated, crucified, and risen in victory over sin and death. Indeed, how is it a gospel, "in which nothing is said of that in which, or of him in whom, its recipients are to believe?"[77]

Of course, Bultmann is not representative of the larger evangelical tradition. This tradition has drawn attention to the doctrine of justification by grace through faith, especially as a forensic or legal declaration that we are right with God because of that which Christ has done for us. Such is a worthy goal. Justification certainly is this, but more needs to be said to

76. See Clark Pinnock, *Flame of Love: A Theology of the Holy Spirit* (Downers Grove, IL: InterVarsity, 1999), 149–84.

77. I add the commas for clarity. Karl Barth, "Rudolf Bultmann—An Attempt to Understand Him," in *Kerygma and Myth: A Theological Debate*, ed. Hans-Werner Bartsch, vol. 2 (London: SPCK, 1962), 96–97.

capture the richness of this concept. Justification also involves more richly union with Christ in the Spirit by faith. Justification by faith is thus not only declaratory but also participatory and relational. It is, in its effect, transformative as well. J. A. Ziesler concludes his extensive study of the biblical terms related to justification by noting that justification is "simply a matter of bringing sinners into a new relationship" along with all of the participatory and transformational implications that this implies.[78] Saving righteousness in the Old Testament (from which we get the notion of justification in the New Testament) is not primarily an abstract norm or a moral virtue. It is God's establishment of a covenant relationship with God's people through divine faithfulness, invoking an analogous faithful loyalty from them.[79] "Jahweh's righteousness was not a norm, but acts, and it was these acts which bestow salvation."[80]

Understood in this way, divine justice is wedded to mercy. God establishes the right by extending mercy to others. The establishment of this relationship with God was thus forensic, or legal, on God's terms alone "as a verdict against which there can be no appeal, as a decision the rightness of which cannot be tested on the standards of other decisions because, on account of the One who made it, it is inherently right."[81] God's making things right with humanity through merciful acts of salvation is radically transformative, a new influx of life and a reorientation of life toward God and the divine glory and purposes. This is why such justice is said to come through the reign of an anointed one (Isa. 11:1-5; 61:1-3), and it is awaited through imagery that implies a gift that brings new life. "Justice will dwell in the desert and righteousness live in the fertile field" (Isa. 32:16). There is no way of understanding what we mean by the justice, or "right relation," of justification on the basis of commonsense notions of justice. It must be understood within the biblical framework of how God overcomes sin and death in order to bring others into the divine embrace. That is how God makes things right. Who is to question that?[82]

---

78. J. A. Ziesler, *The Meaning of Righteousness in Paul: A Linguistic and Theological Inquiry* (Cambridge, UK: Cambridge University Press, 1972), 8.

79. Ziesler, *Meaning of Righteousness*, 40-42.

80. Gerhard von Rad, *Theology of the Old Testament: The Theology of Israel's Historical Traditions*, trans. D. M. G. Stalker, vol. 1 (New York: Harper and Row, 1962), 372-73.

81. Barth, *Church Dogmatics*, II/2, 30.

82. See my more extensive treatment of justification in the Old Testament in Frank D. Macchia, *Justified in the Spirit: Creation, Redemption, and the Triune God* (Grand Rapids: Eerdmans, 2010), 103-30.

What is this new relationship secured in God's justifying us in Christ? First, it is covenantal: it establishes a basis for a new covenant relationship with God, which Jesus, at the Last Supper, said was the meaning of his death (1 Cor. 11:25). As a covenantal concept, justification not only comes through receiving Christ's atoning death by faith (Rom. 3:24) as something abstract; in the new covenantal relationship, which is secured by justification, we receive symbols of Christ's broken body and spilled blood in communion with him and in participation in his death and his life. At the Last Supper, Christ's own description of his death leads to these words: "This is my body, which is for you; do this in remembrance of me" (1 Cor. 11:24). This partaking of Christ in the sacred meal implies that justification by faith comes through receiving Christ himself by faith, for "to all who did receive him, to those who believed in his name, he gave the right to become children of God (John 1:12). Such a union with Christ is initiated under the sign of water baptism (Rom. 6:1–5), which is why Paul, in obvious reference to this rite, tells his readers: "You were sanctified, you were justified in the name of the Lord Jesus Christ and by the Spirit of our God" (1 Cor. 6:11). Justifying faith in union with Christ causes us to participate in him—in his death and in his life—which is the symbolism of baptism (Rom. 6:1–5). In other words, we are justified by faith through the ministry of Christ the Spirit Baptizer.

Therefore, justification comes not just "by faith" as an act of mental assent to an abstract truth. It comes by receiving Christ himself by faith, in living union with him—his death and his life. This rich notion of justification makes it clear that the right relationship with God secured by justification not only highlights Christ's obedient life or atoning death but also his vindication by the Spirit through his resurrection from the dead. He who appeared in the flesh was "justified in the Spirit" (1 Tim. 3:16, ASV). "He was delivered over to death for our sins and was raised to life for our justification" (Rom. 4:25). He was vindicated in resurrection by being declared God's Son by the Spirit (Rom. 1:4). Thus are we also justified in union with Christ by that same Spirit who testifies with our Spirit that we are indeed sons and daughters of God by faith (Rom. 8:15–16). Both "adoption" and "testifying" by the Spirit are forensic metaphors, obviously integral to our legal acceptance in Christ. Both are elements of our baptism in the Spirit by faith (1 Cor. 12:13). Wilhelm Dantine reminds us that justification in the Spirit through union with Christ points us to the "forensic structure" of the Spirit's work in our lives.[83] Baptism in the Spirit by faith in Christ involves a rich experience of

---

83. Wilhelm Dantine, *Justification of the Ungodly* (St. Louis: Concordia, 1968), 116–18.

union with Christ that has not only forensic elements but also participatory and is, in effect, transformative.

Justification is also communal in implication, for our right relation with God through union with Christ also breaks down the barriers between people in order to open the door to a shared life together, a communal justice in the Spirit—in Christ. Referring to Jews and Gentiles, Paul writes of Christ: "For he himself is our peace who made the two groups one" (Eph. 2:14). Justification in union with the crucified and risen Christ reaches for eschatological fulfillment as well, "for through the Spirit we eagerly await by faith the righteousness for which we hope" (Gal. 5:5). Just as Christ was justified or vindicated in resurrection, so will we be in him (Rom. 8:11). Ernst Käsemann helps us understand justification within the context of ancient Jewish apocalypticism, in which the justice attained through justification has to do with the eschatological gift of righteousness connected to the dawning of the kingdom of God and the gift of the Spirit in Christ. The righteousness won for creation by Jesus is the restoration of God's sovereign claim on creation.[84] It is thus not only present but future (Gal. 5:5). Justification is viewed as a powerful act "by which God makes his cause triumph in the world" (180). It is a gift that is not external to us, "but becomes God's gift when it takes possession of us and, so to speak, enters into us" (173). More specifically, "the gift which is being bestowed here is never at any time separable from the Giver. It partakes of the character of power in so far as God himself enters the arena" (174). Indeed, God's power reaches out for the world, and the world's salvation lies in its being recaptured for the sovereignty of God" (182). Connecting justification with kingdom righteousness has the added benefit of including not only an accent on the forgiveness of the sinner but also justice for the victims of sin.[85]

Of course, as John Calvin maintained, we are not justified by the righteousness inherent in us due to the transformative work of the Spirit. In criticizing Andreas Osiander, Calvin wrote against "the absurd dogma that man is justified by faith, in as much as it brings him under the influence of the Spirit of God."[86] Justification is not measured by our progress in the

---

84. Ernst Käsemann, *Perspectives on Paul* (Mifflintown, PA: Sigler Press, 1996), 180. Hereafter, page references to this work appear in parentheses within the text.

85. See Jürgen Moltmann, "Die Rechtfertigung Gottes," *Stimmen der Zeit* 7 (July 2001): 435-42.

86. John Calvin, *Institutes of the Christian Religion*, trans. Henry Beveridge (Grand Rapids: Eerdmans, 1979), 3.11.23. Hereafter, section references to this work appear in parentheses within the text.

Spirit. Though based entirely on the faithfulness of Christ, justification still is received in union with him by the Spirit and by faith, and it reaches for eschatological realization. Therefore, though distinct, justification and sanctification are inseparable for Calvin, because both are accessible by partaking of Christ through the bond of the Spirit (1.3.2). "Christ breathes into his people that they may be one with him" (1.3.1). Justification and sanctification are, for Calvin, both as distinct and yet as inseparable as the heat is from the light of the sun (1.3.1). Baptized in the Spirit, one is justified and sanctified "in the name of the Lord Jesus Christ and the Spirit of our God" (1 Cor. 6:11).

Justification as received by the Spirit in union with Christ is also traceable to Luther. The leading figure in the Finnish interpretation of Luther, Tuomo Mannermaa, proposed that faith in Christ for Luther is not merely intellectual assent but is rather a transformative participation in Christ by the Spirit in union with Christ. Faith participates in "the real presence of the person and work of Christ."[87] Veli-Matti Kärkkäinen draws from this Finnish interpretation of Luther to explore an ecumenical understanding of justification that connects it with *theōsis*. Justification and *theōsis* are not the same metaphor, but they can illuminate one another. He helpfully discusses a broad spectrum of ecumenical Protestant affirmations of this connection (Lutheran, Methodist, evangelical).[88] It is interesting that Luther identifies the righteousness reckoned to us in faith and the gift of the Spirit as "the same thing," presumably because Christ himself (who is our righteousness) is received in the Spirit but also because "grace" is more than a mere "divine disposition"—but is also a divine gift imparted to us. I will allow Luther to speak for himself:

> Now is not the fact that faith is reckoned as righteousness a receiving of the Spirit? So either [Paul] proves nothing or the reception of the Spirit and the fact that faith is reckoned as righteousness will be the same thing. And this is true; it is introduced in order that the divine imputation may not be regarded as amounting to nothing outside of God, as some think that the Apostle's word grace means a favorable disposition rather than a gift. For when God is favorable and when he imputes, the Spirit is really received, both the gift and the grace.[89]

---

87. Tuomo Mannermaa, *Christ Present in Faith: Luther's View of Justification* (Minneapolis: Fortress/Augsburg, 2005), 3–4.

88. Veli-Matti Kärkkäinen, *One with God: Salvation as Deification and Justification* (Collegeville, MN: Liturgical Press, 2004).

89. Martin Luther, "Lectures on Galatians, 1519," in *Luther's Works*, ed. Jaroslav Pelikan (St. Louis: Concordia, 1963), 27:252.

He includes this striking identification of the righteousness reckoned to us by faith with the gift of the Spirit in his commentary (in part) on Galatians 3:21, where Paul says this: "For if a law had been given that could impart life, then righteousness would certainly have come by the law." Luther concludes from this text that the law cannot justify because the law cannot give life, cannot rescue us from the condemnation of death into which we have descended because of our sin. Luther then proposes that the righteousness that justifies us before God is not only won by Christ on the cross and at the resurrection but is also imparted to us in the gift of the Holy Spirit. Reckoned righteousness is indeed incorporated righteousness for Luther: the right relation with God that comes to us through the Christ of Pentecost, who incorporates us into himself and his body by baptizing us in the Holy Spirit. Jürgen Moltmann says: "The Holy Spirit is the righteousness and justice of God which creates justice, justifies, and rectifies. . . . That is why we can in this sense call the Holy Spirit *the justification of life*."[90] Paul Tillich's brilliant insight is also relevant: that justification occurs as God's people affirm by faith not only forgiveness but also "unambiguous life," which takes hold of us in the midst of our fallen and ambiguous existence.[91]

Consistent with this broader Reformation accent, Clark Pinnock locates justification within the soteriological framework of union with Christ by the Spirit. He criticizes those who emphasized justification so much as a legal metaphor that they neglected the significance of Jesus's sojourn in the Spirit for our incorporation into Christ by faith and baptism.[92] A similar approach to justification is advocated by the *Joint Declaration on the Doctrine of Justification* (jointly affirmed by the Catholic Church and the Lutheran World Federation, as well as a growing number of other world Protestant communions) (#15):

> In faith we together hold the conviction that justification is the work of the triune God. The Father sent his Son into the world to save sinners. The foundation and presupposition of justification is the incarnation, death, and resurrection of Christ. Justification thus means that Christ himself is our righteousness, in which we share through the Holy Spirit in accord with the will of the Father. Together we

90. Jürgen Moltmann, *The Spirit of Life: A Universal Affirmation* (Minneapolis: Fortress, 1992), 148.

91. Tillich, *Systematic Theology*, 3:226.

92. Pinnock, *Flame of Love*, 149-84.

confess: By grace alone, in faith in Christ's saving work and not because of any merit on our part, we are accepted by God and receive the Holy Spirit, who renews our hearts while equipping and calling us to good works.

Without this larger soteriological framework, justification by faith can appear as a "legal fiction" or as an abstract declaration of our rightness with God that has no direct relationship to human union with Christ as a participatory reality. Baptism in the Holy Spirit, as the context of justification, can help us avoid this implication. The identity of Jesus as the Spirit Baptizer who incorporates us into his life by the Spirit, under the sign of water baptism, is needed to rescue the doctrine of justification from juridical reductionism. Noteworthy here is Pannenberg's argument that union with Christ by faith as the context of justification can remove a "false objectifying" of justification as detached from our adoption by the Spirit into sonship in Christ.[93] Concerning adoption and regeneration by the Spirit in union with Christ, Pannenberg writes: "There is no reason to *subordinate* these other descriptions to the idea of justification, particularly as Paul himself already presupposed faith fellowship with Christ in the verdict of justification and then developed this theme in terms of adoption into filial relationship with the Father."[94] Justification by faith thus refers to our right relationship with God within the context of union with Christ by the Spirit under the sign of water baptism. As Kevin Vanhoozer has noted, justification as "incorporated" rather than "imputed" righteousness helps us to see how justification is also an ecclesial and social reality, in which our right relationship with God gives rise to the just community.[95]

My intention here is not to twist and turn soteriological categories to fit our favored theological inclinations. Instead, what I am suggesting is a focus on the movement from the cross to Pentecost as the place where Christ ultimately solves our problem, and then a peering through this lens all the way to the nature of the problem itself. More positively, rather than arriving at our own understanding of human salvation and then seeking to decorate it with biblical texts, we should see Christ's mission, in the light of its culmination at the resurrection and Pentecost, as a lens through which

---

93. Pannenberg, *Systematic Theology*, 3:211–36.

94. Pannenberg, *Systematic Theology*, 3:235 (italics in original).

95. Vanhoozer's response to N. T. Wright was given on April 17, 2010, at Wheaton College and is available online: https://vimeo.com/15518450.

we construct our understanding of human salvation. Looking at human renewal through this lens, we note that humanity's basic need is *life*, a life that is the dwelling place of the Spirit in the image of the faithful Son. Reconciliation has incorporation as its goal. Humans are not created as mere servants with divine law at the heartbeat of their existence; they are created by the Spirit of God to thrive as living beings in communion with God and for God's glory (Gen. 2:7). They are meant to be incorporated by the Spirit into the divine life—with all that this implies. "The Spirit of God has made me; the breath of the Almighty gives me life" (Job 33:4). We were made for the divine indwelling—to dwell in God and become living temples of the Holy Spirit. Indeed, one is made by God to seek "the evocative, ecstatic soul which is more itself the more God is in it and it is in God."[96] Earmarked to be the dwelling place of God's Spirit, humanity is also called to bear the Spirit in the image of Christ, the Word of the Father's love according to which they were created. In God, we all "live and move and have our being," for "we are his offspring," meant in the Spirit to take on the image of God's eternal Son (Acts 17:28).

Since sin and death create insurmountable barriers to this destiny of bearing the Spirit in the image of God's faithful Son, a radical solution is required that calls forth the need for the mission of the Spirit Baptizer, the crucified and risen Christ. The last Adam must conquer sin and death so as to be the mediator of life for the new humanity (1 Cor. 15:45; cf. 12:13). Jesus conquers sin and death on the cross in order to open the path for humanity to the Spirit of life. Edward Schillebeeckx suggests that Christ, in his life, death, and resurrection, overcame the enmity between *pneuma* (Spirit) and human *sarx* (flesh) caused by the fall, and he became in his glorified humanity the sacrament of spiritual renewal for all flesh at Pentecost. This is why Jesus would pour out the Spirit only when he was glorified (John 7:39).[97] Hebrews 5:9 says that Christ suffered the fires of judgment "so that once made perfect, he became the source of eternal salvation for all who obey him" (Heb. 5:9). Creation thus groans under the weight of sin and mortality for liberty in the Spirit that only the Spirit Baptizer can bring (Rom. 8:18–25). There is thus an analogy detectible between creation and redemption, since both occur by the Word and in the Spirit. Barth notes that "the relationship between the Spirit and man even in its anthropological sense is to be repre-

---

96. Michael Hanby, *Augustine and Modernity*, Radical Orthodoxy Series (Florence, KY: Routledge, 2003), 3.

97. Schillebeeckx, *Christ the Sacrament*, 26–27.

sented on the analogy of the expressions used in the soteriological context."[98] If we were created by the Word and in the Spirit to live in the love of the Father, salvation must be restored by the incarnation of that Word and his impartation of the Spirit to all flesh. If the fall into sin and death alienates us from the Word and the Spirit, only the offer of that Word to us in the gift of the Spirit can save us.

By looking at Pentecost in the light of all that leads up to it, we are able to surmise that humanity's departure from God does not simply consist of breaking the divine law, but also, more drastically, of denying the very source and flourishing of life in God and with God to which the law bears witness. Sin is by nature a *denial of life* as graced and enjoyed in God. Sin denies the richness of life in the Spirit as lived out in communion, worship, and faithful self-giving. Sin traps one in death and prevents one from choosing life: "Sin issues in the *destruction of the foundations of regeneration*."[99] Sin does break God's laws; more essentially, however, sin denies the *life* to which the law bears witness, the life created by the Spirit through the Word. Sin prefers isolation, idolatry, and self-reliance, all delusionary and unfulfilling. Sin is not just a wrong committed, as though wiping the record clean of wrongs done is sufficient to save us. Sin cannot be quantified in this way, as a mere series of wrongful acts, a record of wrongs that needs to somehow be legitimately erased. Sin is certainly wrong practices, but it is even more deeply a *denial of life*, a condition of separation from God and from divine communion, love, and the flourishing of life that is dedicated to divine purposes. Isaiah 53:6 says: "We all, like sheep, have gone astray. Each of us has turned to his own way." Adam and Eve were alienated from the sanctifying Spirit in the Fall; the last Adam came to give this Spirit back to them and, with the Spirit, a share in his filial relationship with the Father. We are justified, sanctified, and glorified "in the name of the Lord Jesus Christ and by the Spirit of our God" (1 Cor. 6:11; Rom. 8:30).

Of relevance to this "Pentecostal" soteriology, Hebrews 6:4–6 speaks of the danger of falling away from the "heavenly gift" of the Holy Spirit as well as from the "goodness of the Word of God." Hebrews 10:29 also describes sin as, ultimately, trampling "the Son of God underfoot" and insulting "the Spirit of grace." Such a total denial of the Spirit of life is thus analogous to a living

---

98. Karl Barth, *Church Dogmatics*, III/2: *The Doctrine of Creation*, trans. H. Knight et al. (Edinburgh: T & T Clark, 1960), 363.

99. Michael Welker, "The Holy Spirit," *Theology Today* 46, no. 1 (April 1989): 13–14 (italics in original).

death: "You were dead in your trespasses and sins" (Eph. 2:1). There is an integral connection between sin and death that the Pauline metaphor of death as "wages" attempts to capture (Rom. 6:23). More adequate in doing so is the Pauline metaphor of sin as itself a falling away from the glory we were made to share in God as living beings (3:23). We cannot live by bread alone, for we were made for so much more than that, namely, for communion in God. So, if we seek to live by bread alone, we are involved in a living death (death by bread alone [Luke 4:4]). Notice that the gift that saves us does not just result in new life; it *is* new life. In the light of Pentecost we learn that this is life in the Son, life faithful to the Father's loving cause in the world, life in communion and in community, in the expansively diverse work of the Spirit. As Jan M. Lochman maintains, salvation is by nature multidimensional and multicontextual.[100]

Sin, as unholy, denies by its very nature the *Holy* Spirit, and sin, as a path of death, by its very nature denies the Spirit as the Spirit of *life*. Sin spurns the Father, denies Christ, and grieves the Spirit. Sin is the opposite of Pentecost, of the Father as the wellspring of the Spirit, of the Son as the bearer and mediator of the Spirit in his faithful commitment to the Father's cause in the world, and of the Spirit as the eschatological freedom of divine love and witness. The goal of Christ is to bring us back to the self-imparting God of Pentecost, which is rooted in the self-impartation of the incarnation and the cross. The bestowal of the Spirit is precisely where Adam and Eve began their journeys as human beings, and it is where the Christ as the last Adam wishes to restore us and so much more than that: "So it is written: 'The first man Adam became a living being; the last Adam, a life-giving spirit'" (1 Cor. 15:45). It is for this purpose we were made: to trade this earthly body for the risen body that is "swallowed up" (or "baptized") in the life of the immortal Spirit (2 Cor. 5:4), the down payment, or foretaste, of which we now share as bearers of the Spirit in Christ (2 Cor. 5:5). We were made to be the dwelling place of God in the image of the faithful Son, a destiny imparted to us by the crucified and risen Christ at Pentecost.

We are accustomed to viewing sin as simply defying God's holy law. And so it is. But we must also bear in mind that the law serves *life*, the life of the Spirit. The law is thus spiritual (Rom. 7:14). Law characterizes a disciplined devotion to the ways of life in the Spirit, which is why the law arises from the heart, is expressed supremely through love, and can only be followed in the liberty of the Spirit (Deut. 6:4-6; Ezek. 36:26-27). The law cannot save us

---

100. Jan M. Lochman, *Reconciliation and Liberation: Challenging a One-Dimensional View of Salvation* (Philadelphia: Fortress, 1980).

because the law cannot restore us to life: "If a law had been given that could impart life, then righteousness would certainly have come by the law" (Gal. 3:21). Only Christ is the true bearer of the Spirit; only he can mediate life to us as the Spirit Baptizer. The law cannot do this. Only the Spirit as mediated through the faithful Son can open us to the freedom that life in loyalty to the law of God assumes (Ezek. 36:26). In spurning God's law, sin ultimately contradicts the way of the Spirit, the way of the faithful Son, who transforms us in his image by mediating the Spirit of life to us. Indeed, there is a juridical dimension to salvation, which involves us in forgiveness and reconciliation. But the justice of reconciliation through the cross establishes a new covenant that involves life in the Spirit and communion. Pentecost was a celebration of the Sinai covenant within Judaism.[101] But due to Jesus's journey from the cross to Pentecost, it became the celebration of a new covenant between God and humanity lived out in communion with God through the Spirit, a new exodus by the Spirit foretold in Isaiah 40–55.[102]

As divine, the Christ of Pentecost saves out of the abundance of self-giving. Spirit baptism as a root soteriological metaphor reminds us that God did not need to create or save the creation in order to fill up some lack in the divine life. Creation and salvation can thus only be described along the lines of the metaphor used by John the Baptist. The coming Messiah will occasion a virtual river of life from the divine presence that overflows the divine fullness so as to renew the fallen creation. "From his innermost being will flow rivers of living water" (John 7:38, NASB).[103] God creates and saves out of divine fullness and not out of divine need, for "he is not served by human hands as if he needed anything" (Acts 17:25). Barth says that God allows humanity to participate in saving grace "in superfluity." He continues about God and the creature:

> He allows its existence as another, as a counterpart to Himself, and His own co-existence with it. In superfluity—we have to say this because we are in fact dealing with an overflowing, not with a filling up of the perfection of God which needs no filling.[104]

101. Meredith Kline, "Primal Parousia," *Westminster Theological Journal* 40 (1978): 245–80.
102. David W. Pao, *Acts and the Isaianic New Exodus* (Eugene, OR: Wipf and Stock, 2016).
103. This text most likely refers explicitly to Christ in his future impartation of the Spirit. Even if it refers to the believers whose lives will overflow with the Spirit, the implication would at least be that Christ is the one who mediated this Spirit abundantly from God. See Joel Marcus, "Rivers of Living Water from Jesus' Belly," *Journal of Biblical Literature* 117, no. 2 (Summer 1998): 328–30.
104. Barth, *Church Dogmatics*, IV/1, 201.

Drawing from Eastern sources, Eugene Rogers makes this point well, referring to the superfluity of grace in the Spirit's presence, and also how, for this reason, the Spirit is never to be grasped after. The Spirit rests in abundance and overflowing love, first on the Son as the image of self-giving love, but then also through the Son on the creation in order to incorporate it into the Son, in conformity to his image and purpose.[105]

The Christ of Pentecost and Ecclesiology

Christological method will be based on the story of Christ's self-giving that led up to Pentecost as Christ's culminating act in history. But it will also be attentive to what Christ is doing by the Spirit in the world today. This is because Christ opens himself to an ever-expanding ecclesial fellowship as the Spirit Baptizer. (Unpacking this cluster of ideas will be the task of this final section.)

It is important to note from the start that the economy of Christ overlaps with the economy of the Spirit. A Christology of Pentecost might raise the question about whether or not we are honoring the Christian calendar. Doesn't Pentecost belong to the economy or realm of the Spirit in the church calendar? Don't Christmas, Good Friday, and Easter belong to the economy of the Son, or Christology? Are we not confusing the events of the Christian calendar by focusing Christology on Pentecost? Not so. The Spirit is active during Christ's sojourn on earth toward and including the cross and resurrection, and Christ is present and active during the era of the Spirit from Pentecost onward. Though Christ ascended to the Father and is not visibly present, he still addresses and offers communion with us in the Spirit of discernment (Rev. 1–3). Of course, the work of the triune God is undivided. The two economies of Christ and the Spirit overlap most significantly at the point of transition. Pentecost as the transition between the economy of the Son and the economy of the Spirit is just as much a christological event as a pneumatological one. Pentecost is the culmination of the messianic mission and the inauguration of the Spirit's mission—just as important to both economies.[106] It is not to be denied that Pentecost is important to the shape of both missions, both Christ's and the Spirit's. Pentecost moves in both di-

---

105. Rogers, *After the Spirit*, esp. 75–199.
106. John D. Zizioulas, *Being as Communion* (Crestwood, NY: St. Vladimir's Seminary Press, 1997), 130.

rections, from the Spirit to Christ (shaping the direction of Christ's mission pneumatologically from the incarnation to Pentecost) and from Christ to the Spirit (shaping the direction of the Spirit's mission christologically from Pentecost to Christ's return). But there is also overlap between these two economies, since Christ's faithful obedience also brings specificity to the Spirit's leading during Christ's sojourn on earth and the Spirit's witness after Pentecost also plays an important role in Christ's eschatological identity. This overlap is not always fully appreciated.

Not only is Christ's impartation of the Spirit significant for our understanding of the direction of the Spirit's work in the world today, this Pentecost event also decisively determines the mission of Jesus Christ as the Son. John Zizioulas points out that the incarnation makes Christ "historical" in the sense that, at this event, God in the person of the Son enters the flesh of Jesus as the representative person, indeed, in representation of the entire creation. We could add that the Spirit is involved in the incarnation (Luke 1:35) in that the Spirit befriends matter and turns the body of Jesus into the means through which God the Son redeems the world as its representative figure. But not only is the Spirit the means by which the Son incarnates matter (or history) in Jesus Christ, the Spirit—according to Zizioulas—is also the means by which Christ and his economy are "liberated" from bondage to history in order to take history into an eschatological fulfillment, one that conforms to the will of the Father, the risen life of the faithful Son, and the eschatological freedom of divine love in the Spirit.

All of this means, for Zizioulas, that "the Spirit makes of Christ an eschatological being, the 'last Adam.'"[107] As I have noted above, Christ is the last Adam as life-giving spirit (1 Cor. 15:45), or, as in my preferred term, the Spirit Baptizer (1 Cor. 12:13). At the time of the resurrection and Pentecost the risen and exalted Christ becomes the eschatological person: he becomes the doorway to eschatological fulfillment, the new creation. At Pentecost he becomes the Spirit Baptizer. He has not come into flesh and borne the Spirit simply for his own sake but for the sake of the new creation. So also are we renewed in his image, not only to enjoy new life in him but to enjoy it with others (though he is the only mediator through it all). Indeed, his very identity as the Spirit Baptizer is not fulfilled until he imparts the Spirit upon all flesh and brings all flesh into the loving embrace of divine communion, of sonship. In doing so, says Zizioulas, Christ becomes a corporate personality.[108]

---

107. Zizioulas, *Being as Communion*, 130.
108. Zizioulas, *Being as Communion*, 130.

Barth also speaks of Christ's humanity as a "fellow humanity."[109] "Here He is for us and the world in the work of the Holy Spirit: In the gathering and edifying and sending of His community."[110] As the Spirit Baptizer, Christ incorporates a diverse body into himself as one body so that they may all drink of the Spirit in him (1 Cor. 12:13).

This gift of the Spirit given as the culmination of Christ's redemptive work leads to a fellowship in Christ that binds together not only Jew and Gentile but also male and female, bond and free (Gal. 3:28), which is reminiscent of how the Spirit granted at Pentecost crosses boundaries (Acts 2:17–21). Christ the Spirit Baptizer is Christ the head of a diverse body, the firstborn among many brothers and sisters (Rom. 8:29). He is the Messiah and Lord who imparts the Spirit (Acts 2:33–36), the firstborn over creation (Col. 1:15), the one for whom the creation groans as in childbirth in implicit search for freedom from the burdens of sin and death (Rom. 8:29). It becomes clear at Pentecost that his incarnation, baptism, life ministry, death, and resurrection had as their goal the making of Christ into all of these things—and so much more. As Zizioulas shows us, the Spirit resting upon and bestowed by Christ, the last Adam, "contributes to Christ this dimension of communion."[111] Paul Tillich was correct: "Christ is not the Christ without those who receive him as the Christ."[112] The church is to be "the fullness of him that fills everything in every way" (Eph. 1:23). This is because Christ is at Pentecost the Spirit Baptizer. This is his ultimate identity, the Lord and head of his body.

Amos Yong reminds us that Pentecost as a christological event means that Christ must be interpreted in the light of many contexts and voices. He shows how Christ opens the church in Acts to a plurality of voices. Yet the message in Acts does not compromise christological exclusivism (Christ as the only mediator of life).[113] The focus on Christ as Spirit Baptizer opens Christ up to an ever-expanding hospitality of faith and life. Michael Welker says this:

> Indeed, the life of the resurrected one, who constitutes his post-Easter body through the various gifts of the Spirit and in the creative interplay of its members in order to make his presence known

---

109. Barth, *Church Dogmatics*, III/2, 208, 312.
110. Barth, *Church Dogmatics*, III/2, 97.
111. Zizioulas, *Being as Communion*, 130.
112. Tillich, *Systematic Theology*, 2:99.
113. Amos Yong, *Hospitality of the Other: Pentecost, Christian Practices, and the Neighbor* (Maryknoll, NY: Orbis, 2008).

in the world, simply cannot be grasped without a mulitcontextual approach.[114]

Taking the exalted Christ, who incorporates a diversity of others into his life by imparting the Spirit, implies a "multicontextual turn" in christological method, not one that is content with simply speaking about how we are to live in "pluralistic societies," how plurality is on the rise, or how we are to live in the processes of pluralization. No abstract pluralism detached from the exalted Christ will do. Jesus's statement in John 14:2 that his Father's house has many rooms has implications for christological method.[115] A point of departure for the christological method in Jesus as the Spirit Baptizer will take this insight seriously.

As the one who pours out the eschatological Spirit, Christ's identity is open and ever more expansive. Dietrich Bonhoeffer even spoke of Christ as not only existing *for* or *in* the church but of "Christ existing *as* church." Precisely in the penance of the church's members as sinners, "Christ exists as church." He bore the sins of the sinners in himself, within the very heart of God representatively through the incarnation, and he suffered for them vicariously on the cross so that he could redefine their existence as his body.[116] This is what he actualizes at the resurrection and Pentecost. The integral connection now between Christ and the church means that a Christology from below that is focused on Pentecost has the added benefit of taking with utmost seriousness a multicontextual Christology for our time—a Christology on the way. As the Spirit Baptizer, Christ takes us up into himself to experience him and bear witness to him in legitimately diverse ways. And he wears that diverse witness as his colorful robe, integral to his own identity and self-expression in the world.

The Spirit Baptizer thus cannot be expressed in only one dominant tongue or perspective that is put forward so as to gain ascendance over all the rest. There is more than one lampstand surrounding and illuminating the Christ in Revelation 1! One's Christology must, from the beginning, recognize the limitations of its own particular effort to discern and illuminate Christ's identity and significance and will invite others to bring to the table of fellowship their own unique witness. The Christ experienced diversely in

---

114. Michael Welker, *God the Revealed: Christology* (Grand Rapids: Eerdmans, 2013), 53.
115. Welker, *God the Revealed*, 53.
116. Dietrich Bonhoeffer, *Communion of Saints: A Dogmatic Inquiry into the Sociology of the Church* (New York: Harper and Row, 1963), 106–8, 147–48.

the world cannot be an addendum to Christology simply because Jesus came into the world and bore the Spirit precisely so that he could impart the Spirit, and with the Spirit impart himself—to *all flesh*. He came to create space in himself for multiple others in all of their diversity, representatively from the incarnation to the cross and the resurrection, and actually at Pentecost. God willed the multicontextual revelation of Christ from all eternity as the ultimate way in which God would be revealed in him, and the true humanity in him would be inaugurated. Under the banner of Spirit baptism, Christ is one with God precisely in being the God for and with others, and we, in witness to Christ, become in him a people who are with and for others.

The expanding diversity of the body of Christ is the colorful robe that he wears on the way to the fulfillment of history. Wearing this robe, Christ fulfills the history that defines him; but in a way that is still determined by the trajectory of the history that leads up to and includes Pentecost. The Spirit's faithful witness to Christ is still faithful to that history. The church's lack of faithfulness to that history explains in part Christ's transcendence with respect to the church, as well as his challenge to us. It also explains our need for ongoing forgiveness and sanctification. We are his body, but we are also seeking to "grow to become in every respect the mature body of him who is the head, that is, Christ" (Eph. 4:15). This is why Christ's history remains both distinct from and bound to that diverse body that he now bears as the Spirit Baptizer. Christ exists as community in spite of our sin, or as costly grace that calls us continuously beyond ourselves to bear Christ's image by bearing the Spirit. Bound to Christ by such costly grace in the Spirit of holiness, we do not have this Christ at our disposal. The Christ of Pentecost is anchored in his own history as the Spirit-baptized Word of the Father, which means that he identifies himself with us on his terms and toward the fulfillment of his liberating purposes for creation.

To say that Christ imparts himself from his own history as the Spirit-baptized one does not nullify his multicontextual significance as the Spirit Baptizer. For one thing, his entire Spirit-baptized history reaches toward expansive global and eschatological fulfillment. His Spirit-baptized life takes him from rewriting the story of Israel to extending that story to the nations. His birth amongst an occupied people that was under the boot of the Roman Empire—and his betrayal by key leaders from among his own people—locate him uniquely in the place of the oppressed. Yet his offer of himself toward the forgiveness of sinners who repent opens up the possibility of a kingdom justice that reconciles and heals across boundaries of injury and abandonment. How Christ opens the hospitality of the kingdom of God multicontextually reaches for the hospitality of Pentecost and of a globally expanding witness. The Spirit-baptized life of Jesus offers us concrete guidance for discerning how the Spirit Baptizer comes to us and is experienced among us. In imparting the Spirit on all flesh, Christ imparts his own life to the world precisely as his own embodied existence as the beloved and faithful archetype of the new humanity.

In the midst of a diverse conversation, the people of God strive in the Spirit to discern in the light of Scripture whether and in what sense speech about him is in harmony with the Spirit's witness to Christ. One may indeed appeal to what Christ is doing in the world today. After all, "Christ is the same, yesterday, and today, and forever" (Heb. 13:8). Appealing to the voice of the living Christ, however, will be shown, if legitimate, to be consistent with the life of the Spirit- and fire-baptized Christ. Christ spoke to Peter and directed him to the household of a Roman centurion, Cornelius, at the cutting edge of the Gentile mission (Acts 10). When the question arose in Acts 15 about whether or not to accept uncircumcised Gentiles into the messianic fellowship and mission, the disciples could very well have discussed the implications of Jesus's table fellowship (they might actually have done this!). Instead, what the text highlights is the hospitality of the Spirit that Christ opened up to them at the household of a Roman centurion. The expanding multicontextual communion of Christ in the Spirit will, of course, be consistent with Christ's life and work on earth, but that expanding communion will also illuminate the scriptural witness of Christ in creative and diverse ways. Christ's story continues: his hospitality as the Spirit Baptizer is still being extended to the world through the Spirit.

Of course, as I have noted above, he baptizes us in the Spirit from the fullness of his own Spirit-led life as the faithful Son of the Father. He has his own beginning in his crossing of the gulf of sin and death in order to bind himself to the sinful flesh of humanity when he was conceived by the Spirit in the Virgin's womb. He has his own turning point when he steps into the waters of repentance in order to identify himself with sinners and to bear their fire baptism as their Spirit Baptizer. He has his own story of serving and healing, of inviting others to his Father's banquet table, and of going to the cross in self-sacrificial love for the redemption of the world. He has his own voice against the oppressive powers, even—and especially—when he allowed himself to be reduced to silence (Matt. 26:63) in solidarity with those who had their voices silenced or ignored. His story calls Israel to glorify God by bearing witness to the nations of God's justice and mercy, to the nations who come as distant strangers to the household of faith, who hark back to

Christ in remembrance and point ahead to him in hope. This is *the one*, and no other, who comes to us in the impartation of the Spirit and who continues to extend the hospitality of his crucified and risen body to the world. He continues to open his story to us as the all-defining narrative of our own life together in him and in his Spirit. He continues to find in us a unique diversity of witnesses who now represent an extension of his self-expression before the world. His act of pouring forth the Spirit fulfills his sojourn on earth as the beloved and faithful Christ; but this sojourn also provides the foundation from which this fulfillment is to be continually discerned afresh and diversely in the world.

To call and transform us in this way—to make us suitable as his body—Christ has structured his body with the means by which his Spirit can conform us to his love and his justice. As the Spirit Baptizer, Christ grants the church, by his Spirit, core practices that the church "bears" in faithfulness to him.[117] The faith that exalts and follows Jesus is born in the midst of core practices, for faith is a living and practiced reality. Faith is practiced in worship; in the preaching and communal sharing of the word of God; in the sacraments of baptism and the Lord's Supper; in multiple and various spiritual gifts that build up the body of Christ in divine love; in missionary work; and in the promotion of social justice and reconciliation, to name only a handful of obvious examples. People who are in the Spirit are baptized into Christ. They are incorporated into Christ by faith as signified at the waters of baptism. They die to what is sinful or self-centered, but they do not lose what God created them to be. In fact, they were made for this very purpose: to conform to Christ by bearing the Spirit. They merely offer all of themselves by the Spirit in the service of Christ, as Paul did when he let go of his idolatrous attachment to elements of his personal story in order to win Christ and to direct everything in service to him as the author of new life (Phil. 3:1-11). One comes to Christ bearing the gifts of one's social and cultural contexts for his glory and liberating purposes, like the kings of the nations who will bring the splendor of their nations into the heavenly city in honor to Christ (Rev. 21:24). As I noted above, this is what makes the church so diverse—and Christ's robe so colorful. Of course, we will also bring our brokenness to Christ for healing. And we

---

117. I am grateful to Reinhard Hütter for this notion of core practices as gifts from the Spirit that we bear in loving faithfulness to Christ. See his *Suffering Divine Things: Theology as Church Practice* (Grand Rapids: Eerdmans, 1999). A more accessible guide to his thought can be found in his book *Bound to Be Free: Evangelical-Catholic Engagements in Ecclesiology, Ethics, and Ecumenism* (Grand Rapids: Eerdmans, 2004).

will bring the challenges that require an answer. There is a give-and-take in this communion surrounding Christ that aids us in the attainment of wisdom in him.

These gifts that we carry in ourselves as we are baptized into Christ by the Spirit are, however, mediated to Christ through the core practices by which we relate to him and by which he conforms us in the Spirit into his image. In other words, one's cultural or social past exerts a qualified influence on Christology, but one that is still important. The church is the social base of christological reflection. Of course, we cannot totally separate church from culture, nor should we try. Cultural diversification is a wonderful gift of the Spirit of God. God's Word at creation was spoken in the Spirit in diverse ways. So it is at the new creation through the resurrection of Jesus and Pentecost. But the church also subverts culture through its core practices in order to be the instrument of sanctification in service to Christ. Christology has as its social base the churches that are structured by the Spirit to be conformed to Christ, but also wonderfully influenced by a diversity of cultures and ecclesiastical histories. This is the colorful diversity of Christ's body, the body he now bears as the Spirit Baptizer.

The core practices and the faith expressed through them are thus bound and loyal first and foremost to Christ, to the Christ who emerges from his own unique story and now embraces us from that story through the Spirit he imparts to us. Since Scripture, which is also born of the Spirit of Christ, is the primary witness to Christ, this primary witness (practice) remains, by way of the Spirit, the living measure of all other church practices and of the faith expressed through them. How Scripture guides these practices and leads the churches to wisdom concerning Christ will naturally be discerned in the midst of core practices in contextually relevant and diverse ways. But Scripture cannot be dissolved into these church practices.[118] The witnesses whose voices are canonized in Scripture are fundamental to the robes of Christ, to which we are added by grace but also in our hearing and obedience. "We are surrounded by such a great cloud of witnesses" (Heb. 12:1). We join that cloud of witnesses who occasioned the writing of that canonical text as we join in their witness. The Spirit Baptizer speaks through the pages of the text, calling us to add our voices in critical appropriation and witness to those ancient voices. These words of Scripture in his hands could never be a static artifact from the past. Yet the voice of Christ through the Spirit-inspired text must be discerned in its relation to that text itself. Though this

---

118. This is the methodological insight of Kevin Vanhoozer, *The Drama of Doctrine.*

Scripture is discerned and appropriated in contextually relevant ways, the Scripture in the Spirit maintains its own voice distinct from that appropriation as its living measure and guide. Scripture is still the supreme standard and living measure of all Christologies. So, even though there will be diverse Christologies, they will be bound together in united loyalty to one Lord, one faith, one baptism (Eph. 4:5), and one scriptural standard (2 Tim. 3:16).

Conclusion

To conclude this discussion of christological method, a Christology from below does not displace a Christology from above, with its important question about Christ's unity with God and humanity. But christological method will anchor that concern in a Christology from below that highlights Christ's impartation of the Spirit at Pentecost as the point of culmination and clarity. This is the event where the Spirit Baptizer pours forth the Spirit on all flesh and incorporates us into himself—into the life and mission of the triune God. In imparting the Spirit, Christ imparts himself from his own history as the one baptized in Spirit and fire on our behalf. He does this as the Word of the Father's love. This is where Christ's essential unity with God in the divine self-impartation to the world and incorporation of flesh into the divine life is decisively confirmed and revealed. This is where his embodied mediation of the Spirit on behalf of the Father shows him to be quintessential flesh, essentially one with humanity as it was created to be.

A Christology from below will thus settle here at Pentecost as its point of greatest clarity. Each step along the way, from the incarnation to Pentecost, should be discussed in the light of Pentecost—with Pentecost at the horizon. And Pentecost should be understood in the light of each of these steps. Pannenberg is right in noting that the whole is best viewed through the lens of its fulfillment. As for now, this fulfillment is Pentecost, the place of foresight and hope for the apocalyptic revelation yet to come. Pentecost as the christological lens is suggested biblically for us by Jesus's chief forerunner, John the Baptist, who announced that the Christ will bear the Spirit in order to baptize others in the Spirit. But Christ will do so as the one who is himself baptized in the Spirit and fire, in order to take the new creation into himself by the Spirit he imparts. His identity is now conditioned by his body, through which he exists as its head and elder brother. This is who he is and will forever be: the Messiah who is Lord, but also the firstborn of many brothers and sisters.

We are brought into Christ via the Spirit bearing different gifts from our diverse churches and contexts. Christ wears this diverse body as his colorful robe as he continuously offers himself to creation in the hospitality of his broken but risen body. Christological method from below, therefore, has its social base in the churches and its practices that structure the churches' life in Christ, chiefly in faithfulness to the scriptural witness. But the churches incorporated into Christ also have their horizon in the eschatological hope for a world transformed by divine love and justice. Christ's baptizing us in the Spirit will find its ultimate climax when all of us find our mortality fully "swallowed up" (baptized) in his immortal life (2 Cor. 5:4) at his return. The Spirit's outpouring onto all flesh will then find its eschatological fulfillment: the Spirit's witness to Christ gaining its fullness, Christ's body attaining its ultimate fullness of expression, and the Spirit Baptizer fulfilling his final purpose. This is a Christology on the way, anchored in his history as the Spirit-baptized Word of the Father but also reaching beyond history toward eschatological fulfillment.

CHAPTER 2

Challenges to Christology

"God is not free *of* man but *for* man."

—Dietrich Bonhoeffer, *Act and Being*

In the previous chapter I discussed the issue of christological method: how and why we should approach Christology from below with Pentecost as the climactic focus. How this methodological focus on Pentecost illuminates the classical attempts to conceive of the incarnation will need to be taken up in the following chapter. In this chapter I intend to move beyond the strict boundaries of christological method to discuss some further challenges associated with the historical attempt to conceive of Christ as in unity with God and humanity. These challenges will also have methodological implications. The chief challenge to the unity of this genuinely human Christ with God is the challenge of metaphysics, or the nature of God in relation to the nature of the world. It has to do with whether or not Christ can be said to be divine if he is at the same time fully human—and what it means to say that he is divine. The metaphysical challenge to saying that a human can be divine was divine transcendence, or the doctrine of God's uniqueness and sovereign freedom in relation to creation. In particular, if God and creation were contrary to one another in attributes, it would seem conceptually difficult to imagine the human person of Christ as one with God.

The question of Jesus's unity with God also raises the issue of whether this unity is ontological or merely functional (or ontological by being functional). In other words, is Jesus one with God merely in being one with God's saving action in the world, or may we also say that Jesus is one with God in *essence* or with God's being as God? In the modern era, the challenge to Christology went beyond metaphysics. The challenge to Christology took an anthropological turn and had to do with the question of Jesus in relation to human existential enlightenment or, more expansively, communal and social liberation. Finally, the question of Christology has turned most recently to Jesus in relation to the pluralist challenge, an issue of global proportions and one of importance to a Christology that highlights Pentecost. Is faith in Christ alone as savior of the world implicitly contrary to the humility and openness of faith to others? The Christ of Pentecost is indeed open to others, as is his body on earth; and yet this openness highlights him alone as Spirit Baptizer. There are preliminary issues to discuss before we get to the substantive issues of incarnation, Spirit anointing, crucifixion, resurrection, and Pentecost.

The Metaphysical Challenge

The burning question of theological metaphysics was how one can possibly conceive of the divine-human relationship when taking into consideration divine transcendence or freedom from the limitations that characterize creaturely existence. Is the essence of the divine life even knowable? If not, the divine life would seem out of reach to creaturely life. And if what can be known of the divine life is contrary by nature to what we know of creaturely life, then any direct connection of one to the other might seem out of the question. A mediating reality would then seem necessary, one that could participate in both God and finite nature so as to provide a bridge between them. Was Christ this intermediate reality? If so, he would not be God in the same sense as the transcendent deity who must remain distant from us to remain "God." In that case, Christ's very existence would imply a God who remains distant from us, who can never be directly involved with us. God helps us, but only at arm's length, so to speak. Christ would occupy the place of a "middleman," the need for which tragically assumes that God and humanity must remain apart to be free. Gone is the biblical idea that humanity can only be free in God and because God is free for humanity. Gone is the idea that God is free *for* us and not *from* us. Transcendence was in danger here of becoming a divine freedom from us, and not for us. Such was the metaphysical challenge of the ancient world for Christology.

By way of contrast, Scripture presents God as free *for* us. God is self-imparting to creation out of the infinite fullness of divine love, a fullness that never decreases and is ever flowing. The divine transcendence is not meant to remove God from us, or make God a figure alien to life. It is rather meant to explain the infinite freedom of God's sovereign love from all external lim-itation or manipulation. This is the love that is pure grace or has its reason for being in God alone. This is the love that is poured out freely for us in Christ and through Christ in the Spirit of life. Note, for a moment, the full christological hymn of Philippians 2:

> In your relationships with one another, have the same mindset as Christ Jesus:
>
> Who, being in very nature God,
> > did not consider equality with God something to be used to his
> > > own advantage;
> rather, he made himself nothing
> > by taking the very nature of a servant,
> > being made in human likeness.
> And being found in appearance as a man,
> > he humbled himself
> > by becoming obedient to death—
> > even death on a cross!
> Therefore God exalted him to the highest place
> > and gave him the name that is above every name,
> that at the name of Jesus every knee should bow,
> > in heaven and on earth and under the earth,
> and every tongue acknowledge that Jesus Christ is Lord,
> > to the glory of God the Father.

In his seminal examination of this text, Ernst Lohmeyer has determined that it was originally a hymn that was sung as part of an early Jewish Christian eucharistic liturgy. It thus grants us an open window into what the earliest Christians believed about Christ.[1] The one who is in the form of God unites with the reality of human life, becomes a servant, and bears vicariously the death of a criminal. The paradox of grace here is shocking. This is what I have referred to earlier as Christ's baptism in fire. Linking the steps downward is this stunning picture of the self-imparting love of God. The fact that self-giving love drives the steps from the form of God

---

1. Colin Brown, "Ernst Lohmeyer's Kyrios Jesus," in *Where Christology Began: Essays on Philippians 2*, ed. Ralph P. Martin and Brian J. Dodd (Louisville: Westminster John Knox, 1998), 17.

to humanity, servanthood, and criminal condemnation means that the hymn does not intend to present us *simply* with a contrast of opposites between servanthood and lordship. The servant who is exalted as Lord binds them together. As the ideal servant, Christ does not grasp after God; he receives from the heavenly Father with gratitude and obedience. He follows in the way set before him by the Father's cause in the world for the sake of humanity. "For your sake he became poor, so that you through his poverty might become rich" (2 Cor. 8:9). Therefore, Christ's journey to the cross also reveals the love of God for humanity. The journey to the cross represents Christ imaging God for us, doing the most divine thing that the Son of God does. He loves in this way not only to reveal the way of the ideal human servant but also the Lord who gives freely for the sake of our redemption.

The servant is indeed exalted as Lord. "Therefore," says the hymn, "God exalted him to the highest place" (Phil. 2:9). The result is that the creation confesses him as Lord to the glory of the Father. To express it another way, this is divine lordship exercised with sovereign freedom in the direction of self-giving love. This is the lordship revealed from the cross to Pentecost. The love emptied out in the journey to the cross, poured out like a sacred offering through the spilled blood and broken body of Jesus, overflows the barriers of sin and death at the cross (abolishing them) in order to be poured forth through the risen Christ onto all flesh. The eschatological reach and the cosmic expanse of the confession given in Philippians 2 are striking. Though the hymn does not mention the universal expanse of Christ's lordship through his abundant outpouring of the Spirit upon all flesh, it certainly implies that. The ending implies Pentecost and dovetails nicely with Acts 2:33–36 (discussed in the preceding chapter). There Christ is enthroned as Messiah and Lord and then bestows the Spirit on all flesh in order to bring all into the confession that forms the climax of the hymn. It is only by the Spirit that we can confess Jesus as Lord (1 Cor. 12:3).

Christology is the story of how the divine Word of the Father is self-imparted to human flesh from incarnation to Pentecost for the purpose of incorporating all flesh into Christ—that is, into the life of the triune God. The divine capacity to self-impart to all flesh was a big pill to swallow for many in the ancient world, which was true because of the doctrine of divine transcendence: God's eternal and unchanging sovereignty and freedom. As I have noted from the Philippians 2 text above, the irony of this challenge is in the fact that the New Testament reveals God's lordship precisely as the victory and reign of divine *love.*

So what does divine transcendence mean in the context of *this* understanding of divine lordship? What does it mean in the context of a divine love that does not remain self-enclosed but rather, in the eschatological freedom of the Spirit, self-imparts to all flesh across the gulf of sin and death and even beyond the reaches of space and time? That such divine transcendence should be treated in the ancient world as the supreme barrier to God's direct involvement in creation will remain one of the fascinating ironies of theological history.

The precise nature of the challenge arising from the doctrine of divine transcendence depended on how the doctrine was specifically understood. Generally speaking, this doctrine typically involved the basically true notion of God as infinitely or radically "other" (different in being) than creation. God is the origin of all things, and all things are brought into being dependent on God for life. As essentially other than the creation, God is essentially free from its hold or limitations. Some notion of divine otherness was widely thought to exist across the board in both ancient Greek and Jewish thinking, requiring some kind of divine mediation with the world. This mediator was popularly called the Logos (Word) of God, which sometimes accounted for the mind of God, the rational structure of the world, or perhaps the particularly Jewish notion of the creative principle involved in the divine creation of all things. Following John 1 and other texts, Christians connected the Logos to Christ. Various possibilities for understanding the nature of the Logos existed in the ancient world.

Divine otherness means that God is not reducible to an object from the created order. Thus no one can directly comprehend or manipulate God toward human ends. God is not at our disposal. This idea of divine transcendence is very ancient and lies behind the Old Testament condemnation of idolatry (Isa. 40:18–25). In Hebrew Scripture, God is sovereign and free with respect to creation, and God acts to self-reveal and to save on divine rather than human terms. This is the truth value of divine transcendence. Some notion of divine transcendence was characteristic of ancient Greek (e.g., Middle Platonic) and Jewish traditions in the ancient world. Most participants in early Christianity, especially from the third century and beyond, inherited this doctrine in some form or other.

A greater potential for controversy was the development of divine transcendence along the lines of a clearly defined list of divine attributes that were construed at every point in opposition to the created order. This development eventually inspired a definition of divine attributes that negated creaturely attributes. God is infinite while creation is finite; God is immortal while creation is mortal; God is out of the reach of human powers of comprehension while the creaturely realm is at least potentially comprehensible; God is incorporeal while creation is material; God is simple (is not divided, or has no parts, and is fully identifiable with all divine attributes) while creation is complex (has parts, or is able to realize potential attributes and take on additional ones); God is the source of all while everything else is dependent on a higher source for its existence. Especially within a Jewish context, God is Lord of all, while all else is accountable to that lordship. More controversially, God was thought to be immutable, while creation was mutable. God was impassible, while creation was vulnerable to suffering. I say that these last two contrasts were more controversial because they seemed more Greek than Jewish (though these two traditions overlapped in the ancient world). The God of Moses was typically thought to be more compatible with history and its vicissitudes than the God of Plato.

This contrast in attributes was understood among the church fathers as also arising from the limitless fullness and abundance of divine life and power. An attribute like impassibility or immutability "radically affirms and profoundly intensifies the absolute perfection and utter goodness of God."[2] It was also aimed at distinguishing the biblical God from the finite and crude deities of popular mythology.[3] But the contrasts still posed problems when it came to their efforts to understand the incarnation, especially in the light of the crucifixion. The chief question posed by the metaphysical contrasts was how the divine Son could be directly involved in creation given the sharp oppositions assumed between divine and creaturely attributes. In the fourth (to the fifth) century, Theodore of Mopsuestia said of the transcendent divine Son's uniting to human flesh that "it is not possible to limit and define the chasm that exists between the one who is from eternity and the one who began to exist at a time when he was not. What possible resemblance and relationship can exist between two beings so widely separated from each other?"[4] The Christian doctrine of the incarnation, the divine assumption of human flesh, made this problem particularly vexing in the light of the crucifixion.

Any religious vision of the cosmos, however, must connect God with creation in *some* way. How is one to view these two "natures" (divine and

---

2. Thomas G. Weinandy, *Does God Suffer?* (Notre Dame, IN: University of Notre Dame Press, 2000), 110.

3. Weinandy, *Does God Suffer?*, 108–9.

4. Theodore of Mopsuestia, *Catechetical Homilies* 4.6; quoted in Jaroslav Pelikan, *The Christian Tradition: A History of the Development of Doctrine*, vol. 1: *The Emergence of the Catholic Tradition* (Chicago: University of Chicago Press, 1971), 229–30.

human), and how is one to conceptualize their unity in the person of Christ? More specifically, how are we to understand the infinite One and the many finite objects; the immortal One and mortal existence; the incomprehensible One and the comprehensible creation; the incorporeal One and diverse material existence; the One source of all being and contingent reality; the immutable One and mutable existence; or the impassible One and passible existence? In terms of the Christian doctrine of incarnation, how can Christ be both divine and human if the attributes of deity and humanity seem mutually exclusive in nature?

In the religious cosmology or metaphysics of the ancient world, such questions—posed in different ways—made the divine transcendence the supreme challenge of divine mediation. The crucial issue became whether or not the mediator was integral (and indispensable) to the divine self-giving. Christ as the Spirit Baptizer *must be internal to the essence* of God in order to be internal to the divine self-giving at Pentecost. If internal, then it stands to reason that the mediator of the Spirit is one in essence—and not separate in essence—in relation to the God who is the ultimate source of all being. If internal to this God, the mediator would be identifiable with God, one with God's very being in relation to the world. God would then be viewed as directly involved in the world through Christ. This view may be called *mia-hypostatic*, which implies "one essence" uniting the transcendent God and the divine reality that is immanent to the world. The true God self-imparts to the world, and there is potential for an understanding of salvation that involves incorporation or participation in God.

If *not* internal to this God, however, the mediator would then be viewed as external or separate from the essence of the true God, perhaps as a lesser "god" who is in harmony with the divine will and may at most be said to somehow participate in both divine and creaturely realities as a kind of intermediate bridge between them. Implied is a kind of divine hierarchy of "being," or essence, connecting God to the world. For lack of a better word, this view of the mediator may be called *dyohypostatic*, which implies "two different essences" characterizing the difference between the transcendent God and the one who mediates this God to the world. This view regards the mediator as essentially "other" than the true God and hence essentially and radically "subordinate" to the divine life (thus it is also called "subordinationism"). This lesser deity may be "a god," but not "the true God."[5] But

5. For an excellent description of these ancient options, see J. A. Lyons, *The Cosmic Christ in Origen and Teilhard de Chardin: A Comparative Study*, Oxford Theological Monographs

the dyohypostatic view threatens a proper view of the incarnation because it calls into question the idea that the true God self-imparts to flesh, unites with true flesh in the person of the Son in order to rest on all flesh, so as to incorporate it into the divine life. Instead, salvation under the dyohypostatic view tended to emphasize the human need to bring life into harmony with the divine will. The mediator, being separate from the true God in essence, could easily be reduced to playing the role of a mere exemplar of a life in harmony with the will of the true God.

The difference laid out between these two understandings of divine-human relationship had heuristic value but remained in some cases more ideal than real. There were thinkers in the ancient world who did not line up neatly on one side or the other of these two options; elements of both views may be found in their thought. There was indeed agreement among leading thinkers of the ancient world—Greek, Jewish, and Christian—with the idea that the mediator between God and the cosmos is integral to God. In some cases, however, metaphysical challenges occasioned qualification, hesitation, and even contradiction among some of these same thinkers.

The major reason for such qualification, or even contradiction, had to do with difficult metaphysical challenges. First, the source of anything could be considered ontologically or essentially superior, even separate from, what comes forth from it. Within a Christian context, it depended on the thinkers involved—and how consistent they were—as to whether or not this made the Son who was begotten from the Father inferior to the Father in essence. Concerning how the Son's coming forth from the Father was understood in the fourth century, Michel Barnes describes the challenge as the continuity of essence:

> All sides of the early stage of the Nicene controversy could (and did) comfortably describe the production of the second Person from the first as an X from X causal relationship. Expressions like light from light or wisdom from wisdom occur in virtually everyone's writings. Clearly, in themselves, they do not specify that the cause reproduces its own nature or identity in the product.[6]

(Oxford: Oxford University Press, 1982), 90–91. For the difference between miahypostatic and dyohypostatic, see Joseph Lienhard, *Contra Marcellum: Marcellus of Ancyra and Fourth Century Theology* (Washington, DC: Catholic University of America, 1999), 35–46.

6. Michel Rene Barnes, *The Power of God: Dynamis in Gregory of Nyssa's Trinitarian Theology* (Washington, DC: Catholic University of America Press, 2016), 119; quoted in Lewis Ayres, *Nicea and Its Legacy: An Approach to Fourth Century Trinitarian Theology* (Oxford: Oxford University Press, 2004), 23n36.

Origen's idea in the third century that the Son was eternally begotten from the Father supported the essential unity between the Father and the Son. But, as I will note below, Origen also perceived this same generation to imply that the Son was a distinct being who may even be said to have been "created." As many in the ancient world agreed, the generation of the Son from the Father was a mystery. The ancients, in their efforts to fathom this mystery to some extent, did not say that eternal generation needed to imply the ontological inferiority of the one generated. As one may reason, that which came into being external to God is separate from God in essence; but the Son was begotten eternally from the Father within the divine life. The Son could still in this case be regarded as essentially one with the Father. One might refer here to John 5:26, where Jesus says that the Father caused the Son to have life in himself—as the Father does. What is implied here is the unity of being and life between the Father and the Son.[7] Gregory of Nazianzus, in the fourth century, even adds that the eternal Son coming forth eternally from the Father fully shares the glory of the "Unoriginate Father" (the Father who has no origin) since the Son "is of the Unoriginate." Interestingly, Gregory notes that the Son "has the added glory of his generation."[8] Rather than the Son's status as generated eternally from the Father being a lack in the Son, Gregory sees it as an "added glory"! God's self-giving radiates forth from glory to glory! This trajectory of thought is consistent with the God of Pentecost who self-imparts as a river of life.

Second, a strong relational distinction between the Father and the Son caused some to deny that they are of one essence, since it was thought that this unity of essence would imply a material division within the life or being of the transcendent Father. It was thought that, if the Son has the same essence as the Father, the divine essence must have divided in two. A division of the Father's essence would naturally contradict the transcendence, unity, incorporeality, and simplicity of the true God. On the one hand, one way of solving this problem is to deny a personal distinction of the Son and the Father. This solution is commonly called "modalistic," because the difference between the Father and the Son is reduced to a difference in modes of revelation or redemptive action of the one divine person, or agent. Modalism was one version of miahypostatic Christology, but not the only one and not

---

7. See Kevin Giles, *The Eternal Generation of the Son: Maintaining Orthodoxy in Trinitarian Theology* (Downers Grove, IL: IVP Academic, 2012), 205–19.

8. Gregory of Nazianzus, *Theological Orations* iii, trans. Charles Gordon Brown and James Edward Swallow, in *Christology of the Later Fathers*, ed. Edward R. Hardy (Louisville: Westminster John Knox, 2006), 128–214.

the one that ended up defining Trinitarian orthodoxy. On the other hand, one may also attempt to avoid a material division in God by emphasizing the otherness of the Son to the point of assuming two different essences between the Father and the Son from the start. This was the strategy of the dyohypostatic approach to Christology. The effort to maintain unity of essence between the Father and the Son finds support in Origen's idea of the Son's eternal generation from the Father (a begetting without beginning); but the tradition took great care to highlight the mysterious, incorporeal, and spiritual nature of this generation so as to avoid the conclusion that it necessitates a material division in God. The tradition would eventually advocate the orthodox idea that the Son is one in essence with the Father, being "other" only in person, not in essence.

Third, the crucifixion as the goal of the incarnation (Heb. 2:14) made the full deity of Christ especially difficult to swallow metaphysically. It was thought that a unity of essence between the Father and the Son would make God somehow vulnerable to the alienation and decay of death. How can the transcendent and impassible God be united to lowly flesh and even endure suffering and death? How can the Spirit Baptizer suffer the baptism in fire? Specifically, how can the Father be affected in any way by the condemnation, suffering, and death endured by the Son? St. Cyril, the standard bearer of christological orthodoxy in the fifth century, gasped: "Nobody is so mad as to imagine the all transcending nature . . . as capable of suffering."[9] The attempt to grapple with this issue with respect to the crucifixion of Jesus drove an essential wedge, for some, between the Father and the Son. Cyril himself was to resolve this issue by advocating a paradoxical view of the incarnation: the divine Son suffers only "in the flesh" and "impassibly," or in a way proper to God as transcendent and impassible.[10] What this meant requires some unpacking, which I will have occasion to do later. Suffice it to say here that the fundamental intent was to highlight divine perfection, specifically the fact that God loves abundantly in a way that has no limits, including any limits imposed by suffering.[11] God takes up our baptism in fire in order to free us from it for the abundant and overcoming love poured forth through the Son.

Finally, as D. M. Baillie points out, we cannot understand the paradox of the incarnation unless we see an analogous paradox everywhere God's

---

9. Cyril of Alexandria, *De Symbolo* 24; quoted in Paul L. Gavrilyuk, *The Suffering of the Impassible God: The Dialectics of Patristic Thought*, Oxford Early Christian Studies (New York: Oxford University Press, 2004), 161.

10. Gavrilyuk, *Suffering of the Impassible God*, 161.

11. Weinandy, *Does God Suffer?*, 98–99.

gracious presence is given to creation. The divine self-giving and the human reception in all cases, including the incarnation itself, should not be viewed as "delimited, each by the other, and distinguished from each other by a boundary, so that the more of God's grace there is in action, the less it is my own personal action."[12] There is no competition between divine grace and human freedom, so that the more God is involved, the less humans are (or vice versa). The divine involvement *liberates* and *enables* human response. Grace does not cancel or limit it. The unity that the divine Son has with the humanity of Jesus at the incarnation, as this is confirmed and fulfilled at Pentecost, is to be understood in the same way that grace is to be understood, namely, as the divine Son bearing up under finite and fallen creation in order to free and fulfill it by the renewing power of the Spirit, in the Son's own image, and to the Father's glory. Incarnation fulfills the humanity of Jesus; it does not cancel it out or diminish it.

The language of the paradox of grace is helpful, since grace exceeds nature while working wholly within it. So it is with the divine Son, who, in taking on anointed flesh, works in cooperation with the Father and the Spirit to wholly assume flesh and work wholly within it with all of its weakness and suffering, so as—in transcendent freedom—to glorify that flesh as a medium of excessive life to others, thus fulfilling the purpose for which flesh was made, namely, to be the sacrament of Spirit. This is what Pentecost implies about grace. More specifically, Christ's fully human self-giving in fulfilling his redemptive mission shows that he is indispensable to God's redemptive presence and act in history. Christ does this to fulfill the Father's will as well as the Spirit's leading toward renewing the creation in fulfillment of the Father's promise. This framework helps us to deal with the thorny metaphysical problem of how the divine Son could take on flesh, even though flesh is so limited in its capacities. The more radical kenotic (self-emptying) theories suggested that, in becoming incarnated in flesh, the divine Son had to somehow relinquish certain divine attributes (such as omniscience, omnipresence, or omnipotence) that infinitely exceeded human flesh. But how could a divine Son relinquish what is proper to him? This solution seems to create more problems than it solves. The idea (suggested in the preceding chapter) that Jesus, in his fully human self-giving, is shown to be identical (one in person) with the eternal Son of the Father is a helpful one.

In saying that Jesus in his self-giving is identical with the eternal Son (one in person), I have no intention of denying the so-called *extra calvinis-*

---

12. D. M. Baillie, *God Was in Christ* (London: Faber and Faber, 1948), 116.

ticum, or the idea that Christ's human sojourn to Pentecost does not exhaust the life of the eternal Son. This idea has a basis in the patristic witness. Note what Athanasius says about the incarnate Christ: "He was not, as might be imagined, circumscribed in the body, nor, while present in the body, was he absent elsewhere; nor, while he moved in the body, was the universe left void of his working and providence."[13] Of course, the universe was not devoid of the Word's providential work in creation "sustaining all things" (Heb. 1:3) during the life of Jesus. This distinction between the transcendent divine Son and his incarnate presence was advocated in part to solve the problem posed by the more extreme kenotic Christologies. If the eternal Son was transcendent (unlimited in presence and power, which refers to the *Logos asarkos,* or "beyond flesh") while at the same time working fully in and through the limitations of human flesh as the incarnate Christ (the *Logos ensarkos,* or "in flesh"), there is no need to speak of the Son's relinquishing certain divine attributes in becoming incarnate.

Karl Barth embraced this idea early in his career but later qualified it because of the danger it posed of suggesting a bifurcation in the divine Son during his life in the flesh between transcendent and incarnate modes of being the divine Son. This bifurcation posed the danger of leaving the transcendent Son untouched and undefined by the incarnate Son. Moreover, who knows how this "Son beyond the Son" is to be understood? The possibility that the incarnate Son might not be definitive for the transcendent Son opened up a dark and potentially problematic mystery concerning the Son as the Word of the Father. More recently, Thomas Morris proposed the idea of different levels of consciousness as an analogy for understanding the unity of the transcendent and incarnate Son. We are well aware of this concept, since we know that we possess one mind consisting of the more limited conscious and more expansive subconscious dimensions. Analogously, one may assume one mind and capacity of the Son that is both transcendent (unlimited) and incarnate (limited).[14] However we conceive of the Son's transcendence during his incarnate existence, we must emphasize that there is only one Son, one person who takes on flesh for our redemption. The Son revealed in flesh is the only Son there is. What he reveals about God is valid for all time.

---

13. Athanasius, *On the Incarnation* 17, trans. Archibald Robertson, in Hardy, ed., *Christology of the Later Fathers.*

14. Thomas V. Morris, *The Logic of God Incarnate* (Ithaca, NY: Cornell University Press, 1986).

Barth never gave up the idea that the divine Son remains transcendent and free in incarnation. In fact, the Son in cooperation with the Spirit exercises this transcendent freedom precisely in becoming incarnate.[15] God's freedom from creaturely limitations and sin is exercised for this creation in the embrace of divine love. I would add, in line with Barth, that the incarnate Son's eschatological freedom in self-giving for the world as a river of life is shown at Pentecost to be one with the eternal Son's transcendent freedom in self-giving to the Father and the Spirit in eternal communion. Barth went on to suggest that, in the incarnation, the Son's transcendent life and incarnate life is one life, meaning that neither can be defined without reference to the other; furthermore, what we know of the transcendent life of the Son is taken from what is revealed and enacted in the incarnate life given for us.[16] I will deal with the difficult question of how the eternal Son can be one person with two natures, divine and human, in the following chapter. These problems created tensions among those who wrestled with the idea of how the transcendent God is involved in a finite and changing world, which is corrupt and dying. We can only repeat that the solutions were not always neat and consistent. As I noted above, the ancient metaphysical challenges of how the deity could be involved in finite creaturely reality caused many of the same ancient authors who spoke of the mediator as integral to (one in essence with) the divine life to also speak of this mediator as in some sense less than fully divine. The element of ambiguity in the Jewish tradition of God's creative Word, or Wisdom, for example, did leave open some room for variation in answering the question as to its exact status with respect to the transcendent Creator. Philo, the Hellenistic Jewish thinker of the early first century, used the term "Logos" even more often than did the ancient Greek Stoics—thirteen hundred times![17] Is Jewish monotheism abrogated— in Philo's use of the term "Logos"? Is Philo dyohypostatic? He does speak of the Logos as an intermediary reality bridging God and the world.[18] As

---

15. See Darren O. Sumner, "The Two-fold Life of the Word: Karl Barth's Critical Reception of the *Extra Calvinisticum*," *International Journal of Systematic Theology* 15, no. 1 (January 2013): 42–57.

16. Karl Barth, *Church Dogmatics*, IV/2: *The Doctrine of Reconciliation*, trans. G. W. Bromiley (Edinburgh: T & T Clark, 1958), 110.

17. H. Kleinknecht, "B. The Logos in the Greek and Hellenistic World," in *Theological Dictionary of the New Testament*, vol. 4, ed. Gerhard Kittel (Grand Rapids: Eerdmans, 1967), 88.

18. E.g., Philo, *Quis rerum divinarum heres sit* 2–5; quoted in James D. G. Dunn, *Christology in the Making: A New Testament Inquiry into the Origins of the Doctrine of the Incarnation*, 2nd ed. (Grand Rapids: Eerdmans, 1996), 220.

such, the Logos is neither uncreated nor created like us, but somehow exists midway between these two options.[19] This separation of the Logos from God implies that the Logos is a different and inferior being in relation to God. Yet Philo's dominant thought locates the Logos *within* the divine self-giving to the world (implicitly one in essence with it). He regarded the Logos as the divine mind and located the Platonic "forms" as ideas within it. God creates and acts through the Logos in the world without pantheistic implications (such as was true among the Stoics).

In the main, it may still be said that, for Philo, the Logos is one in essence with God: it is God's self-expression. He likened the Logos to that which radiates out from God, like rays from the sun, a favored metaphor used for Christ as the image of God in the New Testament (Heb. 1:3) and beyond—among the church fathers. Such language does not necessitate unity of essence, but it arguably leans in that direction. James Dunn even argues that, for Philo, there is "no thought of the Logos as a real being with particular functions distinct from God."[20] For Philo, the Logos is "God himself in his approach to man, God himself insofar as he may be known by man."[21] Dunn's point is well taken; yet one has to wonder whether, in light of the evidence, his conclusion comes through an overly systematic approach to Philo. Can Philo's less prominent tendency of viewing the Logos as essentially inferior to God be completely subsumed within his dominant idea of the Logos as internal to God? I tend to think not.

Philo's ambivalence is not unique in the ancient world; it also had currency, for example, within ancient Greek thought. In the Greek context, Plato's *Timaeus* provides the background for relating the absolute divine One to the contingent creation. In subsequent Middle Platonic traditions, there was "widespread agreement that the world depends in its order on an absolute and transcendent divine principle," which required a mediating reality to connect divine transcendence with the creaturely world.[22] Stoicism, however, denied transcendence (being pantheistic), viewing the Logos as that which accounts for the "ordered and teleologically oriented nature of the world." It is the power that constitutes all matter—"and works immanently in all things." The Logos is also "a seed that unfolds itself, and this seed is by nature human reason."[23]

19. Philo, *Quis rerum divinarum heres sit* 205–6; quoted in Lyons, *The Cosmic Christ*, 93.

20. Dunn, *Christology in the Making*, 227.

21. Dunn, *Christology in the Making*, 228.

22. See Lyons, *The Cosmic Christ*, 90.

23. Kleinknecht, "B. The Logos," 85.

Early Christology was not immune to ambiguity in its efforts to wrestle with thorny metaphysical problems with respect to God and the world. In the second century, Justin Martyr sought to claim the larger Logos doctrine for Christology and to make his appropriation of the doctrine the dividing line between Christianity and both Greek (pagan) and Jewish heresy. In particular, Justin may be said "to deny the Logos to the Jews, to take it away from them, in order for it to be the major theological center of Christianity."[24] Of course, the Gospel of John used the term "Logos" for Christ before Justin did (e.g., John 1:1–14). Ironically, Justin's appropriation arguably fell short of Johannine orthodoxy. Though Justin writes of the Logos coming forth from the Father, he also speaks of the Logos as separate in nature and inferior to the Father. Richard Norris says this about the Logos in Justin: it "stands as a kind of bumper state between God and the world." Norris asks pointedly why God should need "a middleman to stand between himself and the created order. Does Justin think that God cannot enter into direct relationship with flesh?"[25] Apparently so.

The third-century Alexandrian theologian Origen is the most significant early voice that set up the pivotal christological struggles and developments of the fourth and fifth centuries that led to creedal Christology. Origen viewed the Son as generated (begotten) eternally from the Father. But, as I noted above, this doctrine of the Son as having his origin in the Father did not guarantee a consistent defense of the Son's unity of essence with the Father. Origen did view the Son and the Father as distinct in essence; but he still saw the Son as intrinsic to God. Being intrinsic to God, according to Origen, the Son can mirror the Father for us. The Son radiates from the Father as light from light. Origen hesitated to speak of the Son as of one "essence" (*ousia*) with the Father in order to avoid a material conception of God. Yet Origen could still speak of the Son as "in" the Father.[26] In his antimodalist interpretation of Scripture, Origen thus tended to limit the Son's generation as being from the Father's will rather than essence. Yet it may be that the Father's will is itself "essential" to the Son, according to Origen. Origen denied that there was a time when the Son was not: "There comes into existence, therefore, another power, subsisting in its own proper nature, a kind of breath . . . of the first and unbegotten power of God, drawing from this source whatever existence

24. Daniel Boyarin, *Border Lines: The Partition of Judeo-Christianity* (Philadelphia: University of Pennsylvania Press, 2006), 38.

25. Richard A. Norris Jr., "Introduction," in *The Christological Controversy*, trans. and ed. Richard A. Norris Jr., Sources of Early Christian Thought (Philadelphia: Fortress, 1980), 7.

26. Ayres, *Nicea and Its Legacy*, 22–27.

it has; and there is no time when it did not exist."[27] But, incomprehensibly, his polemic against modalism also caused him to emphasize the essential distinction between the Father and the Son to the point of regarding the Son as something "created." In his commentary on Proverbs 8:22–31 (in which Origen identifies the wisdom that "comes forth" from God as the Logos, or Word, of the Father), Origen refers to the Son as "the firstborn of all creation, a thing created, wisdom."[28] It is not clear what Origen means by this, since it seems to contradict the Son's eternal generation from the Father. We see here an ambivalence in Origen, an intellectual struggle to walk carefully in order to avoid metaphysical pitfalls—similar, in fact, to what we saw in Philo.

In short, for Origen, God was a "shared but graded" reality.[29] How this divine reality could be both properly shared and graded was Origen's chief metaphysical difficulty. To be properly shared, as we will see, we must be able to say that we mean *essentially* the same thing when we speak of the divinity of the Father as when we speak of the divinity of the Son (as well as the divinity of the Spirit). The great insight of post-Nicene fourth-century theology will be to show that this sameness is not necessarily modalistic, because it refers to sameness of essence (*ousia*) and not person (*hypostasis*). To speak of the Father and the Son as *essentially* different powers or agents arguably compromises the monotheism of Scripture and introduces an enormous amount of ambiguity into our notion of God. Indeed, it was not always clear what one meant by the term "God" in the ancient world.[30] Even in cases where the Son was thought to be other than (separate from and inferior to) the Father in essence, the Son could still be called "God" in some lesser sense (as "god"). In the fourth century, when debates concerning the deity of Christ came to a head, it was not uncommon in some parts of the Christian world to distinguish between the Father as the "true" God and the divine Logos, or Word of the Father, as an inferior or lesser god who was thought to be separate from the true God in essence. But how can anyone but the God of Israel impart the Spirit of God to all flesh? How can Christ do this at Pentecost unless he were, as the Nicene Creed would say, "true God from true God"?

---

27. Origen, *On First Principles* 1, 2, 9; quoted in Norris, *Christological Controversy*, 73–82. I am grateful to Lewis Ayres for drawing my attention to this quote and for making this point. Ayres, *Nicea and Its Legacy: An Approach to Fourth-Century Trinitarian Theology* (New York: Oxford University Press, 2004), 27.

28. Origen, *On First Principles* 4. 4. 1.

29. Ayres, *Nicea and Its Legacy*, 26.

30. A point stressed by Ayres, *Nicea and Its Legacy*, 14.

Therefore, the question posed by this ambiguous trajectory is this: Must we deny a proper doctrine of incarnation in order to protect divine transcendence? Does transcendence necessarily prevent the *truly* divine Word or Son from becoming flesh (John 1:14)? Do the oppositions between divine and creaturely attributes prohibit us from intellectually defending the idea of this divine Word or Son as himself identified with a flesh-and-blood life, the anointed existence of Jesus Christ? If one thinks so, it needs to be asked by whose rules we must be driven to such a conclusion. If the gospel tells us that the Word of the Father "was God" (John 1:1), self-revealed and self-imparted as one with the embodied life of Jesus (1:14–16), are we not bound to assume this reality from the start of our theological reflection and just let the metaphysical chips fall where they may, so to speak? We may be forced to accept the possibility of paradox, of a divine strength revealed in creaturely weakness. But isn't such a paradox necessary to any conception of the astounding reach of what we call grace? Any notion of grace will involve saying in some form or other that God's power "is made perfect in weakness" (2 Cor. 12:9) and exceeds—while working within flesh—to free it and to fulfill it.

Yet this paradox does not exist in the nature of God. God is not divided or in tension with Godself. The God who loves the sinner and shows strength and glory through the medium of weakness, or the medium of the cross, is fully one with Godself. Note Barth's compelling words here about what God teaches us about Godself in the event of self-giving, the event of paradoxical grace revealed in Christ, which is worth quoting in full:

> We begin with the insight that God is "not a God of confusion but of peace" (1 Cor. 14:33). In Him, there is no paradox, no antinomy, no division, no inconsistency, not even the possibility of it. He is the Father of lights with whom there is no variableness nor interplay of light and darkness (James 1:17). What He is and does He is and does in full unity with Himself. It is in full unity with Himself that He is also—and especially and above all else—in Jesus Christ, that he becomes a creature, man, flesh, that He enters into our being in contradiction, that he takes upon Himself its consequences. If we think that this is impossible it's because our concept of God is too narrow, too arbitrary, too human—far too human. Who God is and what it is to be divine is something we have to learn where God has revealed Himself and His nature, the essence of the divine. . . . It is not for us to speak of a contradiction and rift in the being, but to learn to correct

our notions of the being of God, to reconstitute them in the light of the fact that He does this.[31]

However, the paradox of the incarnation cannot be denied: "The paradox must be allowed to stand: in the undiminished humanity of Jesus, the whole power and glory of God are made present to us."[32] In taking on our baptism in fire so as to make way for our baptism in the Spirit, God shows strength in the midst of vulnerability and weakness. As a result, a notion of transcendence that would exclude such a paradox in the divine self-disclosure "breaks into pieces."[33] One is open to see "in the powerlessness of the Incarnate and Crucified One the shining forth of divine omnipotence."[34] Our notion of divine transcendence cannot remain unaffected by the incarnation and the cross, as though these are mere intellectual problems that must somehow be altered in order to conform to the commonsense rationality of the ancient world. "I will destroy the wisdom of the wise; the intelligence of the intelligent I will frustrate" (1 Cor. 1:19). God always is the one who loves in freedom so abundantly that it even reaches deeply into the reality of those who spurn that love. Such is God's heart in eternity past, for the Lamb is the one who is "slain from the creation of the world" (Rev. 13:8). There is a fundamental "selflessness" to the divine nature and will that is eternal and that accounts for God's act to both create and redeem.[35] As Kazoh Kitamori maintains, there is revealed in the incarnation and crucifixion an eternal divine will to love without limit, even those who are opposed to this love. This is a love that bears all things in embracing the other.[36] The paradox of grace is built into the divine will and freedom to love, but it does not create in God a self-alienation. "He makes his own the being of the man who is opposed to him; but he does not collaborate in his opposition."[37] Therefore, by becoming human, "he enters into what is alien to him and there remains at the same time true

31. Barth, *Church Dogmatics*, IV/1: *The Doctrine of Reconciliation*, trans. G. W. Bromiley (Edinburgh: T & T Clark, 1956), 186.

32. Hans Urs von Balthasar, *Mysterium Paschale* (Grand Rapids: Eerdmans, 1990), 33.

33. P. Althaus, "Kenosis," *Die Religion in Geschichte und Gegenwart*, 3:1245; quoted in Balthasar, *Mysterium Paschale*, 33.

34. Balthasar, *Mysterium Paschale*, 34.

35. Balthasar, *Mysterium Paschale*, 33–35.

36. Kazoh Kitamori, *Theology of the Pain of God* (Eugene, OR: Wipf and Stock, 2005), esp. 44–49.

37. Barth, *Church Dogmatics*, IV/1, 48.

to himself."[38] And God shows that divine love is capable of identification with these alien others so as to redeem them. God is one with Godself by loving with such freedom. Such is the God of the incarnation, the cross, and Pentecost.

A Christology from below that has Pentecost at its horizon thus grants us resources for dealing with the challenge of divine transcendence. What might transcendence look like as revealed in Christ's journey from the incarnation to Pentecost? It would not do to merely concentrate on divine freedom as a negative concept, a freedom *from* conditioning by creation. God is infinite by *not* being limited by time, immutable by *not* being conditioned by change, and impassible by *not* being subject to suffering. Regardless of what we may think of these understandings of transcendence, the resulting picture of God was arguably abstract and impersonal.[39] The open question becomes: What might transcendence mean in the *positive* sense? Thomas Weinandy emphasizes that the tradition prior to the modern era viewed God as a dynamic and limitless abundance of self-giving grace.[40] This idea of God offers a rich resource for redefining transcendence in a way that conforms to the God of Jesus's sovereign freedom to descend into flesh to bear our baptism of fire in order to baptize all flesh in the Spirit. Gregory of Nyssa says it best: "God's transcendent power is not so much displayed in the vastness of the heavens, or in the luster of the stars, or in the orderly arrangement of the universe or his perpetual oversight of it, as in his condescension to our weak nature."[41]

Barth emphasizes that divine transcendence positively conceived must be gathered concretely from the story of Jesus. "It has to be learned from what took place in Jesus Christ."[42] Fruitful for us is Barth's suggestion that transcendence as revealed in the entire story of Christ has to do most fundamentally with the divine *freedom to love*. He says:

38. Balthasar, *Mysterium Paschale*, 1.

39. Barth, *Church Dogmatics*, II/1: *The Doctrine of God*, trans. L. Parker et al. (Edinburgh: T & T Clark, 1957), 302-5.

40. Weinandy, *Does God Suffer?*, esp. 110.

41. Gregory of Nyssa, *Address on Religious Instruction* 24. I am grateful to J. Warren Smith for drawing my attention to this quote.

42. Barth, *Church Dogmatics*, IV/1, 177. I am grateful to Christophe Chalamet for drawing my attention to this quote. Chalamet, "No Timelessness in God: On Differing Interpretations of Karl Barth's Theology of Eternity, Time and Election," *Zeitschrift für dialektische Theologie*, Supplement Series 4 (January 1, 2010): 34.

As God was in Christ, far from being against Himself, or at disunity with Himself, He has put into effect the freedom of His divine love, the love in which He is divinely free. He has therefore done and revealed that which corresponds to His divine nature. His immutability does not stand in the way of this. It must not be denied, but this possibility must be included in His unalterable being.[43]

God is united in the divine freedom to love so radically and freely that the consequences of human sin are taken up into the divine life and abolished in order to create the conditions for incorporating *this other* into the divine life. Such is the God of Pentecost. Dietrich Bonhoeffer summarizes Barth's point succinctly: "God is not free *of* man but *for* man."[44]

Barth makes the connection between divine freedom and transcendence clear by noting that God loves freely in a way that is unconditional (not limited or conditioned by creation), and this love is transcendent in being free because it has God's gracious self-determination as its sole basis. Barth writes:

The biblical witness to God sees His transcendence of all that is distinct from Himself, not only in the distinction itself, which is supremely and decisively as His freedom from all conditioning by that which is distinct from Himself . . . enters into and maintains communion with this reality other than Himself in His activity as Creator, Reconciler, and Redeemer.

Barth elaborates: "We understand the being of God as moved, although self-moved, as life proceeding from its own center. We understand His loving to be loving for its own sake, an unconditioned, utterly sovereign love, positing its own basis and purpose."[45] Transcendence is "life proceeding from its own center and revealed as unconditional love." This sounds like a description of incarnation in the light of Pentecost. This is what divine transcendence and freedom look like in a Christology from below—with Pentecost at its horizon.

Even more interesting is Barth's point that the Holy Spirit is the principle of divine freedom to love the creation in the incarnation and life of Jesus

---

43. Barth, *Church Dogmatics*, IV/1, 186–87.
44. Dietrich Bonhoeffer, *Act and Being* (New York: Harper and Row, 1962), 90.
45. Barth, *Church Dogmatics*, IV/1, 300, 303.

Christ. He says of Jesus's human conception by the Spirit: "This human existence starts in the freedom of God Himself, in the freedom in which the Father and Son are one in the bond of love, in the Holy Spirit."[46] Yet there is still a difference between God loving internally within the Godhead and God loving the fallen creation, the radically "other." Can God love this creation radically and still be God? Indeed, as Jürgen Moltmann has shown us, the love internal to God is between like and like; but the love that is presumed by orthodox Christology to be poured out from God to creation is between God and what is radically other.[47] Yet it is precisely this difference that points to the radical freedom of God to love excessively, in a way that has no other explanation than the fact that God is revealing in fullness the inner mystery of the divine nature as self-giving love: "In loving the world he is entirely free because he is entirely himself."[48] Kazoh Kitamori adds that it is God's nature to love, even when that love is spurned. Therefore, the incarnation, crucifixion, resurrection, and Pentecost—in short, the impartation of God's Holy Spirit through the Son to fallen flesh—do not contradict the divine nature; they reveal it. So abundantly free is divine love that it is most fully revealed in excessive grace, the grace that overflowed for Israel in order to come upon the sinners among the nations. Rather than the challenge of transcendence erecting a barrier to the incarnation, crucifixion, and Pentecost, it only creates the setting for understanding the inexplicable depth of the divine freedom to love. Barth thus views the incarnation, God's binding himself to flesh in Jesus of Nazareth, as the lens through which to penetrate the depths of God's inner freedom to love and commune as the triune God:

> So when we look at the beginning of the existence of Jesus, we are meant to be looking into this ultimate depth of the Godhead, in which the Father and the Son are one. This is the freedom of the inner life of God, and in this freedom the existence of this man begins in AD 1.[49]

There is for Barth an *analogia caritatis* (analogy of love) between the eternal unity of love forged by the Spirit between the Father and the Son *and* the union of the divine Son and flesh brought about through Jesus's conception by the Spirit in the Virgin's womb.

46. Karl Barth, *Dogmatics in Outline* (London: SCM Press, 1955), 99.

47. Jürgen Moltmann, *The Trinity and the Kingdom* (New York: Harper and Row, 1981), 58–59.

48. Moltmann, *Trinity and the Kingdom*, 55.

49. Kitamori, *Theology of the Pain of God*, 44–49.

More recently, Eugene Rogers expanded on this idea of divine transcendence by referring to the Spirit as perfecting the love shared between the Father and the Son in the Godhead by overflowing this love in freedom. The Spirit displays this abundance by befriending matter and resting on it decisively by resting on the Son—and then beyond to the rest of creation through the Son. Through the Son, the Spirit rests on bodies in excess of the physical, not only in a way that befriends it, but also "redeems, transfigures, elevates, and exceeds it."[50] The implication is that the Spirit is the principle of divine transcendence eschatologically in being the principle of excess, superfluity, and grace.[51] Incorporating the others into himself, the Christ of Pentecost is shaped by this abundantly outpoured Spirit, this promise of the Father, into an ecclesial person, an eschatological person who sums up the new creation in himself. This divine love not only overcomes the barriers of sin and death but also the limits of creation and history. This free and transcendent divine love in the Holy Spirit that springs forth from the Father and is mediated by the faithful Son is based solely in the divine self-determination and is unconditional in relation to creation. This love is eternal, unchanging, and limitless in purity and power. This is what transcendence looks like in the light of a Christology from below—in the light of the incarnation, the resurrection, and Pentecost.

The Scriptural Challenge

The challenge to the true deity of Christ was not only driven by metaphysical considerations. Particularly those who advocated a dyohypostatic Christology felt driven in significant measure by Christian Scripture to do so. One must take this challenge seriously. Rowan Williams says that "Jesus possesses supreme authority but does not simply stand in the place of the God of Israel. He prays to this God as 'Father', 'Abba.'"[52] Jesus did not "simply" stand in the place of the God of Israel in so many words. He did not refer to himself in this way, nor did he encourage others to do so. Yet, when he breathed the Spirit of God upon his disciples and told them to receive the Spirit (John 20:22), wasn't he in some sense standing in the place of the God of Israel? If

---

50. Eugene F. Rogers Jr., *After the Spirit: A Constructive Pneumatology from Resources outside the West* (Grand Rapids: Eerdmans, 2005), 15, 67.

51. Rogers, *After the Spirit*, 71.

52. Rowan D. Williams, "Jesus Christ," in *Dictionary of the Ecumenical Movement*, ed. Nicholas Lossky et al. (Grand Rapids: Eerdmans, 1991), 540.

one responds to Jesus's devotion to the Father in all things by viewing him as a lesser being—as of another, inferior essence—how does one then account for his exercise of supreme authority? How would it be possible, then, for Christ to also present himself as indispensable to the Father's reign and loving cause in the world? Toward this end, Christ gives himself over to the leading of the Spirit and imparts the Spirit to all flesh. He does so as Lord; the Spirit now bears his name (Spirit of Christ) and bears witness to him as Lord (1 Cor. 12:3). The Son is worshiped as such, with the same worship granted to God the Father (Rev. 5:13). Can such things be said of anyone other than the God of Israel? Without an adequate exposure to Jewish monotheism, one might not understand the importance of this question. During his life on earth, the Son did not grasp after equality with God, to be sure, but this would not be consistent with the divine nature. "Although he existed in the form of God," Christ "did not consider equality with God a thing to be grasped" (Phil. 2:6, NASB). The divine way of personal relationship is self-giving toward the end of communion and the sharing of life.

But the challenges to Christ's deity taken from the Bible are complex. More needs to be said. There are texts that identify Christ with the true God and texts that distinguish Christ from God and in ways that imply a dependence on God. In terms of identification with God, Christ is the agent of creation, which is exclusively a divine work (Col. 1:16). Only God upholds all things by the divine Word, but so does Christ, according to Hebrews 1:3. Only God is to be acknowledged as the Savior (Hosea 13:4); yet Christ also saves (Phil. 3:20; Titus 2:13). Only the Creator who made all things by the Spirit (Gen. 1:2), and has redeemed all things, can pour forth the Spirit on all flesh to restore the creation to its original purpose as the divine dwelling place (Joel 2:28–32; Acts 2:17–18). However, we also have the Spirit *from Christ* (1 Cor. 12:13). And the Spirit is the "Spirit of Christ" as well as the "Spirit of God" (Rom. 8:9). Paul, along with the rest of the church, thus regarded Christ as "Lord" of all in the context of worship, which was unprecedented in ancient Judaism in reference to anyone other than the God of Israel (1 Cor. 12:1–3, Phil. 2:9–11). Yet, on the side of distinction and dependence, Paul sometimes reserves the term "God" uniquely for the Father (e.g., Eph. 4:4–6) and does not hesitate, in so doing, to speak of God as the "head" of Christ (1 Cor. 11:3; 15:28). Moreover, Christ is confessed as Lord, but to the glory of the God who exalted him and gave him this name (Phil. 2:9–11).

One finds a similar tension in John's Gospel. Christ is called "God" (1:1; 20:28) and one with the Father (10:30). He is even said to have life in himself, as the Father does (5:26). He breathes forth the Spirit, a striking revelation of his unity with God (20:21). All of this points to Christ's being internal to the divine life and self-giving. Yet it is the Father who places all things under Christ's power (13:13). The Father is the only true God, and the Son is the one who is sent from the Father into the world (17:3); indeed, Christ says that the Father is greater than he (14:28).

This tension is also found elsewhere in the New Testament. We might mention Mark as one last example. In describing John the Baptist's preparation for the coming of Christ (1:1–3), Mark refers to the Baptist as preparing the way for the coming of *the Lord*. Mark does not identify the messenger with Christ, but rather with John the Baptist, with the result that the reader is then led to place Christ in the place of *the Lord*, or the one who is coming to redeem the world, whose way into the world John is said to announce. In the very next chapter, Christ exercises divine authority to forgive sins, and he verifies his authority to do so over the protests to the contrary of his audience (2:6–12). Further into the book of Mark, however, *only* the Father is said to know the end (13:32), and Jesus seems to defer to the Father at one point when speaking of God alone as good (10:18).

When we look at these tensions, it is important for us to keep a few qualifications in mind. First, the Son's appointment by the Father to sonship at his conception (Luke 1:35), baptism (Luke 3:22), and resurrection (Rom. 1:4) does not cancel out an eternal unity of essence between the Father and the Son. The Father highly exalts Christ to lordship as well (Phil. 2:9–11; Acts 2:33–36). Christ is exalted in the Spirit so as to impart the Spirit to all flesh. I agree with James Dunn that such texts are not "adoptionistic," since adoptionism denied Christ's deity (maintaining, as it did, that Christ was only a Spirit-anointed and -adopted man), which could only be read back into the New Testament anachronistically. As Pannenberg has shown us (in the preceding chapter), if the exaltation of Christ by the Spirit reveals that Christ is indispensable to the Father's lordship, such a revelation can be said to imply a "high Christology." In fact, Dunn concurs that this eschatological exaltation of Christ to divine sonship and lordship is a high Christology as well. Since it is revealed in the sojourn of Jesus in the flesh, it is simply different from one that assumes from the start the eternal unity of the divine Son with the Father.[53]

There need not be a contradiction between saying that the divine Son was always one in essence with the Father (and the Spirit) and maintaining that he was exalted and appointed by the Father as the Son and as Lord

---

53. Dunn, *Christology in the Making*, 62–63.

in time. The orthodox tradition helpfully distinguished between the Son's *eternal* unity with the Father (his sharing eternally in the divine life) and his being *appointed* as Son, or enthroned as Lord, in the Spirit and by the Father *in history* (in the flesh). The Son is thus shown to be in the *embodied life* of Jesus what he already is in the Father *in eternity*. The Son thus prays to his Father: "And now, Father, glorify me in your presence with the glory I had with you before the world began" (John 17:5). The glorification in history reveals and realizes for the sake of creation the same glory that existed between the Father and the Son from eternity. These two are not separable, though they are distinct. Athanasius thus notes of the incarnate Christ: "Since the body is his . . . naturally when the body is exalted, he himself as man, because of the body, is said to be exalted."[54] The eternal Son takes on lowly flesh so that, in its exaltation, all of humanity may be exalted with him. Pannenberg's conclusion about Christ is valid: "The idea of his pre-existence does not contradict the fact that his divine sonship will only be revealed eschatologically."[55]

Second, Christ's references to God alone as the source of life, glory, or moral goodness are not intended to refer to Christ's essential inferiority to the Father. Christ's reference to the Father as the only true God and to himself as sent from the Father (in John 17:3) is not meant to essentially separate himself from the Father. On the contrary, the text's purpose is to show that the Son gives life from the Father (John 1:1-5) and, by coming from the Father, "has made him known" (1:18). The life that he has from the Father allows Christ to be the source of life to others (17:4); the glory that he shared with the Father now allows him to show forth that glory in flesh (17:5). The Son's reference to the Father as the only true God (17:3) was for the purpose of verifying that the life and glory that the Son has to share with others is *divine*. Christ does not say that "only the Father is the true God." The text is rather to be translated that the Father is "the only true God." Indeed, the same is said of the Son in John 1:1 and John 1:18! Hebrews also notes that the Father refers to the Son with the title "God": "But about the Son he says, 'Your throne, O God, will last for ever and ever; a scepter of justice will be the scepter of your kingdom'" (Heb. 1:8).

In the Gospel of John as well, the Son is called "God" (1:1, 18). The Son thus calls the Father the only true God in the context of a *mutual glorification* ("glorify your Son that your Son may glorify you" [John 17:1]). Of course,

---

54. Athanasius, *Orations against the Arians* 1.45.

55. Wolfhart Pannenberg, *Systematic Theology*, 3 vols. (Grand Rapids: Eerdmans, 1991–98), 1:265.

only God can share divine life and glory with the world. The prologue to John's Gospel makes this point clear, and it sets up this continuity of life and glory between the Son and the Father by speaking of both the Father and the Son as "God" (1:1–18).

The framework of John's prologue also helps us understand Jesus's statement that the Father is "greater" than he. The point is not the Son's essential inferiority to the Father; instead, it is his unity with the Father, namely, his constant point of reference to something greater than what one can see with the naked eye or hear with the physical ear in searching for the meaning of his entire life and witness. Dunn notes that "the issue is not the *relation* between the Father and the Son . . . but the authority and validity of the Son's *revelation* of the Father, the continuity between the Father and the Son, between the *logos* unuttered and the *logos* uttered."[56] Again, the prologue of John's Gospel would guide the reader to this view of Christ's statement. Isolated from that prologue, one could read it differently, which is why it is wise to keep that framework in view.

A similar framework also helps to explain Christ's reference to God alone as good (Mark 10:18), or as the only one to whom unqualified goodness can be attributed, for God is thus the only source of goodness, the one who stands behind the moral witness of the law of life as the Creator intended it. The emphasis is again on God as the only hope for humanity and on Jesus as having his mission from and in God alone. The person with whom Jesus converses is not calling Jesus "good" so as to affirm his share in God's goodness, an assumption Jesus would then be viewed as correcting (as though he would then be saying, "I am not God!"). It is rather the case that the questioner assumed that Jesus, as a teacher in Israel, could be regarded as the ultimate arbiter of moral goodness, which Jesus corrects by pointing to God *alone* as the source of the law's witness and the weight it places on human life. Jesus's point is anti-establishment. He is not addressing the question of his unity with the Father here, though that question is not absent from Mark. Rather, he is confirming that he represents God and not the temple leadership. His moral authority does not rest on his role as a teacher in Israel, but on God, his Father. One does not regard Jesus as good as a teacher. One regards God *alone* as good, which would then allow a person to discern Jesus's true source of goodness and moral authority. The fact that Jesus draws his moral goodness and authority from God alone, as the only true source of such things,

---

56. James D. G. Dunn, *Christianity in the Making*, vol. 3: *Neither Jew nor Greek: A Contested Identity* (Grand Rapids: Eerdmans, 2015), 353 (italics in original).

(margin handwritten note: then how does this work w/ Christ still being divine?)

does not preclude his unity with God; rather, it provides the only proper framework for discerning that unity.

Third, Christ's finite limitations do not preclude his essential unity with the Father either. Not knowing what the future will hold (John 14:28) is part of Christ's larger human limitation of knowledge. The fact that Christ did not know the time of the end was not the only limitation of his knowledge—not by far. The fact that Christ *grew* in wisdom (Luke 2:52) and *learned* from his suffering (Heb. 5:8) is part of Christ's finitude as a man of flesh and blood. Though Jesus sometimes revealed extraordinary insight, he was obviously limited in knowledge. He shared many of the same limitations that any person of the first century had.[57] But such was needed for our salvation. Christ descended into human weakness in order to grant us a share through his exaltation of the divine freedom and strength. Pannenberg thus points out that the Son's reference to the Father as the only one who knows the future (having sovereignty over the future) was part of the perfection of Christ's free human devotion to the Father's reign, part of Christ's human self-giving to the Father's sovereignty over all things. The creation depended on the Son's perfecting human freedom and devotion in this way in order to perfect creation's dependence on God in all things. When Jesus, as a human, gives the future into the Father's hands, "precisely this fact of Jesus' perfection in dedication to the God of the eschatological future reaches its consummation."[58] This total self-giving to the loving reign of the Father reveals *in human form* the Son's eternal self-giving to the Father's reign, the divine Son being devoted to the Father in a human way, in a way that opens creation to the perfection of its God-intended sonship and daughtership.

To this end, the Son bears the most humble of human limitations. Cyril wrote in the fifth century that Christ "has not refused to descend in such a low position as to bear all that belongs to our nature, included in which is ignorance."[59] Raymond Brown elaborates: "If in the Gospel reports his knowledge seems to have been limited, such limitation would simply show to what depths divine condescension went in the incarnation—it would show just how human was the humanity of Jesus."[60] Those seeking to understand how the eternal Son, who is from all eternity the all-knowing Word of the Father, could simultaneously experience embodied existence and finite knowledge

---

57. See Raymond E. Brown, *Jesus—God and Man* (New York: Macmillan, 1967), 39–102.

58. Wolfhart Pannenberg, *Jesus—God and Man* (Philadelphia: Westminster, 1978), 333.

59. Quoted in Brown, *Jesus—God and Man*, 102.

60. Brown, *Jesus—God and Man*, 100.

through incarnation (without emptying himself of this divine capacity), can consider Thomas Morris's proposal that the Son had levels of consciousness, an infinite and a finite level, analogous to the difference between our more expansive subconscious and more limited conscious mind.[61]

Fourth, the dependence of the Son on the Father and the Spirit as revealed in his embodied life must be balanced by recognition of an *analogous* "dependence" of the Father and the Spirit on him as the incarnate mediator of divine life to others. The Son says of the Father: "He will glorify me because it is from me that he will receive what he will make known to you" (John 16:14). Jesus is the Spirit Baptizer. The Father glorifies the Son so as to reveal that glory through the Spirit to the world. In this text, the Father and the Spirit depend on the Son for what they will reveal to humanity. Does the Father not place all things into the hands of the Son and the Spirit for the fulfillment of the divine reign and redemptive activity in the world? As Athanasius said of the Father, how could the Father have ever been "Wordless"?[62] Or how can Word be spoken without breath? There is no Father without a Son (nor a Son without a Father), and the Spirit of Sonship both anoints the Son (as the Son) and is offered by the Son to creation, making the Son the firstborn over the creation and the elder brother to the rest of humanity.[63] More recently, Pannenberg has highlighted the fact that the Father's deity is shown to be dependent on the Son and the Spirit for the fulfillment of the divine reign on earth. The one-sided emphasis on the Father as the source of all light and life allows for dependence to flow in only one direction, possibly implying some kind of ontological inferiority of the Son and the Spirit to the Father. Pannenberg thus wishes to bring balance to this dependence so that it flows in both directions, from Spirit and the Son on the Father and from the Father on the Son and the Spirit.[64]

Parenthetically, Thomas Weinandy expands on this unity of essence and distinction of persons between the Father, the Son, and the Spirit by depicting the Son's eternal generation from the Father as through the Spirit's eternal anointing *and* the eternal procession of the Spirit from the Father as through the mediation of the Son.[65] The eternal Son was always the anointed Christ, and the eternal Spirit was always the Spirit given in the self-giving

---

61. Morris, *The Logic of God Incarnate.*

62. Athanasius, *Orations against the Arians* 1.24.

63. Athanasius, *Orations against the Arians* 1.34.

64. Pannenberg, *Systematic Theology,* 1:311–12.

65. Thomas Weinandy, *The Father's Spirit of Sonship: Reconceiving the Trinity* (Eugene, OR: Wipf and Stock, 2011).

of the Son. Jesus's anointing by the Spirit in order to give forth the Spirit in history was eternally present in the loving communion of the triune God. As Eugene Rogers puts it, the "Spirit rests on the body of the Son in the economy, precisely because the Spirit rests on the Son in the Trinity."[66] The same is true of Jesus's giving of himself through the mediation of the Spirit. He always did so in relation to the Father from all eternity. The difference at Pentecost is that he is anointed as flesh, and he self-imparts through the Spirit *to the world* for the sake of the world's anointing, the world's sonship. Jesus always was in a sense the Christ and the Spirit, was always in a sense the Spirit of the Son. The Spirit thus mediates the coming of the Word into flesh at the incarnation (Luke 1:35), and the Word mediates the outpouring of the Spirit at Pentecost (Acts 2:33). The journey of Christ from the incarnation to Pentecost is a parable of the eternal God. But this is also the representation and means of the renewed creation. The Son is from all eternity "the Christ," earmarked to be the one who is baptized in the Spirit and in fire so as to be the Spirit Baptizer of all flesh!

Biblical challenges to the Son's unity with the Father did not just come from a reading of specific biblical texts. In the modern era a historical study of the rise of certain christological titles also introduced ambiguity into the Son's role as mediator. This is the case when it came to the title "Christ" (or Messiah, anointed one). Messianic expectations concerning the "Christ" were especially ambiguous in the Judaism of the first century and subject to a range of interpretations, none of which attributed to the Messiah a truly divine identity. Indeed, "the word 'Messiah,' within Jesus' world, does not refer, in itself, to a divine or quasi-divine figure."[67] Interestingly, the Christian adoptionists of the second century and beyond focused on Jesus's anointing as the Christ in order to deny his divine identity. Moreover, it is important to note (as I did in the preceding chapter) that there is no straight line between the Old Testament and the New Testament when it comes to Jesus's actual fulfillment of his messianic mission. New Testament authors granted Old Testament texts that they read messianically, in the light of Jesus, a more expansive horizon of meaning than what was originally intended.[68] There are texts in the Old Testament that may be called "proto-messianic"; Jesus's

---

66. Rogers, *After the Spirit*, 69.

67. N. T. Wright, *Jesus and the Victory of God*, vol. 2 of *Christian Origins and the Question of God* (Minneapolis: Fortress, 1997), 477.

68. See Joachim Becker, *Messianic Expectation in the Old Testament* (Philadelphia: Fortress, 1980). See also Michael F. Bird, *Are You the One Who Is to Come? The Historical Jesus and the Messianic Question* (Grand Rapids: Baker Academic, 2009), 34–35.

messianic identity and mission, however, cannot be found fully formed for us in Old Testament texts.

We need to look elsewhere for the impetus behind how the New Testament authors came to read Old Testament texts in support of Jesus as the Christ. Seminally, John the Baptist is said within the New Testament narrative to have set the terms for how these chosen messianic texts were to be read, which is his function as the forerunner of the Messiah. And his major source of inspiration is not what would come to be viewed as messianic texts but, instead, as the *universal promise of the Spirit*. Unlike John's baptisms in the Jordan River, the coming one will occasion a mighty river of the Spirit in the world, into which he will "baptize" people unto end-time restoration and judgment (Matt. 3:11; Mark 1:8; Luke 3:16; John 1:33). As Christ himself noted in John 7:38, out from him will flow rivers of living water. The novel element in how John the Baptist announces Jesus's messianic installment is precisely in this insight, in which Jesus is shown to be the chosen one because he brings the Spirit with him and will baptize others in the Spirit (John 1:33). The novelty in John's announcement will turn out to be decisive at Pentecost: the one anointed of the Spirit will himself baptize all flesh in the Spirit (John 20:22; Acts 1:5). The John at the Jordan cobbles his announcement together from diverse expectations concerning the coming of the Spirit, but the resulting picture is compelling. Indeed, this linkage John ends up forging between the one who will bear the Spirit and the one who will baptize in the Spirit provides the overall interpretive framework for reading the most striking texts that would be written in support of Christ's deity and universal lordship (John 20:22; Acts 2:33–35). Who else but the Lord of life can impart the Spirit? John ends up providing for us the raw material for our interpretation of Christ's entire messianic identity and mission, and his central idea is that of the Christ as the Spirit Baptizer.

But how will the Christ do this? How will he bear and impart the Spirit in a way that will incorporate all flesh into his own life? Here is where the fulfillment goes even beyond John's expectations, as his announcement went beyond the expectations of the prophets. Christ's baptism of all flesh in the Spirit will not be marked distinctively by judgment, as John implied, for the Messiah will himself bear and overcome the fire of alienation and death so that we can be sanctified by it. Rather, the messianic mission will be most distinctively marked by divine restoration and favor. It will have the healing and restoration of flesh as its hallmark: "For God did not send his Son into the world to condemn the world, but to save the world through him" (John 3:17). In fact, the Messiah will even take on the Spirit precisely in order to himself *bear* and *overcome* the fire that John expected him to immediately light upon the earth. The Messiah will condescend to bear the fires of judgment or death for all flesh in order to rise up and impart to all flesh the Spirit of life (Isa. 53; Acts 2:33–35). The church will come to say that he bears the Spirit in the service of incarnation and crucifixion. He overcomes the fire in his resurrection, is vindicated as the faithful Son in the Spirit, so as to bring divine favor to the earth through the Spirit's impartation. The world is opened up to the favor of his sonship. The beginnings of this trajectory will catch Jesus's forerunner off guard (Luke 7:19). Messianic fulfillment thus moved from unexpected development to unexpected development, carried by the eschatological freedom of the Spirit and explained by an innovative reading of texts. There is no straight line from promise to fulfillment between the Old and New Testaments; rather, it is a line with unexpected turns. Messianic fulfillment is full of surprises over the span of scriptural formation. Only those who can bear the shock of them end up fully understanding what it means to call him the Christ; only those who receive the Spirit from him as Lord will venture to do so.

Even the titles that are directly important to the doctrine of the incarnation and Christ's unity with the Father (such as Son of God, Wisdom of God, and Logos, or Word of God) are also ambiguous in their larger historical setting. The term "Son of God" had a variety of uses in ancient Jewish and Greek settings, and they did not always indicate identification with God.[69] The Logos (Word) Christology in the New Testament is partly dependent on the Jewish notion of the creative Word, or the wisdom of God. Word and wisdom overlap in ancient Judaism (e.g., by the divine Word *and* wisdom, God "formed humankind," according to Wisdom 9:1–2). Divine wisdom, especially as it is witnessed to in the Torah, was the "wise ordering of the world" for those who fear God in ancient Judaism (Dunn, 168–73). Whether divine wisdom is one with God (as God's presence in the world) was not always clear in ancient Judaism, however, as we saw above with regard to Philo. But an argument can be made that even where Word or wisdom is personified in ancient Judaism, it is not dominantly understood as an intermediary "god" separate from the God of Israel. Therefore, Dunn concludes his discussion of this matter by noting that "Wisdom, like the name, the glory, the Spirit of Yahweh, was a way of asserting God's nearness, his involvement in his world, his concern for his people" (Dunn, 176). In line with this tradition, Christ,

---

69. Dunn, *Christology in the Making*, 14–22. Hereafter, page references to this work appear in parentheses within the text.

as the wisdom of God (1 Cor. 8:6), "fully embodies the creative and saving activity of God" (Dunn, 212). In line with the impetus of this tradition, Christ is not treated in the New Testament as an intermediary divine being separate from God. The concept of the "Word" of God is at times personified in the Old Testament (Ps. 33:6; 107:20; 147:15, 18; Isa. 9:8); like wisdom, it depicts "the creative, revelatory, or redemptive activity of God" (Dunn, 219).

But titles such as "Son of God" or "Word of God," whose meanings were ambiguous in ancient Jewish and Greek settings, are taken up and clarified in the life of Jesus as the Spirit Baptizer in a way that causes them to imply his unity with God. Jesus's sojourn on earth as the Spirit Baptizer points in the direction of precisely such identification. In John, the creative Word of the Father acts in unity with the Father in mediating creation and redeeming it (John 1:1–18). The Son of the Father will baptize flesh in the Spirit of life (1:33). The Word (or Son) of the Father is thus superior to the law, which bears witness to him, for he alone channels truth and grace (1:17). As I have noted earlier, Jesus's sonship came to be viewed as eschatologically verified and fulfilled through the Holy Spirit in Jesus's resurrection and exaltation (e.g., Rom. 1:4), which was referred back to both his baptism at the Jordan River (Luke 3:22) and his conception in Mary's womb (1:35)—where he was declared to be God's Son as well. In one sense, his sonship fulfills Israel's (Matt. 2:15; Hosea 11:1). However, Jesus's sonship was also unique in that Israel's—and by implication, humanity's—sonship is shown to be dependent on his (Mark 12:6; Matt. 11:27) (Dunn, 29). In fact, Jesus's relationship to the Abba (Father) to whom he prays also comes to be viewed as unique, giving the impression that though our sonship is dependent on his, his sonship is dependent only on the Father, a relationship that is eventually said to be timeless (John 1:1–18) (Dunn, 27–32, 61). Pannenberg notes that, if Jesus's sonship throughout his life and at his exaltation is shown to be unique and integral to his Father's identity as the Abba, it would be a logical step to assume that Jesus was in some sense always the Son from all eternity and came to the earth through incarnation.[70] Indeed, the Son imparts the Spirit, and the Spirit bears *his* name as the Spirit of Christ, the Spirit of the Son (Rom. 8:9, 15–16). The Spirit ends up drawing us into the benefits of *Christ's* address of "Abba" to his heavenly Father (Rom. 8:9–16). Christ's oneness with the Father and the Spirit makes him irreplaceable and necessary to our communion with the Father in the eschatologically expansive gift of the Spirit. He is the Spirit Baptizer.

---

70. Pannenberg, *Systematic Theology*, 2:368.

This pneumatological and eschatological verification of the Son's unique unity with God in his work as Spirit Baptizer implied that the Son was always one with God, for God is eternal. One cannot "become" one with God in God's self-giving to the world if one is not already and eternally one with God. The one conceived as God's Son in Mary's womb for Luke and Matthew is thus quite rightly, for John, the eternal Logos or Word who was from the beginning not only "with" God, but "was" God (John 1:1). In him was life, the life that was in the Father and is in the Word, as it is in the Father (John 1:4; cf. 5:26), which also explains his identity as the resurrection and the life (11:11), and which qualifies him eventually to breathe the Spirit forth onto others on behalf of—and in unity with—the Father (20:21; 1:33). The Spirit Baptizer (1:33) is thus the divine Word incarnate (1:14): the one and only Son is the Spirit Baptizer who shares fully in God's self-impartation (1:33; cf. 20:21) and *therefore* one with God's eternal being. He is on behalf of the Father the agent of creation (1:3) as well as its rebirth (1:13). Thomas will thus appropriately address him as "my Lord and my God" (John 20:28).

Functional or Ontological?

It is the assumption of many that the scriptural challenge includes an approach to Christology that is functional rather than ontological. In other words, in Scripture, Christ is allegedly only one with God's *actions to save*. Therefore, no ontological unity or unity of essence between Christ and God exists in Scripture. There is an element of truth to this assumption, since even a cursory reading of the New Testament will not yield an attempt to speak explicitly of Christ and God as of one "essence," or nature (though, as we have been saying, that is implied). In fact, functional Christology preserves the truth that Christ's unity with God is seen primarily from his unity with God's presence in action as a dynamic reality that involves Christ's entire mode of human self-giving. What Jesus is, in essence in his relationship to his heavenly Father and the Holy Spirit, comes to visible realization in the active life of Jesus Christ, which culminates at Pentecost, where Jesus's self-giving is shown to be one with the Father's and the Spirit's. "What is known as functional Christology is essentially a Christology in its realization," writes Walter Kasper. Therefore, "functional Christology is itself a form of ontic Christology."[71] Jesus actively images the eternal Son in the world precisely

---

71. Walter Kasper, *Jesus the Christ* (Kent, UK: Burns and Oates, 1976), 166.

by giving of himself to the love of the Father and to the Spirit, who is the promised outpouring of the Father's love in the world. Jesus, and the Spirit poured out through him, particularize God in creation as the "journeying God," to use a phrase taken from Keshab Chandra Sen (1838–64).[72] This God is the incorporating God who takes the creation into the divine life.

But saying that Christ's functional unity with God is essential or ontological requires unpacking. Specifically, how does a Christology focused on Pentecost necessitate this identity of a functional *and* an ontological Christology? Can we justify the link that we have been assuming between Christ's unity with God's redemptive action in the world and Christ's unity with the very being of God as God? Recall Pannenberg's point that Jesus gives himself over to the lordship of the Father in the world in a way that shows himself indispensable to that lordship, an indispensability that is verified in his resurrection from the dead (and at Pentecost). Since the Father's lordship is essential to the Father's very being as God, Jesus's indispensable unity with that lordship implies an indispensable unity with the very essence of the Father. We could add here that the Father's lordship is ultimately proved in his bestowal of the Spirit of life on the dying creation in order to renew it. Since Jesus is shown in his risen and ascended form to have been indispensable to that Spirit impartation, he has shown himself to be indispensable to that lordship. Since that lordship is essential to the Father's and the Spirit's being as God, Jesus's indispensable involvement in the impartation of the Spirit proves his essential unity with the Father and the Spirit. Jesus is one with the divine action precisely in being one in identity and being with God, who is the subject of that action. Christ is one with God both functionally (or one with God's actions in the world) *and* ontologically (or one with the very being of God as the subject of that action).

Bear in mind here that God's action to save is a divine *self*-impartation to flesh. The divine Son unites to flesh at the incarnation as sent by the Father in the power of the Spirit in order to impart the Spirit through his embodied life onto all flesh on behalf of the Father. Therefore, the key insight that justifies the step from a functional to an ontological christological unity with God is the fact that salvation in Scripture is not merely a divine *work*: it is a divine *presence*, a divine self-giving to flesh. One of the fatal flaws of dyohypostatic Christology was the assumption that the true God saves creation from a distance. But this is not the understanding of salvation given in Christ's journey to Pentecost and its ultimate fulfillment at the end

---

72. Williams, "Jesus Christ," 542.

of all things: "Look! God's dwelling place is now among the people, and he will dwell with them. They will be his people, and God himself will be with them and be their God" (Rev. 21:3). The incarnation in the light of Pentecost shows us that God saves by coming to creation, coming to reign and to abundantly pour forth the divine Spirit to all flesh, both of which Christ fulfills at Pentecost (Acts 2:33–36) leading up to the eschatological dwelling of God in creation. Salvation comes via a divine *self*-impartation to the world and the incorporation of the other into the divine life. In the light of salvation as divine self-impartation and incorporation, therefore, even a functional unity between Christ and God's action to save implies that Jesus is indispensable to the divine *self* that is given and is present to creation, which also means the divine self or subject of action at work in renewing creation. As such, Jesus's functional unity with the divine action to save would imply an essential unity with God as the subject of the action, one with the very being of God in relation to the world. Jesus's unity with God's self-giving reveals an indispensability that raises deeper questions about Jesus's unity with all that identifies God *as God*.

All of the above raises a related question concerning whether one can even distinguish between God's being and God's action. The medieval theologians referred to God as *actus purus* (pure action). In the nineteenth century, Friedrich Schleiermacher held to a refined form of pantheism in which God is to be viewed as essentially an action, the action of divine love that governs the cosmos and intends redemption for it. A functional identification between Jesus's embodied life and the divine action is within this restrictive view of God the only identification between God and Christ that is possible.[73] To Schleiermacher's credit, he strained to regard Jesus as permanently indispensable and irreplaceable to God's self-revelation and self-impartation to humanity. Motivating Schleiermacher was thus the issue of what accounts for Jesus's ongoing influence as the mediator of divine love in the fellowship of the church.[74] Not surprisingly, Schleiermacher ended up holding to a modalistic understanding of God in which the divine action from the Father is realized as Spirit through the mediation of Christ in the world. There are no relationships in God; rather, the *God-world link* is the primary relationship. God's being *is* God's action to save in the world. To avoid such pantheistic and modalistic (not to mention deterministic) im-

---

73. See Julia A. Lamm, *The Living God: Schleiermacher's Appropriation of Spinoza* (University Park, PA: Pennsylvania State University Press, 1996), esp. 1–12.

74. Friedrich Schleiermacher, *The Christian Faith* (Philadelphia: Fortress, 1976), 377–79.

plications, we might prefer Barth's idea of an *analogy of love* between God's immanent triune life and God's economic involvement in the world through the incarnation and Pentecost. Though God's being is inseparable from the divine action at the core of creation and redemption, the former cannot be simply collapsed into the latter. God's being is indeed in becoming; but there is still a distinction to be made between them.[75] Therefore, saying that Christ's functional unity with God's action to save is an ontological unity requires significant qualification to be meaningful.

Given the fact that the ontological status of the Logos became so pressing an issue in the ancient world, the church could hardly have avoided it. This question was arguably inevitable, given what the New Testament says about Christ's unity with the Father and with the Spirit, who was poured forth through him and who now bears his name as the "Spirit of Christ" (Rom. 8:9). After all, if Jesus was shown to be one with God's lordship over creation by pouring forth the Spirit on all flesh, it seems faithful to say that Christ's unity with God is eternal—without beginning and without end. Christ was thus integral to God's act of creation, a conclusion that the New Testament draws in several places (John 1:3; Col. 1:16; Heb. 1:3). In Scripture there is an inseparable connection assumed between creation and salvation (which is the new creation). In fact, the creation narrative is told in a way that highlights its connection with the Exodus and the eschatological promise of salvation through the Spirit and the Word of prophecy (Ezek. 37). Given that the Son is proven in his resurrection and at Pentecost to be one with God's sovereign lordship over creation, and given God's self-impartation to creation, it hardly seems possible that the Son's unity with God could be limited by time, could ever have an end or have had a beginning, a point that the New Testament also makes. The Son *is* the beginning and the end of all existing things (Rev. 1:17); he does not himself have a beginning.

The Anthropological Challenge

Over the last two centuries, the dominant view among thinkers is that "the age of metaphysics has come to an end."[76] In making that statement, Pan-

---

75. This is the central thesis of Eberhard Jüngel, *God's Being Is in Becoming: The Trinitarian Being of God in the Theology of Karl Barth* (Grand Rapids: Eerdmans, 2001).

76. Wolfhart Pannenberg, *Metaphysics and the Idea of God* (Grand Rapids: Eerdmans, 1990), 3.

nenberg did not think that the question of being or of existence had ceased having metaphysical significance, even if it was posed solely with reference to science and the empirical world. Indeed, the ancient metaphysical challenges survived into the modern era but tended to take on a distinctively anthropological (especially relational) focus. Bertrand Russell noted that even the turn outward to the cosmos was driven by a deep sense of its existential significance for human life and community.[77] Such probing is metaphysical in the sense that it still implies larger questions about the nature and destiny of humanity with respect to the world or the cosmos. As Paul Tillich reminded us time and again, such probing often implied a grasping after (and being grasped by) "ultimate concern."[78] But the shift of focus to anthropology changed the metaphysical concern. The ancient metaphysical challenge grappled mainly with the issue of how we are to understand divine freedom and transcendence with respect to creation or humanity. But the modern anthropological focus of human questioning has wrestled mainly with the issue of how we are to understand human freedom and fulfillment in relation to God or, perhaps, in the absence of God. And, just as with the ancient metaphysical challenge, Christology was at the heart of the anthropological challenge for Christian theologians, for Christ is the place in Christian dogma where God meets humanity for the sake of all flesh.

At the dawn of the modern era, the French philosopher René Descartes announced the new anthropological interest in basing truth in large part on human self-awareness by announcing, *Cogito ergo sum* (I think, therefore I am). Descartes took seriously the challenge of skepticism concerning the existence of God, but he decided to bend this skepticism in the service of faith. He questioned everything, even his own existence, in order to discover whether there remained one truth that could not be denied and that could form the basis for the trajectory of his thought. This truth was: "I am a thing that thinks."[79] The fact that he thinks establishes the reality of his own existence, for, even if the act of thinking can be doubted, one still has to think in order to doubt it! With the thought firmly in place that thinking validates one's existence, it seemed but a short step for Descartes to argue that the same thinking also validates God's existence, for the horizon of

77. Bertrand Russell, *The Problems of Philosophy* (Oxford: Oxford University Press, 1997), 153–61.

78. Paul Tillich, *Dynamics of Faith* (New York: Harper One, 2009), 1–4.

79. René Descartes, *Meditations on First Philosophy: With Selections from the Objections and Replies*, trans. and ed. John Cottingham (Cambridge, UK: Cambridge University Press, 1986), 69–73.

thought transcends one's finite reach. Descartes discovered within human consciousness an infinite point of reference that he could not explain except to say that it had to correspond to a divine reality that accounts for it. More specifically, Descartes had thought of an infinitely perfect being, which he believed could only have its source in God.[80]

But is this infinite horizon of human thought really God? The nineteenth-century philosopher Ludwig Feuerbach denied that it was, and he was determined to use the Christian doctrine of the incarnation of God in Christ to prove it. For Feuerbach, the infinite horizon of human thought that Descartes thought was God was really a human *self-projection.* "God," for Feuerbach, is alien to real life, a phantom image created out of the depths of human imagination in order to celebrate an idealized picture of ourselves. The problem with this idealization of humanity in the concept of God prevents us from relying on ourselves for the flourishing and meaning of life. For Feuerbach, if Christ is to mean anything to the modern world, he must be the means by which God is eliminated so as to free humanity for self-discovery and self-determination.

Toward that end, Feuerbach constructs his understanding of Jesus within the reality of human self-relation or, more specifically, self-love and self-reliance without God. He starts by locating what is uniquely human in the human capacity for self-relation. A person can self-relate, "that is—he converses with himself." In this self-relation, humanity transcends itself. Since human consciousness has, according to Feuerbach, limitless possibilities, it implies a relationship between a finite mind and its own infinite self-projection. Feuerbach says that "in the consciousness of the infinite, the conscious subject has for his object the infinity of his own nature."[81] This human self-projection is all there is. There is no way for human consciousness to extend beyond the horizon of its own infinite self-projection. Indeed, "man cannot get beyond his own nature."[82] This infinite self-projection is what we have erroneously called "God," which has become the origin and essence of religion. When humans see the face of "God," they are merely looking into the mirror of their own idealized self-image.

For Feuerbach, "God" is this human self-objectification, the projection of ourselves onto an infinite horizon. In this self-relationship between a

80. Descartes's larger argument is found throughout his first three meditations (Descartes, *Meditations on First Philosophy*, 12–90).

81. Ludwig Feuerbach, *The Essence of Christianity*, 2nd ed. (New York: Calvin Blanchard, 1855), 21.

82. Feuerbach, *Essence of Christianity*, 31. Hereafter, page references to this work appear in parentheses within the text.

thinking subject and the infinite horizon of the subject's consciousness, there is ideally "self-verification, self-affirmation, self-love, joy in one's own perfection" (25). More is involved here for Feuerbach than religious feelings, for such ecstasy would merely consist of being intoxicated with one's own plenitude (29). There are also qualities drawn from a person's own nature, "qualities in which he in truth only images and projects himself" (31). Such "qualities" refer specifically to a person's own "thoughts and dispositions." Indeed, "such are a man's thoughts and dispositions, such is his God" (32). "By his God thou knowest the man," says Feuerbach. Likewise, "by the man his God." The two—God and humanity—are "identical" for Feuerbach (33). This is all there is to Christian faith, namely, a way for individuals and human communities to converse with their own self-image (20). Indeed, "man has no other aim than himself" (51). Therefore, the question, for Feuerbach, has to do with how to eliminate the "middleman" of "God," so to speak, so that humanity can understand that in the figure of God they were really loving and enjoying themselves all along. For Feuerbach, humanity can only be free to find self-fulfillment once God is out of the picture.

The way to eliminate God, for Feuerbach, is potentially found in Christ, particularly in the Christian story of the incarnation of the divine Son of God, who became flesh out of love for the human race (see John 1:14; 3:16). If Christ is to be relevant to the flourishing of human self-relation, Feuerbach needed to show how Christ makes the figure of "God" unnecessary to human self-love. How does Jesus eliminate the mythical figure of God from human view so that they can discover the human self-relationship hidden beneath it? Feuerbach finds the key to understanding how Jesus makes God unnecessary in a novel interpretation of *kenosis,* or God's self-emptying at the incarnation for the sake of humanity. God in Christ "made himself nothing"—emptied himself—for us, according to Philippians 2:7. Feuerbach takes this as symbolic of the fact that becoming fully human necessarily implies the elimination of God. For Feuerbach, Christians can come to view the birth of Christ as the laying aside of deity for the sake of elevating humanity. At the incarnation, then, one can discover for the first time that God was really unnecessary to human self-relationship and self-fulfillment all along. In his life, Christ laid God aside and functioned to show humanity that they do not need God anymore to love themselves. They can enjoy their own perfections without the figure of God masking the fact that all they need to do is know themselves.

The incarnation is thus not a reaching for reconciliation *with* God, for Feuerbach; rather, it is a seeking to attain human freedom *from* God. In this scheme Christ is a godless figure who shows humans that destiny is really in their own hands. Therefore, the incarnation is significant for Feuerbach only because, in it, "love conquers God." The result? "As God has renounced himself out of love, so we, out of love, should renounce God." God masks the reality of human self-love and prevents us from recognizing and enjoying it. The result of the incarnation must thus be the renouncing of God, "for if we do not sacrifice God to love, we sacrifice love to God" (81). The divine self-emptying in the biblical story of the incarnation removes "God" from human self-love so that we can love ourselves knowingly and directly. For Feuerbach, Christology becomes nothing more than a form of human self-redemption.

How Feuerbach could have so tragically misread Christology—that is, to empty it of its theological significance—staggers the imagination. His misreading was driven by the misguided conviction that God masks human self-awareness and alienates us from ourselves. The opposite is true. Pentecost reveals that God, as the source of all life, is the one who brings us to the awareness of ourselves as created in the gracious and self-imparting wisdom and love of God. There can be no self-awareness that is not awakened by awareness of God, no flourishing of life that is not from and in God. Divine *kenosis*, or self-emptying, does not eliminate God—so that God leaves humanity to its own resources. Such an idea is a cruel delusion. This divine self-emptying in Christ imparts to us the flourishing of life in the Spirit, the love of the Father in the image of the faithful Son. This divine self-giving frees us to be ourselves as we were created to be and shows us the wisdom by which that life is to be attained and lived. If the metaphysical challenge tempted one to think that God could be free only if freed from humanity, the anthropological challenge under Feuerbach offered an opposite temptation: a humanity that can only be free if freed from God.

Rather than humanity imaging itself under the label of God, as Feuerbach maintains, the incarnation in the light of Pentecost means that God has actually imaged Godself in human form! Christ is indeed the image of the liberated person, but precisely as the divine Son who by the Spirit exercises freedom in uniting in love and grace with humanity for the sake of human freedom. Since humanity was created to image such love by the Spirit, human freedom will be experienced when humans are incorporated by the Spirit into Christ for the sake of bearing his image. Humanity was made for God, and not the "God" projected from humanity, but the self-imparted God in Christ's journey all the way to Pentecost. Fortunately, in Christ, humanity finds God—not its own self-image! In finding God, humanity does indeed find itself, but this self-discovery is due to the fact that humanity was made for God. God pours out the divine life in and through Christ in a way that takes humanity up into a divine love and self-giving for which humanity was made from the beginning. This human self-transcendence of which Feuerbach speaks is thus not humanity confined within its own self-relation but humanity reaching for communion within the divine self-relation for which humanity was created.

The human-projected God imagined by Feuerbach does indeed exist— as essential to what Scripture refers to as *idolatry*. Feuerbach was right about this one thing: this idolatry does partially characterize religion. Feuerbach's version of humanity is, in fact, consistent with the one that Adam assumed when he reached for his own self-exaltation by eating from the tree of the knowledge of good and evil. It is also consistent with the tower of Babel; in fact, it is consistent with any illusion that the eternal horizon for which we implicitly reach is our own self-image. If there is a "god" laid aside at the incarnation of Christ, it is precisely the exalted image of ourselves so cherished by Feuerbach. In reality, a liberating sense of self could only be the self shaped by Pentecost, namely, the self inhabited by God's Spirit and shaped in the image of the crucified and risen Christ.

The temptation to use the figure of Jesus to project outwardly from our own self-image was not confined to Feuerbach. Even the quest for the historical Jesus that attempted to liberate Christology from the bias of church dogma merely caused Christology to take on the new bias of the historians. Albert Schweitzer, in his survey of early modern efforts to write historical biographies of Jesus, noted that "each individual created Jesus in accordance with his own character."[83] This is not to say that genuine gains were not made from an early time in historical research into Jesus, only that the results of that research tended to say as much about the historians as about the image of Jesus that surfaces in their work. This temptation is there for all of us. We all have a tendency to create a Christ who confirms for us our own self-justification, who does not disturb us or make us feel ill at ease.

For all of his theological shortcomings, Bultmann attempted in his Christology to free humanity from self-justification for an opening of the self to God's open future. The anthropological challenge thus took an important turn in Bultmann's existentialist hermeneutic. An existentialist hermeneutic was a way of interpreting Scripture that took seriously questions that arise from human existence in the world. More than any other New Testament

83. Albert Schweitzer, *The Quest of the Historical Jesus* (Minneapolis: Fortress, 2001), 6.

106

scholar of his time, Bultmann was convinced that historical research was all about existential involvement: "History gains meaning only as the historian himself stands within history and takes part in history."[84] Specifically, research into Jesus should involve existential openness to the faith that he offers us as the Word of the Father. For Bultmann, historical Jesus research is not meant to justify one's self-made image; rather, "existential" concerns a personal discovery of authentic existence as given for us in faith.

The existential dimension of historical research is a valid insight. But by collapsing the resurrection of Jesus into the proclaimed word of God, Bultmann neglected to see that the historical Jesus reaches far beyond existential enlightenment to involve larger historical and cosmic dimensions of salvation that are inaugurated in the resurrection of Jesus and in the down payment of the Holy Spirit (2 Cor. 5:1–5). The transformation of creation by the risen Christ was thought by Bultmann to be mythological, so he sought to reinterpret (demythologize) it in the light of a personal discovery of authentic existence. For him, biblical myth "should be interpreted not cosmologically, but anthropologically—or better still, existentially."[85] Faith in Christ is all about discovering authentic existence that is open to God's future and not reliant on this-worldly security.[86] One comes to Christ with an existential interest, a preunderstanding that includes questions driven by existential concerns. One is left, however, with the anthropological reductionism typical of modernity, a reductionism that reduces the resurrection of Jesus to his continued presence after the crucifixion in the preaching of the word as received by faith: "If the event of Easter Day is in any sense an historical event additional to the event of the cross, it is nothing else than the rise of faith in the risen Lord."[87] Nothing else? How Christ is the risen Lord in any realistic sense, that is, if there is no event of his rising again independent of his presence in the church's proclamation, is difficult to fathom. Faith in the light of Pentecost assumes an event of Christ's rising from the dead. Of course, faith in the Christ who imparts new life is existential in significance, but it is also anchored in Jesus's baptism in the Spirit, which climaxes in his resurrection and exaltation as the Lord who imparts the Spirit. Karl Rahner

---

84. Rudolf Bultmann, *History and Eschatology* (Edinburgh: Edinburgh University Press, 1957), 11.

85. Rudolf Bultmann, "The New Testament and Mythology," in *Kerygma and Myth*, ed. Hans-Werner Bartsch (New York: Harper and Row, 1961), 10.

86. Bultmann emphasizes this point in *Jesus Christ and Mythology* (London: SCM Press, 2012).

87. Bultmann, "New Testament and Mythology," 42.

has maintained that there is an inner word that constitutes human nature as made for God and God's self-giving love. This inner word corresponds to the outer word of the incarnate and risen Christ, which is given for humanity, a self-giving that humanity was created to bear.[88] This is what makes Christ relevant not only to existential human enlightenment but also to the renewal of human community, society, and world—indeed, the entire creation. Hence, Pentecostal faith extends far beyond personal enlightenment, as important as that is. Faith in Christ as Spirit Baptizer is also broadly communal and cosmic in significance.

Dorothée Soelle used Bultmann's existential challenge as her point of departure to apply the anthropological challenge to Christology in order to expand it to encompass social liberation. She notes that Bultmann significantly used historical criticism in the service of self-reflection, as a way of entering into the questions concerning historical existence opened up by Jesus as the Word of God.[89] She finds this move of seminal significance to a socially relevant understanding of Christ for our time. But she is critical of Bultmann's "reduction of the question of meaning to individual existence" (48). She continues by criticizing Bultmann's anthropological turn for ignoring the social conditions of the existential preunderstanding brought to one's encounter with the Christ of proclamation: "Existentialist interpretation neglects the conditions of its own pre-understanding. It grounds itself in the experience of the eschatological moment, which transcends all conditions" (45). For Soelle, Bultmann neglects the full historical and social conditions of the preunderstanding that one takes to the biblical text and to Jesus Christ, how one comes to interpret Christ for one's own life. She implicitly asks the question concerning what we mean under the umbrella of human existence. She is grateful for Bultmann's existentialist hermeneutic but wishes to deepen and expand it in order to include the social dimension of the liberation implied in the message of Jesus (esp. 59–63). Enlightenment concerning this existential reality calls for more than individual transformation but also for social liberation and justice as well. Indeed, "only the liberation of all can be a valid liberation for the individual" (67). With some expansion, Bultmann's existential hermeneutic can become, in Soelle's view, a liberation hermeneutic that approaches Jesus from the vantage point of a quest for liberation from

88. A good discussion of this theme in Rahner can be found in Patrick Burke, *Reinterpreting Rahner: A Critical Study of His Major Themes* (New York: Fordham University Press, 2002), 112–14.

89. Dorothée Soelle, *Political Theology* (Philadelphia: Fortress, 1974), 11–18. Hereafter, page references to this work appear in parentheses within the text.

the dehumanizing effects of social injustice and oppression. The anthropological challenge to Christology transitions, under Soelle, into a larger, more socially relevant, project. But she, too, rejects the literal meaning of Christ's resurrection; thus she, too, fails to fully appreciate the larger eschatological and cosmic significance of Jesus as the Spirit Baptizer.

Liberation Christology after Soelle has been a force for the renewal of christological method in the direction of its becoming a critical discipline that challenges idolatrous human ideology, the kind of self-justification that one got with Feuerbach. In the service of this renewal, Jon Sobrino developed his liberation Christology in a way that helps guard against human self-projection and self-justification. In partial dependence on Pannenberg, Sobrino helpfully notes that his own liberation Christology will not neglect its anchor in historical events: "We are going to concentrate on the objective aspect of the Christ event, not on some subjective aspect involving ourselves."[90] He draws on Pannenberg's Christology from below to open up space for developing the social significance of Jesus's lifelong commitment to the coming reign of God.[91] He praises Pannenberg for "a novel historical hermeneutic" for granting Jesus's life devotion to the coming reign of God a mediating role to play in Jesus's identity, but he finds Pannenberg's approach to be "basically explicative, not transformational."[92] Juan Luis Segundo agrees with this conclusion. Though he finds Pannenberg's Christology from below a helpful way of opening up significance to the historical Jesus as being determinative for Jesus's identity, he quickly criticizes Pannenberg for making the dogmatic confession of Jesus's unity with God the fundamental concern. His warning concerning Pannenberg is dramatic: "But beware, readers! Make no mistake here! What question does Pannenberg pose to the historical Jesus *before anything else*? His relationship to the above."[93] In other words, Pannenberg departs from the preoccupation of Christology with the incarnation (from above) only to end up justifying the same dogmatic point of departure via the historical Jesus.

It is true that Pannenberg follows the lead of a Christology from below only to circle back to a Christology from above. But as I observed in the preceding chapter, this circling back to the question of Jesus's unity with God and humanity in Pannenberg's Christology from below is valuable, even

90. Jon Sobrino, SJ, *Christology at the Crossroads* (Maryknoll, NY: Orbis Books, 1978), 2.

91. Sobrino, *Christology at the Crossroads*, 2–9.

92. Sobrino, *Christology at the Crossroads*, 27.

93. Juan Luis Segundo, *The Historical Jesus of the Synoptics* (Maryknoll, NY: Orbis Books, 1985), 29–30.

necessary. The anthropological concern of Christology must be rooted in Jesus's unity with God. How else can he be the one who inaugurates and fulfills the liberating future for humanity in the kingdom of God? James Cone notes helpfully that the Exodus highlights the political dimension of salvation while the resurrection of Jesus accents its far-reaching eschatological dimension.[94] It is Jesus's unity with the inauguration and fulfillment of God's reign for the sake of ultimate mercy, justice, and liberation that proves his unity with God and humanity. There can be no liberation Christology without this unity.

It is understandable that the Marxist commitment to wed interpretation and transformation would lead progenitors of liberation theology to steer Christology in a less speculative and more transformative direction from the beginning. A sympathetic reading of Pannenberg's later *Systematic Theology* (which was not available to Sobrino and Segundo when they wrote) does reveal an anthropological concern that is socially transformative in its implication. Pannenberg writes of how the eternal Word's devotion to the kingdom of the Father is what accounts for the creation of humanity in distinction from God. Humanity was made for this devotion to the kingdom of God, to have their very personhood in the concrete establishment of this kingdom in the world. The implication is that Jesus's lifelong devotion to the kingdom mediates the hypostatic unity of Jesus with the eternal Word of the Father and leads to the divine task of person-building in communion with God and one another. There is rich potential here for a liberation Christology that takes seriously the mediating role of the historical Jesus in God's project to liberate people for a loving and just community.[95] Christ is the ideal person for all time, one with the person of the Word, the person given over to the community of love and justice that God wills for creation.

I wish to add here that, in the light of Pentecost, Christ bears the liberating Spirit to impart the Spirit to others and, with the Spirit, a person-building communion in and with the eternal Word of the Father as well as person-building community in Christ and in the Spirit. Our understanding of the justice of the kingdom of God is not taken first from secular sources but rather from the communal life opened up in the Spirit and in devotion to the way of the crucified and risen Christ. The more expansively the church opens up its witness to the justice of community in the Spirit to the

94. James H. Cone, *The Spirituals and the Blues* (Maryknoll, NY: Orbis Books, 1982), 78–96.

95. Pannenberg, *Systematic Theology*, 2:385–87.

world, subverting humanly destructive structures and ideologies wherever they may be found, the deeper they go into Christ. And the deeper they go into Christ, the more expansive their witness will become. The result is the Christoformistic pneumatic existence that is ecclesial existence, existence in and for the kingdom of love and justice.

Most promising among the Christologies that are consciously committed to a liberation hermeneutic is Elizabeth Johnson's chapter on Christology in her classic book *She Who Is*. She starts this chapter with the conviction that the renewing Spirit has worked among us through Jesus of Nazareth: "Jesus is a genuine Spirit-phenomenon, conceived, inspired, sent, hovered over, guided, and risen from the dead by her power."[96] As the embodiment of divine wisdom and given over to the liberating work of the Spirit in the world, Jesus becomes the true human for all others. Johnson rightly uses this insight to critique "the exacerbated stress on Jesus's maleness in the context of a dualistic anthropology that essentially divorces male from female humanity," placing women's salvation in question, at least the liberating impact of it.[97] As the mediator of life, Jesus becomes the human for all others in a way that liberates the oppressed and the abandoned. The significance of Jesus for the liberated community is this: The characteristic gift of life that comes from God has been mediated to us through the story of Jesus "in a new, unimaginable way, so that the crucified victim of state injustice is not abandoned forever." In the giving forth of the Spirit of life, the risen Christ becomes God's "pledge of a future to all the violated and the dead."[98] This is what a liberation Christology looks like if it has Pentecost at its horizon.

Christology must first be interpreted according to the gospel of the self-giving God and according to the correspondingly liberated human person. The Christ who became flesh in order to pour forth the Spirit of life *upon all flesh* implies an understanding of humanity that lives from the Word of the Father's love and the liberation of the Spirit's witness, rather than from its own resources apart from God. All humanly conceived and exploited hierarchies of privilege are shattered. Jew and Gentile, young and old, rich and poor, male and female—all find their renewed purpose in the way of the crucified Christ and the freedom of the eschatological Spirit (Acts 2:17–18; Gal. 3:28). Indeed, humanity was created when God breathed the breath of

96. Elizabeth A. Johnson, *She Who Is: The Mystery of God in Feminist Theological Discourse* (New York: Herder and Herder, 2008), 150.

97. Johnson, *She Who Is*, 151–54.

98. Johnson, *She Who Is*, 158.

life into them, and they became living souls (Gen. 2:7). We can all say, with Job 33:4, "The Spirit of God has made me; the breath of the Almighty gives me life." We were more specifically made by the indwelling Spirit to share in the life of the Son in communion with the Father, bearing the image of the Son in glory to the Father. For all things were made through the Son and *for him* (Col. 1:16). Humanity is not autonomous, for they "live, move, and have their being" in God (Acts 17:28). We are not autonomous beings who contain within ourselves the infinite source of our own fulfillment. We are made by the Spirit of God to live and love by that Spirit and to find fulfillment in community with others in the path opened up by the Spirit's leading. This is the path of the crucified and risen Christ, who imparts new life to us in the Spirit by imparting himself, incorporating us into his life, the liberating life of the triune God.

The Pluralist Challenge

The anthropological challenge has recently reached global significance. In the light of globalization, the question can be asked about how a Christology of Pentecost speaks to our new awareness of global human diversity and interdependence. Is it not truly significant that Christ's unity with God implied by the incarnation was made clear when God through Christ poured forth the divine presence to *all flesh*? This fact places the most important issue of Christology (Christ's unity with God) directly at the border of the pluralist challenge. We are more aware than ever before of the grand diversity of cultures, perspectives, and faith orientations. We are also aware of how interdependent we are for human flourishing. There are global forces that can doom humanity's future. We need to respect and value each other across the lines that divide us in order to overcome these dangers together. There can be no easy way forward on this path. Genuine repentance and openness to learn, especially by those with the greatest access to privilege and influence, will be required on multiple levels. Christ as the Spirit Baptizer creates the conditions for an ecclesial reality that will not only bear witness to Christ's liberating lordship but will also lend its own influence in a positive way toward the common good.

On the level of dogmatic christological concern, we must take great care in response to global challenges to be faithful to Christ's lordship in a way that is respectful and hospitable to those of other faith orientations (or lack of a consciously held faith orientation) that support the common good. However, it is also important to remain faithful to the ultimate significance of Christ as the one who mediates the incorporation of all flesh in all of its diversity into the divine life. Christ's unity with God implied by the incarnation and confirmed at Pentecost has come under scrutiny, and has even suffered rejection in contemporary theology in the light of the pluralist challenge. In the latter half of the twentieth century, some theologians have raised afresh the entire issue of whether the incarnation is consistent with the pluralistic and expansive reach of God's Spirit in the world. God's global presence in the world seems inclusive. Incarnation, however, seems exclusive. The Gospel of John puts it this way: the one and only Son of the Father, who is God, became flesh to make the Father known (John 1:1–18). Christ is the final Word of the Father for all time—the way, the truth, and the life. No one comes to the Father but through him (John 14:6). There is no other name by which we are saved but Jesus Christ (Acts 4:12). On the other hand, the expansive reach of God's Spirit in the world seems inclusive and diverse, for the Spirit is poured forth upon all flesh (Acts 2:17). But we should also recognize that the Logos of the Father incarnated in Christ is not only particular but implies cosmic universality as well, for "in him all things hold together" (Col. 1:17). This means that the incarnation has significance for all of creation for "all things were created through him and for him" (Col. 1:16). Moreover, the cosmic and eschatological Spirit of God is not only universal but particular as well, anointing the flesh of Jesus so as to transform all of creation in the image and glory of the Son. Both the Word and the Spirit are thus particular and universal in significance.

What happens when the Spirit is cut loose from the universal and final significance of Jesus Christ? The answer is theological pluralism, such as the Christology of John Hick. Hick maintains that our current global awareness of the plurality of faiths makes Christian exclusivism (reducing the way of salvation to Christ alone) untenable, even harmful. Such awareness "undermined the plausibility of the traditional Christian sense of superiority and has thereby set a question mark against its theological core in the dogma of Jesus of Nazareth as God incarnate."[99] Moreover, historical Jesus research has raised significant doubts that Jesus thought of himself as divine. In Hick's view, the dogma of Christ's deity "has dissolved under historical scrutiny" (29). As a result, he views the incarnation of Jesus as a mythological meta-

---

99. John Hick, *The Metaphor of God Incarnate: Christology in a Pluralistic Age* (Louisville: Westminster John Knox, 1993), 9. Hereafter, page references to this work appear in parentheses within the text.

phor of the fact that Jesus's life images God's love for humanity. The worship of Jesus as Lord is mere hyperbole, analogous to a lover exalting the beloved as the "one and only" source of fulfillment in life (9–12).

Hick does not deny that Jesus saw himself as vital to the inauguration of God's reign in the world, but this fact is still, for Hick, "a long way from Jesus thinking that he was God" (31). But, as I noted in the preceding chapter, the resurrection and Pentecost have verified this unity of Jesus with God's reign as eschatologically valid for all time. This is not yet the Son's *homoousios* (unity of essence) with the Father focused on during the fourth century at the Council of Nicaea. But if Christ is indispensable to the coming kingdom, he is indispensable to the Father's lordship, which is essential to the Father's being as God. This implied unity of essence of the Father and the Son is precisely what Easter and Pentecost affirm. This insight is indeed a potential barrier for Hick, because the resurrection and Pentecost point to the fact that the worship of Christ as the lone mediator between God and humanity is more than mere hyperbolic devotion. This essential unity between Jesus and the Father is verified by the resurrection and Pentecost, whether Jesus was fully aware of this in his human journey prior to the crucifixion or not. In the light of Pannenberg's insights, Hick's belief that historical Jesus research devastates incarnation belief is itself an exercise in hyperbole.

It is no small surprise that Hick downplays the significance of the resurrection. His understanding of the incarnation as a mere symbol requires it. Hick thus speculates that Christ's postresurrection appearances were not events in history but rather subjective mental states experienced among his followers, "waking versions" of something akin to near-death experiences (24). The idea that such mental states could launch the Christian movement as early and as dramatically as it did is, of course, open to considerable doubt. This doubt is certainly warranted, especially given the total lack of precedence for the belief in a messianic crucifixion or rising from the dead, a bodily resurrection before the end of history, or a single resurrection that then leads inextricably (and inexplicably) to the raising of all the rest of the dead. Hick is placing a considerable amount of theological freight on the back of this alleged mental state!

To agree with Hick, one would need to believe that all of these theological innovations simply came into existence without explicit scriptural precedence, and very early on, in time to launch the early confession and life of the church as reflected in texts such as 1 Corinthians 15:3–4 and Philippians 2:5–11. Such confessions were certainly not late developments. They predate Paul and seem to have been the tradition that he himself inherited when he joined the Christian movement within a year or two of the movement's beginning (1 Cor. 15:3–4). Hick's assumption that Christ's early failure to return caused his followers later, under Gentile polytheistic influence, to elevate him into a god has been successfully called into question by Larry Hurtado and others. Hurtado shows that the elevation of Christ as Lord and as the inaugurator of the new creation comes at the beginning of the rise of Christianity due to the corporate experience of him as risen and exalted (and, I would add, as the mediator of the Spirit of life).[100] For example, there are very early christological confessions embedded within New Testament texts that involve the presence of faith in him as the risen Lord who is one with God and worthy of worship (Rom. 10:9; 1 Cor. 15:3–4; Phil. 2:9–11). Such texts imply that faith in the risen and exalted Christ as the one who imparts the Spirit of life goes back to the very origin of the Christian faith.

Does it not seem much more likely that the disciples actually experienced Jesus as risen (no matter how "spiritual" or transcendent his body may have seemed) and that they also experienced from him a mighty outpouring of the Spirit that fulfilled scriptural promises, confirmed his lordship and unity with God, and tied his resurrection eschatologically and expansively to the rising of all the saints by the Spirit that dwells in them? Once one moves Christology from Hick's "waking versions" of near death experiences to the risen Christ of Pentecost, the early rise of faith in Christ as the Lord in whom we have the Spirit and future resurrection makes much more sense.

I will deal more extensively with the resurrection in a later chapter. Suffice it to say here that it seems as though Hick never dealt adequately with the charge that the early rise of faith in the risen Christ as Lord is unlikely to have happened without an actual resurrection, given the devastating effect Christ's crucifixion had on his followers. Cleopas expressed the feelings of many when, on the road to Emmaus, he said about Christ's crucifixion: "The chief priests and our rulers handed him over to be sentenced to death, and they crucified him; but we had hoped that he was the one who was going to redeem Israel" (Luke 24:20–21). Hope in Christ was devastated. Hick's response to this assumption that Jesus's death would have prevented the rise of Christianity is that Jesus simply became a martyr and would have been venerated as such by his followers. His death would have even been viewed as having an atoning effect on others (Hick, 23). There are numerous problems connected to this understanding of the rise of Christianity. The

---

100. See Larry Hurtado, *Lord Jesus Christ: Devotion to Jesus in Earliest Christianity* (Grand Rapids: Eerdmans, 2005).

major problem is that the earliest Christians never came to identify Christ as a *mere martyr*. There is simply no evidence that this was the widespread and initial interpretation of his significance. And even if one accepts this idea of Jesus as mere martyr as a premise, how does one explain Christ's meteoric rise very early out of this category to something that transcended it? Moreover, none of the Jewish martyrs among whom Hick groups Jesus was hailed as the Messiah of Israel. None of them were worshiped as Lord of creation, believed to have risen to the throne of God to impart the Spirit onto all flesh, and viewed as the first fruits of the resurrection of all the saints, the inauguration in his very person of the new creation. Which of the Jewish martyrs was granted that kind of dignity—and within a very short time span after his devastating crucifixion?

The only way to deal with the pluralist challenge is to do so in a way that flows from rather than denies the significance of the Spirit Baptizer to creation. The connection we have been discussing between the incarnation and Pentecost is especially relevant to a proper relation of the incarnation to the pluralist challenge. After all, Pentecost is the place where God self-imparts to *all flesh*. As I noted above, it is indeed significant that Christ's unity with God and humanity would become clear at the place where Christ imparts the Spirit to all flesh so as to incorporate all flesh in all of its diversity within himself. When it comes to the revelation of God, we cannot simply relegate Christ to the particular and the Spirit to the universal without significant qualification.[101] Indeed, the Son who mediated all of creation (Heb. 1:3) has, in his anointed journey to Pentecost, opened his life to an expansive diversity of voices so as to grant them a share in his anointing, his baptism in the Spirit. As the Spirit Baptizer, Christ imparts himself by imparting the Spirit, which means that Christ may be found wherever the Spirit is found, explicitly among those who call upon his name but also hidden among those whom the Spirit is drawing, especially among those who suffer and are reaching implicitly for the hope of divine mercy and redemptive justice. The *exclusive* "one and only" Christ in the light of Pentecost is also implicitly and even remarkably *inclusive*. It is for this reason that I have always found Amos Yong to be very helpful in his efforts to show that the light of Christ shines on the hidden presence of the Spirit outside the bounds of the church.[102]

---

101. Veli-Matti Kärkkäinen, *Trinity and Revelation*, vol. 2 of *A Constructive Christian Theology for the Pluralistic World* (Grand Rapids: Eerdmans, 2014), 360.

102. Amos Yong has written much on this subject. A good place to start would be his *Beyond the Impasse: Toward a Pneumatological Theology of Religion* (Grand Rapids: Baker Academic, 2003).

That the Spirit Baptizer was born in humility and went to the cross to bear and overcome the burdens of humanity through suffering love means that Christ's exclusivity cannot be used to bolster some kind of triumphalism. Significantly, Pentecost does not lead to triumphalist celebrations but rather to an open table, a crossing of social barriers, and a challenging message of grace. It leads to humble self-giving for redemption and healing, as well as for recognition of God's presence among the nations drawing them in the direction of God's redemptive and liberating purposes (Acts 17:26–28). Hick's challenge must be taken seriously, even if his Christology falls far short of the dignity that the New Testament affords Christ as divine, and as the global and eschatological mediator of life. This challenge is best met in the light of Christ as the Spirit Baptizer. But to do this, we must not reduce the rising and self-impartation of the Spirit Baptizer to a mental state, and we must not consequently reduce the incarnation to merely one metaphor of divine love among others.[103] The place where God reaches out to all flesh must be developed in the light of what this event shows us about Christ's unity with God. The church proclaims Christ as the Lord of life for all flesh, and it respectfully works together with people of good will across all boundaries for the common good, for we must love and hold in just regard all those for whom Christ has given his life.

Conclusion

A Christology from below in the light of Pentecost helps us to deal with a variety of challenges we face when we take Christ's essential unity with God seriously. The chief challenge discussed in this chapter comes from the question of divine transcendence. God is indeed not limited or conditioned by creaturely life (finitude, mutability, mortality, and so on). Concentration on the disparities between divine and creaturely life caused many to accept a dyohypostatic understanding of the mediator between God and creation, which describes this mediator as essentially external to the transcendent God. Even some who held a miahypostatic Christology in support of the idea that Christ was internal and indispensable to the self-giving of the true God to creation qualified this position with contrary statements. The challenge of transcendence is best grasped in favor of a miahypostatic Christology

103. N. T. Wright, *The Resurrection of the Son of God*, vol. 3 of *Christian Origins and the Question of God* (Minneapolis: Fortress, 2003), 9–12.

through the lens of the reality of grace. Transcendence cannot be viewed as the self-preservation of an abstract and impersonal deity whose attributes represent an interconnected series of negatives—*not* finite, *not* subject to change, *not* subject to suffering. Incarnation in this light seems improbable and even impossible. Deity and humanity seem to cancel each other out. Either the Son is less than human so as to be fully divine or less than fully divine so as to be fully human. But set within the story of Jesus that climaxes at Pentecost, transcendence also becomes that which explains the free and abundant self-impartation of God through grace. Grace is paradoxical, for God's attributes do indeed imply contrasts with creaturely reality. Divine strength bears up under the weakness of flesh so as to redeem and renew it. Transcendence as a positive concept in the light of grace may thus be viewed as the unconditional quality of freedom in the self-impartation of a divine love that is poured forth richly from the Father, through the Son, and in the Spirit. It is the river of love that has its center alone in the eternal self-determination of God to love unconditionally and excessively, in a way that overcomes the barriers of sin and death. By breaking through these barriers, God overflows all boundaries in order to open all flesh, in all of its diversity, to the life of the renewing Spirit, the life of the faithful Son, the life of the triune God.

We must also take the challenge of scriptural interpretation seriously. In the following chapter I will lay out the scriptural case for Christ's's unity with God and humanity. What we noted above, however, is that nothing in the scriptural witness leads to the dyohypostatic conclusion that the Son is essentially separate from and inferior to the being of the Father. Christ's eschatological exaltation by the Spirit to sonship, messianic installation, and lordship does not mean that the Son was not by nature or in eternity one in essence with the Father. It means rather that the Son was to realize in his embodied life by the Spirit and for the sake of our salvation what he had with the Father from all eternity (John 17:5). Moreover, the Son's references to the Father as the only true God or as greater than himself have the purpose of confirming the Father as the source of his authority and mission. Christ's human limitation (for example, not knowing the time of the end) was evidence of the humble existence to which he was willing to descend in order to elevate us in all of our limitations into the transformative work of redemption and renewal.

The functional unity of the Son and the Father is a vital clue to the Son's ontological unity with the Father (unity in essence). The key reason for going beyond the functional to the ontological is the fact that the lordship that Christ fully shares at Pentecost in imparting the Spirit is essential to God. Who else except the Lord can impart the Spirit? In addition, salvation in Scripture comes through God's *self*-impartation to creation, God's very presence to save. Thus a functional unity between Christ's and God's actions to save necessitates a unity between Christ and God as the very subject of salvific actions. Since only God can save (Hosea 13:4), Christ's unity with God's saving action is his unity with God. The journey from the incarnation to Pentecost does not have God saving from a distance; rather, God is *self*-imparting through the Son and by the Spirit.

The metaphysical challenge gave way in the modern era to an anthropological challenge. This challenge was not simply in the fact that the temptation arose to fashion Christ in the image of a human ideal preconceived from sources outside of the biblical witness. Of course, it included that temptation. But the challenge was even deeper than that. If the metaphysical challenge questioned the freedom of God in relation to humanity, the anthropological challenge questioned the freedom of humanity in relation to God. Subsequent to the work of Feuerbach and kindred spirits, the radical proposal was put forward that Christ was the inspiration for conceiving of a humanity that is free by freeing itself from God. If the metaphysical challenge tempted one to think that God is only free if freed from humanity, the anthropological challenge attempted to make an analogous claim but from the other side, namely, humanity is only free if freed from God. Feuerbach used the symbol of the incarnation itself, the chief christological dogma, to make his case. The *kenosis,* or self-emptying, of Christ in becoming human was defined by Feuerbach as the source of humanity's freedom from God. God is only a projection of human ideals that humanity can only own and develop in freedom once the image of God is removed. Of course, Feuerbach had missed what the incarnation actually tells us: that humanity is only free because of God's free self-giving to all flesh in redeeming and renewing love.

Bultmann attempted to steer the anthropological significance of Christ away from human self-reliance and justification to an openness to God and God's future. The anthropological challenge thus encountered us anew within the context of Christian faith in Bultmann's existential challenge and Soelle's expansion of it through her early political theology. Christology took on relevance for humanity's struggle for authentic existence within a world that threatened it at its core. For Bultmann, this world was the world of self-authentication and scientific certainty, but Soelle saw clearly that this world was also structured to preserve the satisfaction of greed, lust, and privilege. As with Bultmann, her own political theology did not take seriously Jesus's resurrection or his larger eschatological significance to creation. Elizabeth Johnson helps us develop a fuller liberation hermeneutic by directing attention to Christ's anointing and impartation of the Spirit of life. Christ's meaning to history and to social humanity is set within the expansive eschatological promise of the Spirit, who forms liberating communities that bear witness to God's love and justice in the world.

Finally, the challenge of pluralism causes us to speak of the Christ of Pentecost in a way that cherishes global diversity and values work across boundaries for the common good. We must love and respect those for whom Christ died and poured forth the Spirit. It is Jesus Christ, however, who alone imparts life in the Spirit and on behalf of the heavenly Father. The Christ of Pentecost is also surprisingly inclusive. In the scriptural witness, incarnation leads to Pentecost, to Christ's impartation of the Spirit to all flesh, to an expanding diversity of voices that reaches beyond the boundaries of the church and draws it outward as the church for others. Pentecost, as the focus of a Christology from below, places the clearest revelation of Christ's unity with God precisely at the event in which God becomes most expansively present to all peoples. This is not to deny that Jesus is the only Spirit Baptizer. But the confession of Christ's lordship because of Pentecost does not lead to a celebration of the church's superiority over others, but rather to an open table, selfless service, and a message of grace. The pluralist challenge can only be met in a way that is faithful to Christ if it is met via the journey from the incarnation to Pentecost, in which God, out of love of humanity, unites to flesh in order to pour forth the Spirit upon all flesh.

PART 2

Christ's Incarnation and Anointing

CHAPTER 3

Christ's Incarnation

"The Spirit gave the Word a body so that those with bodies might receive the Spirit."

—Eugene Rogers, *After the Spirit*

One cannot help but feel the exuberance of John in proclaiming the fact that the "Word of life," who makes all things new, has actually come in the flesh: "That which was from the beginning, which we have heard, which we have seen with our eyes, which we have looked at and our hands have touched— this we proclaim concerning the Word of life" (1 John 1:1). "And this Word became flesh and dwelt among us" (John 1:14), so that "out of his fullness we might receive grace in the place of grace already given" (1:16). For John, this Word "was God" (1:1), but was not removed from us: *he became flesh*. He did not merely appear as a theophany, as something that perhaps seemed like flesh but really was not. He became *flesh*. Neither did he merely indwell flesh as we are indwelt by God; he *became* flesh, conceived of the Spirit for this purpose. Christ as the Spirit baptizer is indeed the Word of life *incarnate*, the Word who is life and has come in the flesh to be the Word or sacrament of life. What it means to say that the divine Word became flesh to impart the Spirit of life is the theme of this chapter.

God created all things as the divine dwelling place: "He stretches out the heavens like a canopy and spreads them out like a tent to live in" (Isa. 40:22). The Son becomes flesh to mediate the divine indwelling. We might take note of Eugene Rogers's statement above as a place to begin to understand this. "The Spirit gave the Word a body!" Why? So that all bodies "might receive the Spirit!" To put it christologically, the Word took on a body from the Spirit in order to mediate the Spirit to all bodies. The incarnational or embodied nature of God's act of self-impartation to the world is one of the unique features of the Christian gospel.[1] The renewal of creation by the divine Spirit is uniquely tied in the gospel to an *embodied* mediation. The divine Son becomes human so that *humanity* could have a share in the *divine* life. Incarnation is fulfilled at Pentecost. Athanasius writes of the incarnation: "Through whom and from whom was it necessary that the Spirit be given other than through the Son, of whom the Spirit is also? But when were we able to receive it, except when the Word became man?"[2] The incarnation anticipates the climactic events that follow (the anointing at the Jordan, the crucifixion, the resurrection, and Pentecost), draws meaning from them, and grants meaning to them. The New Testament makes it clear that the Word finally became flesh so as to grant us the Spirit of life: "This is how God showed his love among us: He sent his one and only Son into the world that we might live through him" (1 John 4:9). To put it differently, the Son becomes human by the Spirit so that humanity might attain sonship and daughtership in him by the same Spirit (Rom. 8:15–16). The eternal Word of the Father became flesh so that out of his fullness we could all receive grace (John 1:14–16). Christ is indeed the "eternal life" that was with the Father and then in flesh "appeared to us" (1 John 1:2). And he not only appeared to us; he gave himself to us as the mediator of life! Indeed, out of Christ's inner-most being flowed rivers of living water so that he would be able to baptize all flesh in the Spirit (John 1:33; 7:38). This seminal connection between the incarnation and the outpouring of the Spirit has the potential of locating the incarnation within the expansive breadth of Christ's significance to the entire creation as the Spirit Baptizer.

The Incarnation and Pentecost

To grasp the importance of this seminal connection, just imagine for a moment Pentecost *without the incarnation,* an outpouring of the Holy Spirit from the Father directly upon all flesh without the mediation of the embodied life of Jesus. The importance of the incarnation comes to glaring clarity once we explore this possibility. Exploring such a theologically unimaginable

1. Veli-Matti Kärkkäinen, *Christ and Reconciliation*, vol. 1 of *A Constructive Christian Theology for the Pluralistic World* (Grand Rapids: Eerdmans, 2013), 24–25.

2. Athanasius, *Orations against the Arians* 1.50, in *The Christological Controversy*, trans. and ed. Richard A. Norris Jr., Sources of Early Christian Thought (Philadelphia: Fortress, 1980), 83–102.

possibility makes us ask, why Jesus? Why his life, anointing, death, and resurrection? Why his exaltation and reign as Lord? Why is Jesus's entire journey in the flesh as the one baptized in fire and Spirit necessary to the impartation of the Spirit to all flesh? Why do we need his embodied life to attain human and cosmic spiritual renewal in God? The incarnation thus touches on the indispensability and eschatological finality of the man Christ Jesus. It touches on the ecumenical significance of Christ for faith in God on a global scale. Why do we need Jesus to bring the promise of the Father, the Spirit of life to all flesh? Why incarnation?

To highlight the need for incarnation, one could begin by noting that the Spirit is mediated and not granted directly. The Spirit is mediated by the Word. The incarnation and Pentecost need each other, because there is never in the biblical drama Word without Spirit, never Spirit without Word. Saint Cyril says of Christ as the Word of the Father: "How can the Word be thought of at all without its own Spirit?"[3] How can there be a Word that is never spoken by the power of the divine breath to its intended recipients? And, of course, how can there be the Spirit of renewal without the Word that grants discernment as to how this renewal is received and fulfilled?

Further, the goal of this renewal is communion or an intimate sharing of life, in God and for God. It is clear from the lens of the incarnation that the Word seeks *embodiment* by the Spirit so that all things might bring glory to God by becoming the dwelling place of this Spirit in the image of this Word. It is the means by which all things are taken up into the eternal communion of the Father and the Son in the Spirit. When God created the heavens and the earth, the Spirit of life hovered over the deep, and God spoke the worlds into existence (Gen. 1:1–3). Humanity became a living soul from the lifeless dust by not only the Word that came forth from the Father but also by the Spirit that shaped the human body into God's dwelling place, a body—and, by extension, a community—that is faithful to that Word and can commune with God through that Word (Gen. 1:27; 2:7; Job 33:4). Prophetic words spoken by the Spirit hark back to creation and foreshadow a grander fulfillment (Ezek. 37:1–14). The creation by the Word and in the Spirit itself foreshadows the timeless fulfillment of incarnation. That Word is later shown to be more deeply a living person who reveals the Father as no other speaking ever could (John 1:1–18). All prophetically spoken words bear witness to this Word, the divine Son of the Father become flesh (John 1:14; Heb. 1:1–2). Such

---

3. Cyril of Alexandria, *Commentary on John*, trans. P. E. Pusey (Oxford: James Packer and Co., 1874), 1:145.

prophetically spoken words merely foretell or look back on *incarnation*, the living person of the Word binding himself to flesh so that all flesh may be redeemed and renewed in him.

Israel received the promise of a prophetic word given in the Spirit precisely at the point of its greatest need. In answer to the question about whether Israel can live again as a people with a promise and a mission, God had Ezekiel prophesy to the "bones" of a people who had had the life drained completely out of them due to their loss of hope: "They say, 'Our bones are dried up and our hope is gone; we are cut off'" (Ezek. 37:11b). In the previous chapter, God had charged Israel with profaning the divine name before the nations. But the Spirit would be given to them, turning their hearts of stone into flesh and enabling them to live according to the law's witness to life. Presumably, they then would be able to hallow the Father's name on earth as it is in heaven (36:22–27). But after confronting their great failure and their dismal situation in captivity, Israel seems devoid of life. The crucial question comes from God to Ezekiel: "Can these bones live?" (37:3). The question is vitally important, for Israel has no future if these bones cannot live again. Ezekiel's response to the question is understandable, "Sovereign Lord, You alone know" (37:3). Only the Sovereign Lord can decide Israel's fate; only the Lord can raise them up through the prophetic Word and by the Spirit of life. Only the Creator can do this. God's answer is that Ezekiel should prophesy to the bones. Israel would live again from the Word of prophecy. But Ezekiel was also to prophesy to the winds, a symbol of the Spirit. The people are reborn only when Word and Spirit come together, as with the original creation. "I will put breath in you, and you will come to life. Then you will know that I am the Lord" (37:6b). Though the coming to new birth here is spiritual rather than literal, it will become this with the rising of the Messiah from the dead! Indeed, God's lordship over creation is shown in the fact that God and God alone speaks forth the Word and breathes forth the Spirit that brought all things into existence and that brings all things to new birth. "I will put breath in you, and you will come to life. Then you will know that I am the Lord" (37:6).

Ezekiel points ahead to a fulfillment that the word of prophecy itself cannot bring to pass. The eschatological renewal of creation will involve more than the word of prophecy. A word of prophecy is inspired by the Spirit, but it does not itself impart this Spirit to others. The Word that imparts the Spirit of God to others must be integral (internal) essentially to the divine *self*-impartation. In other words, the one who imparts the Spirit must be the divine Son, who is proved to be of one essence with the Father and with the

Spirit, whom the Son imparts from the Father. The word of prophecy can bear witness to this impartation, but such a word cannot bring it to pass. Only God can do that; only the divine Son can do that. No human witness can mediate the Spirit and the life of the Son to all flesh.

No *mere* human witness, that is. But what about a human witness that is one in identity or person with the eternal Son who imparts the Spirit? Wouldn't this fleshly witness also be granted a share in the divine Son's impartation of the Spirit to all flesh? And so it is. Incarnation turns the embodied existence of Jesus Christ into the sacrament of the Spirit to all of creation. The divine Word, or the Son of the Father, not only ends up imparting the Spirit *to* flesh but also *through* flesh, a fleshly medium that represents the self-declaration of the Son and the sacrament of the Spirit. This is the only human witness that can have a share in the impartation of the Spirit from the Father to all flesh. In having a share in the impartation of the Spirit, and with it the life of the Son, the fleshly medium of Christ's humanity represents all flesh before God, rewrites the human story, and makes space within itself for all flesh in all of its diversity. In imparting the Spirit in this way, the incarnate Son incorporates all flesh into himself and shapes all flesh in his image. The fleshly medium of this divine self-impartation through the Son and in the Spirit must itself be so united to the divine Son that it has a full share in this divine self-impartation, this divine incorporation. A unity of identity (or person) between the Son and his humanity—in other words, *incarnation*—is required. As the incarnation of this Son, the humanity of Christ becomes the temple into which he incorporates the new humanity and eventually all of creation. All of creation will image Christ in a way that reflects God's glory. The Father's name will be hallowed on earth as it is in heaven. At the conclusion of the new creation, the Lamb is the temple of God's glory, the one who radiates the light of the Father to creation and through creation back to the Father (Rev. 21:22).

Indeed, there is thus a chorus of tongues that proclaim the mighty deeds of God at Pentecost (Acts 2:1–13). These tongues of Pentecost represent an overabundance of prophetic communication that signals the global reach of the gospel and the renewal of all flesh.[4] One could even note that this inspired witness comes with the Spirit of life poured out at that event (the reigning Lord "poured out what you now see and hear" [Acts 2:33]). Throughout the book of Acts, inspired proclamation appears as the telltale

---

4. Michael Welker, *God the Spirit* (Minneapolis: Fortress, 1994), 235. Hereafter, page references to this work appear in parentheses within the text.

sign of the new era of the Spirit (4:31; 10:46; 19:6). But Luke sets up that declaration with Jesus's own words, quoted above, that these voices would be at their noblest *his witnesses*, witnesses to the one who came to fulfill the promise of the Father to all flesh by conquering sin and death and imparting the Spirit of Easter life to others (Luke 24:49). He came from the Father to give us life (John 1:4). John the Baptist testified earlier that he bears witness to the light of God but he is not that light. Only the Word made flesh is the light of God's glory (John 1:1–14). The prophetic witness, as important as it is to Pentecost, is not what ultimately anchors or mediates this eschatological event of renewal. No human word of prophecy can mediate the Spirit and become the eschatological image of the Word for all flesh. Only the eternal Son, or Word of the Father, can do that. This is the Word that conquered sin and death to make way for the Spirit in the world and that was exalted to reign as Lord so as to pour forth this Spirit upon all flesh (Acts 2:33–35). This is the Word that incarnates itself in flesh so as to function as the sacrament of the Spirit to all flesh, turning all flesh into a witness to that Word in the world. This Word is at base the only Word there is, the only Word there ever was, or ever can be. The proclaimed word of the disciples is not adequate to carry that kind of theological freight; neither can our sacraments bear this burden. The Word through whom the end-time outpouring of the Spirit occurs is the Word of all words, the sacrament of all sacraments, the Word become flesh, crucified and risen, the embodied life of Jesus Christ. Our preaching and our sacraments do not mediate; rather, they bear witness to and celebrate the one mediator between God and humanity, the man Jesus Christ (1 Tim. 2:5).

The Word of the Father who mediates the Spirit to all flesh does so through the embodied life of the crucified and risen Christ. Michael Welker has shown that this insight alters how we generally think of spiritual power. The reality of the divine Spirit in relation to creation usually calls up implications of unfathomable power. The incarnation confronts us in this light with an oddity: unfathomable power revealed in humility and weakness. Indeed, "how can this power of God become comprehensible *as power* precisely in this concrete extreme, precisely in this specific person?" (184). Welker responds that in the biblical narrative the Spirit's exercise of power with respect to creation is not something that is meant to remain hidden and mysterious but is to be known "in a way that can be experienced with the senses" (184). The manifestation of the Spirit's power in the midst of Jesus's sojourn to the cross, in the midst of what I have called Jesus's baptism in fire, shows that the power of the Spirit is to be manifested most profoundly in the midst of this powerless man taken captive and crucified on behalf of others. The power that overcomes in the resurrection and will transform the creation is the power of self-giving love, a point powerfully revealed in the journey from the incarnation to the cross. This Spirit of Christ is personally empowering but also directed outwards in ways that build merciful and just communities. I agree with Welker that the embodied life of Jesus represents a "radicalization of the action of the Spirit" (185). This manifestation of the Spirit's power through the embodied Christ affirms the victory of God's strength over the destructive forces of sin and death, but it does so in a way that makes the Spirit's work specific to authentic human community. The Spirit that comes forth through Christ's embodied life directs the people of the Spirit to bear the burdens and sufferings of others in loving solidarity. The community that arises from the exalted Christ's impartation of the Spirit "bears and reflects this power, lets it benefit others, and itself is strengthened in return" (185). The victory of Christ over sin and death is not celebrated through triumphalist self-aggrandizing but rather through baptismal initiation to the way of Christ in the world, through forms of service, and through an open table of fellowship.

When one shifts the designation of Christ from the Word to the Son of the Father (as the Gospel of John does in its first three chapters and Paul does in texts such as Gal. 4:4–7), it becomes clear that the Spirit from all eternity is the Spirit of self-giving communion. Eugene Rogers notes that the Spirit was always "the crowning, celebration, or rejoicing ('perfection')" of the unity between the eternal Son and the Father.[5] In his taking on flesh and his history leading to the cross and beyond, Jesus reveals this sonship and acts to open up its many benefits to creation. At Pentecost this communal invitation is made by the Son and through the Spirit on behalf of the Father. This invitation is rooted in the incarnation, and it finds its *telos* in the impartation of the Spirit. That entire journey serves to grant us discernment of the way of the Spirit in the world:

> But when the set time had fully come, God sent his Son, born of a woman, born under the law, to redeem those under the law, that we might receive adoption to sonship. Because you are his sons, God sent the Spirit of his Son into our hearts, the Spirit who calls out, "Abba, Father." So you are no longer a slave, but God's child; and since you are his child, God has made you also an heir. (Gal. 4:4–7)

---

5. Eugene F. Rogers, *After the Spirit: A Constructive Pneumatology from Resources outside the West* (Grand Rapids: Eerdmans, 2005), 67.

The reference in this text to freedom from slavery to sonship reminds us of the Exodus, where God delivered Israel from slavery in order to make them sons and daughters. For God says, "Out of Egypt I called my son" (Hosea 11:1; cf. Matt. 2:14–15). Christ comes as the eternal Son of the Father; his sonship was foreshadowed by Israel's and reaches beyond in the Spirit to extend that privilege to all flesh. In this case, the Son of the Father takes on flesh in order to recapitulate humanity's entire journey with God in his own faithful journey as the man baptized in the Spirit and fire. He bears the fire of our judgment so that, exalted in the Spirit, he could open up the benefit of his sonship to all flesh by pouring forth the Spirit to all. John Meyendorff highlights this point well in his writing about the incarnation: "With this flesh is the whole of redeemed mankind called to have communion with the Holy Spirit."[6]

But a question remains: Does Jesus possess the fullness of the Spirit from the moment of the incarnation, a fullness that is then progressively unveiled throughout his life? Or is Jesus progressively filled with the Spirit throughout his life? John McKenna has noted that these options are two mutually illuminating points of emphasis.[7] The Spirit fully identifies with Jesus from the moment of the incarnation, in that Jesus, as the incarnation of the eternal Word, yields freely and without resistance to the Spirit from the beginning. Yet that yielding flesh still develops and matures, opening up deeper and more expansive spaces for the Spirit to inhabit. There are key moments or breakthroughs as well as a gradual progression. Jesus's Jordan experience is, after the incarnation, the key event of Jesus's baptism in the Spirit and fire, but that event would also span his entire life, reaching fulfillment at the cross, the resurrection, and Pentecost. Moreover, Jesus's Jordan experience is also anticipated from the beginning because, throughout his human development toward adulthood, he "grew and became strong in the Spirit" (Luke 1:80).[8] His Spirit-filling does not just drop in from above; it also emerges and overflows from below. In the end, Christ is glorified by the Spirit in order to renew others by the Spirit. Jesus said of the Spirit: "He will glorify me because it is from me that he will receive what he will make known to you" (John 16:14). The incarnation by the Spirit anticipates the fullness of the Spirit that will be fully actualized and revealed in Jesus's embodied life at

6. John Meyendorff, *Christ in Eastern Christian Thought* (Washington, DC: Corpus Books, 1969), 10.

7. John H. McKenna, "Eucharistic Epiclesis: Myopia or Microcosm," *Theological Studies* 36, no. 2 (June 1975): 276.

8. I prefer this translation to the one that says he grew "strong in spirit."

Pentecost. The freedom and expanse of the Spirit's outpouring at Pentecost make Christ, already at the incarnation, the anticipation of the eschatological man, the head of his body, and the Lord of the new creation.

The eschatological and cosmic expanse of the Spirit's work unleashed at Pentecost signals to us a divine freedom to love in a way that knows no limit and crosses boundaries, which expands the image of Christ beyond the one to the many. Christ's original circle of witnesses expands to include many more, an expanding "cloud of witnesses" (Heb. 12:1). This "Pentecostal" freedom of the Spirit, then, gets read backwards in order to illuminate the incarnation. The eschatologically free Spirit is present implicitly there as well, for the incarnation anticipates Pentecost. When Mary asks how the Son of God will be conceived in her womb when she is a virgin, "the angel answered, 'The Holy Spirit will come on you, and the power of the Most High will overshadow you. So the holy one to be born will be called the Son of God'" (Luke 1:35). Notice the implied allusion to the Spirit's role in creation overshadowing or hovering over the deep. This vast power of creation is described here in the context of the conception of a lowly child who is to be born into the life of an occupied people as the hope for a world to be transformed by the love and justice of God. The hovering of the Spirit in Mary's womb at the incarnation may be read backwards to creation and forward to Pentecost (and beyond).

In fact, the freedom of the Spirit gets read back into the triune life itself. After all, if the Spirit is revealed in this way at Pentecost, there must be a basis for this not only at the incarnation but within the triune life itself. The Spirit's freedom overflows the circle of love that the Spirit abundantly celebrates and perfects within the triune life in order to open it to the expanse of creation. What Rogers says here pointedly describes that very thing: "There is something about the internal activity that reaches out to involve human beings. Superfluity of the Spirit gets read back into the open Godhead."[9] The mystery of divine freedom by which the Word or Son of the Father became flesh is the freedom of the Father's love and the freedom of the Word to bring that love to expression from all of eternity. But it is also the eschatological freedom of the Spirit that abundantly and excessively celebrates and perfects that love. Barth says of the divine Son's conception by the Spirit in Mary's womb: "This human existence starts in the freedom of God Himself, in the freedom in which the Father and Son are one in the bond of love, in the Holy Spirit."[10]

---

9. Rogers, *After the Spirit*, 76.
10. Karl Barth, *Dogmatics in Outline* (London: SCM Press, 1955), 99.

We can recall Rogers's description of the Spirit's involvement in the bond of love that unites the persons of the Godhead as the "crowning celebration or rejoicing ('perfection') of their unity."[11] As the celebration and perfection of this bond of love, the Spirit is its eschatological freedom and reach, an abundant and free gift that overflows the Godhead to bring creation into being as God's dwelling place and as God's extended witness. There is a longing in the heart of God for the "other" that flows out from the abundant fullness of the divine life and that is fulfilled in the divine self-giving that occurs in and through Christ: "If he longs for this other, it is not out of deficiency of being; it is rather out of the superabundance of his creative fullness."[12] The Word of that love in the power of the Spirit ultimately finds expression throughout Christ's embodied journey from incarnation to Pentecost. Barth thus appropriately views the incarnation, the divine Son being united to flesh in Jesus of Nazareth, as the lens through which to penetrate the depths of God's inner freedom to love and to commune internally as the triune God.[13]

The divine freedom that turns the incarnation into the vehicle for the renewal of creation has no beginning. It always was. As we saw in our previous chapter, it is characteristic of God as sovereign and transcendent. This divine freedom to embody the divine Word in a way that reaches out to incorporate all flesh has no explanation other than the infinite and mysterious depth of God's self-determination. Barth understood this divine self-determination under the rubric of election. For Barth, the Word made flesh is central to our understanding of election. Concerning the eternal Word of the Father, Barth asks, "What choice can precede the choice by which God has of Himself chosen to have with Himself from the beginning of all things the Word which is Jesus?"[14] Any assumption that there is a divine decision that precedes or is other than this Word of the Father opens up an abyss of uncertainty as to who this God is or what this God has eternally willed. Something theologically prior to the divine Word could in theory be anything, even "nothingness, or rather the depth of Satan" (25; see also 65). Jesus Christ is thus "the decree of God behind and above which there can be no earlier or higher decree and beside which there can be no other, since all others serve only the fulfillment of this decree" (25).

---

11. Rogers, *After the Spirit*, 67.

12. Jürgen Moltmann, *The Trinity and the Kingdom* (New York: Harper and Row, 1981), 45.

13. Barth, *Dogmatics in Outline*, 99.

14. Karl Barth, *Church Dogmatics*, II/2: *The Doctrine of God*, trans. G. W. Bromiley et al. (Edinburgh: T & T Clark, 1978), 100–101. Hereafter, page references to this work appear in parentheses within the text.

"Before Him and without Him and beside Him, God does not then elect or will anything" (94).

For Barth, the Word become flesh, in fact, "crowds out and replaces" any notion of an "absolute decree" that allegedly governs the realization of the divine will in history (95). As partakers of the Holy Spirit in Christ, we share in Christ's eternal designation as the chosen Son of the Father and bearer of the Spirit. But Christ, for Barth, is also the image of the electing God, for in election "God ultimately wills Himself" (95). Christ is both "the electing God and the elected man" (174). The divine freedom to self-impart precisely in and through the embodied life of Jesus Christ was an eternally sovereign and free self-determination by God to be God in this and in no other way.[15] Election is thus no speculative idea for it indicates something very real to God. It means that God "as the God of Jesus Christ is a God of men who exists as eternally devoted to man."[16] The source of this love is the Father, the embodied Word of this love is the Son, and the eschatological freedom and overflowing of this love is the Spirit, not only inwardly but also outwardly, to create and to renew the creation in the image of the Son and to the glory of the Father.

Election thus means that the Word was from all eternity self-identified with Jesus of Nazareth, since the Word always determined to be embodied and revealed in this way, as the one who will bear Spirit and fire so as to impart the Spirit upon all flesh. Therefore, when we speak of the eternal Word's "pre-incarnate" state, we must bear in mind that in a sense there never was an identity to the Word that existed entirely apart from Christ's journey from the incarnation to Pentecost. This is not to say that the humanity of Jesus existed before his conception, only that the Word's identity as Jesus Christ would, from God's perspective, always have existed as the self-determination of the Word to be embodied within and for creation.[17] And the creation was made by the Spirit for this Word, to receive it, and

---

15. See Bruce McCormack's brilliant essay "Grace and Being: The Role of God's Gracious Election in Karl Barth's Theological Ontology," in *The Cambridge Companion to Karl Barth*, ed. John Webster (Cambridge, UK: Cambridge University Press, 2000), 92–110. Also helpful is David Gibson, *Reading the Decree: Exegesis, Election, and Christology in Calvin and Barth* (London: T & T Clark, 2012), esp. 1–29.

16. Walter Kasper, *Jesus the Christ* (Kent, UK: Burns and Oates, 1976), 184.

17. See Oliver Crisp, *God Incarnate: Explorations in Christology* (London: T & T Clark, 2009), 56–76; see also Christophe Chalamet, "No Timelessness in God: On Differing Interpretations of Karl Barth's Theology of Eternity, Time and Election," *Zeitschrift für dialektische Theologie*, Supplement Series 4 (January 1, 2010): 21–37.

to be shaped by it, for "all things have been created through him and for him" (Col. 1:16).

All of this means that the divine freedom involved in incarnation for the Word to be declared into flesh by way of the Spirit is not an arbitrary freedom, as though God could very well have decided to abandon the creation. This divine self-determination and the divine nature are mutually contributory in our understanding of the God who unites with flesh in the incarnation.[18] There is no law external to God necessitating the incarnation; but the incarnation does say something about the nature and purposes of divine love, as well as the divine self-determination to be God in this way, the way of the Word made flesh and the Spirit he bears and imparts. The Father through the Word and the eschatological freedom of the Spirit creates "others" (humans) and refuses to abandon them, loving them even in the midst of their unfaithfulness and rejection and going to great lengths to make that love abundantly available so as to incorporate them into the divine life. This complex action cannot be simply one option among others for God.

Truly God

The incarnation involves the true God becoming truly human for the sake of the redemption and renewal of creation. Our task in this section is to speak of Christ as *truly* divine. The Spirit Baptizer must be truly divine in order to impart the Spirit to all of creation, for only the Lord can pour forth the Spirit. One must be careful to theologically contextualize statements about Christ's deity by placing his deity within a Trinitarian context in order to avoid a *Christomonism* that neglects the reality of the Holy Spirit as essential to the divine self-giving and thus important to Christ's self-giving.[19] A Christology of Pentecost would certainly help us to avoid this error. We are hence pressed to say that Christ, as the one who mediates the Spirit on behalf of the Father, reveals his unity of essence with the Father *and* the Spirit.

There are several lines of argument to take in supporting Christ's full deity. The first has to do with a point I have been making all along, namely, that Christ is shown to be indispensable to God's reign as Lord and sover-

---

18. I think Christophe Chalamet, in "No Timelessness in God," strikes the right balance between divine election and divine being.

19. Rowan D. Williams, "Jesus Christ," in *Dictionary of the Ecumenical Movement*, ed. Nicholas Lossky et al. (Grand Rapids: Eerdmans, 1991), 539.

eign self-giving to creation in order to make all things new. Christ's role as savior led the church to assume his deity, since "all Christians shared the conviction that salvation was the work of the Lord of heaven and earth."[20] Such is the tradition's loyalty to Scripture: "You shall acknowledge no God but me, no savior except me" (Hosea 13:4). Christ is also said to save (Matt. 1:21; Acts 5:31; 13:23; Eph. 5:23; Phil. 3:20; 1 Tim. 1:1, 15; 2:3; 2 Tim. 1:9–10; Titus 1:4; 2:13; 3:5–6; Heb. 7:25; 2 Pet. 2:20; 3:2, 18; 1 John 4:14). Only the Lord can defeat sin and death—and pour forth the Holy Spirit upon all flesh. Christ shares fully in this lordship and is confessed as Lord by the Spirit (Phil. 2:11; 1 Cor. 12:3). Since salvation comes by way of God's *self-impartation* to flesh, the incarnate Christ's unity with God's saving action means that Christ must be one with God as the *subject* of salvation. The Christ of the incarnation and Pentecost is one with God; otherwise, how could he impart God and, in doing so, impart himself to us (or, in imparting himself to us, impart God)? As Saint Augustine says of the Christ of Pentecost, "How, then, can he who gives the Spirit not be God? Indeed, how much must he who gives God be God!"[21] Athanasius also says, in addressing Christ, "No one else but you could unite man with the Holy Spirit."[22] Indeed, "being God, [Christ] later became man, that instead he might deify us."[23] So, for Christ to impart the divine Spirit on behalf of the Father, Christ must be divine—the divine Son incarnate. In the light of Pentecost, it becomes clear that Christ as the Word of the Father and the mediator of *new* life also mediated the original creation (John 1:3; Col. 1:16; Heb. 1:3). As the creator, only God can renew the creation, only a fully divine Christ can mediate this renewal in a way that is essential to it.

The second line of argument fastens on key texts that specifically call Jesus "God" or its biblical equivalent, "Lord." In a careful analysis of the evidence, Raymond Brown lists John 1:1, John 20:28, and Hebrews 1:8–9 as "clearly" calling Christ "God."[24] As I have noted above, John 1:1 and 20:28

---

20. Jaroslav Pelikan, *The Emergence of the Catholic Tradition*, vol. 1: *The Christian Tradition: A History of the Development of Doctrine* (Chicago: University of Chicago Press, 1971), 173. This is also the central point of Frank D. Macchia, *The Trinity, Practically Speaking* (Downers Grove, IL: InterVarsity, 2010).

21. Augustine, *On the Trinity* 15.46, trans. Edmund Hill (Hyde Park, NY: New City Press, 1991).

22. Athanasius, *Orations against the Arians* 1.49.

23. Athanasius, *Orations against the Arians* 1.39.

24. Raymond Brown, "Does the New Testament Call Jesus God?," *Theological Studies* 26 (1965): 561–65. Hereafter, page references to this work appear in parentheses within the text.

are implicitly connected as bookends for the Christology of John's Gospel, thereby serving to link Christ's incarnation and his identity as the Spirit Baptizer. In John 1, Jesus as the eternal Word of the Father "is God" (1:1) and becomes "flesh" (1:14) so as to be the Spirit Baptizer (1:33), precisely as the one who overcomes the darkness and imparts life. The lack of the definite article for "God" in the phrase "the Word was God" (1:1) does not imply ontological inferiority in relation to God the Father. The Word is defined first in unity with God *before* the Word is related to creation and incarnation (1:1–5, 14). Throughout John's Gospel, Jesus is featured as the life-giver (e.g., 10:10; 14:6) and even refers to himself as the resurrection and the life (11:25). The incarnate Son is granted to have life in himself, as the Father does (5:26). In 20:22, the risen Christ fulfills his mission by breathing forth the Spirit upon the disciples, which then leads quite appropriately to Thomas's acclamation of him as Lord and God (20:28). The message is clear: the life-giver is divine. The divine Word is incarnated to be the Spirit Baptizer and, as such, is to be worshiped as Lord and God.

The Hebrews 1:8–9 text is significant because it follows Hebrews 1:1–3, where the Son, as the final Word of history, is distinguished from the words of the prophets, because only this final Word is the Son, which means that only he is the very radiance of God's glory, the exact image of God's being, the mediator of creation and of atonement, and the one who sustains "all things by his powerful word," an activity that surely belongs to God alone. As elaboration on this striking passage, Hebrews 1:8–9 then describes the Son's exaltation to the throne to reign. Though the Father is here called the "God" of the incarnate and exalted Son, no inferiority on the part of the Son is implied, because God the Father says of this Son, "Your throne, O God, will last forever and ever."

Brown then lists John 1:18, 1 John 5:20, Titus 2:13, Romans 9:5, and 2 Peter 1:1 as most probably calling Jesus God (554–61). The NIV translates the first half of John 1:18 this way: "No one has ever seen God, but the one and only Son, who is himself God." The key question has to do with the Greek phrase *monogenēs theos* ("the only begotten God" or as the NIV has expanded it, "the one and only Son, who is himself God"). Is this phrase original to the text? Brown notes that the manuscript evidence for this reading is impressive, especially because it is found in the Bodmer Papyri of about 200 CE. This reading of John 1:18 also fits well with the context as it is given in John 1:1. Therefore, there is a very good probability that John 1:18 identifies the Son who came forth eternally from the Father as "God."

First John 5:20 reads:

> We know also that the Son of God has come and has given us understanding, so that we may know him who is true. And we are in him who is true by being in his Son Jesus Christ. He is the true God and eternal life.

To whom does this last phrase concerning "the true God and eternal life" refer? Brown notes that it probably refers to Jesus Christ, because he is the closest antecedent, and God the Father is never referred to as eternal "life" in Johannine literature, though the Son is (John 11:25; 14:6). Moreover, the logic of the passage is that we dwell in the Father by dwelling in the Son precisely because the Son is the true God and eternal life (557–58). There is no stronger link between the incarnation and Pentecost than this. It is precisely because Jesus is the *true God incarnate* that we dwell in God by dwelling in him through the Spirit he has imparted to us. Incorporated into him as the Spirit Baptizer, we drink from his Spirit imparted to us (cf. 1 Cor. 12:13).

Titus 2:13 refers to the "blessed hope," which is "the appearing of the glory of our great God and Savior, Jesus Christ." It is most probable that "God" in this text refers to the Savior, Jesus Christ. The terms "God" and "Savior" are bound together here in the Greek by the conjunction "and" (*kai*). To separate them would not only be awkward grammatically but also theologically, since it seems most unusual in the light of Scripture in general to expect a double epiphany, "God," and then also the "Savior Jesus Christ." This text is especially important because it is the basis of the World Council of Churches' statement of faith, which confesses "the Lord Jesus Christ as God and Savior" (556–57). Jesus is indeed our hope because he is both Savior and God. How could the Savior be anyone else but God?

Another very probable reference to Christ as God is Romans 9:5, which reads: "Theirs are the patriarchs, and from them is traced the human ancestry of the Messiah, who is God over all, forever praised! Amen." The grammar of this text is somewhat ambiguous. One can put a full stop somewhere before the end of the verse so as to detach "God over all" from "Messiah," or Christ (eliminating the NIV "who is," which is not original to the text and serves to link the Messiah with God). But Brown notes that the most natural reading would not divide the verse but rather place a full stop only at the end, which would make "God over all" a description of Christ. He concludes: "Paul calls Jesus God. From a grammatical viewpoint, this is clearly the best reading" (559).

Another high probability for identifying Jesus as God is 2 Peter 1:1. This text addresses its readers as "those who through the righteousness of our God and Savior Jesus Christ have received a faith as precious as ours." As with Titus 2:13, Christ is referred to here as "God and Savior." The grammar of this text parallels Titus 1:4, where Jesus is called "Lord and Savior." This grammatical parallel supports the unbreakable link between God and Savior in Titus 1:2. Brown thus claims that this text could "almost" be categorized among those that "clearly" call Jesus God. Here, as elsewhere in the New Testament, Christ's mediation of salvation occurs *within* the divine self-giving, and not outside of it.

Beyond Brown's informative investigation, one may also mention places where Jesus is called "Lord" in the context of salvation and worship in a way that is appropriate to God alone. Here we may include as obvious examples John 20:28; Acts 2:34–36; 7:59–60; 8:16; 10:36; 11:17; 15:11; 16:31; 19:5; 20:21; Romans 1:4; 1:7; 10:9–16; 11:34; 12:19; 14:8–11; 1 Corinthians 1:2–3; 1:8; 4:5; 8:6; 12:3; 2 Corinthians 1:2–3; 1:14; 8:9; Galatians 1:3; 6:18; Ephesians 1:2; 4:5; 5:19–20; Philippians 1:2; 2:11; 4:23; 1 Thessalonians 5:9, 28; 2 Thessalonians 1:2; 3:18; 1 Timothy 1:2; 2 Timothy 4:8; 2 Peter 2:20; 3:18; Jude 4, 21, 25; Revelation 17:14; and 19:16 ("Lord of Lords"). These texts may be linked to an even larger number that use "Lord" as part of Christ's "proper name." Noteworthy here is the vast number of texts that can be adduced supporting Jesus as Lord. Obviously, this title is original to the church's experience and confession of Christ. Since Lord and God in the context of salvation and worship are equivalent theologically, it is equally obvious that Christ's inclusion in the "God" category among his followers came decisively very early through his exaltation to lordship at his resurrection, a reality defined at its core by Christ's impartation of the Spirit and the Spirit's witness to him as Lord in the lives of believers (Acts 2:33–35; 1 Cor. 12:3; John 17:2). As I noted above, the Philippians 2:11 text is extremely important here as well, since it represents a hymn that predates Paul as part of an ancient Jewish liturgy. As I observed earlier, Larry Hurtado has argued that Jesus's divine lordship goes back to the very beginning of the church members' experience of Christ. Their experience of the risen and exalted Christ caused his followers to expand their understanding of "God" to include Jesus Christ. But they did so without abandoning their monotheism (ending up with a "mutated" monotheism).[25] The confession of Jesus as Lord by the Spirit is arguably the very beginning of Christology.[26]

25. Larry W. Hurtado, *Lord Jesus Christ: Devotion to Jesus in Earliest Christianity* (Grand Rapids: Eerdmans, 2003), 29–78.

26. A point emphasized throughout Dietrich Ritschl, *Memory and Hope: An Inquiry concerning the Presence of Christ* (New York: Macmillan, 1967).

The third line of argument for Christ's unity with God is the fact that he receives the same worship offered (and appropriate only) to God. Philippians 2:11 has all of creation confessing Christ as Lord, precisely in the context of worship. Thomas's acclamation of Christ as Lord and God in John 20:28 would have resonated with many among the Johannine community. Christ's mediation of truth in the book of Revelation causes all of creation to worship him with the same praise offered to God the Father (Rev. 5). Notice especially Revelation 5:13:

> "To him who sits on the throne and to the Lamb
> be praise and honor and glory and power,
> for ever and ever!"

Earlier in that book, John himself falls prostrate before the exalted Christ (1:17). But when he falls down to worship the angel who had been showing him the visions, the angel rebukes him: "Don't do that! I am a fellow servant with you and with your brothers and sisters who hold to the testimony of Jesus. Worship God!" (Rev. 19:10). Yet Jesus *is* worshiped in Revelation, ranking him with God. There is a major difference between the witness to revelation that is external to God (and not worthy of worship) and the witness that is internal to God, essential to God's *self*-disclosure, which is thus worthy of worship. Christ belongs to the latter. The fact that Christ is worshiped is in itself a strong indicator that he is to be regarded as one with God. Some authors have noted that exalted figures like Moses and some angels are sometimes referred to as "god" in ancient Judaism.[27] But which of these figures gave rise to a cultic following that involved the worship of them as Redeemer and Lord of all creation? Which of these figures were worshiped as being themselves the final Word (the only Word) of history? Which among them was praised as the giver of life, the one who imparts the Spirit of God to all flesh?

The fourth line of argument for Christ's deity is made up of the practices of baptism and the Lord's Supper. Matthew 28:19 says that we are baptized "in the name of the Father, the Son, and the Holy Spirit." Note that the Son and the Spirit are listed alongside the Father as the sacred name in which (and under whose authority) we are baptized. These are divine names indicative of one's incorporation by faith and by the Spirit into communion with God

---

27. Bart Ehrman, *How Jesus Became God: The Exaltation of a Jewish Preacher from Galilee* (New York: HarperOne, 2014), 47–84.

and in submission to God's lordship. Athanasius thus argues that we are not baptized in the name of a creature.[28] We are baptized into the divine life, the divine lordship, not of a demigod who rises up from among those created out of nothing, but of the true God and Lord of all!

Likewise, the Lord's Supper is a meal of unity in Christ, communing with him in the Spirit and through him with the heavenly Father. The meal is also a remembrance of the covenant initiated by Christ's broken body and spilled blood. Christ's establishment of the sacred meal at Passover implies an integral connection between him and God, "for Jews ate sacrificial meals in God's presence and, at Passover, in memory of God's deliverance of Israel."[29] Jesus implies that he will be Lord of the new covenant, anticipating not only his coming death but also his rising and his impartation of the Spirit of communion. He will be the Lord of the new exodus and present at the sacred meal taken to remember it. This new covenant meal reflects back on the covenant God made with Israel and anticipates, in the light of Pentecost, the end-time banquet among all of the redeemed from every nation and tongue (Rev. 7:9; 19:6–9). Christ's role in this meal is the central focus of one's remembrance of, and thanksgiving for, God's act of redemption, of one's communion with God, of one's hope for future fellowship in the kingdom of God. Moreover, we dine "in him," incorporated into his sonship by the Spirit. Surely a mere creature could not be the focal point for all of this (cf. 1 Cor. 10:14–17; 11:17–32).

The fifth line of argument is Jesus's "I am" statements, which point to his eternal unity with God. God said, "I am that I am" (Exod. 3:14) to indicate God's eternal and unchanging faithfulness (I am what I always am); it is a name that is future-oriented and is given content in God's lordship and liberating deeds (6:4–6). Jesus made a number of "I am" statements that tie him implicitly to the eternally faithful God. Athanasius notes that Christ does not say "I became" but rather "I am," as though, in all of these things he claims to be, he shares in the changeless faithfulness of the Father in being the source and means of salvation.[30] Christ said, as reported in the Gospel of John, "I am the bread of life" (John 6:35) that "came down from heaven" (6:41). He claimed, "I am the gate" through which people are saved (10:9); "I am the light of the world" (8:12; 9:5); and "I am the resurrection and the

28. Athanasius, *Orations against the Arians* 1.34.

29. Craig A. Evans, "Jesus' Self-Designation 'The Son of Man' and the Recognition of His Divinity," in *Oxford Readings in Philosophical Theology*, vol. 1: *Trinity, Incarnation, Atonement*, ed. Michael Rea (New York: Oxford University Press, 2009), 154.

30. Athanasius, *Orations against the Arians* 1.12.

life" (11:25). He declared that the people were to believe that "I am who I am" (13:19), for "I am the way, the truth, and the life" (14:6). He also maintained, "I am in the Father as the Father is in me" (14:10), in intimate communion: "I am the true vine" (15:5) from which the branches draw life. Christ is the life-giver. Most tellingly, he said, "Before Abraham was born, I am" (8:58), implying that Christ is eternal. The exalted Christ said, "I am the first and the last" (Rev. 1:17) in fulfillment of Isaiah 44:6, which applies these words to God alone ("apart from me there is no God"). These words indicate that Christ does not *have* a beginning and an end, but that he *is* the beginning and end (*telos*) of all else. As divine, he is eternally faithful and unchanging in his faithfulness: "the same yesterday, today, and forever" (Heb. 13:8).

The sixth line of argument for Christ's essential unity with God is drawn from texts that attach possessives to Christ that belonged to God alone, as though "God" and "Christ" were interchangeable terms. For example, the grace of God is also the grace of Christ (Rom. 5:15); the glory of God is the glory of Christ (2 Cor. 1:20–21; 4:4); the reign, or kingdom, of God is also the kingdom of God's Son (Col. 1:13–17); and the church of God is the churches of Christ (2 Cor. 1:1; Rom. 16:16). Most significantly, the Spirit of God is the Spirit of Christ (Rom. 8:9), an interchangeability that would be blasphemous if Christ were not considered identifiable with God, internal to the divine life—to the divine self-giving. Those who make a point of saying that the New Testament tends to defer to the Father when using the term "God" also need to take into consideration the interchangeability between Christ and God that is implied in the New Testament. Though the New Testament may be said to anchor the term "God" in the Father, it also expands the term to include the Son and the Spirit. The incarnation viewed in the light of Pentecost demands nothing less.

The seventh line of argument for Christ's deity in unity with God is the use in the New Testament of Old Testament texts that anticipate *God's* coming to the earth to describe *Christ's* coming as though Christ's coming is identifiable with God's coming. I noted above that the Gospels quote Isaiah 40:3 to identify the voice crying in the wilderness to "make straight in the desert a highway for our God" with that of John the Baptist (Matt. 3:3; Mark 1:3; Luke 3:4; John 1:23). This leaves the reader to identify the coming of God with the coming of Christ. A similar example is Isaiah 43:4–5, which notes that God "will come to save you." The text continues: "Then will the eyes of the blind be opened and the ears of the deaf unstopped." This text is then quoted as fulfilled by Christ's coming to save and to heal in Matthew 11:5. The implication is clear: Christ fulfills God's coming to save. A further example is Joel 2:28–32, which declares that God will pour forth the Spirit onto all flesh to prepare for the coming Day of the Lord. Acts 2:17–21 and 2:33–35 portray Christ as indispensable to the fulfillment of this divine act. He does so at his exaltation to the throne as "Lord and Messiah" (Acts 2:36). Likewise, Jesus says in John 17:2 that he would be glorified and given authority over all peoples in order to impart eternal life to them.

Other examples can be given, but these should suffice to indicate how the followers of Jesus saw *his* coming as fulfilling *God's* coming. In response to these texts, one could maintain that God's presence is simply felt in Jesus's works as with the works of any great saint. But the New Testament makes Jesus's coming *indispensable* to God's coming, as though God comes *because* Jesus comes, and the latter's coming fulfills God's coming, not only throughout his life, but at the resurrection and Pentecost with eschatological finality as the source of redemption for all of creation. Obviously, Jesus fulfills God's coming in a way that reveals him to be essentially one with this God. Jesus's very name is Immanuel, meaning "God with us" (Matt. 1:23). The year of the Lord's favor and the reign of God dawn in the world through his acts of deliverance and the Spirit who works through him (Luke 4:18; Matt. 12:28). When he rises from the dead to impart the Spirit upon all flesh, it becomes clear that the destiny of the entire creation in God is tied to his coming and what he has done. No other view is possible from the lens of Pentecost.

The last line of argument has to do with Christ's divine authority as the final judge, a role reserved for God as the Lord of creation. Craig Evans shows that most of Jesus's "Son of man" sayings reveal Jesus's self-identity with the Son of man figure of Daniel 7, who received authority to reign and to judge on God's behalf. He can forgive sins and is Lord of the Sabbath (Mark 2:7, 28). He is coming on the clouds of heaven to judge at the final day (Mark 8:38; 13:26; 14:61–62). Psalm 98:9 foretells of God's coming to judge the earth, which Christ's coming as judge is said to fulfill in Acts 17:31.[31] Even on a personal level, Christ assumes the power to judge the hearts and actions of people reserved for God alone: "I am he who searches hearts and minds, and I will repay each of you according to your deeds" (Rev. 2:23). He is the Word who "judges the thoughts and attitudes of the heart" (Heb. 4:12). He is the one who bore the fire of judgment in order to renew the creation in the Spirit of life, but his role in occasioning a river of grace both embraces and excludes.

---

31. Evans, "Jesus' Self-Designation," 153–60.

Such lines of argument lay hidden beneath the great triumph of the Nicene Creed in defending Christ's full deity. We should pause to discuss this enormously important fourth-century creed before we proceed to explore Christ's true humanity. The defense of Christ's deity at the Council of Nicaea is important to a Christian doctrine of the incarnation. As I noted in the preceding chapter, there is a difference between a dyohypostatic Christology, which advocates viewing the Father and the Son as two separate essences (commonly called "subordinationism"), and a miahypostatic Christology, which assumes a unity (continuity) of essence between the Father and the Son (and by implication the Spirit). By separating the Son from the being or essence of the Father, dyohypostatic Christology raised the question concerning how the Son could possibly be the self-impartation of the God of Israel to creation. Separated from the Father in essence, Christ is not internal (indispensable) to the self-impartation of the true God. The true God remains at arm's length from creation, untouched by human suffering. This God does not bear up under our baptism in fire so as to baptize us in the renewing Spirit. Salvation tends not to be incorporation or participation in the life of the true God. How does this Christology support the soteriology implied by what Christ does at Pentecost? A miahypostatic Christology has more potential for viewing Christ as the self-impartation of the true God to flesh and the one who incorporates us into the divine life. For the incarnation to support God's self-giving to human flesh, the eternal Son of God must be one in essence with the Father and the Spirit.

I developed in my previous chapter the metaphysical problems that contextualized creedal Christology. I noted that elements of both dyohypostatic and miahypostatic Christology can be found in a single thinker in the ancient world. Most everyone in the fourth century said that Christ was divine light from divine light; but that did not mean that a true continuity of essence was always assumed from one light to the other. The value of the fourth-century Nicene Creed (325 CE) was in helping to bring clarity to the church on this important issue of the Son's relationship to the essence of his Father (and by implication of the Spirit). Though not historic at the time it was crafted, it ended up being so, especially through the advocacy of Athanasius, its most able and passionate defender. Here is the original creed:

> We believe in one God, the Father almighty, maker of all things visible and invisible; and in one Lord, Jesus Christ, the Son of God, begotten from the Father, only-begotten, that is, from the substance of the Father, God from God, light from light, true God from true

God, begotten not made, of one substance with the Father, through Whom all things came into being, things in heaven and things on earth, Who because of us men and because of our salvation came down, and became incarnate and became man, and suffered, and rose again on the third day, and ascended to the heavens, and will come to judge the living and dead, and in the Holy Spirit. But as for those who say, There was when He was not, and, Before being born He was not, and that He came into existence out of nothing, or who assert that the Son of God is of a different hypostasis or substance, or created, or is subject to alteration or change—these the Catholic and apostolic Church anathematizes.

In one fell swoop, this bold support for Christ's full deity (unity of essence with the Father) undermines the dyohypostatic severing of the essential unity between the Son and the Father. This creed is the triumph of miahypostatic Christology: Christ of one essence with the true God. In the Nicene Creed the term *homoousios* is used of the Son, which means that he is of "one essence" with the Father. Significantly, no distinction exists here between the Son as "god" and the Father as "the true God." Christ is "true God from true God." Rejected is an even worse idea: that the Son was created out of nothing. Rather, the Son is "God from God, light from light . . . begotten not made." The common reference to Christ as light from light is granted thereby much needed clarity.

The reference to the Son as "begotten not made" is to an eternal begetting or a generation of the Son from the Father, a generation of the Son without beginning. That the Son is eternally "begotten" distinguishes him in person from the Father. But this distinction does not preclude a unity of essence, which is further supported by the *homoousios* (one essence) of the creed. The creed thus anathematizes those who say of the Son that there was once a time when "he was not," that "he came into existence out of nothing," was of a different "substance," "created," or "subject to alteration or change."

In the light of the preceding chapter, it should be apparent that all of these denials were bold for their time. This creed was not perfect; no creed is. Except for the reference to the Son as "begotten," the relational distinction between the Father and the Son is neglected. The creed had made the essential unity of the Father and Son clear. Yet its failure to adequately describe them as being distinct led some to believe that the creed was a modalist formula. Indeed, Marcellus of Ancyra, who viewed the "Father" and the "Son" as a mere difference in divine actions rather than as personal relations (what may be termed a modalist view of the Trinity), was one of the major voices at the Council of Nicaea. He was a defender of the creed and later a friend and colleague of the creed's chief defender, Athanasius. But this creed was nevertheless a massive step in the direction of clarifying the enormously important unity of essence between the Father and the Son, which, as we have been saying all along, is necessary to a proper understanding of the role that Christ plays in the divine self-giving for all flesh at Pentecost. Only the true God can self-impart by bestowing the Spirit of life to flesh. Only a fully divine Christ can mediate this divine self-impartation.

Why so bold a statement as the Nicene Creed? One might say that extreme measures were needed to deal with an extreme problem. That problem came to focus on a presbyter in the church of Alexandria, Egypt, named Arius. Not all elements of the problem were limited to him; but due to his extremism, he became a lightning rod for a debate that was perhaps inevitable. It was possible for ambivalence to exist among thinkers of the ancient world as they struggled, in the light of divine transcendence, with the problem of how to describe the mediator of salvation as belonging to God, and yet as belonging to creation at the same time. The Father, as the transcendent origin of all things, and as immutable and impassible, caused many to view the one begotten from the Father to bear flesh, suffer, and die, as of *another* essence. Arius was one of those who held this view: he strove to describe the otherness of the Son in relation to the Father as the origin of all things in a way that seemed logical and biblical to him. The Word of the Father is other than the Father, as the origin of all things, by being created. Though the Word was created differently from creation (directly from the Father) and was, therefore, exalted above creation, there still was once, for Arius, when the Son "was not." Others within the dyohypostatic movement who viewed the Word as of an essence different from the Father would not have intentionally gone so far as to say that the Word was created out of nothing. Arius's extreme subordinationism caused him to become embroiled in a debate with his bishop, Alexander of Alexandria, over the nature of Christ in relation to the Father. In declaring that the Son was created out of nothing, Arius would end up calling forth the bold Nicene defense of the unity of essence between the Father and the Son. (Athanasius, Alexander's successor as bishop of Alexandria, later became Arius's most able and passionate opponent.)

On the surface, Arius presents himself as holding to the orthodox faith of the church. In his letter to Emperor Constantine only two years after the Council of Nicaea convened, Arius set forth this as representative of his faith:

We believe in one God, the Father Almighty, and in His Son the Lord Jesus Christ, who was begotten from Him before all ages, God the Word, by whom all things were made, whether things in heaven or on earth; He came and took upon Him flesh, suffered and rose again, and ascended into heaven, whence He will again come to judge the quick and the dead. We believe in the Holy Ghost, in the resurrection of the body, in the life to come, in the kingdom of heaven, and in one Catholic Church of God, established throughout the earth.

This statement on its face would have disturbed few in the fourth century. But in drilling down into Arius's faith, one finds some deeply problematic interpretations of the above statements. In Arius, Origen's best ideas were arguably left behind and his heterodox inclinations concerning Christology were highlighted in bright colors. It is obvious from his other statements that the Word "begotten" (of the Father) "before all ages" was actually, for Arius, a creation "out of nothing" before creation and its ages began.

Why did Arius describe the difference between the Father and the Son in such an extreme way? As I suggested above, his goal was to protect the transcendence of the Father as alone the source of everything good while coming forth from nothing else. The fact that the Son comes forth from the Father meant for Arius that the Son is essentially "other" and inferior to the Father. He had joined others of his day in holding to a dyohypostatic Christology in some sense. The difference for Arius was his aversion to the idea of a generation of the Son from the Father that might allow for some sense of essential continuity of the Son with the Father. He viewed the Greek notion that the Son had "emanated" (or been "belched" forth) from God as a "substratum" of the Father to be a crude or pagan division of the divine life and thus a compromise of divine unity, simplicity, immutability, and transcendence.[32] To replace such speculative notions of the generation or begetting of the Son from the Father with something more biblical, Arius viewed the Son as "created" from the Father *ex nihilo*—that is, out of nothing. For Arius, there was indeed once when the Son was *not*.

To his credit, Arius also did try to regard the Son as superior to the rest of creation: he set the Son apart from all other creatures in that the Son alone mediates their creation. Even Arius's chief opponent, Athanasius, conceded

---

32. *Arius' Letter to Eusebius of Nicomedia* 3–4, in *The Trinitarian Controversy*, ed. and trans. William C. Rusch (Philadelphia: Fortress, 1980), 23–24.

that, for Arius, the Son was a creature like no other.[33] However, claiming that the Son was created before time or with a unique status or purpose would not be enough to capture the lordship of the Son in relation to creation that is so vital for the scriptural witness to the Son's impartation of the Spirit of God from the Father. Romans 4:17 refers to God the creator as the one who "calls into being things that were not." By locating the Son on the side of the "things that were not," Arius ended up stripping us of an adequate way of explaining how the Son participates in what only God can do—that is, *save*. A creature, no matter how exalted, cannot redeem, cannot impart the Spirit of God to creation, and cannot do so in a way that makes the Son himself essential to the divine self-impartation to flesh. Arius could not adequately explain what Christ did at Pentecost.

Arius thus fell short of the richness of what Christ did as the Spirit Baptizer. Arius's lack of attention to the Spirit is widely known and was no insignificant oversight, since the Son's capacity to graciously impart his own life by imparting the Spirit of God compellingly implies a salvific role that the Son exercised as Messiah and Lord at Pentecost. By making the Son a creature created out of nothing, Arius maintained that the Son was only united to the Father in will and purpose and not in nature or essence, and functioned mainly to exemplify God for us. For Arius, the Son did not even know the Father completely, and was rewarded with glory from the Father when he was created only because the Father foreknew he would merit such glory once he became flesh. Rather than being the mediator of God's abundant self-giving to creation, Christ was, for Arius, a mere symbol of a glory granted according to merit. Rather than a source of redemption, the means by which humanity can be incorporated into the divine life and communion, Arius's Christ was merely the exemplar of moralistic good works. Jaroslav Pelikan says that Arius's Christology ended up producing a theological vision in which "God was interpreted deistically, man moralistically, and Christ mythologically."[34]

By reducing Christ to a creature, Arius attempted to not only eliminate a division in God but also remove any possibility of a modalistic lack of distinction between the persons of the Father and the Son, for this would, to Arius's mind, entangle the Father in the limitations and suffering of the incarnate Son. How can there be a unity of essence between the transcendent God, who cannot suffer, and the embodied Son, who can and does suffer in

---

33. Athanasius, *Orations against the Arians* 2.19.
34. Pelikan, *Emergence of the Catholic Tradition*, 1:198.

the flesh? Besides, a unity of essence between an unbegotten true God and a begotten Son made no sense to Arius. This unity of essence between the Father and the Son would, in Arius's view, cause the Son to share the essence of the unbegotten Father and thus to be unbegotten as well, producing two unbegotten causes, a God materially divided: "Nor does he have being with the Father . . . two unbegotten causes."[35] According to Arius, a whole variety of heresies may be clustered with the problems connected to the idea that the Son was "part" of the Father's essence—from Gnosticism to modalism.[36] Arius seemed to be saying that the belief in the sameness of essence of the Father with the Son leads either to a material separation in God (Gnostic emanations) or, in an effort to avoid that, to a lack of a proper distinction between divine persons (modalism). The result would be a compromise of the Father's unique transcendence as alone the unbegotten source of all goodness. For Arius, the only way to avoid this compromise was to simply deny any "true" deity to the Son.

Of course, the eternal generation of the Son from the Father did not necessarily imply such a crudely materialist concept of God, so this generation would result in a division in God. Eternal generation was widely regarded, from Origen onward, as a profound mystery irreducible to materialist or metaphysical conceptuality. Athanasius rightly complained that Arius's followers "think corporeal and earthly things about the Father himself, accusing him of segments, emanations, and influxes" so as to deny that the Son is of one essence with the Father.[37] When it comes to eternal generation, one is dealing with something incomparable and utterly unique, for "the Son is always the peculiar offspring of the Father's substance" (1.29). At its best, the doctrine of the Son's eternal generation from the Father was thought to be internal to God, not external, which makes terms drawn from creation ("originated," etc.) potentially misleading. "'Unoriginated,' writes Athanasius, "was discovered by the Greeks, who do not know the Son" (1.34). Jesus did not teach us to pray, "God Unoriginated" but rather "our Father" (1.34). Athanasius implies that all conceptuality ultimately fails when trying to capture the mystery of what it means to say that the Son was begotten of the Father in a way that views the Son as eternally one in essence with the Father (1.31–34).

35. *Arius' Letter to Alexander of Alexandria* 4.
36. *Arius' Letter to Alexander of Alexandria* 2.
37. Athanasius, *Orations against the Arians* 1.21. Hereafter, references to this work appear in parentheses within the text.

It is important to note here that Arius did attempt to take seriously the full force of Christ's humanity as presented in the New Testament. Arius was focused on those texts that implied the Son's total dependence on the Father or that revealed creaturely limitations of the Son in his embodied state. But rather than view such things as the result of the divine Word descending into limited and weak flesh so that flesh could be exalted in him, Arius read such limitations as in some sense characteristic of the Word himself. Arius was also motivated by a strong desire to accept the reality of the Son's suffering in the flesh. He was strongly motivated by the idea that "god" in this lesser form (as the Son) suffered in the flesh. In fact, it was out of a desire to take in the full impact of the Son's suffering that caused Arius to remove the true God essentially from the Son.[38] But we still need to say that Arius also removed the true God essentially from the Son because Arius could not imagine the idea that the true God could suffer in the flesh. Arius complains about his opponents: "The Father will be according to them compounded, divided, mutable, and a body, and, as far as they are concerned, the incorporeal God suffers things suitable to the body."[39] Perish the thought!

Admittedly, the relationship between God and suffering was a difficult issue among the church fathers. In a thorough study of this issue, Thomas Weinandy concludes that, with few exceptions, the fathers regarded God as essentially impassible in order to distance God from the debilitating nature of suffering as experienced in creation. God does not undergo divergent emotional states, nor does God suffer any loss or lack of perfection or fullness. God does not succumb to anxiety or other debilitating or crippling emotions. God's impassibility was held as important to a proper vision of God's "perfect and dynamic passion," or "perfect goodness and unalterable love."[40] But does this settle the matter for us? Hardly. First, the early fathers by and large do not deny that the divine Son of God suffered in the flesh. Thomas Weinandy summarizes the major thrust of the patristic witness

---

38. Arius did intend to say that "god" in this separate essence as a created logos suffered in the flesh. R. P. C. Hanson highlights this fact by noting: "At the heart of the Arian Gospel was a God who suffered." See Hanson, *The Search for the Christian Doctrine of God: The Arian Controversy, 318–321* (Grand Rapids: Baker Academic, 1988), 121. But this insight needs to be qualified so as not to be misleading. We need to add that, for Arius, the true God cannot suffer, which is why he felt compelled to relegate suffering to a being created by God out of nothing, a being that can hardly be identified as God in any biblical sense of the term.

39. *Arius' Letter to Alexander of Alexandria* 5.

40. Thomas G. Weinandy, *Does God Suffer?* (Notre Dame, IN: University of Notre Dame Press, 2000), 111.

this way: "It is *truly* the Son of God who *truly* is man and so suffers *truly* as man."[41] The Council of Ephesus (430 CE) would, under Cyril of Alexandria's twelfth article, affirm that the Son of God suffered in the flesh. Cyril characterized the impassible Son's suffering in the flesh as a paradox. The divine Son, who has the fullness of divine perfection and has no lack or weakness, bears such things through the incarnation for our salvation. This is the paradox of grace. One could say that Arius could not tolerate such a paradox. For him, the Logos, or the Son of God suffering in the flesh, means that he could not be the true God. He must be of a different and lesser essence.

Arius's effort to protect the transcendence of the true God by relegating the Son to creation out of nothing had catastrophic implications. Unity of essence between Father, Son, and Spirit is thus the most important issue to be protected in Christology. Granted, in the early centuries of the church the distinction of persons in the Godhead was also important and was not properly upheld by all. For Marcellus of Ancyra, a defender of the Nicene Creed, there were no eternal relations in God. The pre-incarnate Logos was for him merely a distinct action of the one God. For Marcellus, the Son is begotten of the Father at the incarnation as the self-impartation of the Father to flesh.[42] Though heretical by the standards of later tradition, Marcellus was still much more orthodox than Arius was. At least Marcellus advocated the full deity and lordship of Christ. It is interesting that, when Bishop Eusebius of Caesarea, a dyohypostatic theologian, urged Athanasius—years after the Council of Nicea—to repudiate Marcellus of Ancyra, Athanasius "neither defended him nor expressed hostility towards him. He only smiled and indicated he [Marcellus] was not far from error, but he considered him excused."[43] I should point out, however, that Marcellus was eventually condemned by the church. But we should also recognize that, by defending Christ's deity, Marcellus could still view Christ as participating fully in the divine self-giving at the incarnation and, by implication, at Pentecost. Christ could still be worshiped as the Lord who imparts the Spirit. It is this point that made Arius's error far more tragic in its consequences than Marcellus's was. Athanasius was right: Marcellus could be "excused" in his error, but Arius could not.

41. Weinandy, *Does God Suffer?*, 175 (italics in original).

42. Joseph T. Lienhard, *Contra Marcellum: Marcellus of Ancyra and Fourth Century Theology* (Washington, DC: Catholic University of America, 1999), 58.

43. As reported by Epiphanius, who brought Eusebius's message to Athanasius, *Panarion* 72.4; quoted in Lienhard, *Contra Marcellum*, 9.

The God of Pentecost abundantly self-imparts, that is, opens the divine life to all flesh. In Arius's understanding, the true God remains removed from the world, sharing only the glory to the Logos that he has come to deserve. It is this portion of the divine inheritance granted from the lofty heights of divine transcendence that the Logos would then share with all fellow creatures. Of the Father's sharing glory with the Son, Arius says: "For the Father having given to him the inheritance of all, did not deprive himself of those things that he had in himself without generation."[44] As I observed in the preceding chapter, divine transcendence is not a divine freedom *from* the world; rather, it is a radical freedom *for* the world that reaches beyond all barriers to embrace those who are unworthy of embrace. It is an infinitely free impartation of divine love that arises from God's sovereign and self-determined purposes. Instead, for Arius, the true God gives from a distance, careful to guard against deprivation by involvement in the world. Arius conceived of the eternal river of life characteristic of the Father's relationship with the Son and the Spirit as revealed at Pentecost as a pond surrounded by NO TRESPASSING signs! There was no abundant river of divine life and love proper to the divine persons to speak of here, neither within the divine life nor analogously between God and creation. Arius concedes that the Son was granted some of the glory from the Father, but only to the degree that a creature *could earn it*. Arius's God is hardly the biblical God of self-giving grace given for us in the incarnation, or the self-imparting God of Pentecost.

Athanasius attacked Arius on many fronts, but none so penetrating as when his writings had Pentecost at the horizon. Nearly all theologians, whether miahypostatic or dyohypostatic, regarded the Son as coming forth from the Father as divine "water from a fountain," or similar metaphors. But Athanasius convincingly made the case that such designations require unity of essence between the Father and the Son. If the Son is of another essence from the Father, how can the Son be the water that comes forth from the Father as the eternal fount of deity? In criticism of Arius, Athanasius thus writes: "God exists and is called a fountain of wisdom and life." He writes further: "Therefore, is not the individual impious who says, 'There was once when the Son was not?' For this is the same thing as saying, 'There was once when the fountain was dry, without life and wisdom.' But this would not be a fountain." In fact, it is, for Athanasius, precisely the loss of essential unity between the Father and the Son that deprives the Father of the fullness of attributes as Father: "But let the thoughtful person note how the perfection and

---

44. *Arius' Letter to Alexander of Alexandria* 4.

fullness of the Father's substance is deprived."[45] The Son cannot be reduced to a mere work of the Father's will, as external to the Father, but rather the Son images the Father as that which springs forth eternally from the Father.[46] So, when it comes to the relationship between the Father and the Son, writes Athanasius, "let them inquire of the sun concerning its reflection, and the fountain concerning what comes from it."[47]

Of course, the Father, Son, and Spirit are not deprived of anything in their self-giving; in fact, they reveal their abundance as the one God precisely in being the self-giving God! In becoming Spirit-baptized flesh, the Word of the Father does not give up what is essential to the divine life as self-giving eternal love. That love is revealed at the incarnation and the cross as limitless in abundance and reach. Taking on the fire of our judgment reveals God's penchant to love faithfully even those who spurn that love, to love so deeply as to join the sinners in the depths of their despair. The divine *kenosis* or self-emptying revealed in the incarnation (Phil. 2:7) is not an abandonment of deity but rather its richest and most expansive expression. If one may speak of a divine "essence," it is "forever 'given' in the self-gift of the Father," "rendered" in the faithful life of the Son, and "represented" as abundant, unconditional love by the Holy Spirit.[48] In becoming flesh, going to the cross, and rising up to impart the Spirit, therefore, God does not fundamentally change. In becoming flesh, God remains faithful to who God is. "God, then, has no need to 'change' when he makes a reality of the wonders of his charity."[49] Divine transcendence reflects the freedom and sovereignty of the divine self-giving of the incarnation, but this transcendence was never meant to become an intellectually insurmountable barrier to the reality of that incarnation. That would be a fundamental misunderstanding of it.

Even some among those of the early to mid-fourth century who were otherwise sympathetic to Arius's radical subordinationism and willing to admit him into communion judged Arius to have gone too far. The greatest dyohypostatic theologian of Arius's day, Bishop Eusebius of Caesarea, reluctantly signed on to the Nicene Creed because he thought that the creed's bold statements were needed to correct the extremism in Arius's thought. When he explained his decision to affirm the creed to his church, he wrote, "It did not appear reasonable" to teach that the Son was created out of nothing,

45. Athanasius, *Orations against the Arians* 1.19.
46. Athanasius, *Orations against the Arians* 1.25.
47. Athanasius, *Orations against the Arians* 1.27.
48. Hans Urs von Balthasar, *Mysterium Paschale* (Grand Rapids: Eerdmans, 1990), viii.
49. Balthasar, *Mysterium Paschale*, ix.

concluding, "we were not accustomed to employing these words."[50] Eusebius also believed that the Son's generation had a beginning but preferred the idea that prior to creation the Son was eternally in the being of the Father "ingenerately in potentiality."[51] He still struggled to maintain some kind of essential link between God and the Logos who mediated God to the world. It is telling indeed that the likes of Eusebius of Caesarea (who viewed the Son as of another essence), Marcellus of Ancyra (who failed to adequately understand the eternal relation between the Father and the Son), and Alexander of Alexandria (whose Christology was closest to what was expressed at Nicaea) all agreed to condemn Arius for saying that the Son was created from nothing. Nicaea was a diverse table! The orthodoxy of that table was generous. But the line that it drew in the sand was important. In imparting the Spirit to all flesh, the Son shows himself to be essentially one with the Lord of creation as well as with the Spirit that he imparts. Nicaea implicitly supported Pentecost.

Truly Human

In imparting the Spirit through the word or sacrament of his embodied life, the Spirit Baptizer also shows himself to be one with human flesh. Christ imparts the Spirit through the declaration or sacrament of his faithful and exalted life. Thomas Torrance says of Christ that "it is in and through our sharing in that human and creaturely being, sanctified and blessed in him, that we share in the life of God."[52] But there are two truths that emerge as important when one says this. First, for Christ, in his resurrection and exaltation, to be the means by which we are exalted in our embodied life, he descended into the full expanse of human capacities, yearnings, and suffering. Moltmann says of Christ that "he humbles himself and assumes the whole and complete being of man, so that everyone can share in him through his human existence."[53] He descends all the way into the depths of our condition under the burdens of sin and death, taking the baptism in fire on our behalf so that we can be exalted. On the other hand, the Son of God in the flesh that

50. *Eusebius of Caesarea's Letter to His Church concerning the Synod at Nicea* 15, in *The Trinitarian Controversy*, trans. and ed. William C. Rusch (Philadelphia: Fortress, 1980), 49–52.

51. *Eusebius of Caesarea's Letter to His Church concerning the Synod at Nicea* 16.

52. Thomas F. Torrance, *Space, Time, and Resurrection* (Grand Rapids: Eerdmans, 1976), 136.

53. Jürgen Moltmann, "The Crucified God," *Theology Today* 31, no. 1 (April 1974): 14.

he shares with us is baptized in the Spirit, which culminates in resurrection and the Spirit's overflowing his exalted state so as to draw us in. This means that he will be unique in his fulfillment of creaturely destiny. He is more human than we are, ideally human for our sakes. It is this descent into our human condition and his ascent in order to save us that will show Christ in his humanity to be both typical and unique for our sake.

As for the typical, Christ's incarnation must involve humanity in all of its capacities and limitations in order to be the source of our transformation and exaltation. Gregory of Nazianzus declares of the Son's assumption of flesh at the incarnation, "What has not been assumed has not been healed."[54] This means that the flesh of Christ must be authentic in every way in order for him to be our representative and healer in every dimension of human existence. If Jesus had no soul, for example, he would not be authentically human: his redemptive journey would not involve the life of the soul. If Jesus were not authentically human in all of our most essential capacities, how can he represent us before God? How can he take up our yearnings and sorrows into the divine embrace? How could he be the declaration or sacrament of our renewal in the Holy Spirit, if he were not genuinely human, the recapitulation of the human race? Recall John Meyendorff's words: "With this flesh is the whole of redeemed mankind called to have communion with the Holy Spirit."[55] In this call to communion, Christ is the source of redemption, the means of renewal, and our moral example, the pattern to follow toward the formation of the just and loving community. But his embodied existence must be flesh—our flesh—or it does not call us at all.

Even a cursory reading of the New Testament will show that Jesus lived a truly human life. Gregory of Nyssa said of Christ that "he who had once decided to share our humanity had to experience all that belongs to our nature."[56] This is so that every dimension of our existence could be taken up into Christ's faithful life and exalted destiny. Hebrews begins appropriately enough with a powerful defense of Christ's deity. He is the exact image of God's very being, the radiance of God's glory. He upholds all things by the power of his Word. God thus addresses him as "God" in handing the divine

---

54. Gregory of Nazianzus, *Epistulae* 101.32; quoted in J. A. McGuckin, "The Strategic Adaptation of Deification in the Cappadocians," in *Partakers of the Divine Nature: The History and Development of Deification in the Christian Traditions*, ed. Michael J. Christensen and Jeffery A. Wittung (Grand Rapids: Baker, 2007), 101.

55. Meyendorff, *Christ in Eastern Christian Thought*, 10.

56. Gregory of Nyssa, *An Address on Religious Instruction* 32, in *Christology of the Later Fathers*, ed. Edward R. Hardy (Louisville: Westminster John Knox, 2006), 309–10.

reign over to him (Heb. 1:3–9). Paradoxically, though, it is precisely to *this* *Son* that Hebrews attributes genuine humanity—with all of its limitations, trials, and sense of dependence on the heavenly Father:

> During the days of Jesus' life on earth, he offered up prayers and petitions with fervent cries and tears to the one who could save him from death, and he was heard, because of his reverent submission. Son though he was, he learned obedience from what he suffered and, once made perfect, he became the source of eternal salvation for all who obey him. (Heb. 5:7–9)

Divine Son though he was, Christ undergoes learning and development, trials and deep sorrow. Every dimension and stage of human life in its development must experience the grace offered through the incarnation: "For he went through every stage of human life, restoring to all of them communion with God."[57]

There is, in fact, every indication in Scripture that Jesus lived the kind of human life that would have been typical for a man of his time and place. For example, he grew in wisdom and stature (Luke 2:52); he was born "under the law" (Gal. 4:4) as a Jewish boy who drank deeply from the streams of Israelite faith and hope; though a precocious student, he nevertheless learned from the teachers of the law in the Temple (Luke 2:46–47). His limited knowledge is obviously an area of his life, like all others, that reveals his human finitude. This includes not knowing the time of the end of the world (Mark 13:32). He practiced his Jewish faith devoutly, being fully devoted to the law of God (Matt. 5:17). He was in every way a man of his time, of his people, and of his social location.

Speaking more broadly, he is also in the lineage of Adam (Luke 3:38), and was thus not ashamed to call us all his brothers and sisters (Heb. 2:11–12). He shared in our humanity in order to share in our death (Heb. 2:14). He suffered not only in his body but also deep within his soul (Mark 14:33–34). Indeed, he suffered from his trials so that he could help others who suffer (Heb. 2:18). He empathizes with our weakness, for he was tried in every way typical of humanity (Heb. 4:15). He was genuinely tempted in the desert, so severely, in fact, that angels attended to him afterwards (Matt. 4:1–11). In

---

57. Irenaeus, *Against Heresies* 3.18.7, in *The Apostolic Fathers: Justin Martyr and Irenaeus*, rev. ed. A. Cleveland Cox, *Ante Nicene Fathers*, vol. 1, ed. Alexander Roberts and James Donaldson (Peabody, MA: Hendrickson, 1994).

the Garden of Gethsemane he was "deeply distressed and troubled," and his soul was "overwhelmed with sorrow to the point of death" (Mark 14:33–34). He cried out from the depths of his human soul (Matt. 26:38–39). He fell to the ground and prayed to have the coming trial of the cross taken from him: "'*Abba*, Father,' he said, 'everything is possible for you. Take this cup from me'" (26:39). The flesh of his followers was indeed weak (26:41). Jesus felt that weakness, too. Such was necessary for our salvation, for he had to experience the depths of human despair so that humanity might eventually be lifted above it. Saint Cyril wrote that "unless he had been troubled and alarmed, no escape from these feelings could have been found."[58] In contrast to the disciples, who were overcome by weakness, Jesus's dependence is on the Father's will, for he concludes, "Yet not what I will but what you will" (26:39). Here he rejects a human will independent of his Father's. He abandons such autonomy and directs his will and destiny completely to his Father. This image of self-sacrificial love against all temptation to the contrary is central to his humanity and helps us understand the victory of the coming Spirit Baptizer in his journey through our baptism in fire.

He also abandons his will to the leading of the Spirit, the Father's cause in the world. Christ saw himself as the inaugurator of the kingdom of God through liberating deeds empowered by the Spirit (Matt. 12:28), and he warned his opponents that ultimate rejection of the Spirit's witness alienates one from eschatological salvation "either in this age or in the age to come" (12:32). So intimately is Christ's redemptive work tied to the Spirit's eschatological witness! Christ's statement, during his trial at Gethsemane, that "the Spirit is willing, but the flesh is weak" refers to the *Holy Spirit* being willing while the flesh of humanity is weak.[59] Christ's disciples gave in to weakness, but Jesus offered himself up to the Father on their behalf "by the eternal Spirit" (Heb. 9:14), even (and especially) at the cross! The struggle at Gethsemane is most likely not the first time Jesus felt human weakness and prayed for the Father to consider rescuing him from the dismal end that he saw at the horizon. But he never abandoned his resolve to follow the will of the Father and the willing Spirit all the way to that horizon. Jesus gave himself over to this path precisely as a man, overcoming human weakness

---

58. Cyril of Alexandria, *In Ioannim* 8; quoted in Paul L. Gavrilyuk, *The Suffering of the Impassible God: The Dialectics of Patristic Thought*, Oxford Early Christian Studies (New York: Oxford University Press, 2004), 164.

59. Lyle Dabney, "Naming the Spirit: Towards a Pneumatology of the Cross," in *Starting with the Spirit*, ed. Stephen Pickard and Gordon Preece, Task of Theology 2 (Hindmarsh, Australia: Australian Theological Forum, 2001), 51–52.

in the process. This is divine strength overcoming human weakness, the Son become flesh in order to give himself to all flesh in the power of the willing Spirit. Because *he* overcame our weakness, we can also now join with him in overcoming it.

Does the struggle of Jesus at Gethsemane imply "two wills" (dyothelitism) in Christ, divine and human, as the orthodox consensus historically affirmed, in rejection of the view that Christ just had one will (monothelitism)? Perhaps not. More convincing is the idea that the struggle involved in Christ's abandonment of his will to that of the Father's is simply Jesus acting as the faithful Son *precisely as human*. That Jesus did not covet suffering is natural to anyone who is not a masochist. Anyone whose journey has a cross looming at the horizon treads toward that horizon only if necessary, only if there is no other way within God's will. The hypostatic union (the union of divine and human natures in Christ) has arguably not advocated anything else than that Jesus has in his humanity "*so far as it is possible for a human*, the very relation of the Son to the Father in the Trinity."[60] Humans loyal to God naturally exercise their will while testing their discernment of the divine will, seeking to avoid suffering unless necessary to that will, and overcoming feelings of weakness all along the way. There is no evidence in Scripture of a divided will in Jesus or of his genuinely wanting to take a path other than God's.

This abandonment of Jesus to the will of the Father and to the leading of the Spirit completely defines his self-sacrificial path to the cross. His cry of dereliction from the cross, "My God, my God, why have you forsaken me?" (Mark 15:34), reveals the extent to which he was willing to go in following the path willed by his Father and led by the Spirit, the path of self-giving love— all the way into the depths of human despair and abandonment. His cry of despair is from Psalm 22, and in quoting from that text, he never abandons his trust in God, as the larger context of Psalm 22:1–5 shows:

> My God, my God, why have you forsaken me?
> > Why are you so far from saving me,
> > so far from my cries of anguish?
> My God, I cry out by day, but you do not answer,
> > by night, but I find no rest.
> Yet you are enthroned as the Holy One;

---

60. David Coffey, "The Theandric Nature of Christ," *Theological Studies* 60 (1999): 425 (italics added).

> you are the one Israel praises.
> In you our ancestors put their trust;
>> they trusted and you delivered them.
> To you they cried out and were saved;
>> in you they trusted and were not put to shame.

Jesus's cry of dereliction is indeed a cry of despair, but one taken from a text still rooted paradoxically in a total abandonment of one's destiny into the hands of God. The cross thus invites all those who are alienated from God to find in their darkest moments the God who is committed to saving them. On the cross, Jesus is caught in the throes of human despair, and he again commits his path to the Father and the way of the Spirit in the midst of staggering darkness. He offered himself by the eternal Spirit (Heb. 9:14). He overcomes our baptism in fire as the faithful Son who bears the Spirit. Bearing the baptism in fire on our behalf, he is the man of sorrows; baptized in the Spirit, he will rise again; exalted to the throne, he will baptize others in the Spirit—turning their trial by fire into a vindicating and sanctifying force.

All of the above implies a uniquely total devotion to the Father's will and the leading of the Spirit in the world. To address this issue of Christ's unique humanity directly, the typical human capacities and burdens that Christ shares with us and for us cannot exhaust the reach of Christ's humanity in terms of its eschatological destiny as the resting place of the Spirit. Christ is meant in his exaltation to bring humanity to its unfulfilled destiny. Thus, according to the Gospel witnesses, there are elements of Jesus's human life that are not typically human. Since Christ is the inauguration of the new humanity, we expect him to be both united to us and different from us. In a way, anticipating the eschatological last Adam, he shows himself to be *more* authentically human than we are. A theological claim of human uniqueness in Christ, though expected, must be carefully examined and properly understood, so that it does not create an unjustified breach between Christ and the human race.

The chief indication of Christ's unique humanity is simply the fact that he is the incarnation of the divine Son, conceived by the Spirit as the holy Son of God in Mary's womb (Luke 1:35). This conception by the Spirit thus implied an eschatological destiny for Jesus that will reach not only to his unique anointing at the Jordan, where the Spirit is given without measure and remains with him (John 1:33; 3:34), but also his conception by the Spirit pointed all the way to the resurrection, where Christ is raised by the Spirit in a way that declares him to be the Son of the Father for all of creation (Rom.

1:4), the Lord who will impart the Spirit to all flesh. This entire trajectory explains Christ's striking impartation of the Spirit to all flesh so as to unite all flesh to himself and to his destiny as the anointed and exalted Son. Jesus's conception by the Spirit in Mary's womb is thus a new creation event that brings God to flesh and flesh to God. The Spirit "overshadows" Mary's womb much as the Spirit was over the face of the deep at creation (Luke 1:35; Gen. 1:2). Christ's assuming of humanity at his conception in Mary's womb is God's act of inaugurating a new humanity, one that will fulfill human destiny in him, as it was always meant to be.

The virginal conception of Jesus in Mary's womb functions as the sign of his conception by the Spirit as the incarnate Son. As such, the virginal conception is also a sign of his eschatological destiny in his embodied life as the sacrament or word of the Spirit for all of creation. But does this sign detach Jesus from humanity as we know it, namely, as taken from the dust of the ground? How is Jesus truly human if he did not have a biological father? Ironically, the creeds include the virginal conception of Jesus by the Spirit in Mary as part of an anti-docetic polemic that was meant to affirm his genuine humanity! Also interesting is the fact that both Matthew and Luke include the account of the virginal conception alongside human genealogies, meaning that "they did not think that the conception ruptured the chain of human descent."[61] It is not certain why the removal of Joseph from Jesus's biological heritage and the compensation for that removal by God's creative Spirit necessarily eliminates Jesus's full human capacities. It is equally unclear why the *inclusion* of Joseph would necessarily have eliminated God's involvement in Jesus's conception as the incarnate Son of God.[62]

The virginal conception of Jesus has been questioned more broadly, however, on historical grounds. As is widely known, miraculous births were reported in the Old Testament (Isaac, Samuel) and in other ancient religious texts as symbolic of an extraordinary life. The virginal conception in the New Testament is unique with respect to the larger religious environment of the ancient world, partly because there is no mention of a sexual act between Mary and a male deity. In fact, Luke's imagery looks more feminine than masculine, a Spirit that "hovers" over Mary's womb, without the participation of a male agent (1:35). The dominant power of the male, widely thought in the ancient world to plant the seed of life in the woman's womb,

---

61. Raymond E. Brown, *The Virginal Conception and Bodily Resurrection of Jesus* (New York: Paulist Press, 1973), 45n63.

62. Brown, *Virginal Conception*, 45.

is removed in order to make way for the Creator Spirit, who overshadows Mary's womb in what might be regarded as nesting imagery. The heavenly Father is not presented here as taking Joseph's place as Mary's sex partner; instead, the imagery is rather like creation, where the Spirit hovered over the waters of the deep to give forth creation. The difference here is that the Creator Spirit does not work in Mary's womb with the primordial deep, or as Romans 4:17 indicates, *ex nihilo*, but rather *ex Maria* (out of Mary) or out of her body, including her willful yielding by grace to humanity's liberating renewal by the Spirit of God. A human reality is assumed here as it is shaped by the Spirit or by both judgment and grace.[63] Any illusion of human self-determination dominating the redemptive process is judged so as to open up the possibility of a new humanity inaugurated by the Son in the Spirit: "Christ has thus invaded the world of Adam and claimed it for himself."[64] In making this claim, Christ says to his Father, "a body you prepared for me" (Heb. 10:5). The Spirit was the agent.

As implied above, the two accounts of the virginal conception by the Spirit (Matt. 1:20; Luke 1:35) are tied to Jesus's reception of the Spirit at his baptism (Matt. 3:16; Luke 3:22) and his resurrection by the Spirit (Rom. 1:4).[65] Jesus's conception by the Spirit as the incarnate Son is tied to his role as Spirit Baptizer. Jesus rises up from the waters of Mary's womb by the Spirit to give us life (John 1:14–16), analogous to how he rises from the waters of the Jordan under the Spirit's anointing, at the time of his baptism, to already grant humanity a share in the liberating Spirit (Matt. 12:28), and to how he rises from the waters of *sheol*, or the grave, at his resurrection so as to give himself to all flesh by imparting the Spirit to others. Obviously, Christ's resurrection by the Spirit and impartation of the Spirit to others cast their light backwards onto Christ's messianic installment at his baptism and further onto his conception by the Spirit in Mary's womb. Because the Word of the Father became flesh, "out of his fullness we have all received grace in place of grace already given" (John 1:16).

If the virginal conception is hard to imagine historically, so should be his messianic installment at his baptism by the Spirit of God and his resurrection from the dead by the Spirit in order to impart the Spirit to others. In

---

63. The contrast between *ex nihilo* and *ex Maria* is taken from Barth, *Church Dogmatics*, I/2: *The Doctrine of the Word of God*, trans. G. W. Bromiley et al. (Edinburgh: T & T Clark, 1978), 186.

64. Karl Barth, *Christ and Adam: Man and Humanity in Romans 5* (New York: Collier Books, 1957), 61.

65. Barth, *Christ and Adam*, 199.

fact, all of these events join together to depict a cooperative work between the eternal Son, the Father, and the Spirit, in which God's abundant and excessive love transforms the flesh of Jesus into a vehicle of immortal life to all flesh. The absence of Joseph's participation in Jesus's conception in Mary's womb is a miraculous sign that allows this conception to signify the abundant, overflowing gift of the Spirit to be granted at Pentecost. Eugene Rogers notes that "the virgin birth seems not only excessive but exorbitant, out of control—and even physically excessive."[66] But so is Pentecost! A single narrative of excessive divine love connects all of these steps on the way to Christ's becoming the Spirit Baptizer.

Admittedly, the fact that the virginal conception only exists in the Gospels of Matthew and Luke may mean that it was not part of the earliest Christian proclamation. If so, this absence may be due to the fact that the story of Jesus's virginal conception was originally handed down as a family tradition, which eventually made its way into the larger Christian tradition.[67] The existence of such a family tradition helps to explain Christ's astonishingly unique claim to authority and relationship to God as *Abba* that seems to have characterized his life, even from an early age (Luke 2:49).[68] This virginal conception may indeed be implied, however, in Galatians 4:4, just as one may also say that the incarnation is implied in the virginal conception texts such as Matthew 1:23 and Luke 1:35. The virginal conception represents part of the larger plot of Christology in the New Testament, so that to ignore it is to miss out on a dramatic part of the story that connects the Spirit's work at Jesus's beginning to Jesus's work at the end, at his resurrection by the Spirit and Spirit impartation.[69]

Therefore, the virginal conception of Jesus by the Spirit has as its *telos* the rising up of Jesus as the last Adam, who is known as the life-giving Spirit (1 Cor. 15:45). This goal means that Jesus's mode of conception signals someone who is both one with humanity and set apart from humanity—for humanity's sake—for he is more fully human than we are and wills to bind us to that destiny by bringing us into union with himself. He is indeed both Spirit-baptized and the Spirit Baptizer, both one with us and utterly unique in order to be for us. Hidden behind these tensions is the divine Word become flesh, the paradox of grace, the paradox of the last Adam who is the

---

66. Rogers, *After the Spirit*, 103.

67. Brown, *Virginal Conception*, 60.

68. Brown, *Virginal Conception*, 46–47.

69. I am grateful here to Oliver Crisp, *God Incarnate: Explorations in Christology* (London: T & T Clark, 1999), 89–91.

life-giving spirit (1 Cor. 15:45). Barth says that Jesus "is the real son of a real mother, the son born of the body, flesh and blood of his mother, both of them as real as all the other sons of other mothers." Yet Barth adds that Jesus is "still a man in a different way from the other sons of other mothers."[70] Here the virginal conception is the sign of the conception of Jesus by the Spirit, the "embryo" of an anointed Messiah, the ideal human, who imparts that anointing as Lord to others (Acts 2:33–36). His being set apart from us indicates a transcending of human nature so as to fulfill it, for ideal humanity is meant to overflow with grace in the image of the Son. He is fully human in being fully divine and fully divine in being fully human.

Christ's uniqueness as signified in the virginal conception is also connected to his universality. Christ's being conceived of a virgin as the eternal Word of the Father and by the Spirit implies that Christ belongs in his very humanity to God's eschatological future for all flesh. His flesh is not just the flesh of a particular man but belongs also to the renewal of all flesh by the Spirit. There is thus a connection implied here between Jesus's particularity and his universality. Born of a virgin from the lineage of David, Jesus is a Jew of his time and place. There are features of his upbringing and life that are peculiar to his ethnicity, religious heritage, time, and place. This fact has implications for his larger mission. The fact that he was born into the realm of an occupied people makes his role as bearer of God's liberating justice in the world especially relevant for our social witness today. The fact that he was born a Jew affirms his place at Pentecost as the Spirit Baptizer, at the pivot point from Israel to the nations in fulfillment of Israel's mission. And yet that pivot point to all flesh is not a mere culminating stage in the Messiah's identity and mission. It defines the thrust and purpose of his entire life. His very conception in the virgin's womb by the Spirit signals it. Christ's conception by the hovering Spirit refers back to creation and ahead to new creation.

The eschatological Spirit embraces concrete historical and cultural particularities and celebrates the best from them but does so in a way that transcends them in order to embrace others, including and especially the otherness of the new creation. The Spirit's anointing in the image of the Son cannot be confined to history—to any time or place. Jesus's virginal conception by this Spirit thus points to the fact that he is human for all others, the one who rises from Israel's history to embrace the nations in all of their own unique callings, only to transcend history itself so as to usher in the new creation. Indeed, as Michael Welker notes of the virginal conception by the

---

70. Barth, *Church Dogmatics*, I/2, 185.

Spirit, "Here the Messiah is born for all times and for all peoples, an event is occurring that cannot be adequately defined and comprehended in biological and political categories."[71] Even though Christ does indeed embody his own particular biological lineage and spiritual heritage as a Jew, he is also, from his very virginal conception, "universally installed by the Spirit before becoming palpably present and public in any physical, social, concrete way."[72]

He is conceived by the Spirit to be the Spirit Baptizer, to bear flesh that will incorporate in itself all flesh. The incorporation of all peoples into himself as his own body by the Spirit has its embryo in the Son's uniting himself by the Spirit to flesh at the virginal conception. Born of Mary, he is one with Israel; but born without Joseph and by the eschatological Spirit, he transcends Israel at the core of his being. He is conceived as God's union with and renewal of all flesh. Precisely as such, he is to be Israel's Messiah, the fulfillment of Israel's calling, for Israel is meant to transcend itself in its faithfulness to God (as are all of us today). All humanity was created analogously to be people for others, persons who thrive from a just and loving communion with others. In transcending his particularity (while not leaving it behind), Jesus ends up fulfilling humanity and not denying it, for all of humanity is made to live by an overflowing grace that ultimately transcends the limits of our times and places to embrace the new creation. The absence of Joseph and the presence of the eschatological Spirit in Jesus's conception do not signal something less than human but rather something more maximally human.

Of course, Jesus could have been conceived by the Spirit as the divine Son without the virginal conception. Jesus's identity as the Spirit Baptizer—his identity and mission as inclusive of all flesh—is not based on the virginal conception; rather, the virginal conception signals or dramatically announces this identity and mission. Barth does us a service by removing from the virginal conception ideas that are not found in the biblical narrative. Nowhere, for example, is Christ's deity or sinlessness founded on the virginal conception per se in Scripture. Christ is conceived in the virgin's womb by the Spirit as the holy Son of God (Luke 1:35), but this virginal conception is not described as something that is demanded by his divine identity or holiness. Instead, Barth helpfully describes the virginal conception as an important *sign* of Christ's coming victory over sin and death rather than the basis on which that victory would be achieved. Barth uses the healing of the paralytic in Mark 2 to illustrate his point. Since that healing was not the basis of the man's forgiveness

---

71. Michael Welker, *God the Spirit* (Minneapolis: Fortress, 1994), 188.
72. Welker, *God the Spirit*, 189.

but rather its sign, so also is Jesus's virginal conception a sign rather than the basis of the Word made flesh by the Spirit in order to conquer sin and death.[73] I would add here that Jesus's reception of the Spirit at the Jordan occurred under the sign of his baptism in water, just as Jesus was conceived by the Spirit in Mary's womb under the sign of the virginal conception. As Barth notes, both the virginal conception and the water baptism were fitting signs of the divine Son brought into the world to renew all flesh by the Spirit of God.[74] Therefore, I agree with Oliver Crisp that the virginal conception is not necessary to the incarnation but it is *fitting* for the incarnation to take place in this way.[75]

Besides Jesus's conception by the Spirit, another unique feature of Jesus's authentic humanity is his sinlessness, which is important to his redemptive mission. Dietrich Bonhoeffer said it best: Christ's incarnation requires that he enter fully into human alienation from God. But "how can he help us out of our trouble, while he is set in the same trouble?"[76] He will sink into this trouble on our behalf but not as one who is by nature captive to it. As the one baptized in the Spirit, Jesus is to also be baptized in the fire of condemnation and death in order to make us in him the sanctified temple of God's presence. He bears the fire of judgment, yet not for his own sin but for ours. We considered him "punished by God, stricken by him," but "he was bruised for our transgressions, he was pierced for our iniquities" (Isa. 53:4–5). His sinlessness was thought by Saint Cyril to make Jesus's Spirit-baptized body fitting as the means by which Christ as the divine Son would pour forth the Spirit to others. Christ thus bore the Spirit in his sanctified body so that the Spirit might through him sanctify us, too. Cyril concludes: "He Who knew no sin, became as one of us, that the Spirit might be accustomed to abide in us."[77]

Christ is the sanctified Son from the moment of his conception by the Spirit in Mary's womb (Luke 1:35). According to Lossky, Christ, sanctified at the incarnation, would make space within himself for "all sin-scarred, fallen human nature."[78] At the incarnation he is the sanctified temple of God's

---

73. Welker, *God the Spirit*, 189.

74. Barth, *Church Dogmatics*, I/2, 199.

75. Crisp, *God Incarnate*, 77–102.

76. Dietrich Bonhoeffer, *Christology* (London: Collins, 1978), 107; quoted in Ivor J. Davidson, "Pondering the Sinlessness of Jesus Christ," *International Journal of Systematic Theology* 10, no. 4 (October 2008): 373n2.

77. Cyril of Alexandria, *Commentary on John* 2.1.32–33, trans. P. E. Pusey (Oxford: James Packer and Co., 1874), 1:142.

78. Vladimir Lossky, *Mystical Theology of the Eastern Church* (Crestwood, NY: St. Vladimir's Seminary Press, 1976), 148.

presence that opens himself to sinners for the sake of their justification and sanctification. Jesus is conceived in Mary's womb as the *holy* Son of God (Luke 1:35), and he claimed to have sanctified himself in life so that others may be sanctified (John 17:19). A body was prepared for him so that he could come to do God's will (Heb. 10:5). He was destined from the beginning as the Spirit Baptizer to become the vindicated and sanctified means by which the creation will be justified and sanctified through union with him. He is the sanctified temple that makes us temples of the Spirit through his redeeming grace (1 Cor. 6:19–20). Thus, as he journeyed to his ultimate trial, "he committed no sin, and no deceit was found in his mouth" (1 Pet. 2:22). He was tempted in ways that were typical of other humans and "yet he did not sin" (Heb. 4:15). He was destined to be the lamb "without blemish or defect" (1 Pet. 1:19), who will take away the sins of the world (John 1:29). He will suffer the alienation of sinful humanity and bear the full brunt of their distance from God. His sinlessness is important to the blessed exchange that takes place between Christ and sinful humanity in which he who knows no sin takes on our sin vicariously so that we can take on his righteousness (2 Cor. 5:21); he was justified so that, united to him in the Spirit, we could be justified (Rom. 4:25; 1 Tim. 3:16); he was sanctified so that, united to him in the Spirit, we could be sanctified (John 17:19); and he was glorified so that, united to him in the Spirit, we could be glorified (Rom. 8:11). Indeed, "you were washed, you were sanctified, you were justified in the name of the Lord Jesus Christ and by the Spirit of our God" (1 Cor. 6:11).

Christ's sinlessness was tied to the faithfulness of the Son in his yielding to the will of the Father and the leading of the Spirit. Appropriately, it is by the Spirit that the Father vindicates Jesus's self-sacrificial life by raising him from the dead. He was condemned by his crucifiers but vindicated by God. Jesus is vindicated in his resurrection as God's faithful Son "through the Spirit of holiness" (Rom. 1:4). He "appeared in the flesh [and] was justified by the Spirit" (1 Tim. 3:16). All of this means that, no matter how we in our limited knowledge might wish to evaluate Jesus's life, God judged Jesus's life to be faithful. God vindicated him as the faithful Son by raising him from the dead. "By the Easter event—but only in the light of it—he was proved to be sinless."[79] The faithful Son who offered himself up for sinners on the cross is vindicated in resurrection and is exalted to the throne so as to reign as Lord and to impart the Spirit to all flesh. He does so to justify sinners in union

---

79. Wolfhart Pannenberg, *Systematic Theology*, 3 vols. (Grand Rapids: Eerdmans, 1991–98), 2:423.

with him and to sanctify the creation in his own image. Thus, Christ's sinlessness is vital to his role as the Spirit Baptizer, and this reality is anchored in the eschatological judgment of the Father.

Christian theologians, therefore, cannot justify or vindicate Christ's sinlessness. Such judgment is out of our hands. But we are compelled to try to understand it theologically as much as possible. How exactly are we to understand this "sinlessness"? Is there not in our efforts to understand it a danger of underestimating the depth to which the Son descended by taking on "flesh" with all that this term implies? As Ivor Davidson puts it:

> What can it mean to say that Jesus of Nazareth, while genuinely human, the inhabitant of a particular historical and cultural space, lived a life that did not exist on the same moral plane as other human lives, and did not exhibit at least some of the same tendencies to error, weakness and failure?[80]

Did Christ have any moral blind spots or insensitivities early on? Did his early focus on Israel mean an exclusion of outsiders? For example, the Christ of Pentecost who comes to share his life with all flesh actually launched his mission almost exclusively within the household of Israel: "I was sent only to the household of Israel" (Matt. 15:24) and instructs his disciples to restrict themselves the same way (Matt. 10:5-6). His open table was thus meant to heal a divide within his own people, specifically between the outcasts and the religious leaders, who were increasingly out of touch with their plight—and often dismissive of it (Luke 14-15). Yet there are striking hints during this time of a broader mission on the horizon. When Jesus first proclaimed his anointing as the Spirit Baptizer, he clashed at his local synagogue with those who rejected his message. By way of response, Jesus pointed to the fact that, amid many Israelites, the only people Elijah ended up healing were Gentiles (Luke 4:24-28). Christ is obviously indicting his own people with this reference. But isn't he also implying the legitimacy of the prophet's reaching out this far? Reading this Lukan text through the lens of Pentecost tempts one to note just such an implication.

Jesus's healing of the centurion's servant from a distance (Matt. 8:5-13) and his ministering to Samaritans are also important. The fact that a woman was among those to whom he ministered was especially surprising

---

80. Davidson, "Pondering the Sinlessness of Jesus Christ," 372.

to his disciples (e.g., John 4:1–26). There seems to have been an unusual openness in Jesus to broader horizons for his ministry; but his initial call to Israel still had strategic significance. He was called to the household of Israel to fulfill the nation's call to witness to the nations of God's goodness. But was this strategic significance all there was to it? Wasn't his early concentration on Israel also indicative of his limitation as a finite human being who needed to grow in his awareness of his identity and mission? Jesus grew in wisdom (Luke 2:52): we must construe the doctrine of his sinlessness in a way that does not deny his finitude—including his growth in wisdom.

However, sinlessness in Christ seems to mean that Jesus's growth in wisdom does not involve downward turns that involve the denial of a divinely ordained path. His growth in wisdom involves a development that fulfills former paths. Noteworthy as an example here is the episode involving the Canaanite woman (Matt. 15:21–28). She cried out continuously for him to help her daughter, to the great annoyance of Jesus's followers. But when the disciples complained to their master, he did not dismiss her; instead, he took the opportunity to engage her:

> Jesus did not answer a word. So his disciples came to him and urged him, "Send her away, for she keeps crying out after us."
> He answered, "I was sent only to the lost sheep of Israel."
> The woman came and knelt before him. "Lord, help me!" she said.
> He replied, "It is not right to take the children's bread and toss it to the dogs."
> "Yes it is, Lord," she said. "Even the dogs eat the crumbs that fall from their master's table."
> Then Jesus said to her, "Woman, you have great faith! Your request is granted." And her daughter was healed at that moment.

On the face of it, Jesus seems at first to want to explain to the woman that he was only sent to redeem Israel. But if this was his only thought, why bother to engage her in conversation at all? Did he do it only to let her down easily? The outcome of the conversation implies otherwise. When Jesus encounters her, she senses her opening and persists. But so does Jesus. He expresses what would have been the sentiment of his disciples in this story. He gives voice to what they must have been thinking. The bread goes to the children who belong to the household of God's covenant and not to the dogs, who do not belong to that household. When she reminds him that the dogs eat the crumbs that fall from the family table, Jesus compliments her for her faith and heals her daughter.

I would not say, as Geza Vermes does, that Jesus was "to a degree, xenophobic" here.[81] On that basis, how could one explain Jesus's praise of the woman's faith at the conclusion of their encounter? His fundamental inclination must have leaned in the direction of showing her favor. Therefore, an about-face or a dramatic conversion on Jesus's part fits neither the text nor the larger Gospel narrative. However, I am also not convinced that Jesus was *only* testing the woman in front of his disciples in order to teach them. It seems that he was indeed testing the boundaries of the disciples' faith, even the faith of his people at that time. Yet, since he was reared in the faith he now tests, he was also pushing at the boundaries of his own evolving awareness of his mission. He certainly seems open and willing to do so, and he does so. I would not deny that the woman challenged Jesus. But the woman's persistence seems to have confirmed in him something that he was inclined toward all along. His own self-understanding as the Spirit Baptizer in Luke 4:24–28 implies as much.

Overall, the above text contains an intriguing exchange that grants us an open window into how Jesus became ever more aware of his Father's will for him in the world, and how he was increasingly willing at every step to push aside limitations placed on him from his own people—his own time and place—in order to yield to what the Father wanted him to become, what the Spirit was leading him to become. This text reveals Jesus's unwavering openness to (and dependence on) the Father and the Spirit in every aspect of his life. But it also shows that, in the process, Jesus was disentangling himself from a systemic problem, as part of his gradual awareness of his far-reaching identity as the Spirit Baptizer, the one who will incorporate and renew all flesh.

The question here is: How does this fact qualify what we say of Jesus's sinlessness? Does his evolving awareness of the full extent of his future mission compromise his sinlessness? Concerning Christ, Ivor Davidson rightly asks: "If, like all human beings, he belonged in a specific web of social relations and a particular context of political and economic realities, was he not implicated in the structural defects and injustices of that environment?"[82]

81. Geza Vermes, *Jesus the Jew: A Historian's Reading of the Gospels* (Philadelphia: Fortress, 1981), 49.

82. Davidson, "Pondering the Sinlessness of Jesus Christ," 372.

Barth makes the bold claim that Jesus did indeed assume flesh under the reign of sin and death, but he overcame it with perfect faithfulness.[83] In Paul Tillich's terms, Christ overcomes estrangement. But it is important to note, as Tillich does, that Christ was not personally bound to estrangement and in need of redemption, as we are. Moreover, though bearing flesh within a fallen world, Christ never acts in ways that would contradict his union with God and self, or his alignment with God's eschatological future for creation. None of his finite limitations adversely affected the fulfillment of his mission, for he overcame whatever barrier stood in the way. His refusal to depart from his Spirit-baptized life with every step of obedience is vindicated by the Father in Christ's passage to exaltation and glorification.

A good place to start in arriving at this idea of Christ's sinlessness is Tillich's general outline of three points that provide us with a framework for understanding this doctrine. First, we must affirm "the complete finitude of Christ." We must not attribute to him, in his embodied existence on earth, infinite freedom or insight. Second, there is also "the reality of the temptations growing out of [this finitude]." Christ is genuinely tempted and assailed. Third, his victory over these temptations, which constitutes his sinlessness, is to be understood theologically as his consistent and unfailing union with God and self. Tillich notes that there are "no traces of estrangement between him and God and consequently between him and himself."[84] Locating this sinlessness within Christ's relationship to God means that Christ has no goodness in himself apart from God; rather, he depends on God for all things precisely as the Son of the Father and man of the Spirit. Jesus thus says at one point: "Why do you call me good? No one is good—except God alone" (Luke 18:19). In commenting on this text, Tillich says:

> He rejects the term "good" as applicable to himself in isolation from God and puts the problem in the right place, namely, the uniqueness of his relation to God. His goodness is goodness only in so far as he participates in the goodness of God.[85]

One has to thus recognize his essential unity with God to understand the ultimate source of his goodness. One could add that Christ's goodness is

---

83. Barth, *Church Dogmatics*, IV/2, *Doctrine of Reconciliation*, trans. G. W. Bromiley (Edinburgh: T & T Clark, 1958), 92.

84. Paul Tillich, *Systematic Theology*, vol. 2 (Chicago: University of Chicago Press, 1957), 127, 126.

85. Tillich, *Systematic Theology*, 2:127.

in his consistent alignment with God's kingdom and liberating future for creation.

Divine and Human

Now that we have discussed challenges to Jesus's full and unique humanity, our concern must turn to how we should understand the hypostatic union, that is, the union of divine and human natures in the one person of Christ. John 1:14 says that "the Word became flesh and made his dwelling among us." Herein lay the ancient debate. On the one hand, when we say with John 1:14 that the Word "became flesh," we are certainly supporting the inseparable union of the Word and flesh. But how do we protect the flesh from being mutated in the process? For example, do we end up proposing that there was a "mingling" of deity and flesh at the incarnation, as the fourth-century theologian Gregory of Nyssa put it?[86] In that case, does Jesus bear authentic flesh? Gregory certainly thought so. As I have noted above, his view of Christ's authentic humanity is clear: "He had to experience all that belongs to our nature" so that he could take all dimensions of our existence up into the renewal of life.[87] Still, it is doubtful that words like "mingling" grant us the resources we need to avoid saying that Jesus's flesh is inauthentic. On the other hand, when we say with John 1:14 that the divine Word "made his dwelling among us," we are surely implying a clear distinction between the divine Word and flesh. But are we protecting their inseparable union at the incarnation? Is the term "indwelling" sufficient to secure this inseparable union? What is to prevent us from understanding this term to mean that God indwelt Jesus in a way that was not qualitatively different from God's indwelling us? What is to prevent us from using this term to keep the divine Son at arm's length from the human suffering and death endured by Jesus?

The burden that the Chalcedonian Definition (451 CE) will seek to carry is to offer us an articulation of the incarnation that honors both the distinction of natures (as truly divine and truly human) and their inseparability in the one person of Christ. The Chalcedonian Definition reads as follows:

86. Gregory of Nyssa, *Address on Religious Instruction* 11, in *Christology of the Later Fathers*, ed. Edward R. Hardy (Louisville: John Knox, 2006), 288.

87. Gregory of Nyssa, *Address on Religious Instruction* 32.

We, then, following the holy Fathers, all with one consent, teach men to confess one and the same Son, our Lord Jesus Christ, the same perfect in Godhead and also perfect in manhood; truly God and truly man, of a reasonable [rational] soul and body; consubstantial [co-essential] with the Father according to the Godhead, and consubstantial with us according to the Manhood; in all things like unto us, without sin; begotten before all ages of the Father according to the Godhead, and in these latter days, for us and for our salvation, born of the Virgin Mary, the Mother of God, according to the Manhood; one and the same Christ, Son, Lord, Only begotten, to be acknowledged in two natures, without confusion, change, division, or separation; the distinction of natures being by no means taken away by the unity, but rather the property of each nature being preserved, and concurring in one Person and one Subsistence, not parted or divided into two persons, but one and the same Son, and only begotten, God the Word, the Lord Jesus Christ; as the prophets from the beginning [have declared] concerning him, and the Lord Jesus Christ himself has taught us, and the Creed of the holy Fathers has handed down to us.

The core idea of the Definition is this: The one "person" (*hypostasis*) of Christ is to be acknowledged in two "natures" (*physeis*) "without confusion, change, division, or separation." The problem of one person acknowledged in two natures (without confusion or separation) has its source in the ancient confession of Romans 1:3–4, where Christ is viewed according to the "flesh" (earthly life) and according to the "Spirit" (raised from the dead). Christ according to the flesh is raised by the Spirit to be the mediator of life. This distinction was read back to Jesus's Jordan experience and conception in Mary's womb, where Jesus as flesh is anointed by the Spirit to be the mediator of life to others. Eventually, these two Christological lenses, flesh and Spirit, were overtaken by the Johannine flesh and Word or the Word become flesh (John 1:14), with the emphasis shifting from the resurrection to the incarnation. The Johannine flesh and Word then later became the "two natures" at Chalcedon.

One senses a move here to something more abstract, and, as I noted in our preceding chapter, this is where a potential problem lies. We dare not forget that these "natures" are actually lenses through which to view the one embodied life given over to the Father and the leading of the Spirit, destined to be vindicated as identical with the eternal Word, or Son of the Father, the means of mediating the Spirit to all flesh. These are not "natures" with opposing properties in need of synthesis; instead, they are the presence of the divine Son in action among us—*divine strength embodied in human weakness*. This is more particularly the person of the eternal Son in the flesh, willing to drink the cup of our alienation and death in order to bring us into the Spirit of communion and life. The paradox of this reality is the paradox of grace, which is apparent in some sense in all of life. All of life implicitly bears witness to what God did in Christ. It was implicit at the point of creation, when God through the Son and by the Spirit overcame the emptiness to call up order and beauty.

Keeping this preface in mind, we can explore the conflict that led more immediately to the Chalcedonian Definition. What led to this idea that the two natures in Christ (divine and human) are united in a way that is unconfused (or distinct) but still inseparable? The fourth-century theologian Apollinaris of Laodicea was understood as "confusing" the two natures in Christ. He perceived the incarnation to have such a strong emphasis on Christ's divine nature that he neglected Christ's human nature to some extent, which one could somewhat crudely refer to as an "absorbing" of the human by the divine, or a "confusing," or "commingling," of the two natures of Christ in favor of the divine. Of course, it goes without saying that an overabundance of deity does not diminish humanity; in fact, it only liberates and fulfills us. Yet this abundance is in the divine wisdom to be poured out through the taking up of flesh like ours in every way typical of human existence, so that human flesh in all dimensions of its existence could be taken up into the divine embrace.

Problematically in this light, Apollinaris concludes that "it is inconceivable that the same person should be both God and an entire man."[88] Instead, for Apollinaris, Christ existed "in the singleness of an incarnate divine nature which is commingled [with flesh]."[89] "O new creation and divine mixture!" he exclaims, "God and flesh completed one and the same nature!"[90] It is not so much the "one nature" that is troubling as the idea of one nature that is a "commingling" of the divine and human, without a proper distinction between them. As I have suggested, the idea of mingling the natures was indeed used elsewhere, but his use of it raised concerns about the need to protect the humanity of Christ from being absorbed through the incarna-

---

88. Apollinaris of Laodicea, *On the Union in Christ of the Body with the Godhead* 9, in *The Christological Controversy*, trans. and ed. Richard A. Norris Jr., Sources of Early Christian Thought (Philadelphia: Fortress, 1980), 103–7.

89. Apollinaris of Laodicea, *On the Union in Christ of the Body with the Godhead* 9.

90. Apollinaris of Laodicea, *On the Union in Christ of the Body with the Godhead* 10.

tion. Christ had to be truly and fully human to be the human sacrament of the impartation of the Spirit to all flesh.

It was against this Apollinarian threat that Nestorius, Bishop of Constantinople, aimed his theological guns. Nestorius's supreme passion was to avoid having the humanity of Christ absorbed into his deity. For Nestorius, this "confusing" of the humanity of Jesus with the Son's divine nature compromised both Christ's humanity and deity.[91] He assumed that dissolving Christ's humanity into his deity would compromise Christ's immutable, impassible deity by exposing it directly to suffering and death. Nestorius attempted to avoid such dangers by radically separating the two natures in Christ, assigning them different functions, and relating them to one another through a mutual cooperation in which both willfully chose one another in a voluntary union. The incarnation is a free, voluntary cooperation between the divine Son and the human Jesus that continues throughout Christ's life. The two natures are "separated in essence, but united by love."[92] To avoid confusing the two natures, Nestorius went to the opposite extreme: separating them from each other to the point that they could function independently of each other and in cooperation with one another.

For Nestorius, the two natures are involved in the freedom of mutual conjunction, interrelation, cooperation, or *synapheia*.[93] Of course, Jesus Christ did display a relationship of devotion with his heavenly Father; however, Nestorius spoke problematically of a loving cooperation and interaction *of the divine Son* and the human Jesus. Thus, for Nestorius, one cannot say that Jesus as a man raised Lazarus from the dead, or that the Logos, or Son, died on the cross.[94] Motivated in part by the desire to distance Christology from ancient religious myths of gods being born of earthly women, Nestorius refused to call Mary the *theotokos,* or God-bearer. Mary does not bear the divine Logos in her womb; the Logos is merely "in conjunction" with the "Christ" she bore.[95] Conversely, to say of the baby Jesus that he was "God wrapped in swaddling bands" would be "blasphemous nonsense!"[96] Nestorius would not even say that the eternal Son was born of Mary; the Son merely passed through Mary in conjunction with the human person

91. John McGuckin, *Saint Cyril of Alexandria and the Christological Controversy* (Crestwood, NY: St. Vladimir's Seminary Press, 2004), 150.

92. Nestorius, *Book of Heraclides* 81; quoted in McGuckin, *Saint Cyril of Alexandria,* 162.

93. McGuckin, *Saint Cyril of Alexandria,* 162.

94. McGuckin, *Saint Cyril of Alexandria,* 152–53.

95. *Nestorius' Second Letter to Cyril,* in Norris, *Christological Controversy,* 137.

96. Nestorius, *Book of Heraclides* 59; quoted in McGuckin, *Saint Cyril of Alexandria,* 154.

of Jesus that was born through her womb. There is no question that, for Nestorius, there were only two possibilities for Christology: either an Apollinarian fusion of the two natures (divine and human) in such a way that the humanity of Christ is dissolved into (or mutated by) the divine, or a radical separation of the two natures in which the Logos indwells and cooperates with the man Jesus. Not only that, but for Nestorius, the two natures may be said to act independently of one another, perform different tasks, have different experiences, and be bound in intimate union through a free and voluntary mutual love. That there could be a third alternative between these two extremes had not crossed his mind.

Though Nestorius attempted to avoid supporting two subjects in Christ, and even in his mature writing advocated beginning with the experience of the one person of Christ, the drift of his thought supports a bifurcation of two subjects in Christ.[97] Most damaging is the fact that one ends up removing the divine Son from Christ's human experiences, especially his suffering and death on the cross. Separating the natures in Christ the way Nestorius does removes the divine Son from our baptism in fire. Gone is the paradox of grace, the paradox of the Spirit Baptizer who bears our baptism of fire. What is the divine Son in Nestorius's thought other than a sympathetic spectator at this fire baptism? Nestorius says that, at the resurrection, the divine Son "stooped down to raise up what had collapsed, but he did not fall."[98] Relating the divine Son to the crucifixion is, of course, a larger problem in the fourth and fifth centuries, but it is especially problematic in Nestorius's handling of it.

Bishop Cyril of Alexandria had the theological talent to confront Nestorius's extreme reaction to Apollinaris, so his theology ended up being the definitive influence on Christology for the Council of Chalcedon and for the fifth century in general. It may be said that what Athanasius was to the fourth century, Cyril was to the fifth. Cyril navigated Christology creatively between the Apollinarian and Nestorian extremes. He started by making the Logos, or Word of the Father, the locus of personhood in the Son. From this Cyril concludes: "To the Logos alone can be attributed the authorship of, and responsibility for," all of Christ's actions.[99] He regards the role of the human soul in the body and the role of the divine Logos in the incarnate

---

97. McGuckin, *Saint Cyril of Alexandria*, 158.

98. *Nestorius' First Sermon against the Theotokos*, in Norris, *Christological Controversy*, 125.

99. McGuckin, *Saint Cyril of Alexandria*, 186.

Christ to be analogous.[100] Yet he attributes a distinct human soul to Jesus.[101] Since the acting subject of Christ is, for Cyril, principally the divine Logos or Son, Cyril does not say that the Son became "a man" at the incarnation, as though the Son, at the incarnation, simply indwelt an autonomous human agent whose humanity is potentially complete even without the incarnation. He writes of the divine Son: "He did not come in a man, but became flesh, that is, became man."[102] He means by this that the humanity of Christ only becomes a fully human person ("man") through unity with the eternal Son. Cyril's Christology was strongly unitive, which means that it had a strong emphasis on Christ as a single subject or person, the divine Son of the Father.

Cyril's unitive Christology means that the crucifixion is the act of the God-human, Jesus Christ, where Christ may be said to have "suffered impassibly."[103] He suffers death on the cross as the God-human in order to impart life to others:

> He surrendered his own body to death even though by nature he is life and is himself the Resurrection (John 11:25). He trampled upon death with unspeakable power, so that he might, in his own flesh, become the "first-born from the dead" (Col. 1:18) and the "first-fruits of those who have fallen asleep" (1 Cor. 15:20).[104]

Impassible suffering is one of a number of paradoxes that the incarnation occasions for Cyril. This paradox is the paradox of grace, the same as the one implied in the fact that the Baptizer in the Spirit must bear our baptism in fire in order to conquer it on our behalf. In a relatively recent opposition to the idea of divine impassiblity, Jürgen Moltmann does not hesitate to speak of divine suffering precisely out of the fullness of life that accounts for God's overcoming love.[105] Moltmann has no difficulty saying that God the Father suffers in the sense that the Father delivers up the Son to suffering, which is something Cyril would not have said. Yet I cannot help but also see

---

100. McGuckin, *Saint Cyril of Alexandria*, 4.

101. *The Third Letter of Cyril to Nestorius* 8, in McGuckin, *Saint Cyril of Alexandria*, 266–75.

102. *Homily Given at Ephesus on St. John's Day, in the Church of St. John*, in McGuckin, *Saint Cyril of Alexandria*, 280–81.

103. *Scolia on the Incarnation* 33, in McGuckin, *Saint Cyril of Alexandria*, 294–95.

104. McGuckin, *Saint Cyril of Alexandria*, 6.

105. Jürgen Moltmann, *The Trinity and the Kingdom* (San Francisco: Harper and Row, 1981), 45.

a connection between Cyril's impassible divine suffering in the flesh and Moltmann's divine suffering out of the fullness of divine life and longing for the other. This is because impassibility was not, among the church fathers, a lack of divine passion; rather, it was the transcendent abundance of divine life that overcomes all suffering.[106] God does suffer in the flesh—does take on our baptism of fire—but in a way appropriate to God.

Cyril's key point is to be found in his insistence that the human sojourn of Jesus, though involving the full range of human capacities, limitations, and experiences, is principally determined by the Logos. This emphasis on the Logos as the principal and dominant determination in the unity of natures does not mean that Cyril diminishes or dissolves Christ's humanity. He seeks in his own way to affirm two natures that are unconfused: "We say that Jesus Christ is one and the same, even though we recognize the difference of natures and keep them unconfused with each other."[107] Note that he says here that we "recognize" two natures when speaking of the one and the same Christ. He does not, however, go so far as to say that Christ exists after the incarnation "in" two natures as metaphysically distinct realities.[108] We "recognize" two natures rather as something akin to abstractions drawn from one embodied life given over to the determination of the one subject of the eternal Son. Thus, rather than speak of the Christ "*in* two natures" as Nestorius would say, Cyril preferred to speak of the one person of Christ as "out of two natures" into one.[109] For Cyril, it is "talking rubbish" to claim that a one-nature doctrine removes Christ's distinct and authentic humanity.[110] There is one nature to the incarnate Christ for Cyril because the humanity of Christ belongs entirely to the divine Logos and yields completely to the divine nature and purpose. The idea here is that of Christ as "deified" in his humanity by the divine Logos, being wholly determined as the Logos's transformative self-expression. As the Word of the Father is the self-expression of the Father, the embodied life of Christ is the self-expression of the divine Word.

Supporting Cyril's Christology is the typically Alexandrian understanding of salvation as the deification of the human (humanity was made to

---

106. Helpful here is Thomas Weinandy, *Does God Suffer?* See also Daniel Castello, *The Apathetic God: Exploring the Contemporary Relevance of Divine Impassibility*, Paternoster Theological Monographs (Eugene, OR: Wipf and Stock, 2009).

107. *Scolia on the Incarnation* 13.

108. *Cyril's Letter to Eulogius*, in McGuckin, *Saint Cyril of Alexandria*, 349–51.

109. McGuckin, *Saint Cyril of Alexandria*, 149.

110. *Second Letter of Cyril to Succensus* 3, in McGuckin, *Saint Cyril of Alexandria*, 359–63.

partake of the divine nature), which is different from the accent on cooperation with God toward the graced life (traditionally connected to Antioch), which informs Nestorius's Christology. Cyril's unitive Christology has as its purpose the idea that the humanity of Jesus is to be the means (we might say "sacrament") of the Son's impartation of the Spirit of life to all flesh. According to Cyril, Adam lost the Spirit by departing from God, so the divine Son became flesh in order to make humanity "worthy of the Spirit again by being restored to our earlier condition." As human, Christ is anointed by the Spirit so that, as divine, he could anoint those who believe in him "with his own Spirit."[111] "For he is sanctified as man and baptized as man, but he sanctifies as God and baptizes in the Holy Spirit."[112] Cyril asks, Why was Jesus's body alone the giver of the Spirit? The answer is: "Because Christ is not a God-bearing man like other saints but rather is truly God, higher than all creation."[113] The humanity of Jesus is like a glowing coal aflame with the self-giving Logos, allowing that incarnate humanity to freely become the means of the Son's impartation of life.[114] In support of Cyril, we might add that the human mission of bearing the Spirit in order to bless others frees and fulfills human nature rather than reducing it. Human personhood is fulfilled by being given over entirely to the divine. As long as all human capacities are noted as participating in the divine life and mission, humanity is not diminished by partaking of the divine nature.

One-nature language does indeed require qualification to avoid an Apollinarian merging of the natures in Christ. Under the influence of Leo's Tome (a letter sent out from Pope Leo I), the Chalcedonian Definition ended up avoiding it. But Cyril intended by it a Christoformistic anthropology that describes humanity as created to image the personhood of the eternal Son by bearing the Spirit. It is not intellect or will that is ideally most core to ideal personhood, but "the act of divine power which first creates man" to image the Son. Therefore, to say that there is one nature to Christ that involves an unconfused divine and human union is a testimony to this Christoformistic anthropology.[115] This view of the incarnation has Jesus's humanity finding its eschatological fulfillment and ultimate freedom *as human* through the incarnation. It is not that we need to keep Jesus's humanity separate from the divine Logos (as an autonomous acting agent) in order to preserve the

---

111. *Scolia on the Incarnation* 1, in McGuckin, *Saint Cyril of Alexandria*, 295.

112. *Scolia on the Incarnation* 34, in McGuckin, *Saint Cyril of Alexandria*, 330.

113. *Scolia on the Incarnation* 24, in McGuckin, *Saint Cyril of Alexandria*, 317.

114. *Scolia on the Incarnation* 9, in McGuckin, *Saint Cyril of Alexandria*, 301–2.

115. McGuckin, *Saint Cyril of Alexandria*, 206.

fullness and freedom of Jesus's humanity, as Nestorius assumed. Complete human autonomy is an idolatrous delusion. Rather, it is through the incarnation, in union with the divine Logos by the Spirit, that Jesus's humanity gains its fullness and freedom. For Cyril, to continue to speak of two natures after the incarnation is to give in to the illusion that human autonomy with respect to God is needed for human fullness and freedom.

How much of Cyril's vision is actually supported by the Chalcedonian Definition is debated, in part because the Definition lacks clarity. What does it really say? The term *hypostasis* (person) at Nicaea simply meant "nature," or what unifies Christ and the Father (and, we might add, the Spirit). By the time we reach Chalcedon, the term—through the rise of Trinitarian theology—had taken on the meaning of "person," not exactly in the sense we mean the term today (as a self-conscious ego) but still in a way that carried the significance of a subject or agent of action. Natures (*physeis*) were thought to have distinct properties that distinguished one reality from another. But beyond these seminal thoughts, it is not clear what the Chalcedonian Definition meant by the terms "one person" (*hypostasis*, and how it is to be defined) and two "natures" (*physeis*, how they are to be understood). For this supposedly being a Definition, it does not define much![116]

Chalcedon simply wanted to avoid the extremes of Apollinaris and Nestorius. Its major function was to sweep away undesirable alternatives in order to open debate for how the deity and humanity of Christ are to be positively understood. This challenge is met historically in subsequent commentary on the Definition, specifically by using Cyril to clearly identify the eternal Logos of the Father as the person of Christ, who unites human nature to himself.[117] There are, indeed, elements from Leo's Tome in the Definition, which did, in fact, use the Nestorian sense of "in two natures." I agree with John McGuckin, however, that the bulk of the Definition owes much to Cyril. In the Definition, Mary is the *theotokos* (God bearer) with the softer language of Christ as "*acknowledged* in two natures" (rather than existing or subsisting in two natures). The softer language is Cyrillian, since he tended to see the distinction of natures after the incarnation as acknowledged theologically rather than actually distinguishable in reality. The Definition then proceeds

---

116. See Sarah Coakley, "What Does Chalcedon Solve and What Does It Not? Some Reflections on the Status and Meaning of the Chalcedonian 'Definition,'" in *The Incarnation*, ed. Stephen T. Davis et al. (New York: Oxford University Press, 2002), 143–63, esp. 162.

117. See Robert W. Jenson, *Systematic Theology*, vol. 1: *The Triune God* (New York: Oxford University Press, 1997), 132–33.

to list the adverbs that describe the relationships of the natures: uncon-fusedly, unchangeably, indivisibly, inseparably—all of which are from Cyril.[118]

Though the natures are not to be confused (*contra* Apollinaris), neither are they to be separated (*contra* Nestorius). But this still does not tell us much about whether or not the Definition sides with Cyril in making the one person of Christ the eternal Logos. There was undoubtedly room for the Cyrillian notion of the one person as the divine Logos, and this would not have dissolved the human personhood of Christ, but fulfilled it. It is conceivable that the human personhood of Christ as subject is fully human precisely by being the self-declaration of the eternal Logos. As Pannenberg has shown, Jesus is revealed to be identical with the eternal Logos precisely in being given over entirely to the Father and the Spirit for the sake of the world, as the Logos has eternally been. Bonhoeffer agrees: "This person's being God is not something added onto the human being of Jesus Christ."[119] This is not to be conceived of as a cooperation between the man Jesus and the eternal Logos. The man Jesus has no such independence from the Logos's devotion to the Father or the leading of the Spirit. Rather, the humanity of Jesus has no existence other than as the self-declaration of the Logos in human flesh for the sake of the world. Viewed from one angle, Christ is human because he is wholly given over to God; viewed from another angle, Christ is the eternal Logos as the subject of Christ's entire life of self-giving. It is thus the Cyrillian and not the Nestorian trajectory that is most promising for a Christology today that *acknowledges* one person "in two natures" without treating these natures as two abstract "entities" that require unification.

On a more positive note, Chalcedon not only clears the way for or-thodox theological construction; it preserves a certain amount of mystery, a level of apophatic reticence needed for humble dialogue.[120] There is no question that this reticence allows us to be sensitive to the subtle ways in which Chalcedon respects the limits of language to capture the incarnation. Sarah Coakley observes that the language of Chalcedon excludes extreme positions that threaten Christ's full humanity or full deity, "but without any support that this doctrinal regulation thereby *explains* or *grasps* the real-ity towards which it points."[121] Michael Welker also makes this point in a

---

118. McGuckin, *St. Cyril of Alexandria*, 227–43.

119. Dietrich Bonhoeffer, "Lectures on Christology (Student Notes)," *Dietrich Bonhoeffer Works*, vol. 12: *Berlin, 1932–1933* (Minneapolis: Augsburg Fortress, 2009), 353; Michael Welker, *God the Revealed: Christology* (Grand Rapids: Eerdmans, 2013), 273.

120. Coakley, "What Does Chalcedon Solve?," 162.

121. Coakley, "What Does Chalcedon Solve?," 161 (italics in original).

compelling way by drawing from Dietrich Bonhoeffer. In his early lectures on Christology, Bonhoeffer notes that the four adverbs ("unconfusedly, unchangeably, indivisibly, inseparably")—in relating the two natures—seek to show that one cannot treat these two natures in the same way one would treat objects, things, or facts.[122] He thus "picks up these concepts of nature (or two natures) and then immediately bursts them."[123]

Yet Cyril requires clarification, too. The matter of the incarnation is more complex than merely saying that the eternal Son is the person of Jesus Christ. This is certainly true, but it must be declared in a way that allows us to call Christ's person genuinely human as well, something to which Cyril would not have been opposed. Seen from one angle, Jesus is human in being wholly given over to the Father as the self-declaration of the Logos, or Son; but, viewed from another angle, Jesus is the divine Son as wholly given over to the Father, as wedded to humanity through incarnation. Each is defined with reference to the other and, in God's eternal self-determination, it was always meant to be that way. But it is the eternal Son who takes the initiative in the incarnation. Every aspect of the human life of Jesus is identical with him, because the eternal Son has willed that it be so; has willed to be the one who incarnates this flesh; has willed that Jesus of Nazareth be defined as the self-declaration of himself for the sake of humanity. This divine decision does not cancel out the human subject, but fulfills it, for humanity was created to be the incarnation of the Son and to image or reveal the Son by the anointing of the Spirit.

Human personhood was created to be fulfilled by the cross, the resurrection, and Pentecost, to participate in God's abundant self-giving to creation. As the dwelling place of the Spirit, humanity is called to be distinct from the Logos; however, precisely in the Spirit, humanity was also made for the Logos—for incarnation. This fact makes Jesus the only archetypical human. The term *anhypostasis* refers to the fact that Jesus has no human personhood apart from the person of the eternal Son; *enhypostasis* means that Jesus only has human personhood in the person of the eternal Son. Barth says of Jesus's human flesh at the incarnation that "the flesh not only could not be the flesh apart from the Word, but apart from the Word it could have no being at all."[124] Being fully human means being one in person with the eternal Son for the purpose of fulfilling the

122. Bonhoeffer, "Lectures on Christology," 343; Welker, *God the Revealed*, 271.
123. Welker, *God the Revealed*, 271.
124. Barth, *Church Dogmatics*, I/2, 136.

promise of the Father, namely, imparting the Spirit and the image of the Son to all of creation.

Karl Rahner helps us understand the hypostatic unity of the divine Word and flesh in the incarnation precisely under the rubric of the outpouring of divine love. As divine love revealed, the Word of the Father expresses himself when he empties himself, which is why the Word is eternally earmarked for incarnation. Human nature was originally made in the image of that Word, of his self-giving love.[125] "Man *is* insofar as he gives up himself."[126] Thus, for Rahner—and implicitly for Cyril and Pannenberg—"when the Word becomes man, his humanity is not prior. It is something that comes to be and is constituted in essence and existence when and in so far as the Word empties himself."[127] Personhood is shown in Christ to be fulfilled by self-giving in order to embrace the other. This is the kenotic human person who is not fulfilled until he or she opens that fulfillment to others. Divine transcendence is revealed in the eschatological freedom to love that is embodied in the Son and mediated by the Son (overflowing his self-sacrificial life) to the world in the outpoured Spirit. We mimic Christ when, by believing in him out of our innermost being, the blessings of life in the Spirit flow (John 4:14; 7:38). We are eternally merely participants in this humanity. His alone is the genuine article.

It is important that the hypostatic union (one person of Christ acknowledged in two distinct natures—divine and human) means that Jesus has in his humanity "*so far as it is possible for a human*, the very relationship of the Son to the Father in the Trinity."[128] Of course, God has attributes that infinitely exceed those of the human life of Jesus. As I noted in the preceding chapter, Thomas Morris has suggested that we think of this unity of the transcendent and incarnate Son along the lines of an analogy drawn from different levels of human consciousness, such as one's conscious and subconscious mind. For example, the conscious mind is not aware of all that is present in the subconscious mind. So one could think of Jesus's fully human mind and action as wholly expressive of the transcendent mind and life of the divine Son, but in a more *limited, human* way, or without entirely expressing all of the divine capacities until glorification.[129]

---

125. Karl Rahner, "On the Theology of the Incarnation," in *Theological Investigations*, vol. 4: *More Recent Writings* (New York: Crossroad, 1982), 116.

126. Rahner, "On the Theology of the Incarnation," 110 (italics added).

127. Rahner, "On the Theology of the Incarnation," 116.

128. Coffey, "The Theandric Nature of Christ," 425 (italics added).

129. Thomas V. Morris, "The Metaphysics of God Incarnate," in *Oxford Readings in Phil-*

The kenotic Son bears kenotic humanity so as to plunge into the depths of human despair. The infinite power of the self-giving love that characterizes the Son in his eternal relationship with the Father will not be fully revealed until the climactic moments of Christ's life. In exalted form, overflowing with life for all flesh, Christ reveals that "God was pleased to have all his fullness dwell in him" (Col. 1:19). He bears weak and limited flesh into the depths of alienation in order to bring flesh into this liberating fullness. The eternal Son is not diminished by the incarnation; instead, he is revealed by it, for the infinite freedom of his love is a freedom *for* us and not *from* us. Likewise, the humanity of Jesus is not diminished by the incarnation; it is rather fulfilled by it. Yes, the Son experiences in this union all that opposes God. God bears all things in loving us. The eternal Son experiences what opposes his very essence in order to bring that essence to the fullness of self-disclosure as the essence of a love that bears all burdens for the sake of others. And the humanity of Jesus is taken up into what transcends humanity in order to become the revelation of a humanity that is oriented toward the other in steadfast love. This seems to be the intention behind the doctrine that was fully articulated in the seventh century by John of Damascus: the *communicatio idiomatum* (communication of properties) occasioned by the incarnation between the eternal Son and the human life assumed by the Son.[130] The one person of the divine Son has the transcendent properties of deity, but in the incarnation he claims the properties of humanity in the impartation of divine love to humanity. In the process, the Son, who has divine properties, can experience suffering and death in the flesh, and the flesh can experience exaltation in order to overcome death and be the sacrament of life to all flesh.

Conclusion

The triune God incorporates creation into the divine life at Pentecost through the Word made flesh and the impartation of the Spirit by the Word to all flesh. As the Logos made flesh, Christ was fully divine, internal to God, and thus essential and indispensable to the divine self-giving to all flesh.

---

osophical Theology, vol. 1: *Trinity, Incarnation, Atonement*, ed. Michael Rea (New York: Oxford University Press, 2009), 211–24.

130. The best explanation of this doctrine is given by Charles C. Twombly, *Perichoresis and Personhood: God, Christ, and Salvation in John of Damascus*, Princeton Theological Monographs (Eugene, OR: Pickwick, 2015).

He who bore the Spirit of life bore our death so as to bring us life. The chief concern of Christology is, therefore, to preserve Jesus Christ's essential unity with the Father and the Holy Spirit in order to remain faithful to Christ as the anointed Spirit Baptizer, the incarnation of the divine Son. For only the Lord can redeem us from death and restore us to life. The incarnation means that the eternal Son would take on humanity to be the Spirit Baptizer for all of creation. The human personhood of Jesus would be fulfilled precisely in being wholly identified with this Son, as the disclosure of the person of this Son, this one who pours himself out from his never-ending fullness so that others may be filled. Christ's humanity is typical of flesh in our fallen world, since Christ must bear our flesh so as to redeem and renew all flesh in every dimension of its existence. However, since Christ's humanity is ideal, it is also unique, conceived by the Spirit under the sign of a virginal conception and lived out in sinless faithfulness to his Father—and destined for exaltation. In a sense, Jesus is more fully human than we are.

Humanity can never be ideal exactly as Christ is. We cannot be united to the eternal Son as Jesus was. His flesh was uniquely united to the Son so that he alone could be the quintessential human, the eschatological Adam who is the life-giving Spirit Baptizer for all flesh (1 Cor. 15:45; cf. 12:13). All true human dignity reflects him in some way. By receiving the Spirit from him, through faith in him, we become shaped in Christ's image in communion with him, each of us yielding in diverse ways and from diverse contexts in witness to Christ by the Spirit. We are becoming persons in him. But our personhood will always be qualified as derivative and in witness to his, never one with the eternal Son, as his is. Like John the Baptist, we are not the light of truth; he alone is that (John 1:8). In union with Christ and in living witness to him, humanity finds true freedom and authenticity. Humanity was made to be the dwelling place of the Spirit in the image of the Son. We were formed from the formless and lifeless dust by the Father's Word and by the living breath of God (Gen. 2:7). In the words of Job 33:4, "the Spirit of God has made me; the breath of the Almighty gives me life." All of humanity was made to be God's offspring, to live in filial relationship with God's Son, to live in and from God's Spirit (Acts 17:24–28). Pentecost becomes the fulfillment of creation. The sound of a mighty rushing wind breathed forth through the embodied life of Jesus (the declaration, or sacrament, of the new humanity) brings into being the messianic community as the Spirit-baptized witnesses to the exalted Christ as Lord of all.

CHAPTER 4

The Jordan and the Life of Jesus

"So the Spirit of God descended upon him . . . that we might be saved."

—Irenaeus, *Against Heresies* 3.9.3

We can join with James Dunn in saying without hesitation that "the decisive change in the ages was effected by the Spirit coming down upon Jesus."[1] This entire chapter will allow us to circle around the significance of that statement. Why was Jesus's reception of the Spirit of such pivotal significance to the era of salvation? Note Walter Kasper's insight that "the mediation between God and man in Jesus Christ can be understood theologically only as an event 'in the Holy Spirit.'"[2] Jesus's reception of the Spirit at the Jordan is thus a pivotal salvation-historical event because Jesus's entire mission will be fulfilled in and through the Spirit. Jesus's reception of the Spirit after his baptism and the life that follows is enormously significant to salvation history.

Note the key Scripture text depicting Jesus's reception of the Spirit: "Just as Jesus was coming up out of the water, he saw heaven being torn open and the Spirit descending on him like a dove. And a voice came from heaven: 'You are my Son, whom I love; with you I am well pleased'" (Mark 1:10–11). The scene is the Jordan River, where John the Baptist had just baptized Jesus. John announced earlier that one would come after him, not to baptize people with water as John had done, but rather to "baptize" people in the Holy Spirit and fire (1:8). He observes: "The man on whom you see the Spirit come down and remain is the one who will baptize with the Holy Spirit. I

---

1. James D. G. Dunn, *Baptism in the Holy Spirit*, Studies in Biblical Theology, Second Series 15 (London: SCM Press, 1970), 26.
2. Walter Kasper, *Jesus the Christ* (Kent, UK: Burns and Oates, 1976), 249.

have seen and I testify that this is God's Chosen One" (John 1:33), for on him the Father bestows the Spirit "without limit" (3:34). This event is rooted in the incarnation and finds its confirmation and purpose at Pentecost. Jesus is baptized in the Spirit in order to baptize all flesh in the Spirit.

Christ received the Spirit that we might be saved. How so? The Spirit rests on Christ in order to rest on us through him. In resting on us through Christ, the Spirit enables us to participate in Christ's life and destiny. This means that the Spirit's resting on Christ at the Jordan not only launched Jesus's public ministry but is a salvation-historical event in its own right. Rooted in Jesus's conception by the Spirit in Mary's womb (Luke 1:35) and reaching for the climactic moments of Jesus's work (24:49; Acts 2:33–36), Jesus's anointing by the Spirit at the Jordan is an utterly unique moment in the history of salvation. How unique? John 3:34 tells us that the Spirit rests on Jesus *without limit*, and 1:33 indicates that the Spirit rests on Jesus *permanently*. Kilian McDonnell explains: "Jesus, therefore, fully and permanently possesses the Spirit, and can impart the Spirit after the resurrection . . . out of his own fullness."[3]

Resting on the Son fully and permanently, the Spirit overflows Christ's fullness at Pentecost in order to draw us into union with Christ by faith. Indeed, with regard to Christ, "God gives the Spirit without limit" (John 3:34). John baptized in the Jordan River, but the Spirit that rests on Christ will not be thus localized or have such boundaries. Christ is excessively filled with the Spirit in order to grant all flesh a share in his rich and boundless abundance. Christ's reception of the Spirit at the Jordan eschatologically transcends the historical moment as the abundant and overflowing bestowal of the Father's love through the medium of the life of the faithful Son. Irenaeus writes: "So the Spirit of God descended upon him . . . that we might be saved by receiving from the abundance of his anointing."[4] Pointing to the eschatological destiny of Jesus as the source of life (the firstborn from the dead), Paul says, "For God was pleased to have all his fullness dwell in him" (Col. 1:19).

This fullness is abundant and overflowing. It crashes through the barriers of sin and death and permeates every dimension of Jesus's humanity with the glory of God. Not only that, but it overflows Jesus's exalted body in order to come upon all flesh. Christ grants the abundant rains of the Spirit

---

3. Kilian McDonnell, *The Baptism of Jesus in the Jordan: Trinitarian and Cosmic Order of Salvation* (Collegeville, MN: Liturgical Press, 1996), 11.

4. Irenaeus, *Against Heresies* 3.9.3; quoted in M. C. Steenberg, *Of God and Man: Theology as Anthropology from Athanasius to Irenaeus* (Edinburgh: Bloomsbury T & T Clark, 2009), 36.

to be poured down everywhere from heaven, which leads to rivers or floods on earth that will water the soil and cause diverse forms of life to spring forth (Ezek. 47:1–12). Indeed, out of him will flow rivers of living water (John 7:38), and drinking from these streams will satisfy the soul to the point that we will ultimately never thirst again. Baptized in the Spirit, we drink of the Spirit from Christ (1 Cor. 12:13). Jesus said to the woman at the well: "Whoever drinks of the water that I will give him shall never thirst; but the water that I will give him will become in him a well of water springing up to eternal life" (John 4:14). Jesus is the ultimate source of the Spirit's fullness—once and for all time.

But how will Jesus be able to impart the Spirit out of his fullness—once and for all time—given the fact that the crucifixion is at his horizon? *The Spirit remains with him.* In Isaiah 59:21, God promises Israel that the Spirit to be imparted to them will not depart from them: "My Spirit, who is on you, will not depart from you." This promise is fulfilled with Jesus, Israel's Messiah. In the fifth century, Cyril of Alexandria helped us understand why this is true and what this promise means. For Cyril, the Spirit remains with Jesus (John 1:33), because the Spirit on Jesus will have no reason or occasion to depart from him. Jesus is indeed the eternal Word of the Father, who was eternally and essentially one with the Spirit. But he was also sinless in his sanctified body. The Spirit's remaining with Christ distinguishes Christ from the rest of humanity, from whom the sanctifying Spirit departed due to sin. Cyril says of the Spirit's remaining with Jesus at the Jordan: "And it abode upon Him. For it had fled from us by reason of sin, but he who knew no sin became as one of us, that the Spirit might be accustomed to abide in us, having no occasion of departure or withdrawal in him."[5]

It staggers the mind to think that Jesus sinks into the abyss of human alienation at the cross as the one who never ceases to bear the Spirit. Because the Spirit never leaves him, Christ's sinking is described as a self-offering—"by the eternal Spirit" (Heb. 9:14). He then rises from this baptism in fire in order to baptize us in the Spirit. Jesus's unique bearing of the Spirit not only points to ultimate fullness but also to eschatological permanence and finality, for the Spirit rested on Jesus to remain with him (John 1:33). Christ is meant to be the firstborn of the new creation, the one who is of final and universal significance for the creation's redemption and renewal. Baptized in the Spirit, we drink of the Spirit from his fullness (1 Cor. 12:13). That Jesus

---

5. Cyril of Alexandria, *Commentary on John* 2.1.32–33, trans. P. E. Pusey (Oxford: James Packer, 1874), 1:142.

"fully and permanently" bears the Spirit is the key to understanding the salvific significance of Jesus's reception of the Spirit at the Jordan (the theme of this chapter).

The Spirit-baptized Christ, Incarnation, and Pentecost

In the preceding chapter we explored the doctrine of the incarnation, the Word becoming flesh. Here I wish to ask, Could we imagine the incarnation without Christ's reception of the Spirit at the Jordan? By way of a preliminary answer, note what Eugene Rogers says about the incarnation: "The Spirit gives the Son a corporeal body in order that she might alight upon it."[6] Jesus says to the Father, "a body you prepared for me" (Heb. 10:5), a body prepared as the means of redemption and renewal for creation. Rogers's comment means that the incarnation has as its penultimate purpose the Jordan experience. Rogers adds that the faithful Son lives by the leading of the Spirit, and imparts the Spirit through his embodied life (faithful and exalted) so as to conform all flesh to his own image as the Son. The Spirit at Pentecost will then seek to "find" the Son throughout communities incorporated into Christ and throughout the sanctified creation.[7] Christ's conception by the Spirit in Mary's womb leads to his baptism in the Spirit and in fire at the Jordan. The incarnation reaches Pentecost only through the mediation of this life, baptized in this way. The Jordan River is the key to this baptism.

As I noted in the preceding chapter, the Jordan relates to the incarnation by implying that the incarnation is an event of both the Word and Spirit. The Word becomes flesh through the Holy Spirit. The mediation of the Spirit at the incarnation is sanctifying, for Jesus is conceived as the holy Son of God (Luke 1:35). David Coffey maintains that neither the Son's uniting to flesh nor the sanctification of this flesh is logically prior to the other. They are two sides of the same event. The incarnation is an event of the sanctifying Spirit.[8] It is an event that spans Jesus's entire life. "This being is this One in His history, and this history is His being."[9] Conceived by the Spirit as the holy Son of God, Jesus will be filled with the Spirit at the Jordan without measure

6. Eugene F. Rogers Jr., *After the Spirit: A Constructive Pneumatology from Resources outside the Modern West* (Grand Rapids: Eerdmans, 2005), 62.

7. Rogers, *After the Spirit*, 62.

8. David Coffey, "The Theandric Nature of Christ," *Theological Studies* 60 (1999): 406.

9. Karl Barth, *Church Dogmatics*, IV/1: *The Doctrine of Reconciliation*, trans. G. W. Bromiley (Edinburgh: T & T Clark, 1956), 128.

and permanently. Jesus's conception by the Spirit prepares for the unique reception of the Spirit at the Jordan. The eventfulness of the incarnation as a dynamic reality throughout Jesus's life is connected to the eschatological work of the Holy Spirit, which "freely and wholly" constitutes Jesus as "mold and receptacle for God's self-communication."[10] Yet, though Jesus's Spirit baptism is anticipated at the incarnation, it decisively occurs and is manifested at the Jordan River. Hence the key to the Jordan is Jesus's being filled with the Spirit. The incarnation and the Jordan *mutually* define one another: each is necessary to the other.

Though anchored in the incarnation, Christ's baptism in the Spirit at the Jordan anticipates the ultimate effects of the Spirit's work that occur at Christ's resurrection and exaltation, for Christ is raised by the Spirit of holiness as the Son of the Father (Rom. 1:4). Can we imagine the journey from the incarnation to the resurrection without the mediation of the Jordan and the life ministry of Jesus that is launched there? What would the image be that gets imparted to creation at Pentecost if not the image of Jesus's anointed and faithful life? Moreover, Paul calls the body of the resurrection a "spiritual," or better, a "Spirit body" (1 Cor. 15:44). He also describes it as mortal existence being "swallowed up" (or baptized) into immortal life (2 Cor. 5:4). The resurrection itself is the ultimate baptism in the Spirit (Rom. 1:4)! Therefore, the Jordan River as the place where Jesus rises from the waters baptized in the Spirit to share God's favor with the many anticipates the resurrection, where Jesus rises from the dead to baptize others in the Spirit. Vladimir Lossky thus quotes Nicholas Cabasilas concerning the effects of Christ's journey from the incarnation through the Jordan to his death and resurrection: "The Lord allowed men separated from God by the triple barrier of nature, sin, and death, to be fully possessed of him."[11]

The Jordan-Pentecost connection is key to Christ's identity and salvific mission. Christ's reception of the Spirit at his baptism is vital to the restoration that the entire sojourn of Christ will bring to humanity. Kilian McDonnell writes that, "if the loss of the image in Adam is tied to the loss of the Spirit, then the restoration of the image can only be linked to the return of the Spirit."[12] This restoration occurs through the life and image of the Son. The Jordan points ultimately to Pentecost as the solution to the

---

10. Kasper, *Jesus the Christ*, 251.

11. Nicholas Cabasilas, *De la vie en Christ* 3; quoted in Vladimir Lossky, *The Mystical Theology of the Eastern Church* (New York: St. Vladimir's Seminary Press, 1976), 136.

12. McDonnell, *Baptism of Jesus*, 71.

human problem. Adam and Eve were created to be the dwelling place of God's Spirit (implicitly) in the image of the Word by which all things were created (Gen. 2:7). Any illusion that we—our capacities or deeds—are at the base of life and its flourishing is roundly rejected in Scripture. One recalls Jeremiah's faulting Israel for harboring the idolatrous delusion that they have the source of life in their own hands: "My people have committed two sins: They have forsaken me, the spring of living water, and have dug their own cisterns, broken cisterns that cannot hold water" (Jer. 2:13; cf. 17:13). But the new creation will thrive from these very springs that come forth from God (Rev. 7:17). By reading the salvation story through the lens of the Jordan-Pentecost connection, one may discover an important way of understanding the identity and mission of Christ.

This Jordan-Pentecost connection helps us appreciate Irenaeus's remark that the Holy Spirit rested on Jesus at the Jordan and remained on him in order to "get accustomed to dwell in the human race, to repose on men, to reside within the work God has modeled working the Father's will in them and renewing them from oldness to newness in Christ."[13] He advocated a theory of recapitulation in which Christ sums up in his entire life journey, not only the story of Israel in its relationship to God, but also that of the entire human race: "He summed up in himself the long history of the human race and so furnished us with salvation in a short and summary way, to the end that what we had lost in Adam . . . we might recover in Christ Jesus."[14] More specifically, the same Word and Spirit that shaped Adam and Eve to begin with have now in Christ "brought about a living and completed humanity, which embraces God in his completeness." Referring to the eternal Word and the Spirit as the left and right hands of God, Irenaeus notes that, in Christ, "Adam never escapes those hands of God" by which he and Eve were made.[15] Colin Gunton eloquently puts the matter this way: "Through his Son and Spirit, his two hands, the Father both prevents the creation from slipping back into the nothingness from which it came and restores its teleology, its movement towards perfection."[16] Irenaeus writes of the Christ, who "gives his life for our life, his flesh for our flesh, that he pours out the

13. Irenaeus, *Against Heresies* 3.17.1, in *The Apostolic Fathers: Justin Martyr and Irenaeus*, rev. ed., A. Cleveland Cox, *Ante Nicene Fathers*, vol. 1, ed. Alexander Roberts and James Donaldson (Peabody, MA: Hendrickson, 1994).

14. Irenaeus, *Against Heresies* 3.18.1.

15. Irenaeus, *Against Heresies* 5.1.3.

16. Colin Gunton, "The Spirit Moved over the Face of the Waters: The Holy Spirit and the Created Order," *International Journal of Systematic Theology* 4, no. 2 (July 2002): 197-98.

Spirit of the Father to unite God to humanity and bring them into commu-nion."[17] In effect, Jesus, as the one baptized in the Spirit, rewrites the story of humanity's journey with God that was focused on Israel so as to open up an eschatologically more expansive and diverse future for them by sharing the Spirit with them, and with the Spirit sharing his own faithful life, and sharing the love and good favor of the heavenly Father.

Jesus's lifetime of devotion that begins at the incarnation is publicly de-clared and launched at the Jordan, and it culminates at the cross. This life is ultimately glorified so as to be the fitting image into which the creation will be transformed by the bestowal of the Spirit (John 7:38–39). M. C. Steenberg summarizes Irenaeus's thought in a way that appropriates just such salvific significance to Jesus's anointing at the Jordan: "Without the unction of the Spirit, Jesus is not Messiah; rather that without the Spirit the incarnate Son is not fully redeemer, since he who redeems recapitulatively does so by uniting humanity to the full life of God."[18] Jesus baptizes in the Spirit by means of an anointed life, a life that is vindicated and perfected as faithful and fitting for the new creation at his resurrection and then opened up to creation at Pen-tecost. As I noted about the incarnation in the preceding chapter, there can be no unmediated bestowal of the Spirit at Pentecost. The Spirit is bestowed through the mediation of the embodied, faithful life of the Messiah, Jesus Christ our Lord. Both the incarnation and Pentecost involve the Jordan, and the Jordan involves the incarnation and Pentecost.

Unfortunately, the salvific significance of the Jordan was neglected to an extent in the early centuries of the church. The theologians from the early centuries and beyond who combated the adoptionist heresy (which regarded Jesus as merely a Spirit-anointed man) were sometimes wary of highlighting Jesus's reception of the Spirit at the Jordan as of central significance to his identity and mission. Though impressive patristic evidence can be mustered from the fourth and fifth centuries granting the reception of the Spirit at the Jordan a significant role to play, the classic creeds of the church (Apostles' Creed, Nicene Creed, and the Chalcedonian Definition) do not mention it, nor Christ's bestowal of the Spirit at Pentecost, for that matter. The creeds focus theologically on the eternal Son's taking on flesh at the incarnation in order to die and rise again. While this confession is orthodox as far as it goes (cf. Heb. 2:14), it does not go far enough. It is also important to recapture the significance of the Jordan-Pentecost connection that comes to light in

17. Irenaeus, *Against Heresies* 5.1.1.
18. Steenberg, *Of God and Man*, 36–37.

John the Baptist's announcement of the coming Christ (cf. Luke 3:16) and its fulfillment in texts such as John 20:22 and Acts 2:33–36. As I have noted in earlier chapters, John the Baptist foretold of one who would bear the Spirit in order to baptize others in the same Spirit. Christ at his exaltation was made "both Lord and Messiah" (2:35–36) to fulfill this purpose. He is made Messiah as the one who receives and bears the Spirit, Lord as the one who imparts the Spirit to all flesh.

The neglect of the Jordan in ancient creedal developments must be resisted in contemporary Christology. N. T. Wright correctly notes that the problem here is not only the neglect of the Jordan experience but also the entire anointed life of Christ that is launched at that event. When we look at the creeds and notice how they leapfrog from the incarnation to the crucifixion, we say, "Not so fast!"[19] A Christology from below, however, will not neglect Christ's anointing at the Jordan and the faithful life that flows from this, because this is where all of our talk about the Word becoming flesh becomes a substantive claim that is concrete, discernible, and historically mediated. In short, the Son, or Word, of the Father, who receives and pours forth the Spirit at Pentecost, does so through a life that was given over and offered up completely to the divine redemption and renewal of creation. Without the launching of this life at the Jordan and its fulfilling at the crucifixion and resurrection, the incarnation lacks its fulfillment and Pentecost its embodied means of mediation. Thomas Torrance observes that, though the Word made flesh was in a sense forged (past tense) at the incarnation, it is also "a historical event, a dynamic event, a real happening in the time of this world which is coincident with the whole historical life of Jesus."[20] Upon Jesus's reception of the Spirit at the Jordan, the Word's elevation of humanity by the Spirit in uniting with flesh continues and reaches a turning point at the Jordan, at Jesus's reception of the Spirit. Poised in between incarnation and the climactic moments of Jesus's life, the reception of the Spirit at the Jordan and Jesus's anointed life play a significant role in his identity and redemptive mission. The Jordan and the Spirit- and fire-baptized life that proceeds from that event will hark back to the incarnation and will reach in anticipation for the crucifixion, the resurrection, and Pentecost for decisive fulfillment and confirmation.

19. N. T. Wright, *How God Became King: The Forgotten Story of the Gospels* (New York: HarperOne, 2016), 3–24.

20. Thomas F. Torrance, *Incarnation: The Person and Life of Christ* (Downers Grove, IL: InterVarsity, 2008), 67.

The Spirit-baptized Christ and Israel

The life of Jesus launched at the Jordan is revealed with added specificity, a point that especially has to do with the need to face the full brunt of Jesus's particularity as the Messiah of Israel. This is where John the Baptist, an enigmatic figure, plays a vital role. There is no denying that all four Gospels and Acts place him at the threshold of the new age of the Spirit, announcing the coming of the Messiah. He is the chief forerunner. What he announces concerning the coming Messiah, therefore, deserves more attention than it has received in dogmatic Christology. John himself holds more significance for Christian theology than the role typically assigned to him—as the one who practiced pre-Christian baptism. He did that, but it is of secondary significance. John's announcement exceeds the significance of his water rite, and the Messiah's baptizing of all flesh in the Spirit is not just a description of the salvific significance of the Christian water rite that will follow his impartation of the Spirit. Water baptism is a sign of Spirit baptism, but Spirit baptism cannot be contained by the water rite. It describes Christ's eschatological reach to all flesh through the outpouring of the Spirit. It not only involves our initiation into Christ's body by faith and water baptism; it leads up to our mortal life's being "swallowed up by life" (2 Cor. 5:4). Just as Jesus was appointed the favored Son by the Spirit at his resurrection, as anticipated by his incarnation and anointing, so we will become adopted as sons and daughters in his image at our resurrection, as anticipated by our initiation to Christ by faith (Rom. 8:15–23).[21] John's announcement reaches ahead, all the way to the Christ of the new creation.

So significant is John's announcement of the coming Messiah that Luke even anchors the Baptist's role as forerunner to his existence in the womb, for John reacts in his mother's womb by leaping at the presence of the woman who will bear Jesus in her womb (Luke 1:41). And Jesus only moves toward the culmination of his mission once he has reaffirmed the significance of John as the pivotal witness of the final age of the Spirit to be ushered in by the Messiah: "Then what did you go out to see? A prophet? Yes, I tell you, and more than a prophet" (Matt. 11:9). Though John, before his death, questioned the adequacy of Jesus's healing ministry to fulfill the role of the one

---

21. See my development of this theme in Frank D. Macchia, *Baptized in the Spirit: A Global Pentecostal Theology* (Grand Rapids: Zondervan, 2006). I seek in part to develop James D. G. Dunn's argument that Spirit baptism is the root metaphor of the entire salvific work of the Holy Spirit in the New Testament. See Dunn, *Baptism in the Holy Spirit*.

who will baptize in the Spirit and fire, Jesus responded without hesitation that John was no reed swayed by the wind (Matt. 11:7). His significance as Jesus's forerunner endures.

John the Baptist's announcement of the coming one looks ahead to Jesus as the future Spirit Baptizer. John is the one who recognizes the significance of the Spirit's descent on Jesus, installing him as the Messiah (John 1:33). This means that John's baptism, even of Jesus, is not the central feature of the narratives that refer to him as the Baptist, though it provides important context for what occupies the center of concern. Of central importance are the descent of the Spirit and the eschatological promise of this gift offered to humanity through the Messiah. Christ's water baptism is but a sign of this eschatological reality that is dawning before John's eyes. James Dunn notes that "an examination of each of the four Gospels makes it quite plain that Jesus's baptism at the hands of John was not the principal interest."[22] The Fourth Gospel does not mention it. John's baptism is in no case necessary to the gift of the Spirit, not even after the Day of Pentecost (Acts 19:1-3).[23] But John's baptism is still a fitting sign of the faith and hope that reaches for the Spirit. John's greatness in the context of this hope is in setting the terms by which the identity and work of the Messiah are understood. John's great insight is this: Jesus will bear the Spirit to baptize in the Spirit.

In baptizing the Messiah, John the Baptist "does not belong within the kingdom; he stands before it."[24] John was filled with the Spirit like prophets of old, but Jesus was also conceived by the Spirit in the womb to be the one who will bear the Spirit in order to impart the Spirit to others. Indeed, "John's baptism was essentially preparatory, not initiatory, a prophetic symbol of the Messianic baptism."[25] But it is Christ's reception of the Spirit that is "the decisive change in the ages."[26] It represents the gift that Christ will give to others in the future, which is fittingly contrasted to John's water rite: "I baptize you with water, but he will baptize you with the Holy Spirit" (Mark 1:8). The contrast is between John and Jesus, "the antithesis of preparation

---

22. Dunn, *Baptism in the Holy Spirit*, 33.

23. A point made by Wolfhart Pannenberg, *Jesus—God and Man* (Philadelphia: Westminster, 1977), 140.

24. Knox Chamblin, "John the Baptist and the Kingdom of God," *Tyndale House Bulletin* 13 (October 1963): 7-15, quoting W. Marxsen, *Der Evangelist Markus* (Göttingen: Vandenhoeck and Ruprecht, 1956), 31.

25. Dunn, *Baptism in the Holy Spirit*, 17.

26. Dunn, *Baptism in the Holy Spirit*, 26.

and fulfillment, of shadow and substance."[27] The contrast between shadow and substance, however, also involves a positive relationship between the two: the shadow also reaches for and points toward the substance. The key connection of this substance is between Jesus's reception of the Spirit at the Jordan and his impartation of the Spirit at Pentecost. It is not simply between Jesus's baptism by John and Christian baptism in general. The latter issue of water baptism is of secondary significance (just as the sign is to the substance that it signifies). The role of Christian baptism in Christ's impartation of the Holy Spirit is indeed an important issue that we will explore later. The argument of Barth—and, more recently, of Dunn—is particularly convincing at this point: that a water rite cannot formalize Spirit baptism. Water baptism is an important sign of Spirit baptism, confirming and bearing witness to it. But the sign must not dominate our theological discussion; rather, it is the reality to which the sign points.

Jesus's reception of the Spirit at the Jordan is eschatological in significance, since the arrival of the Spirit was regarded as an end-time event (Joel 2:28–29). The eschatological features of the event are introduced after Jesus's baptism at John's hands and are connected instead with the arrival of the Spirit. This descent of the Spirit is the eschatological moment. The heavens part, and God's voice can be heard making an announcement about Jesus as the beloved Son, both of which indicate an event of apocalyptic or ultimate significance.[28] And the Spirit appears in the form of a dove, which is reminiscent of the Spirit brooding on the waters of creation and the sign of new creation in the story of Noah.[29] "Eschatology begins at the Jordan."[30] Though John's baptism and Jesus's anointing by the Spirit are closely related, "it was not the water-baptism which initiated into the Messianic office, but only the baptism in the Spirit."[31]

The eschatological reach of Jesus's receiving of the Spirit at the Jordan, however, should not eclipse the immediate setting that surrounded Jesus's Jordan experience. Here is where the symbolic significance of John's baptism of Jesus can help us, especially if we fully grasp how it depicted the hope for the forgiveness and renewal of Israel. Indeed, the neglect of the Jordan in classical Christology has arguably aided in the historic loss of emphasis

27. Dunn, *Baptism in the Holy Spirit*, 19.

28. John Nolland, *Luke 1–9:20*, Word Biblical Commentary 35A (Dallas: Word, 1989), 162.

29. Donald Hagner, *Matthew 1–13*, Word Biblical Commentary 33A (Dallas: Word, 1993), 58.

30. McDonnell, *Baptism of Jesus in the Jordan*, 148.

31. Dunn, *Baptism in the Holy Spirit*, 35.

on Jesus's *Jewish* identity and mission. Of course, the incarnation texts do not exclude this aspect of Jesus's identity and mission. Matthew 1:1 starts with "Jesus the Messiah, the Son of David," and the genealogy that follows confirms the significance of his Jewish heritage. So also in Luke, the angelic messenger tells Mary that God will give her son "the throne of his father, David" and he will "reign over Jacob's descendants forever" (Luke 1:32–33). Jesus is "born of a woman, born under the law," according to Paul (Gal. 4:4). But if one rushes from Jesus's birth past the Jordan to the cross, the resurrection, and Pentecost—to the place where Christ as Messiah and Lord transcends the limits of time and place so as to pour out the Spirit upon *all flesh*—it is easy to give a mere nod to Jesus's mission to the household of Israel before leaving that quickly behind in favor of his global and cosmic significance. Barth reminds us:

> The Word did not simply become any "flesh," any man humbled and suffering. It became Jewish flesh. The Church's whole doctrine of the incarnation becomes abstract and valueless and meaningless to the extent that this comes to be regarded as something accidental and incidental.[32]

Not only is Jesus's Jewishness religiously significant in its own right, but it also has social significance. Jesus's liberating significance for the church's social stance is informed by the particularity of his birth as a man in solidarity with others who lived under occupation. Significant also in this light is his reaching out to the least of these, and even to those who, like the tax collectors, exploited the least of these on behalf of the empire, so that they, too, might repent and participate in God's redemptive justice in the world. The community baptized in the Spirit will later not be built to protect the social privilege that comes with being male over female, free over bond slave, or one race over another (1 Cor. 12:13; Acts 2:17–18; Gal. 3:28). The "all flesh" of Jesus's own identity as flesh includes them all, but not at the loss of meaning concerning how that reconciliation takes shape from the context of Jesus's concrete Jewish life and mission to the downtrodden and sinners within Israel—and, ultimately, among the nations.

If we ignore Jesus's concrete Jewish particularity, the important message of Jesus's flesh as belonging to *all flesh*, which becomes clear at the resurrection and at Pentecost, suddenly seems abstract, lacking the guidance that

---

32. Barth, *Church Dogmatics*, IV/1, 166.

his particularity provides. Jesus's story emerges from a past narrative that is canonical and thus vital to how the story reaches its climax. The global and cosmic significance of Christ is important to faith, but it should not be promoted at the cost of the particular significance of Jesus as the "king of Israel" (John 1:49). Jesus's flesh as belonging to all flesh occurs at the fulfillment of Israel's mission, in Israel's self-transcendence through its Messiah so as to open up to the unique calling of the nations and to serve it, and in the openness of the nations to the unique gift of Christ to which Israel's Scripture had given witness. This fulfillment occurs through the hard and difficult crossing of barriers in order to realize the just and merciful reconciliation that the grace of the cross and of Pentecost provides. The barrier between Jew and Gentile is broken down in Christ by the cross (Eph. 2:14) so that "through him we both have access to the Father by one Spirit" (Eph. 2:18). The "all flesh" of Pentecost that is already anticipated at the incarnation will be bought with a price and realized through painful and rewarding conversion. This "all flesh" cannot be a mere theological assumption that is taken for granted from the start.

John the Baptist emerges in the Gospel narratives as the voice crying out from the desert for Israel to recognize that the time of purging and renewal was at hand. John's baptism was in fact significant as a drama of Israelite hope. Though tied perhaps indirectly to the purification rites practiced at Qumran, John's baptismal rite is nevertheless unique.[33] John's water rite was open to all, was tied to repentance, and apparently did not require repetition. The call to repentance was prominent, especially as it was aimed at the leaders of Israel, with warnings of coming judgment. This practice placed John the Baptist at odds with the Temple cult. It was as if John were saying to his audience, "You can have, here and now, what you would normally get through the Temple cult."[34] The Jewish leadership was thus negative toward John and only held back from openly opposing him for fear of popular backlash (Matt. 21:25-26). The Temple was at the center of Israel's spiritual and political life, so Jesus's implied replacement of it was significant. (I will pick up this issue again later in our discussion.)

Here it is important to note that Jesus's reception of the Spirit as the favored Son of the heavenly Father sets in motion the renewal of Israel,

---

33. Raymond Brown, "Three Quotations from John the Baptist in the Gospel of John," *The Catholic Biblical Quarterly* 22, no. 3 (July 1960): 294.

34. N. T. Wright, *Jesus and the Victory of God*, vol. 2 of *Christian Origins and the Question of God* (Minneapolis: Fortress, 1997), 160.

which includes the fulfillment of Israel's mission to bless all nations. The Spirit poured out as a mighty river knows no boundaries, but challenges and enriches diverse lands and peoples—that is, all flesh (Joel 2:28–29; Acts 2:17–18).[35] The nation of Israel thus cannot be blessed in its own renewal unless the conditions are met for the fulfillment of the witness to all nations.

> May God be gracious to us and bless us
> > and make his face shine on us—
> so that your ways may be known on earth,
> > your salvation among all nations. (Ps. 67:1–2)

Israel's mission was to fulfill the promise given to Abraham to bless the nations (Gen. 18:18) by proclaiming the things God has done (Ps. 9:11; 67:2; Isa. 12:4), to praise God among the nations (Ps. 18:49), that the nations may glorify God (Ps. 45:17). God will be exalted among the nations (Ps. 46:10), and God will do all of this particularly through his servant, upon whom the Spirit will rest to bring justice to the nations (Isa. 42:1). Paul notes that the seed through which Abraham's blessing, the gift of the Spirit, will come is ultimately Christ, born of Israel (Isa. 44:1–3; Gal. 3:14–16). It will be through Christ that Israel will bless the nations. Eschatological Israel revealed through the church will witness to *him* among the nations (Acts 1:8).

Jesus's particularity, however, cannot remain within Israel's boundaries, not if is true to God's promise to the world—and thus to that particularity at its core. That promise is focused on the coming Messiah and the coming Spirit that he will bear and impart. Because the Messiah bears and imparts the cosmic and eschatological Spirit, no nationalism can contain this Messiah without betraying him. No nationalism can seek to domesticate the will of the Creator in pouring forth the divine favor through the Messiah to all nations, for that would quench the Spirit. Jesus will thus bear the Spirit and the trial by fire not only to rewrite the story of Israel but also the story of Adam and Eve (and their seed) for whom Israel came as a missionary force. Christ will recapitulate the story of the human race by first recapitulating Israel. He bears the flesh of Israel, but also the flesh of the entire human race. Barth expresses the connection between the Jesus of Israel and the Jesus for all flesh in the following way:

---

35. For an excellent discussion of this point, see Michael Welker, *God the Spirit* (Minneapolis: Fortress, 1994), 134–42.

As God's act He willed that it should be done by him personally, by Him as the one Israelite who was elected, ordained and born, and who lived to do this, as the Israelite who was also Israel's Judge and Deliverer, its Messiah, the eschatological Son of David, the goal of its whole history, in his own person the fulfilled purpose of the mission of Israel to the nations.[36]

The nations will not be subordinate to Israel in their experience of God, nor merely represent an extension of their history and experience. The nations have their own unique histories with God that parallel Israel's and that will be blessed by Israel's history, especially by the Messiah born from Israel (Acts 17:24-28). And so Israel will be blessed as well. The kings of the nations will bring the splendor from their own peoples' responses to God into the heavenly city in honor of Christ for all to enjoy (Rev. 21:24).

Jesus would fulfill Israel's mission as the Spirit Baptizer. Matthew sets up John's announcement of this at the Jordan River by connecting Jesus's faithful sonship with Israel's. Matthew recounts how Mary and Joseph fled with the child Jesus to Egypt to escape the murderous threats of Herod. After Herod's death, they brought Jesus back from Egypt to Palestine in fulfillment of Hosea 11:1: "Out of Egypt I called my son" (Matt. 2:15). Jesus's rising up from Mary's womb and from the waters of the Jordan (foreshadowing his rising up from the grave) fulfills Israel's being raised up by God from Egyptian bondage.

But Matthew does not include the very next verse from Hosea 11 (v. 2):

> But the more they were called,
>   the more they went away from me.
> They sacrificed to the Baals
>   and they burned incense to images.

Since, according to Hosea 11:2, Israel failed to fully attain the liberty of sonship granted in the Exodus, the burning question left unanswered at the time of Christ's coming to earth concerns who will ultimately fulfill the faithful sonship to which Israel was called. This is the question that Matthew and the other Gospel writers wished to answer as they recorded the moment when Christ entered the Jordan to be baptized by John. As Jesus rises from the

---

36. Karl Barth, *Church Dogmatics*, IV/4: *The Doctrine of Reconciliation*, trans. G. W. Bromiley (Edinburgh: T & T Clark, 1969), 63.

waters of the Jordan, the heavenly Father announces that Christ is indeed the beloved Son with whom the Father is well pleased (Matt. 3:16–17). That God raised Israel up from Egypt for the liberty of favored sonship and daughtership is now fulfilled as Jesus rises from the Jordan under the anointing of the Spirit and the Father's declaration of Christ's beloved sonship. That event will be fulfilled at the resurrection, by which Christ is declared to be the faithful and beloved Son by the Spirit of holiness (Rom. 1:4). But since Israel was called to witness to Adam's seed, Adam's sonship is also to be fulfilled in all of this (Luke 3:38).

Since Israel's Exodus from Egypt is tied to the gift of sonship, the coming of the faithful Son fulfills the freedom of the Exodus and imparts the freedom and renewal promised in the giving of the Spirit. Both the blessing of Jacob (from Abraham) and the fulfillment of the law are said to come through the outpouring of the Spirit (Isa. 44:1–3; Ezek. 36:26). Matthew only quotes Hosea 11:1 in reference to Jesus (and not verse 2, concerning Israel's unfaithfulness) because Jesus is the *faithful Son* (Matt. 3:17). Jesus fulfills Israel's election and faithfulness to God. "Here I am—it is written about me in the scroll—I have come to do your will, my God" (Heb. 10:7). He was obedient unto death (Phil. 2:8). Like Joseph of old, Jesus's adoptive father is named Joseph, and he hears of Jesus's conception in the womb of his betrothed via a dream. Joseph was "faithful to the law" (Matt. 1:19); Mary's faithfulness was even more striking than that of her betrothed, since she offered her very body to the coming of the Messiah and stood to suffer the most from public shame had Joseph sent her away. All that she says in response to the news of her potentially difficult role in the birth of Jesus is, "May your word to me be fulfilled" (Luke 1:38). Mary and Joseph both exemplify Israel's faithful hope while awaiting the coming promise of renewal. All of this is to say that Israel's election and faithfulness foreshadow Christ's. In Israel's piety, the nation foreshadows the coming Christ; but in its failures it finds in him their hope for redemption and renewal, the fulfillment of their eschatological destiny as free and faithful sons and daughters of God in Christ.

Jesus's participation in John's baptism was also participation in Israel's prophetic drama of hope. John's baptismal ministry had its significance in directing this drama, one that is connected mainly to the Jordan River's historic significance. If it were not for this drama, the Jordan would be an unlikely place for John's baptismal ministry to flourish. It was not conducive for mass baptisms. The water there was difficult to access in the winter months, and its relative shallowness raised questions about its adequacy to meet common standards of purity. The Jordan's location was significant for this prophetic drama of hope, because that river was historically important to Israel's crossing into the Promised Land. It seems that John's baptism was a drama of a new Israel leaving its sins behind and reemerging from the Jordan a renewed people.[37] This baptismal drama was thus symbolic of a people who were welcoming the coming era of the Spirit, even to the degree that John would make it part of his proclamation of the kingdom (Mark 1:4; Luke 3:3). This led Morna Hooker to say, "No real parallel to John's baptism has been discovered in contemporary Jewish practice."[38]

Baptized by John, Jesus enters into this drama of hope that defines the ministry of the Baptist and those who participated in it. He claims this drama as his own, so that, rising from the Jordan filled with hope, he may welcome the Spirit on behalf of Israel, on behalf of the human race. Bearing the Spirit, he may transform the journey into a path to renewal by imparting the Spirit. By receiving the end-time gift of the Spirit as he emerged from the water, Christ transformed John's ritual of hope into a sign of apocalyptic fulfillment, something that John's baptism, no water rite, could ever give—only the arrival of the Spirit (Acts 19:2).

Christ walked through John's drama of hope and transformed it, because he was not merely a member of Israel; he was the Spirit Baptizer, the nation's Messiah who bore the eschatological Spirit for the sake of renewing all flesh. The one declared to be the beloved Son passed through the water of the Jordan to receive the promised Spirit, to be baptized in the Spirit and fire. He entered the desert to have his sonship tried by fire for forty days, analogous to the Israelites' passing through the water of the Red Sea when they were freed from Egypt and—as sons and daughters of God—were tried in the desert for forty years. Jesus relived Israel's drama as the faithful Son. Where Israel failed, he will succeed. His trial in the desert also recalls the temptation of the first human parents in the Garden. His victory over the Tempter will win their salvation. He will prove to be the Lord of life who imparts his faithfulness to all others. He chose twelve disciples to symbolize eschatological Israel (the twelve tribes), which would, in Christ and by the Spirit, bear witness to the blessing of Abraham to all nations. But Christ is not one of the twelve, because he does not merely bear witness to the coming renewal; he imparts it. He is not the twelfth. He stands apart from them as

37. Colin Brown, "What Was John the Baptist Doing?," *Bulletin for Biblical Research* 7 (1997): 37–50.

38. Morna Hooker, *The Gospel according to St. Mark*, Black's New Testament Commentaries (Peabody, MA: Hendrickson, 1991), 39; quoted in Brown, "What was John the Baptist Doing?," 41.

the one who will be their Lord; he transcends them as the one who founds and will bring their witness to fulfillment; he is the last Adam, the life-giving Spirit (1 Cor. 15:45). They will discover a new Israel, a new humanity—from and in him. And the twelve are absolutely dependent on him to join the renewed Israel that will witness to the opening of the life of the Spirit to all flesh (Matt. 11:27; John 14:6–7; Acts 1:8). He will bring the forgiveness and the renewal in the Spirit for which the faithful remnant of Israel grasps at the culmination of its historic journey with God.

The Spirit-baptized Christ and the Coming of God

I have made the point all along that Jesus's role as mediator of the Spirit implies his deity. This insight finds its early expression in John the Baptist's announcement of the coming Messiah. In the Old Testament, the Lord is said to pour out the Spirit in the latter days (Joel 2:28–32). Moreover, messianic expectation came to focus on the coming one who will be anointed of the Spirit. John the Baptist's announcement implicitly combined both expectations into one figure, thereby granting clarity as to how the Lord will pour out the Spirit. The one anointed of the Spirit will occasion a river of the Spirit into which he will baptize others. The Messiah, who bears the Spirit, will also be the Lord who pours out the Spirit (cf. Acts 2:33–36). John thus prepares the way for the coming of the Lord: "Make ready the way of the Lord" (Mark 1:3). The text of Isaiah 40:3, from which Mark 1:2–3 is partially taken, makes it clear that the messenger fulfilled by John the Baptist prepares the way for the coming of *God*. John is thus not the light of life, but the Christ as the coming of God into the world *is* (John 1:1–9). The Spirit Baptizer will impart the Spirit of the heavenly Father because he is to be identified with God. Christ's baptism in the Spirit installed him as the Messiah who fulfills Israel's hopes that God will come to reign and to renew Israel—in fact, all flesh. God fulfilled this hope through Christ in the reality of the Spirit, because the kingdom, or liberating reign of God, is not a place but a presence, God's presence in the world through the Messiah and the liberating Spirit. "If it is by the Spirit of God that I drive out demons, then the kingdom of God has come upon you" (Matt. 12:28). Though Jesus will not bestow the Spirit on all flesh until Pentecost (and beyond), the liberating power of the Spirit can already be felt through him during his life ministry. The Spirit is at the essence of God's liberating reign. Paul thus points out that the kingdom of God is not primarily experienced in food laws (or *any* ceremonial laws) but rather as "righteousness, peace, and joy in the Holy Spirit" (Rom. 14:17). Jesus's acts of deliverance in the power of the Spirit thus confront people already with the liberating power of the kingdom (Matt. 12:28). G. R. Beasley-Murray notes that it was "as Bearer of the Spirit that Jesus was the instrument of the divine sovereignty—or, as we may equally say, the bearer of the kingdom."[39]

Indeed, John's announcement of the coming kingdom involves the coming of *God*. It is for this reason that Jesus's reception of the Spirit at the Jordan was of such historic significance. Matthew introduces the Baptist: "In those days John the Baptist came, preaching in the wilderness of Judea and saying, 'Repent, for the kingdom of heaven has come near'" (Matt. 3:1-2). The phrase "in those days" indicates the beginnings of an epic turning point in the coming of the kingdom of God. But the verse that follows indicates both his greatness and his limitation in this dawn of the kingdom:

This is he who was spoken of through the prophet Isaiah:

"A voice of one calling in the wilderness,
    'Prepare the way for the Lord,
    make straight paths for him.'"

The text from Isaiah 40:3 speaks of a voice calling to prepare the way for the coming of the Lord. In this text John the Baptist is the voice calling out from the desert to prepare for the presence of the Lord, who will come to reign and to bring new life to those who repent. John's greatness is in his being identified as this end-time voice of witness and preparation. But John is not the coming Lord. His baptism cannot bring new life, cannot fulfill its own promise. The Gospels want the reader to place Jesus as the coming Lord who will fulfill that for which John and his baptism prepare.[40]

John's proclamation of the coming kingdom (Matt. 3:2) is in fact essential to his role in preparing for the coming of the Lord, for in the Old Testament and Judaism, "the coming of the kingdom of God means the coming of God."[41] Indeed, "in the announcement of the dawning kingdom we find the persistent emphasis that YHWH is, at last, returning to Zion. He will do again what he did at the Exodus, that is, come to dwell in the

---

39. G. R. Beasley-Murray, "Jesus and the Spirit," in *Mélanges Bibliques*, ed. A. Descamps and R. P. A. Halleaux (Gembloux, France: Duculot, 1970), 463.

40. Richard B. Hays, *Reading Backwards: Figural Christology and the Fourfold Gospel Witness* (Waco, TX: Baylor University Press, 2014), 20-21.

41. Kasper, *Jesus the Christ*, 78.

midst of his people."[42] The coming of the Lord in the figure of the Christ at the Jordan had naturally come much earlier via the Virgin's womb. Christ's declaration as the Son in the womb, overshadowed by the Spirit, adumbrates what happens at the Jordan (Luke 1:35). The significant incarnation text of John 1:14 further notes that the Word of the Father, who "was God" (John 1:1), will now become flesh to "dwell among us" (or, "tabernacle" among us). The Spirit fills Jesus at the Jordan as the divine glory filled the tabernacle of Israel (Exod. 40:34–35). The coming kingdom or reign of God is the coming of God to reign, and this coming will bring widespread restoration and judgment.

The coming of the Spirit Baptizer fulfills those texts that speak of the coming of God, who will reign by means of a vast impartation of the Spirit to restore or to judge. The gift of the Spirit is one of the chief marks of the new age of salvation ushered in by the coming Lord. Note Joel 2:28–32:

"And afterward,
  I will pour out my Spirit on all people.
Your sons and daughters will prophesy,
  your old men will dream dreams,
  your young men will see visions.
Even on my servants, both men and women,
  I will pour out my Spirit in those days.
I will show wonders in the heavens
  and on the earth,
  blood and fire and billows of smoke.
The sun will be turned to darkness
  and the moon to blood
  before the coming of the great and dreadful day of the LORD.
And everyone who calls
  on the name of the LORD will be saved;
for on Mount Zion and in Jerusalem
  there will be deliverance,
  as the LORD has said,
even among the survivors
  whom the LORD calls."

This latter-day outpouring of the Spirit will overflow all social boundaries, smashing through illusions of privilege based on age, sex, or social class (see

42. Wright, *Jesus and the Victory of God*, 616.

Acts 2:17–18); Paul adds race as well (Gal. 3:28). This end-time impartation of the Spirit will set up God's final self-disclosure to Israel and the world: "I will no longer hide my face from them, for I will pour out my Spirit on the house of Israel" (Ezek. 39:29). God is ultimately defined by the Messiah who bears the liberating Spirit, whose life is shaped and led by this Spirit and is ultimately disclosed when raised up in order to be imparted through an overflowing stream of divine love (Acts 2:33–36).

This end-time bestowal of the Spirit begins with the Messiah. Note also Isaiah 59:19–21:

> From the west, people will fear the name of the LORD,
>   and from the rising of the sun, they will revere his glory.
> For he will come like a pent-up flood
>   that the breath of the LORD drives along.
> "The Redeemer will come to Zion,
>   to those in Jacob who repent of their sins,"
> declares the LORD.
>
> "As for me, this is my covenant with them," says the LORD. "My Spirit, who is on you, will not depart from you, and my words that I have put in your mouth will always be on your lips, on the lips of your children and on the lips of their descendants—from this time on and forever," says the LORD.

Matthew 12:18 (taken from Isaiah 42:1) reaches back to Jesus's baptism in the Spirit at the Jordan (where Jesus is declared to be the beloved Son who pleases the Father):

> "Here is my servant whom I have chosen,
>   the one I love, in whom I delight;
> I will put my Spirit on him,
>   and he will proclaim justice to the nations."

The above text (from Matthew 12:18) then explains Jesus's remark in 12:28 that the kingdom of God is already being felt in his acts of deliverance by the Spirit. Gregory of Nyssa expresses it best when he says that Christ is the King and the Spirit is the kingdom that is inaugurated through and in him. The larger quote is: "The Spirit is a living and a substantial and distinctly subsisting kingdom with which the only begotten Christ is anointed and is

King of all that is."[43] The kingdom of God is already felt through Jesus and makes ultimate demands on Jesus's audience even before his fateful crucifixion (Matt. 12:28). But this reality only anticipates the resurrection and Pentecost, for the Father pours forth the Spirit through Christ when Christ is glorified (John 7:39).

One can appreciate the seamless flow of life that leads to the fulfillment of Christ's reign as Lord when he shows himself to be the Lord of life by imparting the Spirit to all flesh. As the giver of life on behalf of the Father, Christ will reign—not sin and death. The Jordan is key to what will happen at Jesus's exaltation and impartation of the Spirit as Lord. Ephrem the Syrian even wrote (in the fourth century CE) of Jesus's conception by the Spirit in Mary's womb as "hurrying" toward his reception of the Spirit at the Jordan, which itself "hurries" toward his crucifixion and resurrection from the dead. He viewed these events as "bridges" to the renewal of creation through the Lord Jesus Christ at Pentecost.[44] One may also speak, as does James Shelton, of expanding waves of the Spirit's arrival through the Son that spans Jesus's life ministry and culminates at Pentecost.[45] Whether bridges or waves, these events move toward eschatological fulfillment because they anticipate that fulfillment and can already grasp it in a way that is unique to these events. Nothing can stop the expanding and overflowing of the Spirit from the Father and through the Son, who reigns as Lord!

The Spirit-baptized Christ and the Temple

Christ brings God to earth because, as the divine Son of the Father, he takes on flesh and bears the Spirit as the new temple of God on earth. The Temple in Jerusalem was the seat of Jewish political power. Christ's eschatological lordship as the bearer and future imparter of the Spirit is thus significant for the Temple's destiny. Jesus's announcement of the judgment coming to the Jewish Temple is connected to his identity as the new center of the divine

43. Gregory of Nyssa, *On the Lord's Prayer* 3; quoted in Kilian McDonnell, *The Other Hand of God: The Holy Spirit as the Universal Touch and Goal* (Collegeville, MN: Liturgical Press, 2003), 226.

44. McDonnell, *Baptism of Jesus in the Jordan*, 168–69; McDonnell's book is a masterful reflection on the soteriological significance of Jesus's reception of the Spirit at the Jordan.

45. James B. Shelton, *Mighty in Word and Deed: The Role of the Holy Spirit in Luke–Acts* (Eugene, OR: Wipf and Stock, 2000), esp. 165–78.

presence and favor among humankind. Jesus's cleansing of the Temple was symbolic of this judgment. Note Luke's account of the incident:

> When Jesus entered the temple courts, he began to drive out those who were selling. "It is written," he said to them, "'My house will be a house of prayer'; but you have made it a 'den of robbers.'" (Luke 19:45–46)

The Temple merchants sold sacrificial animals to pilgrims who came for worship, and in the process of making sales they exchanged foreign currency. Jesus overturned some of the tables of the money changers in symbolic protest of what he may have considered less than acceptable rates of exchange. But his protest was fundamentally spiritual. The Temple was to be a "house of prayer." The full line of the Old Testament text (Isaiah 56:7) at the base of Jesus's statement is: "a house of prayer for *all nations*." The Temple was to be a place from which the life and light of God's presence was to shine outward to all people through countless lives that were wholly given over to the kingdom of God in the world. For Jesus, the less than ethical financial dealings at the Temple were obviously merely a symptom of a deeper distance from God and from the justice and compassion of God's kingdom.

Jesus did not mean to simply protest the Temple cult and leadership; he also meant to signal its eschatological destruction and replacement. Indeed, it is significant that Mark and Luke place the cleansing of the Temple in close proximity to Jesus's prediction of its coming destruction (Mark 11:15–19, in relation to Mark 13; Luke 19:45–48, in relation to Luke 21). In continuity with John's ministry, Christ's protest at the Temple signaled a coming shift at the very center of Israelite life. The coming time of redemption and renewal through the Spirit would not be centered on the Temple. Instead, it would be focused on Jesus, the new "temple" of God's presence. Quoting N. T. Wright, we can note the following points about Jesus's cleansing of the Temple:

(i) Jesus intended to symbolize the imminent destruction of the Temple.
(ii) He believed that Israel's God was in the process of judging and redeeming his people, not just as one such incident among many but as the climax of Israel's whole history.
(iii) The judgment on the Temple would take the form of destruction by Rome, which (like Babylon according to Jeremiah) would be the agent of the wrath of YHWH.

(iv) The specific reasons for this judgment were, broadly, Israel's failure to obey YHWH's call to be his people . . . more narrowly, Israel's large-scale commitment to national rebellion, coupled with her failure to enact justice with her own society, not least within the Temple-system itself.

(v) . . . This critique, though, was itself part of Jesus' eschatological programme.[46]

Significantly, when the Jewish leaders press Jesus as to what gives him the authority to challenge the Temple cult and leadership, he responds in obvious reference to his own embodied life as the eschatological, or final, temple of the Spirit: "Destroy this temple, and I will raise it again in three days" (John 2:19). Jesus implies that the Jewish leaders were attempting to cling to the old Temple system, which involved their hold on power in Israel's religious and civil life. In that attachment they would seek to destroy Jesus as the new temple of God's presence, who bore the Spirit to bring the eschatological renewal to Israel. But the God who would destroy the Temple to which they clung would raise the temple of Jesus's body that they would seek to destroy. Jesus had the authority to announce judgment on the Temple because, as the future Messiah and King, *he* was the new center of God's presence and reign; *he* would bear the Spirit to give the Spirit; *he* would be the new locus of prayer—not only for Israel, but also "for all nations." His authority over the Temple was shown later in his triumphal entry into Jerusalem. N. T. Wright expresses this point well: "Within his own time and culture, his riding on a donkey over the Mount of Olives, across Kidron, and up to the Temple mount spoke more powerfully than words could have done of a royal claim."[47]

The Spirit-baptized Christ and Prayer

As the Spirit-baptized Temple of God, Jesus is the center of a new address to God as *Abba,* or Father. Basic to his Spirit-baptized life is prayer. Luke specifically mentions that Jesus was *praying* after he was baptized, and as

46. Wright, *Jesus and the Victory of God,* 417–18. An important discussion of these issues that one can read alongside Wright's discussion is E. P. Sanders, *Jesus and Judaism* (Philadelphia: Fortress, 1985), 61–76. Wright agrees with many of Sanders's conclusions, except Wright views the announcement of the coming destruction of the Temple as eschatological, replaced by Christ himself, while Sanders believed that Jesus foresaw the Temple's being rebuilt.

47 Wright, *Jesus and the Victory of God,* 490.

the heaven opened and the Spirit first descended on him (Luke 3:21). This fact gives the impression that the Spirit's descent on him and the Father's announcement that Jesus is the beloved Son were perhaps in part a response to Jesus's addressing his Father in prayer. Jesus's sonship is obviously connected to his prayerful devotion to both his Father and the Spirit's leading. Jesus's prayer life was basic to his unique experience of his heavenly Father as *Abba* and his experience as the one on whom the Spirit rests permanently and abundantly. Parenthetically, Paul notes that the Spirit cries, "Abba, Father" through those who are in Christ, because of him (Rom. 8:15-16). *Abba* was obviously to be viewed as a personal address to God as Father; it was exercised by Christ as the one and only Son and as the quintessential man of the Spirit. Jesus's *Abba* prayer is thus distinctive.

Joachim Jeremias exaggerates when he claims that addressing God in individual prayer as *Abba* was utterly unique to Jesus. It would have been more accurate to say that the *prominence* of such individual address in Jesus's spiritual life was unique.[48] However, it was not just the prominence of Jesus's *Abba* addressing of God that is noteworthy; more importantly, the sense in Jesus that all others address God this way *only because of him*. The Gospel of John bears abundant witness to this assumption (John 1:12; 5:23; 5:43; 6:37-46; 10:30; 10:38; 14:6-10; 15:1-2; 15:23; 15:26; 16:3; 16:15; 16:23; 17:2; 17:11). In John's Gospel, Jesus is the "one and only" sent from the Father to reveal him (1:18). But Jesus's indispensability to the experience of God as Father is not restricted to the Fourth Gospel. Matthew 11:27 is an example of a synoptic witness to the same thought: "All things have been committed to me by my Father. No one knows the Son except the Father, and no one knows the Father except the Son and those to whom the Son chooses to reveal him." In this text Jesus is the only one who shares intimate knowing with the Father and becomes the only one who can share that knowledge with others. Only he is the baptizer in the Spirit who incorporates all flesh into himself and into his *Abba* prayer to the Father (cf. Rom. 8:15-17). Jesus's consciousness of his unique relationship with his heavenly Father emerges very early in Jesus's sense of self (Luke 2:49-50). After discussing whether or not Matthew 11:27 is historically authentic to Jesus, Dunn concludes that its authenticity cannot be dismissed out of hand given the distinctiveness of Jesus's *Abba* address in Matthew and the other synoptic Gospels (11:25-26).

---

48. James D. G. Dunn, *Jesus and the Spirit: A Study of the Religious and Charismatic Experience of Jesus and the First Christians as Reflected in the New Testament* (Philadelphia: Westminster, 1975), 22-23.

"Jesus taught his disciples to share in some sense in his '*Abba*-relationship' with God, sent them forth to participate in his mission of proclaiming the kingdom to Israel . . . and regarded his table fellowship as a foretaste of the life of the kingdom."[49] Jesus thus raised his *Abba* prayer as unique and as a gift that would bless others. Jesus is the Spirit Baptizer.

Prayer plays an enormously important role in Jesus's life in the Spirit as the Son of the Father: "Jesus often withdrew to lonely places and prayed" (Luke 5:16). Such constant prayer indicated a life wholly given over to the reign of the Father and the leading of the Spirit. His challenge to seek *first* the kingdom and righteousness of God above all else (Matt. 6:33) occurs first in the model prayer given for us earlier in that chapter of Matthew. This life quest is tersely characterized in the Lord's Prayer. The opening two words of the Prayer reveal Jesus's willingness even before Pentecost to open up the benefits of his sonship to others. Though Jesus alone is properly allowed to call God his Father, he opens this address up to his followers as well, instructing them, in relation to him, to pray "our Father" (6:9). In a sense, the entire gospel is implied in these two words. How can we be allowed to share in Jesus's *Abba* prayer except by grace? Prayer is thus not a public display for self-aggrandizement (6:5–6). Though importunate, prayer is also not a human achievement secured by force of will and verbal repetition (6:7–8). Instead, prayer is a humble and grateful participation in the gift of addressing God as *Abba* in and with Christ.

The model prayer from Christ thus starts in a Christ-like posture of grateful and devout dependence on God as *Abba* "in heaven," meaning, as the sovereign provider of all good things (Matt. 6:9). The prayer then moves effortlessly from gratitude to yearning. The prayer yearns for God's name to be hallowed on the earth, harking back to Ezekiel 36, which refers to the hallowing of God's name by Israel among the nations, once Israel receives the Spirit of God that turns hearts from stone to flesh (36:22–27). Jesus's baptism in the Spirit will make him the sanctified locus of restored glory to God on behalf of Israel, glorifying the Father on behalf of and before the nations. Christ himself becomes the locus of restored persons and restored community, a diverse and abundant communion of life in God. The fact that the restoration of the Spirit in Ezekiel 36 grants humanity a heart of "flesh" is significant. This turning of human hearts from stone to flesh implies the fulfillment of their very humanity in the reception and witness of the Spirit.

Christ is baptized in the Spirit at the Jordan in order to hallow the Father's name with his human life on earth—as it is in heaven. Christ under-

---

49. Dunn, *Jesus and the Spirit*, 32, 36.

goes this realization of his sonship so that believers can pray "our Father" with him and yearn with him for the hallowing of the Father's name that will come from a life filled and led by the Spirit in the image of the Son (see Rom. 8:15–16). As the incarnate Son and bearer of the Spirit, Christ is the renewed temple of God, where God's name is hallowed. The Christ behind the Lord's Prayer is to be the Spirit Baptizer, incorporating us into his temple life! The kingdom defined by this Messianic gift of the Spirit is not to be defined by human wishes or wants but rather by the will of the Father. The Father's will is yet to be realized from heaven to the earth in the completion of Christ's work (Matt. 6:10).

The Lord's Prayer, then, shifts from vast issues related to the realization of the kingdom of God "on earth" to a realm that is more personal and particularized. The Prayer asks for "daily bread," which was symbolic of all that sustains one's physical well-being (Matt. 6:11). Jesus fasted during his time of trial in the desert out of a conviction that one "shall not live on bread alone, but on every word that comes from the mouth of God" (4:4). He was not thereby disparaging bread, only living by bread *alone*, as though bread is to be regarded as sufficient to life. To live by bread alone is for Jesus a living *death*—death by bread alone. Christ thus fasts in the desert as a protest action meant to symbolize a rejection of this death and a reaching for life as God intended it. He fasts from a feeling for the urgency of his impending mission to grant this life to a dying nation, and a dying world. Jesus's need in the desert was to focus in that moment and for that time on the surpassing importance of spiritual preparation for the challenges ahead. He was willing to sacrifice for the coming kingdom of mercy and justice that the Father would bring. Christ's model prayer is consistent with this spiritual discipline. The *Abba* prayer of Jesus's sonship, of his devotion to the Father, and of the leading of the Spirit, does not start with bread, nor is it dominated by such material concerns. But bread still has a legitimate place in a flourishing human life, and Jesus does not exclude it. But he places it within the larger sense of grateful dependence on God for all things shared by those who are dedicated first and foremost to the liberating reign of God in the world. Consistent with the Lord's Prayer is the kingdom spirituality Jesus describes later in that sixth chapter of Matthew (6:25–34) concerning the need to seek *first* God's kingdom and righteousness (6:33) and not to worry about food, clothing, or what tomorrow might bring (6:31, 34).

The Lord's Prayer then concludes with the communal request for forgiveness, but one that the community praying in the Son and by the Spirit vows has already been shared with one another (Matt. 6:12). This is not to say that the community's reception of grace from Christ is earned by, or arises from, acts of grace toward one another. Of course, all grace shared with one another comes from Christ. But the community's *continued* requests for grace from God necessarily assumes that the grace already sustaining the community is freely shared among its participants. Christ places a weighty assumption before us here. We ignore it at our own peril, as the warnings attached to the end of the Lord's Prayer in Matthew indicate (6:14–15).

In the last place, the Prayer asks the Father not to lead us into temptation; we request deliverance instead (Matt. 6:13). Jesus suffered temptation and trial, our baptism in fire, so that we might know the deliverance that comes through our baptism in the Spirit. Praying alongside Jesus means that we do not covet such trials, neither do we request them. We pray to avoid them, just as Jesus did in the Garden. But should they come, we are thankful to Christ's submission to the Father's will. We are grateful to God for the redemption that Christ's trial brought us, for transforming this trial into an occasion for sanctification.

The Spirit-baptized Christ and the Justice of the Kingdom

The messianic river of love affects social groups and political realities through redemptive justice, a justice that is built from liberating grace but leads to the overthrow of dehumanizing and unjust social privilege. Jesus's Spirit-baptized prayer life starts with the desire that the Father's righteous reign be realized *on earth*, as it is in heaven. This desire is eschatological, but not as an escape into the heavenly realms beyond creation, beyond the injustices and hardships suffered within creation, within human society, in the here and now. According to Jürgen Moltmann, the yearning for God fulfilled by Christ is not only a *Transzendenzfrömmigkeit* (otherworldly piety) set over against a *Solidaritätsfrömmigkeit* (a this-worldly solidarity with the poor and the oppressed).[50] Both options in isolation from each other contradict the incarnate Christ, who bore the Spirit to usher in the mercy and justice of God's reign. Helpful here is Moltmann's point that hope for "the blessedness of the soul without the new earth, is really just as godless as the this-worldliness which wants its kingdom without God, and the earth

---

50. Jürgen Moltmann, *Kirche in der Kraft der Geistes: Ein Beitrag zur messianischen Ekklesiologie* (Gütersloh: Gütersloher Verlagshaus, 1975), 309.

without the horizon of salvation."[51] Hope for salvation that is entirely other-worldly is just as "godless" as a quest for a this-worldly kingdom that neglects God's eschatological promise of redemption and renewal. Moreover, there is no reducing salvation to only one dimension of human experience such as the personal over against the corporate, or vice versa. As Jan M. Lochman shows so well, salvation is multidimensional and multicontextual.[52] In general, though the ultimate swallowing up of mortal life by the immortal Spirit of God exceeds the limits of time and space, it does not leave behind the justice of God's kingdom to be realized in this realm. Christologically, we say something similar when we maintain that the risen and exalted Christ does not leave the historical Jesus behind. So also, the eschatological horizon of the kingdom in the power of the transforming Spirit for which we yearn does not leave behind the this-worldly justice for which Jesus prayed and acted. Jesus will baptize all flesh in the Spirit via the sacrament or declaration of his Spirit-baptized flesh.

Jesus as the Messiah and Lord, as Baptizer in the Spirit, is the one who fulfills justice. This fulfillment is related to the point made above about Jesus as inaugurator of God's coming kingdom. There is no question but that Jesus proclaimed the good news about the kingdom of God (Matt. 4:23; 9:35; Mark 1:14; Luke 4:18–19; 4:43; 20:1). He especially proclaimed repentance and dependence on God for mercy and grace in all things (Matt. 4:17). Jesus calls sinners to repentance but not without challenging the unjust and exclusionary practices that degraded the poor and the outcast. His calls to repentance were not generic but rather contextually specific. The lepers and the Pharisees did not receive exactly the same challenge in every respect. The oppressor was called to repent by letting go of privilege and by seeking to bless and empower others. The oppressed were called to repentance in a way that was liberating or that released them from self-destructive resignation and called them to a humanizing vocation.[53] Revenge is replaced by the challenge of openness to forgive, even one's fiercest enemies (Matt. 5:44). Such openness to forgive the enemy is not a form of resignation to injustice, for, though the will to forgive is unconditional for Jesus, actual reconciliation is conditioned on the other's willingness to accept the liberating and just direction of the kingdom of God.

51. Moltmann, *The Church in the Power of the Spirit: A Contribution to Messianic Ecclesiology* (New York: Harper and Row, 1977), 283.

52. Jan M. Lochman, *Reconciliation and Liberation: Challenging a One-Dimensional View of Salvation* (Minneapolis: Fortress, 1980).

53. See Miroslav Volf, *Exclusion and Embrace: A Theological Exploration of Identity, Otherness, and Reconciliation* (Nashville: Abingdon, 1996), 113–14.

The willingness among the liberated oppressed to embrace the oppressor breaks the cycle of violence and opens the possibility of reconciliation on other than the oppressor's terms. Miroslav Volf notes:

> Repentance thus empowers victims and disempowers the oppressors. It humanizes the victims precisely by protecting them from either mimicking or dehumanizing the oppressors. Far from being a sign of acquiescence to the dominant order, repentance creates a haven in God's new world in the midst of the old and so makes the transformation of the old possible.[54]

The kingdom of grace and love proclaimed and inaugurated by Jesus stood for justice, a redemptive justice that transformed and reconciled people. The direction of this graced life set in motion by this kingdom is one of self-giving love and mutual regard. It results in community, a community baptized in the Spirit and incorporated into Christ (1 Cor. 12:13). The good news of Christ thus opposes the power of sin in its oppressive effects on people's lives—both personal and corporate. The proclamation of the kingdom involves the good news concerning the year of the Lord's favor among the poor and oppressed (Luke 4:18–19). To completely spiritualize these terms is to rip them loose from their ancient settings. We must bear in mind that Zacchaeus's acts of justice toward the poor were vital to his kingdom repentance (Luke 19:1–11). The repentance of a tax collector, someone despised by the religious elite, was more important to God than the self-assurance of the religious leader. One is justified before God by such repentance (Luke 18:9–14). The conversion of Zacchaeus challenged the complainers to convert as well. Conversion was communal, and it called for a merciful and just community.

Through Christ's redemptive work, justice is restored between God and humanity and among believers in community with Christ and each other. The Spirit Baptizer will incorporate us into a community, a just and mutually edifying community governed by liberating love, in which there is neither Jew nor Greek, bond nor free, neither male nor female (cf. 1 Cor. 12:13; Gal. 3:28; cf. Acts 2:17–18). Distinctions do not disappear, only the assumption of privilege based on those distinctions. This community seeks to bear witness in word, in a shared life, and in external witness of the goodness of God. One could also speak of signs of kingdom justice already present in the world that implicitly bear witness to the shared Spirit, human dignity, and gracious

---

54. Volf, *Exclusion and Embrace*, 116.

generosity that are to be affirmed in Christ. Not only Zacchaeus, but later also Cornelius, had already begun to live by and for such things, even before they came to see them as fulfilled in Christ (Luke 19:1–10; Acts 10).

The righteousness and healing of God's kingdom is both now and not yet. Christ's proclamation of the kingdom assumed that God was not only breaking into human history through his Spirit-led ministry (Matt. 12:28), but that this reality was not yet fulfilled in its effect on creation. He was not yet the Spirit Baptizer, and the full effect of that act on creation was far from realized. Like a seed buried beneath the ground—not yet visible as a full-grown tree—so is the kingdom of God dawning in the ministry of Jesus, in his presence, proclamation, and acts of deliverance (Matt. 13:31–32). The kingdom of God is still a mystery in the world: its presence is having an effect but not one that has reached its full purpose in transforming creation. Yet those who came to detect the presence of the kingdom in Jesus and the presence of the Spirit working through him were called to give all in conformity to Christ's way in the world. Like someone who sells all to purchase a plot of land that has a hidden treasure buried beneath it, it is also true of those who have discovered the presence of God's reign breaking into the world through Christ and the Spirit and will give all to receive it and live by it (Matt. 13:44). Those who follow Christ must carry the cross with him, which means giving of themselves through him, entirely to the reign of God's self-giving love and justice in the world (Matt. 16:24; Mark 8:34; Luke 9:23).

The rich young ruler balks at the challenge of giving everything he has to the poor in order to follow Christ. The ruler's entire life was defined by the privilege and power granted to him by the riches he had inherited—and to which he had given himself. How could he be expected to let all of this fall to the ground like dust so that he could now be totally redefined at the core of his existence by the kingdom purposes being inaugurated in the world by Christ? The ruler's rejection of that radical change caused Jesus Christ to remark about how difficult it is for those entangled in riches to have their entire lives redefined by God's purposes in the world. Jesus concludes, however, that all things are possible with God (Luke 18:18–30). In the very next chapter, the story of Zacchaeus, a wealthy tax collector, proves this point. By the time Zacchaeus joyously encounters Christ, he has already taken steps to disinvest himself of everything that might hold him back from giving of himself to God's kingdom that is dawning through Christ in the world (19:1–10).[55]

---

55. The verbs in 19:8 indicate that he is already involved in giving to the poor.

The righteousness of God's reign breaking in through Christ fulfills the law. The law of God requires total love for God (Deut. 6:4) and neighbor (Lev. 19:18). But the injustice of sin and oppression also gave rise to the need for redemptive justice, the conditions for which are set up through a divine mercy that reconciles people with God and with one another. This divine mercy transforms them in the direction of genuine repentance and self-giving for the fulfillment of God's will for the earth. The righteousness to which the law bears witness is most basically a divine act that is carried out in history in God's redeeming and renewing presence. It is also covenant faithfulness to the cause of divine justice both within Israel and in the world. Peter Stuhlmacher explains:

> "God's righteousness" in the Old Testament and early Judaism means, above all, the activity of the one God to create welfare and salvation in the creation, in the history of Israel, and in the situation of the (end-time) judgment.[56]

The hope for the time of righteousness in the Old Testament was thus also merged with the promise of the coming servant of God upon whom the Spirit will rest, as well as the coming outpouring of the Spirit itself. The righteousness to which the law also bore witness is pictured as coming with imagery used of the arriving Spirit, as a coming rainfall or a mighty river that will renew life (Isa. 45:8; Amos 5:24; Hosea 6:3; 10:12). The Old Testament envisions the fulfillment of the law as coming through the resting of the Spirit on God's chosen servant in order to bring a restoration that interconnects justice, mercy, and knowledge of God.

Three major texts can be quoted as a background to Christ's Spirit-anointed ministry in support of justice: Isaiah 11:2-5; 42:1-7; and 61:1-6.[57] Two of these texts are cited in the Gospels in commentary on Jesus's reception of the Spirit at the Jordan, and one of the texts is implied as an important background to this event. Note initially Isaiah 11:2-5, and 9-10:

> The Spirit of the LORD will rest on him—
> the Spirit of wisdom and of understanding,
> the Spirit of counsel and of might,

---

56. Peter Stuhlmacher, *A Challenge to the New Perspective: Revisiting Paul's Doctrine of Justification* (Downers Grove, IL: InterVarsity, 2000), 19.

57. Michael Welker, *God the Spirit*, 108-17.

the Spirit of the knowledge and fear of the LORD—
and he will delight in the fear of the LORD.
He will not judge by what he sees with his eyes,
    or decide by what he hears with his ears;
but with righteousness he will judge the needy,
    with justice he will give decisions for the poor of the earth.
He will strike the earth with the rod of his mouth;
    with the breath of his lips he will slay the wicked.
Righteousness will be his belt
    and faithfulness the sash around his waist. (Isa. 11:2–5)

They will neither harm nor destroy
    on all my holy mountain,
for the earth will be filled with the knowledge of the LORD,
    as the waters cover the sea.
In that day the Root of Jesse will stand as a banner for the peoples;
    the nations will rally to him, and his resting place will be glorious.
(Isa. 11:9–10)

Though the above text is not cited in the Gospels in reference to Jesus's reception of the Spirit at the Jordan River, it nonetheless provides us with important background to that event. The Spirit of the Lord will rest on the servant, who becomes a storehouse of wisdom, understanding, counsel and might. From these powers of the Spirit he will provide justice for the needy and the poor—by restoring to them their God-given dignity and purpose. He will also judge the unrepentant wicked by the same breath of his mouth by which the Spirit bearer restores those who repent. John the Baptist would say, "He will baptize in the Holy Spirit and fire!" When the knowledge of the Lord covers the earth as the waters cover the sea, the nations will rally around God's servant on whom the Spirit rests (11:9–10). Second, take note of Isaiah 42:1–7:

"Here is my servant, whom I uphold,
    my chosen one, in whom I delight;
I will put my Spirit on him,
    and he will bring justice to the nations.
He will not shout or cry out,
    or raise his voice in the streets.
A bruised reed he will not break,

and a smoldering wick he will not snuff out.
   In faithfulness he will bring forth justice;
he will not falter or be discouraged
      till he establishes justice on earth.
      In his teaching the islands will put their hope."
This is what God the LORD says—
      the Creator of the heavens, who stretches them out,
who spreads out the earth with all that springs from it,
      who gives breath to its people,
      and life to those who walk on it:
"I, the LORD, have called you in righteousness;
      I will take hold of your hand.
I will keep you and will make you
      to be a covenant for the people
      and a light for the Gentiles,
to open eyes that are blind,
      to free captives from prison
      and to release from the dungeon those who sit in darkness.

This text is cited in Matthew 12:18–21 to explain Jesus's installation at the Jordan River as the Spirit Bearer. God takes delight in the one on whom the Spirit rests. He will bring justice to Israel and to all nations, but not in the usual ways. He will not shout out, nor will he raise his voice, in the streets. He will not buy into the standards of commonsense morality, nor gain power through a political uprising. Instead, he will enter into human despair in order to offer grace and new beginnings through the Spirit of life, breaking the hold that it has on the human psyche and on human communities. He will be ranked among the bruised reeds, but he will not be broken; he will be ranked among the smoldering wicks, but he will not be snuffed out (Isa. 42:2–3). He will end up teaching the knowledge of the Lord and bringing hope (42:4); he will be a light to the nations (42:6); his justice will be both merciful and liberating (42:7). The Spirit Baptizer will bring justice to the nations through the witness of communities that subvert the injustices of the world by testifying to Christ's liberating reign both in their shared life and through acts of public witness.

Finally, take note of Isaiah 61:1–6:

The Spirit of the Sovereign LORD is on me,
      because the LORD has anointed me

to proclaim good news to the poor.
He has sent me to bind up the brokenhearted,
    to proclaim freedom for the captives
    and release from darkness for the prisoners,
to proclaim the year of the LORD's favor
    and the day of vengeance of our God,
to comfort all who mourn,
    and provide for those who grieve in Zion—
to bestow on them a crown of beauty
    instead of ashes,
the oil of joy
    instead of mourning,
and a garment of praise
    instead of a spirit of despair.
They will be called oaks of righteousness,
    a planting of the LORD
    for the display of his splendor.
They will rebuild the ancient ruins
    and restore the places long devastated;
they will renew the ruined cities
    that have been devastated for generations.
Strangers will shepherd your flocks;
    foreigners will work your fields and vineyards.
And you will be called priests of the LORD,
    you will be named ministers of our God.
You will feed on the wealth of nations,
    and in their riches you will boast.

This text is also cited by Jesus in his commentary on the reception of the Spirit at the Jordan (Luke 4:18–19). The one on whom the Spirit rests will mean good news to the poor and the oppressed. His proclamation of the year of the Lord's favor that brings liberty to the downtrodden means vengeance on those who oppose grace. But those who mourn will be comforted; the poor, the broken-hearted, and the captives will find a new beginning in the bearer of the Spirit and the liberating reign of God that will come forth from him. Jesus quotes from this text in his own commentary on his future role as the Spirit Baptizer (Luke 4:18–19). The combination of Spirit and fire that John uses dovetails in Jesus's ministry with references in the above text to a divine favor that liberates the oppressed and comforts those who mourn while judging those who oppose this grace. But this mercy will extend to all: to the oppressed among the poor and to the tax collectors who exploited them on behalf of a heartless empire. But they must repent and change direction in partaking of it. Kingdom grace is free, but it demands everything in being received. Jesus exhorts his audience to count the cost before receiving it (Luke 14:25–33).

There are several general points that can be gathered from all three of these Old Testament texts. First, all of them locate the coming time of renewal with the resting of the Spirit on the servant of God. This event somehow provides a new era of justice, mercy, and knowledge of God. From the resting of the Spirit on Christ, the dimensions of this redemptive justice will be administered. Second, God will take delight in this Spirit-anointed servant and will place authority to bring about the coming renewal and judgment.

Third, the Messiah will not gain authority in the usual way of gaining political strength (crying out in the streets); he will not appeal to commonly held moralities with all of their one-sided or biased perspectives; he will not accumulate power by manipulating or oppressing others. Instead, he will side with those who are neglected and crushed. But he himself will not be crushed. From this path of overcoming love, he will offer a redemptive justice that imparts the knowledge and wisdom of God as embodied in Christ's sojourn on earth. He will open up to creation its capacity to know God, to hallow God's name, and to experience the redemptive justice that comes with the restoration of human community in God and for God.

Fourth, the powers of the Spirit impart this knowledge and wisdom in a way that is excessive and abundant, flooding the earth as the waters cover the sea. The nations will be brought into this redemptive justice that is granted through the life of the Spirit and the ministry of the chosen servant.

Fifth, though renewal will be potentially universal, those who have been most neglected and beaten down will be the ones most notably lifted up. The poor and oppressed are granted special focus as recipients of justice, that is, not a condescending charity but a liberating and redemptive justice that fulfills the human community and vocation. This element is important to the witness of the law of God, for "a judicial structure which is not constantly oriented toward the integration of the weak and disadvantaged, does not deserve the great name of 'righteousness.'"[58] In general, through the Spirit-anointed servant of God, the "establishment of universal righteousness in

---

58. Welker, *God the Spirit*, 110.

connection with justice and mercy brings with itself a knowledge of God that redounds to the benefit of Israel and the nations."[59]

One must interpret Jesus's baptism in the Holy Spirit at the Jordan against the backdrop of this rich Old Testament set of expectations concerning the coming justice of the kingdom of God through the anointed servant. This set of expectations reveals the larger framework for understanding John's conviction that the coming one will baptize in the Spirit and fire, or will bring both renewal and judgment. But how will Jesus do this? How will he provide this river of the renewing Spirit in the world? And most baffling, how will he light a fire of judgment if he himself is counted among the smoldering wicks being snuffed out by the dark powers that deny the life of the liberating Spirit? Bear in mind that the justice he brings is redemptive justice that offers mercy and transformation to all who repent. This fact implies that the fire Christ brings will first be carried by him in order to provide the redemptive source necessary for the just community.

The above insight means that Jesus will step into this role as the Baptizer in Spirit and fire, to be sure, but not in a way that John—or many others— could have entirely foreseen. He will bear the Spirit to bring the good news to Israel and the nations, to lift up the downtrodden and create communities of the Spirit dedicated to the path of the crucified one in the world. But he will do this precisely by bearing the fire of judgment that will come upon the world himself. The justice and righteousness that he will bring to the world will have significant political implications—but precisely because it is redemptive. It will be rooted in the redemptive love and justice of the cross, of a God who suffers with and for suffering humanity to redeem and to heal, to shape humanity into the image of the crucified and exalted Christ by self-imparting to all flesh.

The Spirit-baptized Christ and the Law

In the above discussion of the justice to be inaugurated by the Spirit Baptizer, I mentioned that this justice would fulfill the law of God. But more needs to be said about this point. According to Jesus, the law is fulfilled in loving God and the neighbor with one's entire life (Luke 10:27), restoring glory and honor to God in the world, and realizing redemptive justice in and through human community. The law bears witness to the demands of divine love and righteousness in such ways, but the law cannot impart these realities.

---

59. Welker, *God the Spirit*, 116–19.

"For what the law was powerless to do, because it was weakened by the flesh, God did by sending his own Son in the likeness of sinful flesh to be a sin offering" (Rom. 8:3). Not only is the sin offering of Christ by the Spirit of God needed to fulfill the witness of the law (Heb. 9:14), but so is the gift of the Spirit of life that creates new life and new communities of justice in the world: "For if a law had been given that could impart life, then righteousness would certainly have come by the law" (Gal. 3:21). The law bears witness to a new reality in the world that it cannot impart itself. Only God, through the Messiah and through the gift of the Spirit, can impart it. This is why Paul refers to the redemptive righteousness of the kingdom of God as an eschatological reality dawning in the world—but still future: "For through the Spirit we eagerly await by faith the righteousness for which we hope" (Gal. 5:5). So Ezekiel gives us the crucial prophetic word about the fulfillment of the law: "And I will put my Spirit in you and move you to follow my decrees and be careful to keep my laws" (Ezek. 36:27). The Spirit rests on Jesus in order to bring to humanity an unprecedented revelation of God in the world, but only through the redemptive path of Jesus and the gift of the Spirit poured forth from him will this knowledge become reality in us.

The law bears witness to weighty matters of human personal and communal life. It is in this light that we can understand Jesus's clash with Jewish leaders for emphasizing "minor" matters of the law that justify the status quo of Temple life and politics, while neglecting the weighty matters to which the era of the Spirit, through the Messiah, is bearing witness in the world:

> Woe to you, teachers of the law and Pharisees, you hypocrites! You give a tenth of your spices—mint, dill and cumin. But you have neglected the more important matters of the law—justice, mercy and faithfulness. You should have practiced the latter, without neglecting the former. (Matt. 23:23)

But the problem is worse than that, for some leaders used external devotion to ceremonial laws to cover a heart that was far from the will of the Father for the world: "You clean the outside of the cup and dish, but inside they are full of greed and self-indulgence" (Matt. 23:25).

Jesus clashes with those in the scribal tradition about how to interpret the law and where to place their priorities. He opposed that tradition by healing on the Sabbath (Mark 3:1–2) and dining with those considered unclean (Luke 15:1–2). Why were the Temple elite not doing this? He introduces these new practices through a revelation that is final or connected to the bearing and imparting of the end-time presence of the Holy Spirit in the world, or of the liberating reign of God in the world (both of which amount to the same thing). He sharply opposes scribal interpretations with an unprecedented authority, saying "truly" before everything he says, implying a finality to what he says: "For truly I tell you, many prophets and righteous people longed to see what you see but did not see it, and to hear what you hear but did not hear it" (Matt. 13:17). He also uses the phrase "I say unto you" as though he needs no higher authority beyond what the Father has given him and what the Spirit confirms and verifies. What higher authority can there be than that (Matt. 5:21-22, 27-28, 31-32, 33-34, 38-39, 43-44)? He is not opposing Moses here. I. Howard Marshall notes that there is a "good case that Jesus was essentially attacking the scribal interpretation of the written law and not the law itself. On the contrary, he was sharpening the demands of the law."[60]

Jesus's teaching on the law was meant to have a shock effect on those who had succumbed to commonsense notions of morality that were contrary to the ways in which God's kingdom was finding embodiment in Christ's liberating ministry. Informed by his mission to proclaim good news to the poor and the oppressed, Jesus spoke in beatitudes, and they suggested a series of unexpected reversals in social life. The poor in spirit and the destitute will belong to the kingdom; those who mourn will be comforted; the meek (or powerless) will have the earth as their inheritance; those who thirst for righteousness will be filled to overflowing; those who give out of mercy, even if presently unappreciated, will receive the full benefit of mercy one day; and those who are persecuted for the sake of justice may be displaced from the kingdom of the world, but they will belong to the kingdom of God (Matt. 5:3-7, 10). In other words, because of the kingdom of God that Jesus is inaugurating, things are not always as they appear and will turn out different from what many may expect. One recalls here not only Jesus's mission to proclaim good news to the poor and oppressed (Luke 4:18) but also the reversals of his mother's song of praise when he was yet unborn (Luke 1:46-55). Note, especially, these reversals:

> He has brought down rulers from their thrones
>   but has lifted up the humble.
> He has filled the hungry with good things
>   but has sent the rich away empty. (Luke 1:52-53)

60. I. Howard Marshall, *The Origins of New Testament Christology* (Downers Grove, IL: InterVarsity, 1976), 48.

After Jesus notes the reversals in his Sermon on the Mount, he hammers the audience with stunning exclusions: only the pure in heart can see God; only the peacemakers can be called his children! Jesus does not demand perfection, but he does assume a life orientation that yearns for God and for the accomplishment of God's will on earth. Toward this end, Jesus demanded that due attention be granted to motives, and not only external actions (5:21–30). He wanted his audience to see anyone who was in need as a neighbor, another human whom one is to love as one loves oneself. To make his point, Jesus told a parable in which the respected leaders of Israelite society pass by a man bleeding on the side of the road. The hero of the story, the one who goes out of his way to help the man in need, is a Samaritan, someone who would not have been held in high esteem in Israelite society (Luke 10:25–37). Jesus even demands that divine love be willed for one's most hated and feared enemies (Matt. 5:43–48). Jesus would do the same; he even prayed from the cross for his crucifiers: "Father, forgive them, for they do not know what they are doing" (Luke 23:34). Ultimately, the witness of the law to the love of God and neighbor is fulfilled at the cross.

Therefore, an unprecedented finality to Jesus's fulfillment of the law places him above the rest of Israel, even above Moses himself: "Jesus has been found worthy of greater honor than Moses" (Heb. 3:3). "For the law was given through Moses; grace and truth came through Jesus Christ" (John 1:17). Hence, Moses is surpassed but not denied. Jesus has not come to abolish the law and the prophets but to fulfill them. Heaven and earth may pass away but not the words of the law and the prophets "until everything is accomplished" (Matt. 5:17–18). Jesus saw himself as standing at that point of ultimate accomplishment. The eschatological reach of the law's fulfillment ("heaven and earth may pass away . . .") points not only to the cross but also to the resurrection of Jesus, to the gift of the Spirit at Pentecost, and ultimately to the fulfillment of Pentecost in the Spirit's work throughout the world in fulfillment of Christ's final reign. The eschatological reach and finality of the Messiah's reign as the Spirit Baptizer provides the background for understanding his distinctive authority when speaking of the meaning and fulfillment of the law: "He taught as one who had authority, and not as their teachers of the law" (Matt. 7:29). If the meaning of revelation is fulfilled in the eschatological promise of final salvation, only the Spirit Baptizer who will bring it to pass can proclaim it with final authority.

As the one who was ushering in the era of salvation, Jesus also spoke with unprecedented authority in other areas of life. He said to a dead girl, "I say to you, get up!"—and it's enough to raise her from the dead (Mark

5:41). He commanded the storm ("Quiet, be still!"), and it obeyed (4:39). He said without hesitation to the lame man, "Your sins are forgiven" (2:5), and he did not back down when someone complained that only God possesses such authority. In fact, Jesus healed the man to prove he had that authority on earth (2:11). He commanded evil spirits to leave, "and they obeyed him" (1:27). The demons recognized his eschatological significance as final judge, and they pleaded not to be tortured (5:7). One's relationship to God's kingdom depends on one's relationship to Christ (Matt. 7:21), for Christ alone is of ultimate significance: "If you believe in God; believe also in me" (John 14:1). "I am the way and the truth and the life. No one comes to the Father except through me" (14:6). "Jesus stands alone; he has no equals," because Jesus spoke "as if he were God."[61]

Jesus's place at the point of fulfillment for the witness of both the law and the prophets is dramatically illustrated for us at Jesus's transfiguration. Jesus took Peter, James, and John to a "high mountain," and there he was "transfigured" before their very eyes. "His face shone like the sun, and his clothes became as white as the light" (Matt. 17:2). There is little question that a vision was offered here that anticipated the exalted Christ of eschatological glory, as is implied by Jesus's instructions that the disciples not tell what they had seen until Jesus was raised and exalted (17:9). It is significant that Moses and Elijah, the chief symbols of the former witness of the law and the prophets, appear in conversation with Jesus (17:3). But only he reveals eschatological glory. The text does not give us the content of that conversation. But given Jesus's eschatological significance, the implication is that it involves the yielding of what is former to what comes to fulfill it. Peter's desire to build shelters for all three is quickly interrupted by the Father's voice, which highlights the entire point of the event: "This is my Son, whom I love; with him I am well pleased. Listen to him!" (17:5). The voices of Elijah and Moses are fulfilled in him. The announcement of Jesus's eschatological sonship that had been given at the Jordan River is reaffirmed. Jesus's path to his baptism in the Spirit that will find its fulfillment in his death, resurrection, and impartation of life is assured. That path will be severely tested, to be sure. But a glimpse of victory is already given. The disciples will lose sight of it momentarily. But the Lord will restore it to them, all in due time. They will then be able to look back to the experience of Jesus on the Mount and say that the words of the law and the prophets are shown to be "completely reliable" because of Christ (2 Pet. 1:19–21).

---

61. Marshall, *Origins of New Testament Christology*, 50–51.

The Spirit-baptized Christ and Table Fellowship

Baptized in the Spirit, Jesus already begins to create analogues of the new communities of redemptive justice and love that his outpouring of the Spirit at Pentecost will bring about in the world. Jesus's table fellowship was a unique feature of his mission and requires greater attention here. Jesus told a parable about a rich man who invited the coveted members of society to come to his wedding feast, only to receive excuses about why they could not attend (Luke 14:18). As the hour for the wedding grew near, the host instructed his servants to go out into the streets to invite the undesirables: "Go out quickly into the streets and alleys of the town and bring in the poor, the crippled, the blind and the lame" (14:21). The irony of the story is that these folks ended up being the best ones to invite. After the so-called undesirables came in, and there was still room for more, the host instructed the servant to invite even more—"that my house may be full" (14:23). Indeed, there is room for many more, and the more who come, the merrier. This is the kingdom that Jesus inaugurates in the world with his table fellowship.

Jesus's table fellowship was intended as a banquet of the coming kingdom. Indeed, his first miracle was at a wedding feast, where he turned water into wine and broke custom by giving the guests the best wine at the end of the feast (John 2:1–11). The eschatological kingdom of God is not drudgery or a lifeless set of obligations; rather, it is a liberating fulfillment that can only be received and celebrated gratefully. And in this celebration God saves the best wine for last. In the final hour before the celebration, we are to go out and invite the destitute of the earth so that the community of the Spirit in the temple of the Son may be full and rich in a just and loving communion. The kingdom places demands on humanity, requiring total commitment. But Christ's yoke is easy and his burden light (Matt. 11:30), because the way of Christ comes first as a gift in the liberating power of the Spirit. Only in the power of that gift of love, and only in the spirit of gratitude and celebration can the demands be understood in their proper light.

Jesus sought to bring not only the poor to his table, but also the tax collectors who once oppressed them. He also invited those religious leaders who rejected both the poor and the tax collectors, but not all of them responded favorably. That Jesus ate with tax collectors and sinners was a common complaint lodged by the religious authorities (Luke 15:1–2). The parable of the prodigal son is a key text here. The story begins with the younger son making an unusual request: "Father, give me my share of the estate" (15:12). So the father divides the estate between the two sons. Rather than mimic the generosity of his father, the younger son does the opposite. He squanders his inheritance on a self-absorbed binge and, in the process, shows no respect for his family nor for the generosity with which they have treated him. It takes a famine and real destitution for the young man to come to his senses. Perhaps he had taken way too much for granted, for even his father's hired hands are now better off than he is (15:17). He would now return to the household of his father and announce, "Father, I have sinned against heaven and against you" (15:18), that is, against the generosity that comes from above and against the family that channeled that blessing to him. Feeling unworthy to be called his father's son, he also planned to include a plea to be accepted, if need be, as one of the hired hands (15:19). Perhaps from there he could pay back some of the inheritance that he had squandered. The young man is willing to do whatever it takes to walk the path to redemption. But upon his arrival, before he even has a chance to give his speech of contrition, the father is moved with compassion upon seeing him approaching from a long way off, and runs to greet him. He throws his arms around his son and kisses him. Rather than ask what happened to the money—or complain about how the son had squandered it—the father ignores the issue entirely and welcomes the wayward son back with a royal welcome: the best robe, a ring, new sandals, and a feast fit for a king. All that matters is that the boy who was lost is now found, one who was dead is now alive.

The older brother enters the scene at this point, and he has a very different reaction to the return of his younger brother. To his mind, his kid brother's transgression and consequent unworthiness are paramount. He refuses to join his father in the welcoming party for his brother. Obviously perplexed by the older son's absence from the celebration, the father approaches him and implores him to join the party. But the older son wastes no time airing his grievance. He, in his turn, is baffled by the banquet being lavished on his undeserving brother, while *his* worthy accomplishments have gone relatively unnoticed. He feels terribly unappreciated: "Look! All these years I've been slaving for you and never disobeyed your orders. Yet you never gave me even a young goat so I could celebrate with my friends" (Luke 15:29). And just look at the celebration you're having to welcome this ungrateful scoundrel back into the fold! What does someone have to do to get a party around here! Be ungrateful? Betray the family honor?

The father immediately sets the angry son straight, and in a way that cuts right to the core of the key issue at stake. The family is not based on what one deserves or does not deserve: "Everything I have is yours," he says (15:31). No amount of extravagance displayed at a celebration can match that. It is rather about a deeper sense of justice that is merciful and seeks the restoration of lost bonds of love and mutual regard. It is about a merciful justice that celebrates the restoration of the lost: "But we had to celebrate and be glad" (15:32). But it is also about accountability. When the older brother refers to "this son of *yours*" in the midst of his complaint, the father responds with "this brother of *yours*" (15:30, 32). The compassion of God's kingdom is not mere sentiment. It arises from insight into how we are bound together by God's image and God's calling. It awakens in us the idea that to betray each other is to betray ourselves. The only way for the older brother to find grace is to grant it to the younger one—to whom God has made him accountable. The outcast son is the tax collector, and the resentful son is the religious leader who opposed Jesus's open hospitality. And Jesus is the faithful elder Son who has gone into the far country to find us, to bear our shame and alienation so as to bring us home to his Father's household. As the Spirit Baptizer, Jesus incorporates others into himself in order to open up the Father's banquet to them all. He conditions his own existence in becoming our head and elder brother in this way, the last Adam that opens the mercy and justice of the kingdom to all flesh.

The Spirit-baptized Christ and Healing

After Jesus's experience at the Jordan, he defined his Spirit-baptized life as a life that would proclaim the year of the Lord's favor, a time of grace that would be manifested in the overcoming of the dark powers and the healing of the sick. The vast number of texts about Christ's healing ministry leaves no doubt that this was a major part of his life's ministry (Matt. 4:24; 8:16; 14:14; 15:30; 21:14; Mark 1:34; 3:10; 6:13; 6:56; Luke 4:40; 5:15; 6:18). With the Spirit of God remaining with him and granted abundantly upon him, Jesus sensed that sonship brought with it a unique consciousness of spiritual power, "the power of God flowing through him to overcome other superhuman power, evil power, to restore and make whole."[62] When Jesus was accused of casting out demons by the power of Satan, Jesus responded by saying that, besides lacking discernment, this charge made no logical sense. How can a kingdom survive if it is divided against itself (Matt. 12:25–27)? "But if it is by the Spirit of God that I drive out demons, then the kingdom of God has come upon you" (12:28). Now that makes sense. A spiritual force that casts out the dark

---

62. Dunn, *Jesus and the Spirit*, 47.

powers and makes people whole must be a sign that the liberating reign of God is at work. Jesus is committed to restraining evil and spreading liberty; he will tie up the strong man and plunder his house (12:29).

Jesus placed a strong emphasis on the faith of the person receiving the healing, though the primary issue is doubtless Christ's authority to heal (e.g., Mark 2:8–12). Though the healing ministry of Jesus is not just a social issue, the social dimension of healing cannot be ignored. In being healed, these people were humanized and brought into loving communities. Jesus's healing ministry anticipated the communities of Pentecost dedicated to the healing and humanization of all persons without regard to social privilege (e.g., Acts 2:17–18; 1 Cor. 12:13; Gal. 3:28). Eschatologically speaking, the healing ministry of Jesus showed his authority over the demonic realm as well as over the powers of nature. His healing ministry thus anticipated the "powers of the age to come" (Heb. 6:5) that will be manifested in his resurrection. Therefore, Jesus's healing ministry is not simply an accommodation to an ancient worldview but is rather a permanent part of the church's devotion to the ministry of Jesus Christ.

Jesus's miracle-working was well known enough to make an impression on Jewish leaders. The Pharisee Nicodemus came to Jesus in secret to engage him because of the impressive signs of God's power that were active through Jesus: "Rabbi, we know that you are a teacher who has come from God. For no one could perform the signs you are doing if God were not with him" (John 3:2). Jesus immediately shifts attention to the point of the miracles, which was to bear witness to the kingdom of God dawning in the world: "Very truly I tell you, no one can enter the kingdom of God unless they are born of water and the Spirit" (3:5). It is unclear what Jesus meant in this context with "born of water," though spiritual rebirth under the sign of the water rite may be indicated. Being born of the Spirit (3:8) means being "born not of natural descent, nor of human decision or a husband's will, but born of God" (1:13). The Spirit of God working through Christ is liberating and must be welcomed with repentance and complete dependence on the way of God's self-giving love in the world. The change that this requires is radical, involving a completely new sense of self and direction of loyalty. The signs and wonders that come through Christ in the power of the Spirit bear witness to the power of divine love and to its eschatological horizon.

This commitment to the larger purposes of God in the world meant that Jesus was not in favor of sign-seeking as an end in itself. The greatest sign granted to Israel will be the sign of Jonah, a cryptic reference to Jesus's future resurrection from the dead and the witness that will go forth from that event on Pentecost, just as Jonah came out of the belly of the fish, the belly of death, to proclaim repentance to Nineveh (Matt. 12:38–45). Jesus provides a sign of his victory over sin and death in the raising of Lazarus, but this startling event only caused the leadership of Israel to seek to kill him. The reason was that the leadership of Israel thought Jesus's miracles might have the potential to inspire a mass movement on Jesus's behalf, a people's movement that could stir the wrath of the Roman Empire: "Here is this man performing many signs. If we let him go on like this, everyone will believe in him, and then the Romans will come and take away both our temple and our nation" (John 11:47–48). In other words, the leaders, in an effort to spare their Temple, would seek to destroy Jesus, who is in reality the new temple of God, the new locus of the divine presence and favor. Their conclusion? "It is better . . . that one man die for the people than that the whole nation perish" (11:50). Ironically, the signs that were intended to direct attention to final salvation through Christ ended up merely being used as a reason for killing him. Rather than snuffing him out, however, this murderous act would only bring about God's intended fulfillment for Christ's life. Christ was not to gain power by raising his voice in the street but by laying down his life for the sake of others.

The Fire-baptized Christ

This laying down of life would be Christ's baptism in fire. "Our God is a consuming fire" (Heb. 12:29). Humanity is created for immersion in the Spirit of life to embody in community the image of the Son; the consuming fire of God's holy presence is meant to purge and renew humanity, but it becomes more thoroughly devastating in the context of alienation from God. Hans Urs von Balthasar notes, about Christ after the Jordan experience, that "he who is to baptize in the Holy Spirit and fire . . . presses towards the baptism of the Cross which he must receive."[63] Christ's baptism in the Spirit that will save humanity involves his baptism in the fire of death and alienation from God. Jesus's self-sacrifice will be how he endures and transforms humanity's baptism in fire. It is the baptism of his death (Mark 10:38–39). This baptism in fire will call Christ's very identity as the Spirit-baptized Son of the Father radically into question and will set the stage for the vindication of his resurrection from the dead by the Spirit (Rom. 1:4). Hebrews 5:8–9 summarizes

63. Hans Urs von Balthasar, *Mysterium Paschale* (Grand Rapids: Eerdmans, 1990), 92.

the matter well: "Son though he was, he learned obedience from what he suffered and, once made perfect, he became the source of eternal salvation for all who obey him." He took on our baptism in fire but was not destroyed by it. As the Son of the Father and man of the Spirit, he emerged from it only perfected by the experience, perfected in resurrection so that he could impart new life to us all, so that the fire of God could now be experienced as a sanctifying force. The baptism in fire is thus inseparable from the Son of God's baptism in the Holy Spirit.

We will explore the meaning of Christ's death and resurrection (the ultimate baptism in fire and Spirit) in the following chapter. Here we need to explore the background to these events and, especially, how the life of Jesus led up to them. As I have noted throughout our discussion thus far, John the Baptist announced at the Jordan that the coming one will not only bring a torrent of the Spirit of restoration but also flames of judgment. Such messianic woes unleashed upon the earth are foretold in the Old Testament. Look, for example, at Isaiah 66:15–16:

> See, the LORD is coming with fire,
>   and his chariots are like a whirlwind;
> he will bring down his anger with fury,
>   and his rebuke with flames of fire.
> For with fire and with his sword
>   the LORD will execute judgment on all people,
>   and many will be those slain by the LORD.

And Isaiah 30:28:

> His breath is like a rushing torrent,
>   rising up to the neck.
> He shakes the nations in the sieve of destruction;
>   he places in the jaws of the peoples
>   a bit that leads them astray.

Now compare such verses with John the Baptist's announcement of the one who is coming, the one whose way the Baptist is preparing:

> I baptize you with water for repentance. But after me comes one who is more powerful than I, whose sandals I am not worthy to carry. He will baptize you with the Holy Spirit and fire. His winnowing fork is

in his hand, and he will clear his threshing floor, gathering his wheat into the barn and burning up the chaff with unquenchable fire. (Matt. 3:11–12)

How the Messiah will pour forth a river of the Spirit that will engulf people is, in the light of the above texts, not only hopeful but also ominous—a baptism in Spirit and *fire*. John the Baptist announced one baptism of two different effects, a baptism in the Spirit unto restoration and in fire unto judgment, as John's parallel statement indicates: "His winnowing fork is in his hand, and he will clear his threshing floor, gathering his wheat into the barn and burning up the chaff with unquenchable fire" (Matt. 3:12). Unless this text has a double meaning, which seems unlikely, the Spirit points to restoration and the fire to devastating judgment. This is not to deny that the Messiah's baptism is still in a sense one baptism—of "Spirit-and-fire."[64] After all, the Spirit is involved in both restoration and judgment. One need not deny that both effects come by way of the Spirit. Perhaps it would be more accurate to speak of two effects of the Messiah's baptizing in the Spirit, namely, of "Spirit" (restoration) and of "Spirit-fire" (judgment). To avoid confusion, the decision was made to use the shorthand "Spirit" (restoration) and "fire" (judgment). The "river" of the Spirit mediated by the Messiah will bring the Spirit's restoration to those who repent and the fire of judgment to those who oppose this flourishing of life. The fire baptism no doubt turns into a purgative force under the Messiah's incorporation of it into his own redemptive work, but it is unlikely that John had this possibly positive understanding of fire in mind. There is no explicit indication in his announcement that the fire is a positive force; we need to incorporate this additional dimension into John's announcement from other sources.

There was to be an integral connection between Jesus's bearing humanity's trial of fire and his bringing humanity into the baptism of the Spirit. No one could have imagined it then. But was the idea so farfetched? If one examines the terrifying vision of Daniel in 7:11–14, one notices that the Son of man rises on the cloud to the throne of the Ancient of Days, with evil forces on earth below. The implication is some kind of victory and vindication as ruler of the nations: "He was given authority, glory and sovereign power; all nations and peoples of every language worshiped him" (Dan. 7:14). So Jesus, as the one to be fully baptized in the Spirit of renewal and in the fire of judgment, prays to his Father: "Father, the hour has come. Glorify your

---

64. Dunn, *Baptism in the Holy Spirit*, 11.

Son, that your Son may glorify you. For you granted him authority over all people that he might give eternal life to all those you have given him" (John 17:1-2). This Johannine text has Daniel 7 as its implicit background.

John the Baptist expected, instead, that the Messiah would bring judgment to those who oppose the liberating work of the Spirit. He saw the coming trial of judgment as imminent. He predicted that the axe was already being laid to the very root of the tree. Everything was about to come down, and nothing would be left standing. Thorough judgment was already on its way; nothing that does not grow from repentance and yearning for God's kingdom would remain. Those lives not bearing the fruit of repentance "will be cut down and thrown into the fire" (Luke 3:9). Christ will "burn the chaff with unquenchable fire" (3:17). Hence, when inhabitants of a Samaritan village refused to welcome Jesus, James and John asked whether they should call down fire from heaven to destroy them (9:54). Let the fire be lit! Apparently, they thought it was about time to start igniting the baptism of fire on the earth. Jesus rebuked them, though he later added that a fire was coming upon the earth and that he himself wished it were already kindled (12:49). It is understandable that Jesus would wish the fire to be already kindled and the reign of God fulfilled on the earth. But he knew that the fire had to rest first on him: "But I have a baptism to undergo, and what constraint I am under until it is completed!" (12:50). This baptism of his death is the baptism in fire of which John the Baptist spoke; but little did John know that it was to rest first on the Son of the Father himself. He bears it for the world. He must bear it so that fallen humanity can receive the Holy Spirit from him as a sanctifying force.

Jesus's baptism by fire did not begin on the cross; it culminated there. Jesus moved in the direction of this baptism already at the Jordan River. By stepping into Israel's need to repent in the waters of his baptism at the Jordan, he symbolized the direction in which his reception of the Spirit would take him as the future Spirit Baptizer. He stepped into solidarity with sinners in their need to repent, or in their fallenness—not only in their hope but also in their brokenness. He did not need to repent or convert; but he stepped into those waters of repentance in identification with those who did need to convert.[65] He took his public step toward the cross, for "the events at the Jordan and at Golgotha are interrelated as beginning and end" (*CD*, IV/4, 15). As this beginning, he is already anticipating taking the sin of all of humanity

65. Barth, *Church Dogmatics*, IV/4, 59. In the next few paragraphs, references to the *Church Dogmatics* (*CD*) appear in parentheses within the text.

upon his shoulders. At the Jordan he is already the man of sorrows. Barth movingly describes this reality of Christ's taking the burdens of the world upon his shoulders:

> No one who came to the Jordan was as laden and afflicted as He. No one was as needy. No one was so utterly human, because so wholly fellow-human. . . . He stands alone in this, He who was elected and ordained from all eternity to partake of the sin of all in His own person, to bear its shame and curse in the place of all, to be the man responsible for all, and as such, wholly theirs, to live and act and suffer. (*CD*, IV/4, 59)

But the trial by fire will not destroy Jesus Christ. It may already be said of the Jordan River that the "creaturely sun sinks into the ocean, but is not quenched."[66] As this "sun" (or "Son") rises from the Jordan, he prefigures his own rising from *sheol* at his resurrection. His reception of the Spirit at the Jordan launches Jesus Christ's life, not only baptized in the Spirit but also baptized in fire, the fire of judgment that belongs to humanity and, as such, belongs to the Son of man, Jesus Christ. Indeed, "the *descent* of the Spirit is mirrored by the *consent* of that Son" to identification with sinners for the sake of their redemption.[67]

It is the very same Spirit that fills Jesus as the beloved Son of the Father that then leads Jesus into the wilderness to have this sonship radically called into question (e.g., Matt. 4:1). This is the beginning of sorrow, the time of testing, threatening darkness, and ultimately of death under the charge of blasphemy and treason. Thus, stepping out of the Jordan, Jesus is driven by the Spirit into the desert to confront Satan and the kingdom of darkness so as to begin taking on humanity's fire baptism. While we humans are called upon to resist temptation, Jesus is called to confront it. "He has to suffer it on the offensive and not on the defensive, just as later he goes with open eyes to the death of the cross, to Jerusalem" (*CD*, IV/1, 261).

His temptation is not superficial, and the stakes are high. Without his faithfulness, Israel's mission to the nations would have remained unfulfilled, and instead of representing all of humanity in bearing the baptism in fire

---

66. McDonnell, *The Baptism of Jesus in the Jordan*, 51. This is an overarching theme of McDonnell's book.

67. D. Lyle Dabney, "Naming the Spirit: Towards a Pneumatology of the Cross," in *Starting with the Spirit: The Task of Theology Today II*, ed. Stephen Pickard and Gordon Preece (Hindmarsh, Australia: Australian Theological Forum, 2001), 47 (italics in original).

for them, "He would have left them in the lurch at the very moment when He had made their cause His own" (*CD*, IV/1, 262). In fact, "the destruction of the cosmos could not have been arrested, and man would inevitably have perished" (*CD*, IV/1, 261). The temptation is thus serious, cutting necessarily to the very core of Christ's identity: "If you are the Son of God . . . ," says Satan (Matt. 4:3), as if the issue were seriously open to question. The tempter will cunningly attempt to lure Christ into defending his sonship in ways that would ironically end up forcing him to abandon it. Jesus refuses to play along. He does not seek to defend his sonship; instead, he seeks to affirm his path of obedience, perhaps for the sake of his own self-awareness and strengthening in preparation for his role as the faithful Son and redeemer. By turning attention away from defending his sonship and toward devotion to his Father, he was engaging in the only proper defense of his sonship possible. This is a path in which he will grow: "He learned obedience through what he suffered" (Heb. 5:8). His baptism in the Spirit as the faithful Son directs his response to the threatening baptism in fire. In the throes of darkness and alienation he does not cease being faithful. Christ does not succumb or yield the field. He is destined to be the Spirit Baptizer. To attain that end, he must endure all trials as the one baptized in Spirit-fire.

The first temptation occurs in response to Jesus's fasting for forty days in the desert. Satan challenges Jesus's fasting by pointing him to his alleged right to self-preservation: "If you are the Son of God, tell these stones to become bread" (Matt. 4:3). What would Christ prove by starving himself? Would he not prove something far more glorious if he asked the Father to miraculously feed him? What a symbol of the Father's care for him! Surely, the favored Son of the Father can depend on the Father to meet his physical needs. No one could be faulted for doing that. Wouldn't Jesus later pray for daily bread? Indeed he would. But the priority of his prayer would be for the Father's will to be done on the earth as it is in heaven. Bread is important to human life, but, precisely as human, Christ was also made for more than bread. The will of the heavenly Father has the priority.

The priority given to the Father's will is a lesson that Israel was challenged to learn. Deuteronomy 8:2-3 describes how God humbled the Israelites in the desert in order to teach them that one is not to attempt to live by bread alone. Israel grumbled for bread in the wilderness and only with difficulty endured their spiritual trial (Exod. 16:2-3). Jesus ended up rewriting that story by putting himself in the place of Israel and reliving that drama on behalf of the whole human race. After all, confronting the tempter in the desert recalls Adam's temptation in the Garden as well. As a protest action, Jesus has foregone eating bread entirely in order to symbolize the all-surpassing value of giving one's life to the will of the Father and the leading of the Spirit. What a challenge it is for us today, in our consumer society, where "more" is constantly thought to be "better." Or where those who have no bread are ignored so that our feasting might proceed free of guilt.

Indeed, there are moments when we must refuse bread for the sake of a spiritual discipline that meets the human need that is even more essential—to follow the larger purposes of the Father. It is this spiritual discipline that makes life most worth living. In Jesus's case, his spiritual discipline was vital to his identity. How could he be the Word of the Father who will mediate the Spirit to all flesh had he placed physical nourishment above the needs of God's words in the desert? How could he later be the bread of life when imparting himself to us as the Spirit Baptizer if he had denied his mission for the sake of physical bread in the desert?

In the Gospel of Matthew's order, the second temptation by Satan challenges Jesus's identity once again ("If you are the Son of God . . ."; Matt. 4:6). This time Satan asks Christ to climb to the highest point of the temple and then throw himself down. God has promised in Psalm 91:11–12 not to let the righteous strike their foot against a stone (Matt. 4:6). God would spare them; so also Christ, Satan says, if he is indeed the favored Son. The Father surely would not abandon him—that is, if Christ were indeed the Son of God. The point is that the baptism in fire must cause Jesus to throw himself into the place of the abandoned, but not this way. It must be done in the way willed by the Father. Jesus's response again is memorable: "Do not put the Lord your God to the test" (4:7). The Son is the one to be tested in the desert, not the Father. The Son's role is not to test the Father but rather to obey the Father by faithfully enduring testing so as to follow the path of suffering love, the path also of the Spirit's leading. Instead of Jesus's giving himself over to death on the cross for the Father's cause of redeeming and renewing humanity, thus vindicating his faithful sonship, the temptation was for Jesus to betray this cause much earlier by throwing himself down from the temple "to fulfill his own self-justification before God."[68] To prematurely cast himself down so that the Father would save him and prove his status as a righteous man is a form of self-justification, a form of grasping after equality with God, something he refused to do (cf. Phil. 2:6). It would be a form of self-justification that avoids the cross, his true baptism in fire. The Son will only be justified through resurrection by the Father (1 Tim. 3:16; Rom. 1:4), not by asserting

68. Barth, *Church Dogmatics*, IV/1, 263.

his own right but by giving of himself to death for the right of others in fulfillment of his Father's will.

In the final test, the Son's identity is not directly questioned; but his loyalty to the Father is, which amounts to the same thing. Satan cannot get the Son to accept illegitimate tests of his identity as the Son of the Father, but in a last-ditch effort to derail the Son's journey to the cross, Satan tries to get him to switch loyalty altogether. Satan offers him the kingdoms of the world "and all their splendor" (4:8), if only the Son would worship him. But the Son's mission was to redeem the nations so that they might ultimately lay their splendor before the Father (Rev. 21:24). As a result of fulfilling *that* mission, the Son will indeed be given authority over all peoples in order to grant them eternal life (John 17:2; Acts 2:33–36). But he will gain this rule not by grasping for it, but by giving himself up for the world's redemption. At the end of time, the kings of the nations will enter the heavenly city and will walk by the light of the Lamb and will bring the splendor of the nations into it. The Son will indeed have the splendor of the nations but only to the glory of the Father. He will receive this splendor only as the light of the world that has conquered the darkness and not yielded to it, the light of faithfulness and truth (Rev. 21:24). Bowing a knee to the forces of darkness would sink creation into the abyss. The splendor would vanish. Jesus thus answered Satan in the desert in the only way possible for him to remain true to himself: "Worship the Lord your God, and serve him only" (Matt. 4:10). There can be no other victory over the trial than this, and no means of changing the world in the flood of the Spirit than this. Any other path would end in utter destruction.

It is interesting that, when Jesus asked his disciples, midway through his mission on earth, who they thought he was, Peter made his significant confession: "You are the Messiah" (Mark 8:29). But when Jesus warned that he had to "suffer many things" that would cause his path to end in rejection and crucifixion, "Peter took him aside and began to rebuke him" (Mark 8:32). Apparently, Peter found this baptism in fire to have been an unimaginable path for the one destined to be exalted by God above the nations. Of course, Peter's response is understandable. There was no Jewish tradition of a crucified Messiah. Such an idea at that time was preposterous; hence it is not Peter's reaction that is surprising here but rather Christ's: "Get behind me, Satan!" Why would Jesus find in Peter's rebuke a challenge from Satan?

Perhaps Satan was once again attempting to derail Jesus's journey to fulfill the Father's will by luring him toward a false glory without the cross, but this time through the words of Peter. Jesus was in effect saying to Satan that such challenges did not work in the desert, and they would not work now, at this decisive midpoint of Jesus's mission, even if the vehicle be the well-intentioned words of a trusted disciple. As for Peter, he was obviously an unwitting participant in this temptation, merely speaking from a condition of partial blindness, which must have represented where everyone besides Jesus was at that point. Provocatively, just prior to Peter's confession, a blind man was healed, but only partially at first. He saw people "like trees walking around" (Mark 8:24) and only somewhat later gained full clarity of sight. One is tempted to see this miracle as placed strategically in the narrative in order to function as a parable of Peter's confession of Christ as Messiah. At first Peter's vision is only partial. He sees Jesus as the Spirit-baptized Messiah clearly enough. But he does not yet see him as the one who must also bear humanity's baptism in fire. He did not yet understand that "even the Son of Man did not come to be served but to serve and to give his life as a ransom to many" (Mark 10:45). Jesus's death would be a ransom or an offering given for the freedom of humanity from the bondage of sin and death. Peter's sight concerning Jesus's path would clear up at the resurrection and Pentecost, but not until then. And the same holds true for Jesus's other disciples. When their sight would become clear concerning Jesus's path, their sight would be clear concerning their own path as his followers. "For whoever wants to save their life will lose it, but whoever loses their life for me and for the gospel will save it" (8:35).

The tragedy of the rejected and abused Son is a strong theme in the Gospels. Although he made the world, the world did not recognize him. He came to his own, the people of Israel, but even they did not receive him (John 1:10–11). Jesus told a parable about a landowner who built a vineyard with a winepress and a watchtower. He then moved to another location and rented out his property to tenant workers. At harvest time, he sent his servant to receive his crop, but the tenants "beat one, killed another, and stoned a third" (Matt. 21:35). When the owner of the land sent more servants, they were treated in the same way. Then the owner thought he would send his son. Surely, he thought, the tenants would respect him. But they ended up killing his son as well. There would be no limit to their rebellion! Therefore, Jesus asked, what would the owner do to such tenants? The answer is clear: "He will bring those wretches to a wretched end." And then he would rent out his vineyard to responsible tenants. Jesus then quotes from Psalm 118:22–23:

The stone the builders rejected
    has become the cornerstone;
the Lord has done this,
    and it is marvelous in our eyes. (Matt. 21:42)

Jesus tells the religious leaders that the kingdom of God will be taken away from them and given to people who will produce the fruit of repentance and receive the coming time of renewal (21:43–44).

It is clear from this parable that Jesus considered his entire sojourn to Jerusalem as in one sense a path to final rejection and murder at the hands of the Jewish authorities, with whom he had clashed, and a heartless empire more interested in domination and taxes than justice. How his heart breaks when he laments over Jerusalem after he made his triumphal entry into that city (Luke 19:41–42). Jerusalem was meant to be the center from which God's people would bless the nations; it was not meant for occupation by a power-hungry empire. The king of the Jews was meant to grant justice to the nations. How can he now be crucified at the hands of a chief center of Gentile power? Christ ends up as the faithful Son who is condemned as a blasphemer and a traitor, but he bears the shame for the sake of lost Israel—and of lost humanity. He suffers their baptism in fire so that he, as the one baptized in the Spirit, could rise and ascend to be the Spirit Baptizer, not only for those who placed their hope in him but also for many more who were most vigorous is condemning him. But only those who repent can join in his wealth of spiritual blessing. The thrown-away stone has become the cornerstone, but only those who join themselves to him in repentance and faith will be renewed. Those who continue to oppose the grace of the promised Spirit offered through him will dash themselves against that rock to their own destruction. "Anyone who falls on this stone will be broken to pieces" (Matt. 21:44). But Jesus is the first to be broken for their sakes, so that they might yet be mended. This is the significance of Jesus's baptism in fire for the good news of the Gospel.

Jesus approaches the eve of his baptism in fire with the Last Supper. (We will look at that sacred meal again in our next chapter.) Suffice it to say here that Christ's chief statement concerning the meaning of his death occurs at this meal, a point that is not always recognized. The occasion of the meal refers back to the Passover meal depicting Israel's passage from death to life, which is why Jesus says that he will not eat this Passover with his disciples again "until it finds fulfillment in the kingdom of God," when he opens life to a dying humanity (Luke 22:15–16). Jesus implies that his broken body and spilled blood will facilitate this passage from death to life. Jesus fittingly describes his death as covenant-making, implying that his death will be a passage to a new community freed from death and open to new life in the Spirit.[69]

---

69. This is Michael J. Gorman's major point in *The Death of the Messiah and the Birth of the New Covenant: A (Not So) New Model of the Atonement* (Eugene, OR: Cascade Books, 2014).

Christ's baptism in fire is meant to lead to a baptism in the Spirit of new life and communion, not only through water baptism and in the breaking of bread but in other practices of the Spirit, such as proclamation, discipleship, spiritual gifts, and mission.

John the Evangelist places Jesus's washing of his disciples' feet in the place of the Lord's Supper, highlighting an event connected to the meal rather than the meal itself. In doing this, John grants us unique insight into the total event. Christ shares himself with his disciples as the servant Messiah who establishes a community bound together by the love that is leading Jesus to the moment of his greatest trial (John 13:1). But the event of foot-washing was not merely symbolic of humble servanthood; it was more deeply symbolic of the cleansing that will later occur through incorporation in him ("if you remain in me and I in you," 15:5). Therefore, the stakes are high in Peter's refusal to let Jesus wash his feet: "Unless I wash you, you have no part with me" (13:8), Jesus says. It will not be until later that they will understand the significance of this enigmatic act and the statement that explains it: "You do not realize now what I am doing, but later you will understand" (13:7). Jesus even encouraged the disciples to continue the practice of foot-washing to commemorate their cleansing and how Christ opened up to them his servant path to the cross. Early in the history of the church—and for some traditions down to the present day—churches viewed foot-washing as a postbaptismal act of reflecting on the cleansing effects of incorporation into Christ, as a kind of bridge ritual, so to speak, between water baptism and the Lord's Supper.[70] Implicit in this act is the idea that we are cleansed through incorporation into Christ the Spirit Baptizer.

Throughout the events of leading up to the cross, Jesus's heart is heavy, which was especially true at the Last Supper. "Truly I tell you, one of you will betray me—one who is eating with me" (Mark 14:18). Christ had in mind Judas, not Peter; but Peter is targeted by Christ as one who will indeed deny him three times before that fateful hour of suffering on the cross (14:27–31). Jesus will be the abandoned man of sorrows. He then enters the Garden of Gethsemane bearing this burden already, knowing full well that he must walk this path to his end alone. He is plunged into a grief "that overwhelms from all sides (*peri-lupos*), so great that it leads him in advance, in

---

70. For an excellent treatment of this topic, see John Christopher Thomas, *Footwashing in John 13 and the Johannine Community* (Edinburgh: T & T Clark, 2004). See my theological response to this book in Frank D. Macchia, "Is Footwashing the Neglected Sacrament? A Theological Response to John Christopher Thomas," *Pneuma* 19, no. 2 (Fall 1997): 239–49.

the midst of life, 'right into the death' which it represents by anticipation."[71] This troubling of Christ's soul is needed, for he must be the man of sorrows who suffers all things typical of human flesh in order to redeem flesh in all of its dimensions. "In appropriating the experiences of humanity, the Word directed them toward the salvific end and rendered them life-giving."[72] In the midst of this despair, Jesus thus turned to his Father. In John's Gospel, he prayed for the sake of his followers; he sanctified himself in truth so that they may be sanctified (John 17:19). His future role as Spirit Baptizer was obviously before him. He would gain authority over the nations so as to grant them new life (17:2). To this end he yearned for the glory that he had always shared with the Father (17:5).

These expressions of hope were not to be used to lessen in any way the despair that gripped him at his core. He turned to his *Abba* prayer at this time of need: "'*Abba*, Father,' he said, 'everything is possible for you. Take this cup from me. Yet not what I will, but what you will'" (Mark 14:36). In doing this, he remained faithful to the Father. "He only prays. He does not demand."[73] This request was thus not a reversal of the faithfulness shown in the desert during his temptation. There he resisted the efforts of the tempter to derail him from his path to the cross. Here he questioned the Father concerning the necessity of that path. He did not for a moment consider a deviation from the will of his Father. He faced the reality of the cup he knew he had to drink. He felt the waters of judgment engulfing him like Jonah in the belly of the great fish (Jonah 2:5):

> The engulfing waters threatened me,
> > the deep surrounded me;
> > seaweed was wrapped around my head.

Jesus's plight was even worse than this, for Jesus did not just face his own death. Indeed, he didn't even merely face the threat of a martyr experiencing the sacrifice of his life for his faith. He faced the judgment of God against all of humanity, against creation as a whole, a creation he now bore and represented. He had to feel its sorrow. He had to feel its threat and its despair, down to his bones. He had to express it, wrestle with it. But he did so as one who

---

71. Balthasar, *Mysterium Paschale*, 72.

72. Paul L. Gavrilyuk, *The Suffering of the Impassible God: The Dialectics of Patristic Thought*, Oxford Early Christian Studies (New York: Oxford University Press, 2004), 171.

73. Barth, *Church Dogmatics*, IV/1, 270.

was faithful. He could not deviate from the path he had taken his entire life. His prayer in the Garden did not change this, for there was no sin involved in sincerely questioning what the will of God was. Jesus threw himself completely into his path of sorrow in order to take it up into the path of renewal. The path of Spirit baptism could not bypass the baptism in fire. There could be no other way. Christ could not be the Spirit Baptizer if he did not allow himself to sink beneath the waves of despair and condemnation. He could not be the Lord of the church's sacred meal if he did not drink of the bitter cup of death. He sought in his final hour confirmation of what he, in his heart of hearts, already knew: "Yet not what I will, but what you will" (Mark 14:36).

Earlier, he said of his disciples' lack of diligence that the Spirit is willing but the flesh is weak. All flesh is weak. And Jesus had to submit the weakness of his own flesh to the will of his Father and to the work of the willing Spirit in order for there to be hope for all of humankind at their points of greatest weakness (Heb. 4:15). This willing Spirit is the Holy Spirit. The Spirit of God is *willing*, willing to lead one to a genuinely *Abba* prayer and willing to lead in the way willed by the Father. Christ would follow the willing Spirit all the way to the cross, for Christ was the one "who through the eternal Spirit offered himself unblemished to God" (Heb. 9:14). His sonship would be defined by his baptism in that willing Spirit. Ironically, his baptism in the fire of death was necessary to his baptism in this willing Spirit, for the Spirit led him to the cross. It was the only way that Jesus could prove to be the human icon of the faithful Son as a man totally defined by that willing Spirit, and thus by the Father's own suffering love for humanity.

Jesus's *Abba* prayer reaches its greatest challenge at the cross. "My God, my God, why have you forsaken me?" (Mark 15:34). Is this an *Abba* prayer? The larger context of Psalm 22, from which this prayer is taken, implies an *Abba*-like relationship with God:

> "He trusts in the LORD," they say,
>   "let the LORD rescue him.
> Let him deliver him,
>   since he delights in him." (Ps. 22:8)

Yet, the fact that this prayer goes out to "God" rather than *Abba* is still significant, since it opens the prayer of the Psalm to humanity as a whole.[74] With-

---

74. Raymond E. Brown, *An Introduction to the New Testament* (New York: Doubleday, 1997), 147.

out losing faith in his *Abba* to sustain him, Christ sank into the deepest pit of despair possible within the human race. The result is a baptism in fire that transforms it into a purgative force for those who will find their existence by the Spirit in him. (I will discuss Christ's death in the following chapter.)

Conclusion

Jesus's baptism in the Holy Spirit or reception of the Spirit at the Jordan is an important event that picks up the thread of the incarnation and ties it meaningfully to the massively important events at the climax of Jesus's mission: crucifixion, resurrection, and Pentecost. As the faithful Son of the Father, Jesus bears the Spirit without measure and permanently, for he will offer his life by the Spirit at the cross and rise up by the Spirit to be the Spirit Baptizer. Jesus's baptism under John functions as a prophetic sign of his reception of the Spirit at the Jordan, much as the virginal conception of Jesus in Mary's womb functioned as a sign of the incarnation. That water baptism was the place where Jesus's reception of the Spirit was contextualized. He accepted the Spirit from the Father in fulfillment of Israel's hopes and the hopes of humanity at large. He also received the Spirit under the weight of Israel's failure and shame—and of those of humanity at large. But he is also the Lord who will bestow the Spirit on others. He is the living Temple of God, the man of prayer who opens the benefits of his prayer to others. He is the one who fulfills the law and can thus speak with unprecedented authority concerning it. He will fulfill justice as the man of the Spirit who will create communities of love and justice in the world that call into question all that contradicts the righteousness of the kingdom of God. His table fellowship reveals a kingdom that is like a celebratory feast. He heals the sick as a sign of his coming renewal of creation.

All of this began at his conception by the Spirit in Mary's womb and his anointing by the Spirit at the Jordan. Under the sign of John's water rite, Jesus was baptized in the Holy Spirit, more precisely, baptized in the Holy Spirit and fire. Baptized in fire, he stepped into the shoes of those who must repent, of Israel and the nations in their need of God. His trial by fire began in the desert and would span the rest of his earthly life and culminate in his death. He was the falsely rejected and accused man of sorrows throughout his life. Baptized in the Spirit, however, he fulfilled hope by bearing the Father's love as an enduring and abundant source for the redemption of others, especially those most neglected and abused. The impact he had on others during his life anticipated the victory of his resurrection from the dead and the abundant self-giving to which this victory leads at Pentecost.

Jesus's baptism in the Spirit and fire grants content to the direction of the incarnation and sets up the culmination of the crucifixion and resurrection. They grant content to the life that is opened up to all flesh at Pentecost. What Barth writes about what the life of the Spirit-baptized, Spirit-filled Christ teaches us represents a fitting way to complete this chapter:

> God the Father, of what is meant by the presence of the Spirit in fullness. On the contrary, we must be content to recognize what is divine and worthy and well pleasing and spiritual at the very point where it is human history—in the happening of this history, in the way of Jesus of Nazareth, and therefore in his human essence. This does not make everything clear at a stroke. It brings us to the beginning of a way on which we have to accompany this history, recognizing the divine in the human. But we shall know that when it is a matter of knowing what is truly divine there can be no evading the child in the crib at Bethlehem, the Tempted in the wilderness of the Jordan, the one who prayed in Gethsemane, and the man on the cross at Golgotha. This is how it is when the Son of the Father becomes a guest in the world under His unqualified Yes and wholly participant in His Spirit. Here in the flesh there dwells the eternal Word, and His glory is seen—in the exaltation of human essence which takes place here and in this way—and in nowhere else and in no other way.[75]

75. Barth, *Church Dogmatics*, IV/2, *Doctrine of Reconciliation*, trans. G. W. Bromiley (Edinburgh: T & T Clark, 1958), 95–96.

PART 3

Christ's Crucifixion,
Resurrection, and Self-Impartation

CHAPTER 5

Christ's Death and Resurrection

"He who is to baptize in the Holy Spirit and fire . . . presses towards the baptism of the Cross which he must receive."

—Hans Urs von Balthasar, *Mysterium Paschale*

N. T. Wright tells a story of a king who demanded that his archers shoot the sun. Of course, all those who tried failed. How can an archer reach the sun with an arrow shot from the earth? But the youngest of the archers was yet to take his turn at the impossible task. He appeared at the king's garden at noon, right at the time when a reflection of the sun shown brightly on the surface of the pond that lay in plain sight of the king. Aiming at the reflection, the young archer hit the sun dead center, splintering it "into a thousand glittering fragments."[1] So it is with the transcendent God of Christian Scriptures: unreachable by the arrows of human violence and oppression, but vulnerable when imaged in human flesh. Of course, one could say, with Kazoh Kitamori, that there is "vulnerability" deep within the heart of God, namely, the penchant to love even those who spurn that love in the most extreme ways. And so we find in God the theological root of the incarnation and the cross.[2] But this vulnerability is actually a strength, for God thereby enters into the depths of human rejection and sorrow in order to open up the possibility of life and love in much greater abundance than any evil that might be erected against it.

---

1. N. T. Wright, *The Resurrection of the Son of God*, vol. 3 of *Christian Origins and the Question of God* (Minneapolis: Fortress, 2003), 11.

2. Kazoh Kitamori, *Theology of the Pain of God* (Eugene, OR: Wipf and Stock, 2005), esp. 44–49.

God actually uses the cross to bring about the triumph of the resurrection and the wonderful gift of Pentecost. In my view, what stands out in the above story about shooting the image of the sun, therefore, is how the image of the sun, once shot, splinters into many embers of light. One is reminded of Jesus's own parable about how a seed, once it is dead and then put into the earth, will sprout into a plant that will give off many other seeds (John 12:24). Jesus's death opens his life to the many, *fulfilling justice* by honoring the Father *on their behalf.* He honors the Father precisely by giving himself over to the Father's cause in the world. His resurrection vindicates this sacred self-offering. Jesus dies so that, by rising, he can give birth to many brothers and sisters through the Spirit he imparts. At the cross the barriers of sin and death are removed so that Christ could pour forth the Spirit upon all flesh. In fact, the Spirit overflows his journey in order to draw others in. The cross makes way for the Spirit through the vindication of the resurrection. He was "vindicated in the Spirit" (1 Tim. 3:16) and raised for our justification (Rom. 4:25). Sinners are thus justified in the embrace of the Spirit of life.

"The right to send the Spirit into the hearts of fallen men was acquired by atonement."[3] Indeed, Paul says: "He redeemed us . . . so that by faith we might receive the promise of the Spirit" (Gal. 3:14). By his own sanctification through the fires of judgment he can sanctify us. Hebrews 5:8–9 expresses it best: "Son though he was, he learned obedience from what he suffered and, once made perfect, he became the source of eternal salvation for all who obey him." Christ bore our baptism in fire so that, perfected in glorification, he could impart new life to all flesh, so that mortality could one day be "swallowed up by life" (2 Cor. 5:4). Under the sign of water baptism "you were washed, you were sanctified, you were justified in the name of the Lord Jesus Christ and by the Spirit of our God" (1 Cor. 6:11). In this chapter we will explore how Christ's death and resurrection culminates in his journey through his baptism in Spirit and fire and provides the basis for Pentecost.

The Cross and Pentecost

The crucifixion of Jesus is the way by which God overcomes humanity's baptism in fire and removes the barrier of sin and death so as to make way for granting the Spirit to *fallen* flesh. Christ descended into the clutches of

---

3. George Smeaton, *The Doctrine of the Holy Spirit* (London: Banner of Truth Trust, 1958), 135.

sin and death, but he did not go alone. He went bearing the Holy Spirit—the Spirit of life. The Spirit remained with him in all of the Spirit's excessive abundance and eschatological reach. The willing Spirit remained with him, the Spirit whom Jesus followed at his trial in the desert to his trial in the Garden of Gethsemane, all the way to his trial on the cross. Christ offered himself in *death* precisely by the *eternal Spirit* (Heb. 9:14), who is the power of an *indestructible life* (Heb. 7:16). The Son of the Father, who bore the Spirit of life, rose from death in order to bring those captive to death into life.

The removal of this captivity is for all flesh in all of its diversity. This diversity has no limits, for even those thought to be unclean Gentiles may receive the Spirit by grace, the grace of the cross, for Christ broke down the barrier between Jew and Gentile on the cross (Eph. 2:14), so that "through him we both have access to the Father by one Spirit" (2:18). Indeed, Christ "redeemed us in order that the blessing given to Abraham might come to the Gentiles through Christ Jesus, so that by faith we might receive the promise of the Spirit" (Gal. 3:14). Galatians 3:1–5 indicates that the major topic of the chapter is the reception of the Spirit by faith, which Paul connects intimately to the gift of justification that he mentions in Galatians 2:17. "Did you receive the Spirit by the works of the law, or by believing what you heard?" (3:2). The blessing of Abraham is the blessing of the gift of the Spirit along with the forgiveness of sins. Note Isaiah's description of the blessing of Jacob that comes down from the promise given to Abraham:

> "But now listen, Jacob, my servant,
>   Israel, whom I have chosen.
> This is what the LORD says—
>   he who made you, who formed you in the womb,
>   and who will help you:
> 'Do not be afraid, Jacob, my servant,
>   Jeshurun, whom I have chosen.
> For I will pour water on the thirsty land,
>   and streams on the dry ground;
> I will pour out my Spirit on your offspring,
>   and my blessing on your descendants.'" (Isa. 44:1–3)

The cross makes way for the blessing of Abraham, the gift of the Spirit, to be given to fallen flesh. How the barriers of sin and death are overcome and removed so that humanity may be forgiven and receive the Spirit of life is the core meaning of the atonement. A deeper understanding of this concept, however, introduces us to a rich complexity of issues, to which we now turn.

No one in the ancient world would have connected crucifixion with a life-enabling event. Crucifixion was an extreme form of execution meant to crush a dissident in public in a way that would eliminate any resistance the authorities perceived in the populace against the laws or purposes of the Roman Empire. More deeply, the cross is an act of human rejection of God. Who would have thought that such an act would become the place where divine love overcomes condemnation for the sake of the renewal of creation? What a deeply significant thought this is that God would choose to be decisively revealed right at the place where God is most profoundly rejected and mocked. God's presence ends up where one might least expect it, at the cross, the place of condemnation, alienation, and shame. But how else could it be? Isn't this the place where we need God the most? That God would meet us decisively here is the most striking feature of the Christian gospel, and it helps to explain why this message *is* a gospel. When one realizes that this event of condemnation and death would make way for the gift of righteousness, life brings hope right where it is needed the most. No matter how deep the pit of despair or hopelessness may be, we know from the cross that God's love is deeper still (as Corrie Ten Boom reminded us).

Yet such a prospect is difficult for many to grasp, since the experience of abandonment and alienation is often a reason for questioning the divine existence, or love for humanity. Here is where the reality of the cross challenges commonsense discourse about God. Who would have thought that the Messiah would come to earth to die, and not just to die, but to be executed at the hands of the Romans and at the behest of his own national leadership? Who would have thought that the Lord who promised to pour out the Spirit on all flesh would first suffer the death of one accused of blasphemy, presumably a betrayal of the very Spirit who was thought to rest upon God's anointed? Who would have thought that the one destined to bless the nations with the Spirit of truth and rule over them with divine mercy and justice would be put to death by a pagan empire for treason? It is difficult for many today to imagine how scandalous the cross was, given the fact that the symbol of the cross has been romanticized over time as a token of religious devotion and frequently worn as a piece of jewelry. One cannot deny that the cross can legitimately be a sign of spiritual devotion. But one must always bear in mind that this cross is also a shocking event of condemnation and shame, having the same impact then as the term "gallows" would have to our ears today. As

James Cone has written, the crucifixion was like a "lynching," and we must apply it to our lives and social history first and foremost as that—before we come to see it as a symbol of divine love and hope.[4]

As shocking and offensive as it was, the crucifixion of Jesus Christ is a climactic moment in his mission and for reasons that are core to the gospel. "For I resolved to know nothing while I was with you except Jesus Christ and him crucified" (1 Cor. 2:2). As the climax of Jesus's baptism in fire, the crucifixion occupies a key place in his future role as the Messiah and baptizer in the Spirit. As we saw in the preceding chapter, from the moment Jesus received the Spirit at the Jordan River, he set out on his mission to also bear the fire baptism of humanity. In bearing the Spirit for humanity, Christ bears also the fire of judgment. And he does so in order to take humanity into the Spirit's renewal. Kevin Vanhoozer writes that the cross is the new Exodus that leads to the possibility of entering the "promised land of the Holy Spirit."[5] Christ went before us and goes with us through the passage from death to life. Baptized in the Spirit, we are buried and raised with him under the sign of water baptism.

Let us consider that conclusion, drawing together a number of threads that are already woven in at various places. First, the cross—along with the resurrection—is the source of *justification.* As I have noted above, Christ was condemned in death but vindicated in resurrection as the beloved and faithful Son of the Father (1 Tim. 3:16; Rom. 1:4). He sinks into condemnation and is vindicated in life for others. He was delivered up to death for our transgressions, but he was raised for our justification (Rom. 4:25). In the light of the resurrection we realize that he was, in death, glorifying the Father as the faithful Son and man of the Spirit, at the very time that his own people and the empire were condemning him, at the very time that he took upon himself our condemnation before the Father. He passes from condemnation to vindication for us so that we, in union with him, may also by faith pass from condemnation to vindication. As he was vindicated by resurrection, so are we vindicated by resurrection. But the Spirit of Easter life presently bears legal witness to us that we are already sons and daughters of God (Rom. 8:16). We are already in a right relationship with God in union with Christ by faith, vindicated as such already in the Spirit.

---

4. James H. Cone, *The Cross and the Lynching Tree* (Maryknoll, NY: Orbis Books, 2013).

5. Kevin J. Vanhoozer, "The Atonement in Postmodernity: Guilt, Goats, and Gifts," in *The Glory of the Atonement: Biblical, Historical, and Practical Perspectives*, ed. Charles E. Hill and Frank A. James III (Downers Grove, IL: InterVarsity, 2004), 399.

Second, the cross in the light of the resurrection is the source of *new life.* Precisely by the crucified Christ! The necessity of Christ's death in the impartation of life is symbolized in his remark that "unless a kernel of wheat falls to the ground and dies, it remains only a single seed. But if it dies, it produces many seeds" (John 12:24). In other words, Christ must die in order to be the sprouting seed that multiplies into many other seeds. By bearing sin and death, he removes the barriers that stand in the way of his impartation of life. New life is born through the cross. He bears our mortality so that in rising again he can transform our mortal bodies into immortal existence in his image. This idea informs Paul's use of the dying and sprouting seed metaphor:

> It is sown in dishonor, it is raised in glory; it is sown in weakness, it is raised in power; it is sown a natural body, it is raised a spiritual body. If there is a natural body, there is also a spiritual body. So it is written: "The first man Adam became a living being"; the last Adam, a life-giving spirit. (1 Cor. 15:43–45)

Notice Paul's progression of thought in the above quotation: through the seed that dies, new life sprouts forth—from dishonor to glory, from weakness to power, from nature to immortality in the Spirit. Then comes the climax: the death of the natural seed gives rise to a spiritual plant that has the capacity to multiply many other seeds that sprout forth in analogous forms of new life. Out of the fullness of Christ's life poured out for us and vindicated at the resurrection, Christ imparts new life to others. The one who died in dishonor and weakness now meets us in faith as a glorious and powerful mediator of new life ("life-giving spirit").

Third, Christ said in reference to his coming death that he *sanctified* himself in truth so that others may be *sanctified* (John 17:19). The faithful Son sanctifies himself in Spirit and truth (cf. John 4:24) throughout his baptism in fire. He did so in his faithfulness during Satan's temptations in the desert. As the man of the Spirit and faithful Son of the Father, he sanctified himself in truth in resistance to the deceptive efforts of the enemy to sway him from his faithful path to the cross. The same is true during every test that the Son faced on his path to the Garden of Gethsemane and all the way to the cross. Heather Oglevie notes that "the death of Christ was the critical moment of his earthly life, his moment of entire commitment and self-consecration."[6]

---

6. Heather Oglevie, "Entire Sanctification and the Atonement: A Wesleyan Demonstration," *Wesleyan Theological Journal* 50, no. 1 (Spring 2015): 40.

Christ's acceptance of our baptism in fire becomes the means by which he learns and exercises obedience (Heb. 5:8). Recall that the "hallowed be your name" petition of the Lord's Prayer (Matt. 6:9) alludes to the hallowing of God's name that will occur among the nations when God pours forth the Spirit upon the faithful so that they might have hearts of stone turned to hearts of flesh and fulfill the witness of the law (Ezek. 36:22–27). As the man of the Spirit and the faithful Son of the Father, Jesus hallows the Father's name in his entire journey to the cross (his baptism in fire) so that others may be able to hallow the Father's name as bearers of the sanctifying Spirit in him. The Spirit baptism of believers at Pentecost is a sanctifying event, as the tongues of fire imply (Acts 2:3).[7] By baptizing Gentiles in the Spirit, Christ "purified their hearts by faith" (Acts 15:9). Christ's entire baptism in fire leading to the cross may be viewed as providing the conditions for his mediation of his own sanctified life to others at Pentecost.[8] Going through the fire with him changes it from a destructive to a sanctifying force.

Fourth, the healing power of the cross in the light of the resurrection *anticipates Pentecost as well.* How can the event that breaks Jesus's body and spills his blood become the basis for the healing and renewal of our bodies and our communities? The resurrection and Pentecost explain it by pointing to the cross as the triumph of life over death. Like the seed that is planted and breaks open in order to give forth new life, the breaking of Christ's body leads to the mending of ours. Indeed, "by his wounds you have been healed" (1 Pet. 2:24). Christ's very blood mixed with water flowed from the wound in his side on the cross (John 19:34), which has been taken as symbolic of his future pouring forth of the Spirit for the healing of others.[9] Indeed, by Christ's very wounds, we today receive healing in the midst of our own suffering, an implication of the Spirit's outpouring through the crucified and risen body of Jesus. Matthew 8:17 anchors Jesus's healing ministry in the classic atonement prophecy of Isaiah 53:4:

> "He took up our infirmities
>   and bore our diseases."

---

7. See Glen Menzies, "Pre-Lukan Occurrences of the Phrase 'Tongues of Fire,'" *Pneuma* 22, no. 1 (Spring 2000): 27–60.

8. Oglevie, "Entire Sanctification and the Atonement," 38–52.

9. Note, e.g., Nicholas Ludwig Count von Zinzendorf, *Ein und Zwanzig Discurse über die Augsburgische Konfession, 1748, Der achte Discurs, Hauptschriften,* vol. 6 (Hildesheim: Georg Olms Verlagsbuchhandlung, 1963), 159–61.

Though Matthew quotes this text in reference to Jesus's healing ministry, it surely anticipates the healing that Christ will provide by his death in relation to the resurrection and Pentecost. Healing today, however, only anticipates our resurrection from the dead, which is the ultimate healing. Christ's bearing and overcoming of our baptism in fire, our baptism of suffering and pain, turns his broken body into a *healing force*.

Fifth, the cross opens the path to *communion between God and humanity* caught in the throes of alienation and death. The cross is the basis of the participation of humanity in the Son's communion with the Father in the Spirit. As I noted earlier, it is interesting that the chief description of Christ's atoning death, given by Christ himself, he gave during the Last Supper, where he established a ritual meal that would henceforth provide the context for joint communion with the risen Christ and among his followers after they are incorporated into him through baptism in the Holy Spirit (1 Cor. 12:13). Baptized in the Spirit under the sign of water baptism, we drink of the Spirit under the sign of the Lord's Supper (1 Cor. 12:13). The various accounts of the Lord's Supper agree that Jesus referred to his death as covenant-making, an event that would open to others the communion between God and humanity representatively established at the cross (Matt. 26:17–30; Mark 14:12–26; Luke 22:7–38; 1 Cor. 11:23–26).[10] His spilled blood and broken body symbolize Christ's unqualified and total self-giving to bring alienated humanity into the communion of a new covenant community. His blood is spilled, but it will only lead to the drinking of a cup that symbolizes the nourishment of the Spirit. His body is broken, but it will only lead to the breaking of the bread as a symbol of new life granted to the many who now unite around Christ as bearers of his Spirit. His body is broken and his blood spilled to establish a new covenant involving a diverse and liberating communion of life in the image of the crucified Christ (e.g., 1 Cor. 11:25; 12:13; Gal. 3:28). Luke informs us that the meal is celebrated in the fulfillment of the kingdom of God, having an eschatological reach that implicitly overflows all limits of time and space (Luke 22:16). Christ's share in our alienation opens up our share in the *communion of divine love*—with God and, in God, with others.

Though the cross is liberating as the source of redemption, we must not lose sight of the fact that, at this event, Christ sank into the abyss of condemnation and death. In fact, the cross is so liberating precisely because Christ entered into such an abyss at that event. The metaphor of Christ's death as a

10. Michael J. Gorman, *The Death of the Messiah and the Birth of the New Covenant: A (Not So) New Model of the Atonement* (Eugene, OR: Cascade Books, 2004), 43.

"baptism" implies a connection with John's baptism in fire (Luke 3:16; 12:50). Divine judgment is referred to in Scripture as a mighty river: "His breath is like a rushing torrent, rising up to the neck" (Isa. 30:28). The depth of despair into which Christ sank at the cross is unfathomable. Wrath can drown one under the waves: "Your wrath lies heavily on me; you have overwhelmed me with all your waves" (Ps. 88:7). The experience of Jonah (as recorded in Jonah 2:3–6) is also telling in this context. Notice how the sea symbolizes the overwhelming wrath of God:

> You hurled me into the depths,
>> into the very heart of the seas,
>> and the currents swirled about me;
> all your waves and breakers
>> swept over me.
> I said, "I have been banished
>> from your sight;
> yet I will look again
>> toward your holy temple."
> The engulfing waters threatened me,
>> the deep surrounded me;
>> seaweed was wrapped around my head.
> To the roots of the mountains I sank down;
>> the earth beneath barred me in forever.
> But you, LORD my God,
>> brought my life up from the pit.

Jonah's being hurled into the sea is parallel to being "banished" from God's "sight," the engulfing waters with the depths of the earth that "barred" him from God forever. The sea is symbolic of the judgment of God that engulfs him. When Jesus referred to his coming death as a "baptism" or a "submersion," one calls to mind something like the imagery above. Jesus did, in fact, refer to his coming death and resurrection as "the sign of Jonah." As Jonah was swallowed up by the sea and the great fish for three days, so also will Christ be swallowed up by condemnation and death for the same amount of time. As Jonah rose up from this threat, so will Christ (Matt. 12:39–40). The church's confession of Christ's being "raised on the the third day" (1 Cor. 15:4) recalls the Jonah-Christ connection. Jonah's judgment is likened to a sinking into the abyss. I am proposing that the death of Jesus be viewed along the lines of such a plight. The Son of man allows himself to be swallowed up by condemnation and death, but he does so as the man of the Spirit and beloved Son of the Father. Though submerged, he is not destroyed. He will rise victorious:

> You will not abandon me to the realm of the dead,
> you will not let your holy one see decay.
> You have made known to me the paths of life;
> you will fill me with joy in your presence. (Acts 2:27–28)

The holy one will rise from the baptism in fire exalted as the one baptized in the Spirit for our sakes, so that he could be the source of life to us. Death as judgment for sin that swallows up its victims beneath its waves will itself be swallowed up by the sovereign Lord: "He will swallow up death forever. The Sovereign LORD will wipe away the tears from all faces" (Isa. 25:8). Mortality is "swallowed up by life" (2 Cor. 5:4).

Atonement and Representation

The cross in the light of the resurrection makes way for the impartation of the Spirit by overcoming the barriers of sin and death. But the cross does so by honoring God on behalf of fallen humanity. Christ is the faithful self-offering to the Father on humanity's behalf. In the light of Pentecost, it is especially clear that, in offering himself on our behalf, he opens his life to us in all of our diversity. He does not merely represent us as an undefined mass. He does not simply represent us as fallen creatures. He also represents us in all of our diverse hopes and yearnings for God. In the light of Pentecost, the representation of the cross opens Christ's life to all flesh in all of its diversity, which is why the cross leads to the giving of the Spirit and to communion in the Spirit among the many.

A theme that seems to run throughout all of the various meanings of the cross discussed above is *representation*, which is also called "substitution." Jesus dies in our place—for us. That the death of Jesus is in some sense "for us" runs throughout the New Testament as a description of the atoning significance of the cross. He was delivered over to death "for us all" (Rom. 8:32) or "for me" (Gal. 2:20). He tasted death "for everyone" (Heb. 2:9); he laid down his life "for the sheep" (John 10:11) or for his friends (John 15:13). He suffered "for you" (1 Pet. 2:21). More to the point, he bore our sins in his body on the cross (1 Pet. 2:24). He also died "for our sins" (Rom. 4:25; cf.

Gal. 1:4; 1 Cor. 15:3), or "once for sins" (1 Pet. 3:18). Most of these texts imply some kind of vicarious suffering for our sins, or suffering in our place, what some call "substitutionary atonement," since the sin and death endured by him belonged properly to us and not to him (e.g., Heb. 4:15). He took our place in order to provide for a just relationship between us and God so that we, in all of our fallenness, could still be recipients of the Holy Spirit. Christ is raised by the Spirit of holiness (Rom. 1:4) so that fallen creatures could receive this sanctifying Spirit, we who are worthy of the fire of judgment. In terms of election, Christ was elected to perdition on our behalf so that we could in him be elected to grace. "God from all eternity ordains this obedient One in order that he might bear the suffering which the disobedient have deserved."[11] The Spirit-baptized was ordained to bear our baptism in fire in order to take us up into his life in the Spirit.

The church has always read the following text (Isa. 53:4–6) as indicative of this kind of representative atonement:

> Surely he took up our pain
>   and bore our suffering,
> yet we considered him punished by God,
>   stricken by him, and afflicted.
> But he was pierced for our transgressions,
>   he was crushed for our iniquities;
> the punishment that brought us peace was on him,
>   and by his wounds we are healed.
> We all, like sheep, have gone astray,
>   each of us has turned to our own way;
> and the LORD has laid on him
>   the iniquity of us all.

The above text is part of the fourth servant song in Isaiah, and it is unique. Isaiah 40–55 contains a strong emphasis on the restoration of the people of God, implying a new Exodus motif that Luke uses to describe the Messiah's impartation of the Spirit.[12] However, though the renewal of Israel as a nation is arguably present in Isaiah 40–48, afterwards the theme shifts to the restoration of Zion. This change shifts the attention away from the nation:

---

11. Barth, *Church Dogmatics*, II/2: *The Doctrine of God*, trans. G. W. Bromiley et al. (Edinburgh: T & T Clark, 1957), 167.

12. David W. Pao, *Acts and the Isaianic New Exodus* (Eugene, OR: Wipf and Stock, 2016).

"Israel is not identified with the servant of the Lord anywhere in these latter oracles."[13] The above text is also part of a shift of emphasis from the exaltation to the suffering of the servant of God. Most distinctively, however, this suffering is vicarious, or *for others*. This emphasis "is without parallel either in the other songs, or outside them in the surrounding oracles."[14] There is a possibility that the above text in its historical context referred to the prophet behind the text as written by his disciples. Though possibly inspired historically by the life of the prophet, the text reaches implicitly beyond to an ideal servant.[15] In the above text, it is *our* iniquity and judgment that is laid upon and endured by the faithful servant and not *his*, a testimony to the sinless nature of his faithful sojourn on earth. Such is not descriptive of Isaiah (Isa. 6:5). The suffering servant stands apart from the sinners. In the light of New Testament fulfillment, he endures and overcomes the fire of alienation and condemnation for us, for our justification and renewal (Isa. 53:11). The servant is the Lord who dies for the sins of the world, to take all flesh with him from death to life.

We must exercise caution, however, when speaking of Christ as representing humanity on the cross, especially when such terms as "substitution" are used. Pentecost makes it clear that humanity is not reduced to insignificance by Christ's representation on the cross. Christ represents us in a way that takes a share in us, not only in our sin and death, but also in all of our God-given particularity in order to invite us to communion in the Spirit. If we are not careful, the term "substitution" can end up wrongly implying that humanity in all of its uniqueness and particularity is negated and replaced by the flesh of Jesus in the process of human reconciliation with God. The "for us" of the crucifixion involves the "with us" of Christ's partaking of human life in all of its particularity. He is Immanuel, "God with us" (Matt. 1:23). We mean here "with Israel" in the history of its journey toward God, in all of its most profound hopes and openness to God, as well as its devastating failures and despair. Christ joins them in the waters of repentance at the Jordan in order to bring them to the fulfillment of their God-intended journey. Christ will die as their king due to being rejected by those in power, only to rise in fulfillment of the nation's historic mission (Rom. 11:12). Since that mission is open to the nations in all of their unique particularity under God, we also

13. Peter Wilcox, "The Servant Songs of Deutero-Isaiah," *Journal of the Study of the Old Testament* 42 (1988): 84.

14. Wilcox, "Servant Songs," 96.

15. Wilcox, "Servant Songs," 97.

mean here that God is also "with the nations" in their seasons and wanderings in search of God, in all of their unique openness and failures as well (Acts 17:24–28). Placing this "with us" before the "for us" helps to safeguard against an understanding of the "for us" that eliminates humanity in all of its diversity from the larger event of human reconciliation with God.

The key to Wolfhart Pannenberg's theology of atonement rightly begins with "the fellowship that Jesus Christ accepted with all of us as sinners and with our fate as such."[16] Of course, Christ's baptism in fire is Christ's communion with human flesh in its alienation from God. But his baptism in the Spirit takes up our God-given hopes and yearnings as well. And it is precisely the Spirit-baptized Christ who goes to the cross. At the cross, Christ takes into himself our despair *and* hopes, alienation from the divine life *and* yearning for God, situation of oppression by evil *and* quest for freedom. In doing so, he opens the way through the crucifixion and resurrection for all of humanity to partake of him, to share in his communion with the heavenly Father, as well as his life in the Spirit. Miroslav Volf helps us see that God opened the divine life on the cross to humanity, making space for humanity within the divine life in a way that does not destroy what we were made by the Spirit and the Word to be: human beings in all of our diversity. God does this in order to fulfill justice by extending to all of creation the divine embrace. Volf observes: "Note the first two dimensions of the passion of Christ: self-giving love which overcomes human enmity and the creation of space in himself to receive estranged humanity."[17] This is how we view the cross through the *lens of Pentecost*.

The background to understanding what Pannenberg means more precisely can be found in his doctrine of creation. As we noted earlier, Pannenberg argued that humanity's distinction and orientation toward the heavenly Father and Creator is possible because humanity was created by and for the eternal Word, who is eternally distinct from and oriented toward the Father. Humanity is also distinct from and oriented toward the Word by being created in and for the Holy Spirit.[18] The Holy Spirit, as the principle of anointing and proliferating diversity, respects human particularity and diversity and allows for humanity to offer a diverse witness to the divine Word—to the glory of the Father. As the man of the Spirit, Christ is the

---

16. Wolfhart Pannenberg, *Systematic Theology*, 3 vols. (Grand Rapids: Eerdmans, 1991–98), 2:427.

17. Miroslav Volf, *Exclusion and Embrace: A Theological Exploration of Identity, Otherness, and Reconciliation* (Nashville: Abingdon, 1996), 127.

18. Volf, *Exclusion and Embrace*, 385–86.

one-and-only who opens his life to the many. The basis for this opening is the journey from the incarnation to the cross. Christ already represents us in a way that makes space in himself for the diverse many who will come. What all of this means is that the eternal Son's representation of us before God on the cross (or, if you will, his death in our place) does not reduce us to insignificance. Of course, we are only present there by grace, by God's action on our behalf. But Christ redeems us in all of our uniqueness and particularity. Indeed, "with your blood you purchased for God persons from every tribe and language and people and nation" (Rev. 5:9). Notice how his redemption of us mentions our unique backgrounds and heritages. We are not mere objects of redemption like cardboard figures or an indiscriminate mass. He partakes of us as our representative in a way that invites us to find redemption in his quintessential humanity, which is a humanity that makes room for us in all of our diversity, but also opens us to the many others, in a way that reflects how he is open. We discover personhood in him in a way that fulfills its diverse seeds in us. The cross in the light of Pentecost demands nothing less.

Unfortunately, Christ as representative humanity has sometimes been understood in such a way as to accent only human alienation from God. The colorfully diverse human yearning for God can easily be dismissed in this light as empty idolatry. Representation from this one-sided interest must demolish humanity in order to create them from the broken flesh of Christ anew, with no sense of God-given continuity between creation and redemption. Sin and sinful existence are indeed demolished at the cross, but not humanity as created for God and inherently and uniquely hoping for God. When Christ was baptized by John the Baptist, he joined himself to Israelites in the waters of repentance but also of hope, searching for the renewal of the Spirit. When he descended to his death on the cross, he had manifestly joined himself to all flesh. This is not to say that humanity in any way merits what Christ does for us on the cross. But it does mean that, in suffering and dying for us, Christ represents us in a way that not only removes the barriers of our sin and death but also renews and perfects our diverse hopes, which are inspired by the Spirit of creation. Fearing the error of viewing the cross as the triumph of the human spirit over all that oppresses it, it was tempting to understand the cross as the place where humanity is set aside, implying "the total disappearance of our independent humanity."[19] Pannenberg regards Karl Barth as the chief advocate of this

---

19. Volf, *Exclusion and Embrace*, 431.

displacement theology of representation. Barth says that the cross "negated us, cancelled us out."[20] Inspired by Dorothée Soelle, Pannenberg referred to Barth's language here as representing "a totalitarian understanding of representation."[21]

As a corrective, it becomes important to claim that Christ's representation of humanity on the cross did not lead "to a violating of the independence as persons of those that are represented." For Pannenberg, Christ's representation of humanity on the cross was the "definitive actualizing of our destiny" in a way that "leaves room, however, for the individuality of others." Pannenberg notes that by taking part in humanity's particular existence, "Jesus made room for that of others." But he adds, "We see by his conduct that others in their individual particularity can share in filial relation to God and the inheritance of his kingdom only through the death of Jesus."[22] Humanity is fulfilled and not cancelled out by the one for whom they were created by the Spirit in all of their uniqueness. Humanity is transformed in the process of creation and redemption at the cross, refashioned in that image of the Word for which they were made. This is done for them, something that they could in no way do for themselves, but it involves them as created by and for the faithful Word and the diverse witness of the Spirit.

The idea that we die and are reborn in the Son because of the cross and the resurrection is true, but it needs qualification. Following Calvin, Barth emphasizes the demolition of the "old man" of sin on the cross so that the new person could be born in us. Note what Calvin says: "By our participation in it, his death mortifies our earthly members so that they no longer perform their functions; and it kills the old man in us that he may not flourish and bear fruit."[23] Though this point is true, it is one-sided. Volf says that the self, in being reborn in Christ, is not annihilated—only "de-centered." The self-centered self "dies" but only by being de-centered, not annihilated. The self is de-centered in order to be re-centered on Christ.[24] But in being de-centered and re-centered, the self finds the fulfillment for which it was

20. Barth, *Church Dogmatics*, IV/1: *The Doctrine of Reconciliation*, trans. G. W. Bromiley (Edinburgh: T & T Clark, 1956), 253; see Pannenberg, *Systematic Theology*, 2:432.

21. Pannenberg, *Systematic Theology*, 2:432. See Dorothée Soelle, *Christ the Representative: An Essay in Theology after the Death of God* (Philadelphia: Fortress, 1967).

22. Pannenberg, *Systematic Theology*, 2:432–34.

23. John Calvin, *Institutes of the Christian Religion*, 2.16.7; quoted in Andrew R. Hay, "The Heart of Wrath: Calvin, Barth, and Reformed Theories of Atonement," *Neue Zeitschrift für systematische Theologie und Religionsphilosophie* 55, no. 3 (2013): 371–72.

24. Volf, *Exclusion and Embrace*, 70.

made and for which it yearns. But being de-centered and re-centered does not obliterate the unique particularity of how we were created. This unique self is sanctified in glory to God.

Though Pannenberg's corrective is enormously helpful in showing us how to link the cross to Pentecost, his critique of Barth is not entirely fair. For Barth, the cross is not only the Son of man's going out into the far country but also his coming home.[25] But the crucial issue in Pannenberg's critique is whether or not Barth intended Christ's representation of humanity on the cross to consist of the cancellation of humanity and its radical rebirth, *without any continuity* sustained by God from creation to new creation. Barth does imply some sense of continuity sustained by God (though, rightly, not by us) in his reference to how the condescension of the Son of God in the journey to the cross exalts humanity "with all its possibilities and limits into the completely different sphere of that totality, freedom, correspondence and service."[26] Thus, despite occasional comments to the contrary, Barth does not simply demolish humanity at the cross; his position is more complex than that.

The point here is that the cross is a liberating event, not a totalitarian one. In Revelation, Babylon is criticized for selling human beings as slaves (Rev. 18:13), but Christ is praised for purchasing for God "persons from every tribe and language and people and nation" (5:9), people in all of their God-given diversity. Babylon reduces people to mere property, cancelling out their distinctness before God. But Christ's representation of humanity on the cross redeems our God-given humanity in all of its unique particularity in a way that does not cancel it out. Rather, Christ represents "persons" not one-dimensional figures or property to be exploited, "persons from every tribe and language and people and nation." Even in heaven, these redeemed persons are described as "from every nation, tribe, people and language" (7:9). Even their heavenly existence still does not cancel out their unique particularity as persons. Their diverse and unique humanity is preserved, not blotted out by Christ's representation of them on the cross.

It is vital to realize that the cross represents all of humanity in all of its diversity as *one body* in Christ, the Head. It is for this reason that Paul could write that it is the cross that broke down the barrier between Jew and Gentile

---

25. Barth, *Church Dogmatics*, IV/2: *The Doctrine of Reconciliation*, trans. G. W. Bromiley (Edinburgh: T & T Clark, 1958), 21.

26. Barth, *Church Dogmatics*, IV/2, 30.

and made them one so that they both "have access to the one Spirit" (Eph. 2:14–18). There is thus continuity between the cross and the diverse and unifying event of Pentecost. The cross implies *Spirit-baptized communion.* The cross is a covenant-making event that reaches for the formation of a new community in Christ—unified by Christ and in Christ. This is how the cross anticipates Pentecost. This is how it anticipates the pouring out of the Spirit upon all flesh and the breaking down of the barriers between God and all of humanity, as well as among all peoples in a loving and just communion (Acts 2:17–18; 1 Cor. 12:13; Gal. 3:28). The cross breaks down the barrier between person groups so that they may all receive the Spirit as one body in Christ (Eph. 2:19–22).

Christ redeems humanity in a way that liberates them. He used the metaphor of a *ransom* (Mark 10:45), which meant a payment or offering made to deliver someone from captivity. The point of the ransom metaphor is not so much the payment, as though God needs to be paid off to show humanity mercy. Instead, the point is that the self-offering of Christ in fulfillment of the Father's will frees humanity from its captivity to sin and death. Old Testament sacrifices were important to Israel's worship and were symbolic of the need for a mediator. But these sacrifices could not overcome the barrier of sin and death; they could not represent God's act of reconciling the world to Godself. Only the one who comes from God to do God's will can fulfill this act of atonement. Take note of Hebrews 10:5–10:

Therefore, when Christ came into the world, he said:

"Sacrifice and offering you did not desire,
    but a body you prepared for me;
with burnt offerings and sin offerings
    you were not pleased.
Then I said, 'Here I am—it is written about me in the scroll—
    I have come to do your will, my God.'"

First he says that "sacrifices and offerings, burnt offerings and sin offerings you did not desire, nor were you pleased with them"—though they were offered in accordance with the law. Then he says, "Here I am, I have come to do your will." He sets aside the first to establish the second. And by that will, we have been made holy through the sacrifice of the body of Jesus Christ once for all.

The above text may be called "the key to a clear understanding of all that the writer of Hebrews says about Christ's sacrificial death."[27] The context leading up to this text emphasizes the fact that, by offering himself, Christ provided redemption for humanity once and for all time: "He has appeared once for all at the culmination of the ages to do away with sin by the sacrifice of himself" (9:26). Quoting Psalm 40:6–8, the above text explains why the Son's self-offering is sufficient for all people and for all time. He is the one who perfectly fulfills the Father's will, the Father's cause in the world: "I have come to do your will, my God" (Heb. 10:7). Christ's offer of his embodied life for humanity makes the sacrificial system and everything connected to it passé. Christ is now the new means of communion and worship, the new temple of God's presence.

Christ's self-offering is not merely a variation in Israel's worship that is on a par with what occurred before. His self-offering was God's plan for Israel and for the world from the very beginning, the hidden meaning of all that had transpired before and the basis of all that will occur in the future. Christ is the new temple of the Holy Spirit that has hallowed the Father's name on behalf of humanity. He did so on the cross, breaking through the barrier of sin, and overcoming the judgment of death in his resurrection. He did this on the cross in order to impart the Spirit and incorporate into himself an ever-diverse body of worshipers who will glorify the Father in and through him, their great high priest.

Though Christ's representation of humanity is vital to the atonement, the redemption theme shows that the atonement is principally a divine act, representative of God's self-giving love to humanity: "This is how God showed his love among us: He sent his one and only Son into the world that we might live through him" (1 John 4:9). To be consistent with the event of the incarnation through to Pentecost, it is important to say that God is, throughout the event of the cross, the principal player in the atonement. Paul makes this point crystal clear when he notes "that God was reconciling the world to himself in Christ, not counting people's sins against them" (2 Cor. 5:19). God removes the sin barrier and overcomes alienation and death in order to reconcile humanity to the divine life in all of its fullness. In Christ, God overcomes the fire of God's own judgment in order to baptize sinners in the renewing Spirit.

Of course, all that Christ does, he does as the man of the Spirit, totally given over to the Father's cause in the world. The priority of the divine action

---

27. Gareth Lee Cockerbill, "Structure and Interpretation in Hebrews 8:1–10:18: A Symphony in Three Movements," *Bulletin for Biblical Research* 11, no. 2 (2001): 193.

does not remove the human character of this action. Christ's fully human journey through the baptism in fire as the one baptized in the Spirit is necessary to humanity's being representatively brought into the divine life from crucifixion to Pentecost. After all, Jesus is the last Adam, truly human as well as truly divine. In Christ, God recapitulates the human race in him in order to provide another way of being human, one that fulfills the original divine intent for creation. Humans parted from the faithful Son of the Father who created them, and they spurned the Holy Spirit whom they were meant to bear in the Son's image. Christ fulfills that journey for the human race. He bears flesh and bears the Spirit in faithful fulfillment of the Father's will. Christ representatively reconciles humanity to God on the cross precisely by becoming, in his death and resurrection, the quintessential human, the embodied declaration, or sacrament, of the Father's love toward humanity. This is what humanity was always meant to be, the revelation of God's self-imparting love to the world.

However, Jesus Christ's act of representation is human precisely in being the divine Son. I will explain this idea through several logical steps that will place the cross in the context of the resurrection and Pentecost. First, when Christ offers himself in glory to the Father on the cross, he does what the eternal Son has always done—namely, he glorifies the Father (John 17:5). But, at the same time, he fulfills what humanity was made to do, for humanity was made to image the Son in glory to the Father. Second, since the Father is the source of self-giving love to the world, the Father is supremely hallowed or glorified when the favored Son bears the Spirit in devotion to that loving cause. There can be no self-offering in glory to the Father that is not also a self-offering in fulfillment of the Father's promise of renewal through the Spirit (Luke 24:49). Christ's glorifying the Father on behalf of humanity on the cross thus reaches for resurrection and Pentecost, where Christ imparts the Spirit to all flesh. Again, Christ is doing on the cross what the eternal Son has always done, namely, offering himself to the cause of the Father's outpoured love to the world. But, since humanity was made for this same purpose, Christ, in being the divine Son on the cross, also fulfills the obligation of the human race. This is what motivated the Son's coming into flesh, to fulfill the purpose for which flesh was made, precisely by being the divine Son ("I have come to do your will, my God"; Heb. 10:7).

In revealing the divine Son's devotion to the Father's outpoured love to the world on the cross, Christ also represents the ideal human, who is created for that same cause. He represents us on the cross, fulfills glory that we owe the Father in a way that overcomes sin and death and opens a path to the

Father on our behalf. He also opens his own life to us as the faithful Son: he did it on the cross, but it was as the climax of his entire life of obedience and dedication to the Father and to the leading of the Spirit that the Father promised to the world. By representing us on the cross, Christ provides the basis of an invitation for humanity to enter into communion with him as the last Adam, the life-giving Spirit (1 Cor. 15:45). The cross represents the bringing together of the faithful God and the consequent faithful human sustained by the divine Spirit. The cross provides the basis for Pentecost, where the invitation is made: the Spirit poured out through the Son—and the Word going out—that we should come and drink from the waters of life. Come and bear the image of the faithful Son.

Divine Love and Justice

Perhaps the most significant effort to understand how the Son represented humanity on the cross is Anselm's famous satisfaction theory of atonement as expressed in his eleventh-century classic *Cur Deus Homo* (*"Why the God-Man?"*). For centuries this was by far the most influential theory of the atonement in the soteriology of the West. The core of the doctrine was the effort to understand how the death of Christ removed the sin barrier between God and humanity without compromising divine justice, or in a way that fulfilled justice and moral rectitude for creation. Why was this doctrine called the "satisfaction" theory of atonement? During the Middle Ages, satisfaction consisted of a payment made to make amends for a wrong committed and an honor offended. It came to represent an element of the doctrine of penance: that is, it was a penitential act that followed contrition of the heart and confession as part of one's spiritual healing. Anselm applied this concept to the atonement. He argued that humans willfully offended God's honor by sinning and submitting to the domination of the devil. Thus, in denying the honor due to God as Creator and Lord, humans had a heavy debt to pay: "So then, everyone who sins ought to pay back the honor of which he has robbed God; and this is the satisfaction which every sinner owes to God."[28] Yet the payment of this debt is impossible for humanity, for all have sinned and fallen short of divine glory (Rom. 3:23). Humans cannot free themselves from the magnitude of this offense, nor from the devil's grip or the bond-

---

28. Anselm, *Cur Deus Homo* 1.11, in *St. Anselm: Basic Writings*, trans. S. N. Deane (La Salle, IL: Open Court, 1968). Hereafter, references to this work appear in parentheses within the text.

age of sin and death. And they cannot undo the moral disruption caused throughout the divine-creature relationship.

Can God just overlook sin and forgive humanity without the cross? Anselm admits that God is bound to no law, but Anselm is quick to add that God is committed to solving this problem in a way that is appropriate to the divine relationship with creation. For this reason God will not just overlook the wrongs committed or the debt owed. If God overlooks sin, "there is no longer any difference between the guilty and the not guilty, and this is unbecoming to God" (1.12). And if God overlooks the affront to the divine honor that sin brings, and forgives humanity without serving justice, "God would not be just to himself . . . and this is too impious even to think of" (1.13). The crucial issue is that, for Anselm, "God's compassion cannot contradict God's justice for God to be consistent with himself" (1.24). Anselm rejected the idea that the debt must be paid to the *devil* to bring about justice; the devil does not deserve payment. Rather, humanity owes the debt to *God*, for the offense was made against God. Only God is properly Lord of creation, and only the granting of honor to God as Lord constitutes the moral unity and harmony of creation. For Anselm, humanity does not need to pay the devil off, but humanity is obliged to makes things right with God by overcoming the devil's bondage and giving God glory as the only true Lord.

But how can sinful humanity restore honor to God by conquering the devil and adequately glorifying God as Lord? Only humanity owes this debt and only humanity can pay it. But how can they? This is the trap in which humans find themselves. They are obligated to do something that they cannot do. Anselm finds in the God-man the only possible solution. As human, Christ can take up humanity's obligation to overcome the devil and give proper honor to God; as divine, he has the power to do it. As both divine and human, Christ fulfills justice on behalf of humans to God so that they could be reconciled without compromising divine justice.

In evaluating Anselm's significant theological achievement, I find it important to note that his satisfaction theory places its overwhelming emphasis on the representative act of honoring the heavenly Father on humanity's behalf. The Father is nearly assumed everywhere to be on the receiving end of Jesus's meritorious self-offering on behalf of humanity. It is because of this that Gustaf Aulen famously accused Anselm of making the atonement through Christ essentially an act of human merit.[29] By way of response, I

---

29. Gustaf Aulen, *Christus Victor: An Historical Study of the Three Main Types of the Idea of Atonement* (New York: Macmillan, 1969), 143–45.

must observe that Anselm does not totally exclude atonement as a divine act. He suggests that Christ, as divine, had the power to restore honor to the Father and, by implication, to himself and to the Spirit. Anselm says of Christ: "Since he is very God, the Son of God, he offered himself for his own honor as well as for that of the Father and the Holy Spirit" (2.18). Indeed, by providing Christ as the offering owed to God on humanity's behalf, "God recovers his right" (1.13). Contrary to Aulen's criticism, Anselm even describes the divine activity as a victory over the devil's hold on creation.

In drawing attention to this matter of divine honor, Anselm raised an issue that is important to biblical theology. As I pointed out above, Christ on the cross overcomes sin and death and, at the resurrection, restores glory to the Father on behalf of humanity. However, how Christ restores honor to God on humanity's behalf is an issue that requires careful evaluation. Walter Brueggemann shows us that there is a basic tension in the Old Testament between divine honor and pathos, or between divine self-regard and regard for others. There are texts in which God acts primarily out of a desire to preserve the divine honor or glory in the world, for example, by sanctifying God's great name (Ezek. 36:23) or supporting God's holy name (39:25). "This is what the sovereign LORD says: It is not for your sake, people of Israel, that I am going to do these things, but for the sake of my holy name, which you have profaned among the nations where you have gone" (36:22). In fact, God will pour forth the Spirit so that Israel could honor the divine name before the nations once more (36:26–27). In Exodus 14:4 and 17, God says that he will deliver Israel "to gain glory for myself over Pharaoh." It might even appear here that "Yahweh in effect has no interest in Israel, but Israel is a convenient ready-at-hand vehicle for the assertion and enactment of Yahweh's self-regard."[30]

But these texts that emphasize the divine self-regard look different when they are set in relation to other texts in which the divine pathos or loving regard for Israel and the nations takes precedence and is the overarching goal, even to the extent that God is willing to suffer indignity and humiliation in acting to give of the divine life in the effort to embrace sinners. Even judgment is exercised in the desire to fulfill this goal. God will "punish" Israel for sacrificing to the Baals (Hosea 2:13), but the goal is to "allure" her into the desert, where God will speak tenderly to her and give her back her vineyards

---

30. Walter Brueggemann, *Theology of the Old Testament: Testimony, Dispute, Advocacy* (Minneapolis: Fortress, 2005), 308; see also 303–8. Hereafter, page references to this work appear in parentheses within the text.

(2:14). The purpose is to recover that first love that Israel had with God at the time of the Exodus: "She will respond as in the days of her youth, as in the day she came up out of Egypt" (2:15). Judgment serves the purposes of suffering love in drawing God's people to repentance and renewal. In the process, God suffers the indignity of pursuing unfaithful Israel as a husband goes after an unfaithful spouse (Hosea 1–2) or a parent a rebellious child (Hosea 11:1–4). Such indignity is suffered in pursuing the nations as well. God compels a stubborn prophet to show compassion to a ruthless people like the Ninevites in the book of Jonah, even though they are far from deserving it. Jonah is deeply offended by the seeming lack of "justice" in this shameless act of divine mercy, which is why he refused to go to Nineveh in the first place: "I knew that you are a gracious and compassionate God, slow to anger and abounding in love, a God who relents from sending calamity!" (4:2). Jonah had not realized that glorifying God involves not only devotion to God in worship but also devotion to God's pathos for the world.

Brueggemann notes that in the Old Testament "Yahweh moves back and forth" between self-regard and regard for others, between "sovereignty and pathos" (309). The Old Testament ends up resolving the tension through a notion of God's saving deeds in which Yahweh is honored and glorified precisely by acting redemptively out of love for others. God's justice is fulfilled in redemptive deeds that show mercy (Isa. 45:8, 23–24; 51:6–8; Ps. 71:19; 89:17; 96:13; 98:9; 111:3; Dan. 9:16–18). God is honored in redeeming out of love for others; in fact, such convergence of honor and pathos "is the staple of Israel's faith" (306). Brueggemann concludes that this convergence "should be regarded as normative for theological interpretation and be allowed to govern other texts" (309). Brueggemann then connects this hermeneutical conclusion to the message of the cross. He refers especially to Jürgen Moltmann's "cruciform discernment of the character of God . . . who completely risks sovereignty in solidarity" (311). Moltmann did indeed criticize Anselm's implied image of the heavenly Father as a patriarch whose overarching concern is the restoration of his honor for its own sake. On the contrary, Moltmann suggests that the Father shares in the suffering love of the triune God by handing the faithful Son over to the path of the cross.[31] *Pentecost* helps us see that this is how God is honored and justice is served at the cross.

Though Brueggemann did not explore the issue of divine honor in the Old Testament with Anselm's atonement theology in mind, his discussion is

---

31. Moltmann does this throughout *Trinity and the Kingdom: The Doctrine of God* (Minneapolis: Fortress, 1983).

obviously relevant to how we evaluate Anselm. He implicitly shows us that Anselm's atonement theology had indeed touched on an issue of importance to a biblical theology of God and redemption. Anselm was right to assume that God's honor and glory as Creator and Lord were rejected in the human fall into sin and death. In spurning the righteousness of God's reign, humans spurned God's honor as Creator and Lord. This offense not only alienated humanity from God; it also contradicted God's redemptive purposes for creation. Rather than glorifying the Creator as Lord, humanity succumbed to idolatry (Rom. 1:21–23) and to the domination of the devil. Therefore, the recovery of God's rightful place as Lord of creation is a legitimate concern to bring forward in any theology of atonement that is sensitive to biblical soteriology.

Anselm saw Christ on the cross as fulfilling penitential satisfaction on behalf of humanity. Anselm was not completely wrong in this. Christ did indeed enter the waters of repentance and hope at the Jordan River to bind himself to us so as to honor the Father on our behalf. But, preoccupied with the doctrine of penance, Anselm lacked the theological resources to bring his core insight to adequate expression. First, it seems that Anselm never fully appreciated the Old Testament's subordination of divine honor to divine pathos, which Brueggemann grasped so well. For Anselm, the restoration of divine honor and dignity is the highest form of justice: "God maintains nothing with more justice than the honor of his own dignity."[32] For Anselm, God sends Christ to restore divine honor in order to save humanity. But what if we flip the relationship between divine honor and pathos, putting pathos first? Rather than saying that the highest form of justice is the divine honor and that God fulfills it in a way that saves us, why not say that the highest form of justice is the offer of mercy to humanity and that God is honored by doing this? Divine justice includes both honor and pathos (mercy), of course, and the two are inseparable. But it does matter which one has the priority. In Anselm's picture of God, one gets the impression of a God who requires satisfaction and honor to save. If one puts divine pathos first, one can give the impression of a God who self-imparts mercifully so as to be honored only in this way. Jesus glorifies the Father as the Spirit Baptizer who faithfully devotes himself to the Father's outpoured love in the world.

Anselm contextually reads Scripture in service to a commonsense morality, which does not make the offended lord very noble by the moral stan-

---

32. Anselm, *Cur Deus Homo* 1.13.

dards of the gospel. In Anselm's day, it was not a lord's obligation to make amends for an offense by someone lower on the social scale or to act so as to free the offender from the difficulty caused by the offense. The offender is the only one morally obligated to do so. For this reason, for Anselm, God can have no legitimate dealings with the devil at the cross, not even to overthrow him by means of divine power, because God is not the one who is morally obligated to do so. In fact, it would be inappropriate for God to do so; God has no legal obligation to contend with the devil in any sense. Since humanity submitted to the devil, only humans can legitimately make cause against him. Anselm observes:

> God was in no need of descending from heaven to conquer the devil, nor of contending against him in holiness to free mankind. But God demanded that man should conquer the devil, so that he who had offended by sin should atone by holiness.[33]

As Gustaf Aulen says about Anselm, the love of God is "regulated" by Anselm's notion of justice "and is only free to act within the limits that Justice marks out."[34] But much is lost by this restriction. By way of response, Aulen rightly makes the overcoming love of God the prior and overarching meaning of the cross:

> The New Testament idea of redemption constitutes in fact a veritable revolution; for it declares that sovereign divine love had taken the initiative, broken through the order of justice and merit, triumphed over the powers of evil and created a new relation between the world and God.[35]

God determines what is appropriate to the divine action, and it is the action itself that guides us in making this determination. God follows the way of mercy from beginning to end. The logic of punishment is the logic of equivalence (the "wages of sin is death"), but the logic of grace is the logic of overflowing abundance. The cross serves Pentecost by being the place where God abundantly shows mercy by opening up for humanity a life filled with the Spirit and dedicated to the Father's cause in the world. "See what

33. Anselm, *Cur Deus Homo* 2.19.
34. Aulen, *Christus Victor*, 79.
35. Aulen, *Christus Victor*, 155.

great love the Father has lavished on us, that we should be called children of God" (1 John 3:1).

Lastly, Anselm did not adequately grasp the fact that Christ hallowed the Father's name before the nations on humanity's behalf by representatively bearing the Spirit through the fire of judgment so as to offer himself for the fulfillment of the Father's cause in the world. Bear in mind that, in Ezekiel 36:22-27, God gave Israelites the Spirit so that they would not profane God's name before the nations but rather hallow God's name by doing God's will. Christ represents Israel and the nations by being the faithful Son who bears the Spirit in representation of us all. Christ honors the Father on humanity's behalf by joining himself to the Father's cause in the world, fulfilling the promise of the Father to overcome the barriers of sin and death with the goal of *bestowing the Spirit to all flesh* (Luke 24:49). There is no other way to hallow the Father's name than to say, "Your kingdom come, your will be done, on earth as it is in heaven" (Matt. 6:10)—and to give your life to make it happen. The vision to be preferred is rather of the divine Son proceeding through the fire of human rejection and alienation in order to overcome that fire through self-giving love, so as to turn it into a sanctifying force. His worship of the Father is one with his devotion to the Father's cause. God is honored in the victory of this suffering love.

A Christology from below will follow Jesus's sojourn through fire as the man of the Spirit in order to determine how the righteousness of the kingdom of God will be fulfilled. We do not find a tallying of merits here, but instead the victory of an indestructible life over the forces of darkness that hold humans captive: "If it is by the Spirit of God that I drive out demons, then the kingdom of God has come upon you" (Matt. 12:28). The justice of the cross is the victory of divine love that does indeed take up the human cause (which is God's cause) and does so with relentless resolve. The inner logic of the cross finds its culmination at Pentecost, the place where the triune God self-imparts in a way that takes others into the divine embrace. Christ's representative victory on the cross finds its goal there.

Part of the problem for Anselm is that he did not have Pentecost adequately in view when he wrote on the atonement. As a result, he portrays the atonement as *only* an objective, legal transaction between the Father and the Son that finds its completion at the cross. Of course, the cross does indeed have objective significance, since Christ *representatively* involves all flesh in his redemptive act, while Pentecost also opens Christ to an *actual* incorporation of others into himself. But the representative involvement has as its goal the actual incorporation. As Pannenberg states the matter, Christ's atonement is objective but not closed.[36] He goes so far as to say that "the righteousness of God comes to fulfillment as we let ourselves be reconciled to God through the atoning death of Jesus Christ."[37] "The Spirit thus brings the mission of the Son to completion."[38] The event of the cross as a redemptive and reconciling event extends its power through the Spirit to bring others into its sphere. The cross is a legal act in a way that resembles the law court of Yahweh, in which enactments overcome the evil opposition and bring about what is enacted. At the Last Supper, Jesus's own description of the significance of his death implies as much. Jesus interpreted his death as covenant-making, as establishing the basis for a new communion of life that will be established after his death through the baptism in the Spirit.[39]

So there is no need to abandon the objectivity of the cross and resurrection as a reconciling act in order to maintain the equally valid link to Pentecost as their goal. Pentecost has objective significance too, for it is there that Christ brings us into union with himself, so that the goal of the cross in representing all of humanity in all of its diversity as one body may be actualized. One cannot reduce Pentecost to a subjective experience of the Spirit, as Abelard did. One cannot assume that atonement only occurs when we are subjectively converted to the divine love. The New Testament speaks of the cross as exemplifying divine love in a way that also includes Jesus's role in bearing our sin and death so as to break their hold on us that we may have life (1 Pet. 2:20–25). However, though his view is one-sided, Abelard is not to be totally dismissed either, for the atonement is indeed a reality that extends beyond its objective basis to form reconciled and reconciling communities shaped by the image of Christ, or by the love of God, and thus the redemptive justice of the kingdom. Jesus Christ, in the power of the Spirit and in faithfulness to the Father, extends his self-sacrificial life to us and invites us to take part (Gal. 2:20). Toward this end, Jesus baptizes in the Holy Spirit (Acts 2:17–18; 1 Cor. 12:13; Gal. 3:28).

---

36. Pannenberg, *Systematic Theology*, 2:428.
37. Pannenberg, *Systematic Theology*, 2:455.
38. Pannenberg, *Systematic Theology*, 2:436.
39. See Gorman, *The Death of the Messiah and the Birth of the New Covenant*.

Love and Wrath

The cross as a representative act involves Christ's bearing the fire of judgment on our behalf. What does this mean? Anselm's theology of atonement included Christ's satisfaction of God's wrath, but Anselm did not emphasize it. This point was highlighted later by the Reformers and subsequent thinkers, such as Jonathan Edwards. Though in need of careful definition, this concern is legitimate. As I have been saying all along, Jesus did bear our baptism in fire, the baptism of judgment. In fact, if Christ bore our fire baptism on the cross, the baptism of his death, some notion of his taking upon himself divine judgment for us would need to be involved. Isaiah 53:5 declares that "the punishment that brought us peace was upon him."

But how are we to understand this bearing of divine judgment or wrath? What is divine wrath? The interpretation of divine wrath as a *divine disposition* has led to the idea that wrath is simply divine anger. There are texts that do support this connection. The nation of Israel is said to have been "swallowed up" or drowned in the "divine wrath," which is defined further as divine anger:

> Without pity the Lord has swallowed up
>> all the dwellings of Jacob;
> in his wrath he has torn down
>> the strongholds of Daughter Judah.
> He has brought her kingdom and its princes
>> down to the ground in dishonor.
> In fierce anger he has cut off
>> every horn of Israel.
> He has withdrawn his right hand
>> at the approach of the enemy.
> He has burned in Jacob like a flaming fire
>> that consumes everything around it. (Lam. 2:2–3)

The tension raised by such texts is between God's compassion and his divine anger concerning sin. Talk of divine "anger" is obviously anthropomorphic, though it does bear witness to a divine passion for the fulfillment of divine purposes for creation. The divine anger to which such texts bear witness is naturally not like ours. It is not subject to fluctuation or loss of control according to shifting circumstance, nor is it driven by self-centered concerns. God's anger is by contrast consistently resistant to flagrant sin out of enduring faithfulness to the welfare of creation, is tempered by divine patience, and is subordinated to the purposes of divine love. For example, Moses asks God (in Exod. 32:11): "Why should your anger burn against your people, whom you brought out of Egypt with great power and a mighty hand?" God eventually responds with this description of the divine identity: "The LORD, the Lord, the compassionate and gracious God, slow to anger, abounding in love and faithfulness." Though a warning is added against unrelenting and unrepentant sin, compassion is promised to those who repent (Exod. 34:6-7). By way of fulfillment, Jesus, after receiving the Spirit, proclaimed the year of the Lord's compassionate favor (Luke 4:19) on his way to the cross to overcome sin and death for humanity.

The anthropomorphic idea of divine judgment as divine anger must be qualified but not dismissed. God is not overtaken by emotions as we are. But divine love is passionate, like a holy flame, and so is the divine rejection of the sin that destroys us: "God is a consuming fire" (Heb. 12:29). God passionately hates sin, not only because of divine holiness but also because of divine love for us, for God knows what sin does to us. God hates sin out of a holy love—for our sakes. Divine love is thus a redemptive and holy love. God's holy love is faithful and omnipotent because it cannot be seduced by evil. It does not conform to evil nor yield the field in any way to its threat to plunge the creation into the abyss. God wills to plunge creation into the renewing Spirit, "so that what is mortal may be swallowed up by life" (2 Cor. 5:4). When Christ allows himself to be plunged into this abyss, when he accepts the baptism in fire (in death), he does so destined to overcome it with self-giving love. Divine love thus opposes and overcomes evil for our sakes.

Defining divine wrath simply as divine anger, however, is theologically reductionist and potentially distorting. Wrath is not simply internal to God, a mere element of the divine passion, confined to isolated incidents of punishment. Divine wrath is significantly more objective and vast, theologically speaking. That is, from a theological perspective, wrath is much more prominently to be viewed as the condition of alienation from the divine life along with all that goes with that: gracelessness and death itself. It is the consequence of sin as a denial of grace and a rejection of the life that God abundantly and freely pours out for us. It is the consequence of the wayward journey away from God. Note Isaiah 53:4-6:

> Surely he took up our pain
> and bore our suffering,
> yet we considered him punished by God,

stricken by him, and afflicted.
But he was pierced for our transgressions,
   he was crushed for our iniquities;
the punishment that brought us peace was on him,
   and by his wounds we are healed.
We all, like sheep, have gone astray,
   each of us has turned to our own way;
and the LORD has laid on him
   the iniquity of us all.

Noteworthy is the fact that the "punishment" with which the servant allowed himself to be "afflicted" (v. 4) and "crushed" (v. 5) is the direct result of our "iniquity" being laid upon him. This iniquity is itself a journey *away from* God: "We all, like sheep, have gone astray, each of us has turned to our own way" (v. 6). The prodigal son's virtual demise was essentially his wayward journey into the far country. The punishment laid upon the faithful servant is precisely the darkness and alienation of that wayward journey.

The Father laid this judgment upon the Son by delivering him up to the wayward path of the sinners. Romans makes this point clear: the divine wrath revealed from heaven (Rom. 1:18) is realized when God "delivers" humanity up to the degradations and distortions of the wayward path (1:24–28). But God also "delivers" up the faithful Son to that very same state of alienation for our justification (4:25) and blessing (8:32). In the light of Pentecost, we may say that Christ's baptism in fire represented his full submersion into the human condemnation and alienation of sin, which ends in death. This is the divine wrath endured by the Son, to which the Father delivered and the Spirit led him. This is the divine wrath that the divine Son bears up under in order to exchange that fire for a purgative baptism, the baptism in the Holy Spirit. And the Son does this in devotion to the Father's cause in the world. This is the victory of the cross, the victory of the resurrection, and the victory of Pentecost, where that love is abundantly poured out from the Father and through the Son in the form of the vivifying and sanctifying Spirit.

The popular version of the penal theory of atonement in evangelical circles, however, typically highlights the Father as burning with anger toward humanity. To turn that anger away from humanity, the Son accepts it upon himself. This version—without further explanation and qualification—has eventually led to the modern emphasis on Jesus's role in the atonement as one of vicarious suffering, and the Father's role as the angry avenger who is appeased or assuaged by that sacrifice. For example, look at the lyrics of the following popular chorus, entitled "Jesus, Thank You":

The mystery of the Cross I cannot comprehend,
The agonies of Calvary.
You, the perfect Holy One, crushed Your Son,
Who drank the bitter cup reserved for me.
Your blood has washed away my sin,
Jesus, thank You.
The Father's wrath completely satisfied,
Jesus, thank You.
Once Your enemy, now seated at Your table,
Jesus, thank you.[40]

In singing this song, we are made to ponder the negative role reserved for the heavenly Father. Though Jesus is thanked for graciously drinking our bitter cup and inviting us to his table, the role reserved for the heavenly Father is entirely negative. The Father crushes Jesus, who serves to satisfy this divine anger for us, presumably so that the Father would be able to justly embrace us as sinners. One could take this to mean that the Son is not devoted to the Father's cause in bringing humanity into line with it; instead, the Son is devoted to humanity's cause in order to convert the Father to it!

I do not wish to be unfair to the songwriter of the "Jesus, Thank You" chorus. No chorus or song can say everything theologically. But the chorus does perhaps inadvertently contribute to a larger problem in evangelical theology. Neglecting a positive role for the Father has historically been a problem in evangelical atonement theology, one that is traceable to the relative lack of a positive role for the Father in Anselm's theory. Merely saying that the angry Father sent the Son to appease his anger is not enough to grant divine love its rightful place in our understanding of atonement. Though it is clear from Anselm's *Cur Deus Homo* that the Son is sent to fulfill justice for creation by restoring honor to the Father on our behalf, the Father otherwise plays a largely passive role, namely, having divine honor satisfied. Once one includes within this vision a heftier role for the appeasement of the Father's wrath, the result can become a view of the Father's role in the atonement as passive and the Son's as active, the Father's role as having wrath assuaged and

---

40. Pat Sczebel, "Jesus, Thank You" (Colorado Springs: Hosanna Music/Sovereign Grace Worship, 2003).

the Son's role as assuaging it. We could as a result fail to take adequately into consideration Martin Hengel's point that the New Testament broke with the martyr cults of the ancient world precisely by defining atonement as God's gracious act of reconciling the world to the divine life rather than merely assuaging God's wrath.[41]

An example of this problem may be found in the famous sermon by the eighteenth-century theologian Jonathan Edwards, entitled "Sinners in the Hands of an Angry God." His sermon overwhelmingly accents God the Father's sovereignty, holiness, and wrath toward humanity. He describes God's attitude toward humanity this way:

> The God who holds you over the pit of hell, much as one holds a spider, or some loathsome insect over the fire, abhors you, and is dreadfully provoked: His wrath toward you burns like fire; He looks upon you as worthy of nothing else, but to be cast into the fire.[42]

Does God look at humanity in the same way as we might look at loathsome insects to be tossed into the flames? By introducing Jesus as the one who came to change this by taking the Father's wrath for us threatens to place the Father and the Son at cross purposes. Perhaps we should then alter John 3:16 to say that God so *hated* the world that Jesus had to come to assuage that wrath, so that whoever believes may be saved! God does not need to be converted to humanity. God's penchant to love even those who spurn that love is the biblical foundation for understanding the cross. The divine love is thus eternal and unchanging (James 1:17). Christ as the Lamb was indeed slain from the foundation of the world (Rev. 13:8). It was always the case that "the cross of Christ is etched in the heart of the triune God."[43] It is humanity that needs converting, and Pannenberg is correct: "The world must be reconciled to God, not God to the world."[44]

There is thus a continuity of purpose to redeem out of love for humanity among the Father, the Son, and the Spirit that can be lost in Edwards's version of the penal doctrine of atonement. Moreover, nonviolent atonement maintains that the Father in penal theories of atonement comes off looking

---

41. Martin Hengel, *The Atonement: The Origins of the Doctrine in the New Testament*, trans. John Bowden (Philadelphia: Fortress, 1981), 31.

42. Jonathan Edwards, "Sinners in the Hands of an Angry God," http://www.religionfacts.com/christianity/library/edwards_sinners.htm, accessed October 18, 2011.

43. Volf, *Exclusion and Embrace*, 127.

44. Pannenberg, *Systematic Theology*, 2:437.

like an oppressive and violent patriarchal figure who abuses his Son out of anger against humanity. Jesus appears to be a passive victim who submits to the Father's violent wrath so that others can avoid it. Friedrich Schleiermacher understandably observes that this theory of atonement is fashioned out of "the crudest human conditions" and is applied from there to God.[45] Dorothée Soelle has more recently been a key voice behind an even more negative response. She calls the God of this atonement theory "sadistic" and the Christ of this theory "masochistic."[46] Others followed Soelle in calling the penal atonement theory divine or cosmic "child abuse." Rather than encouraging oppressed people to affirm their God-given dignity and resist abuse, this theory of atonement can seem to support violence and passive submission to it. Joan Carlson Brown and Rebecca Parker thus say: "The image of God the Father demanding and carrying out the suffering and death of his own Son has sustained a culture of abuse and led to the abandonment of victims of abuse and oppression."[47]

These voices must be taken seriously. The penal theory as it is popularly stated draws from less than biblical portrayals of God. If one emphasizes Jesus's coming to assuage God's wrath against humanity, or somehow to turn God mercifully toward humanity, how does one then fit this with the Father's love for humanity that went into the coming of Christ into the world and totally defines the Son's entire mission as sent of the Father (John 3:16–17)? From the womb to the cross, Jesus is the Word of the Father! After all, in bearing our baptism of fire in order to pour forth the abundant Spirit of life, Jesus is fulfilling the promise of the Father in the world. And if Jesus is fully divine, one in essence and will with the heavenly Father, how can one portray the Father as wrathful toward humanity and Jesus as coming out of love for humanity to turn the Father's wrath away from us? We are compelled, in the light of texts such as John 3:16–17, to describe love and grace as the primary and all-encompassing divine action, a point confirmed at the cross. Everything else is to be viewed in service to this. Rather than say that the Son satisfied the Father's wrath, one should say that the Son satisfied the Father's *love*.

The cross is indeed an act of forgiveness. At the cross, God does not count our sin against us (2 Cor. 5:19), does not allow it to be an insurmount-

---

45. Friedrich Schleiermacher, *The Christian Faith* (Philadelphia: Fortress, 1976), 176.

46. Dorothée Soelle, *Suffering* (Philadelphia: Fortress, 1975), 9–32.

47. Joan Carlson Brown and Rebecca Parker, "For God So Loved the World?," in *Christianity, Patriarchy, and Abuse: A Feminist Critique*, ed. Joan Carlson Brown and Carol R. Bohn (New York: Pilgrim Press, 1989), 8–9.

able barrier to reconciliation and the promise of the Spirit. No legal requirement needs to be met—other than what God's redemptive action establishes as covenantal. That was the case at the time of the Exodus and at Sinai, and that was also the case at the cross and at Pentecost. God does not allow displeasure at human sin and the condition of alienation and death to be insurmountable barriers. The divine love for humanity overcomes all of these barriers in order to offer humans grace, reconciliation, and incorporation. At the cross, God overcomes God's own wrath to self-impart to humanity in grace. Christ represents *God* in bearing the baptism by fire in such a way that the baptism in the Spirit—in divine love—triumphs for the sake of humanity.[48] The Son on the cross gives himself over to the Father's cause in the world and honors the Father in this way. Christ represents humanity in this act, too, for Christ's human yielding to the Father's cause and the Spirit's leading is shown to be the fulfillment of what it means to be ideally human, namely, to bear the Spirit in the image of the faithful Son.

This is not to say that we should eliminate the overcoming of divine wrath at the cross. We should not forget H. Richard Niebuhr's admonition about the need to avoid a theology that advocates a "God without wrath, who brought people without sin into a kingdom without judgment, through the ministrations of a Christ without a cross."[49] The light cast on Jesus's sojourn to the cross helps us see that his baptism by fire is to be viewed in the light of his baptism in the Spirit, and vice versa. This means that Jesus's taking on of our sin and death is to be viewed as a reality to be overcome by his Spirit-baptized life as the faithful Son of the Father, destined to be the one with whom the Spirit remains, the one raised from the dead, the one who will bestow new life through his crucified and risen body. This also means that he is baptized in the Spirit precisely to identify with sinners in the depths of their despair, in order to overcome evil with good and bestow new life on others. In other words, Pentecost shows us that, bearing divine judgment on the cross, Jesus is the one through whom God overcomes God's own wrath through the eschatologically free and indestructible flame of love we call the Holy Spirit. The idea of the triune God overcoming our baptism in fire in order to baptize us in the Spirit helps us to avoid the potential problems associated with the penal theory of atonement discussed above.

48. See Andrew R. Hay, "The Heart of Wrath: Calvin, Barth, and Reformed Theories of Atonement," *Neue Zeitschrift für systematische Theologie und Religionsphilosophie* 55, no. 3 (2013): 361–78.

49. H. Richard Niebuhr, *The Kingdom of God in America* (New York: Harper and Row, 1953), 193.

There is no possibility of finding in the parable of the prodigal son a sadistic father or a masochistic son (Luke 15). The father in the story does not wish to inflict harm. In contrast to the elder son in the parable, who wishes for punishment for his outcast brother, Jesus may be said to journey to the far country of condemnation and alienation in order to bring the sinner back home to the hospitality and generosity of the Father's love. It is the Father who sends the faithful son to the far country to begin with, and it is the Father's love that defines the entire journey. In Christ, God bears up under the sin that affronts and assails the divine will and purpose for creation, in order to extend grace to the sinners. This is why the love extended is suffering love, which joins with the sinners at the core of their despair in order to break them free of its hold. It is this love in the fullness and freedom of the Spirit to which the elder Son is committed and gives himself over to fulfill. And he does so in honor of the Father and the Father's cause, for only in the fulfillment of this cause is the Father glorified. Thus, in glorifying the Father on behalf *of* humanity, the Son simultaneously reveals the generosity of the Father's love *to* humanity. What is implied here is not divine sadism and human masochism, but divine love as a liberating force that calls us in all of our vast diversity to the Father's banquet table.

Surprised by Joy

"The death of Christ blooming into resurrection was God's breathing again into Adam."[50] In Christ's resurrection, the Spirit overcomes sin and death so as to overflow onto others. Christ rises as the life-giving spirit (1 Cor. 15:45). For this purpose, Christ opens space in himself for others in all of their diversity. But how can this potentiality become an actuality without the resurrection? The resurrection and exaltation vindicates and perfects Christ's faithful life so that his embodied existence could be the Word or Sacrament of the Spirit to creation. Who could have anticipated this event? The movement from crucifixion to resurrection was not obvious to anyone among Jesus's followers before it occurred. How could it have been? The cross seems to contradict everything the resurrection would seem to stand for. Rather than vindication, the cross implied condemnation; rather than life, the crucifixion implied death. The devastating shock of crucifixion thus

---

50. Paul Mallia, "Baptized into Death and Life," *Worship* 39, no. 7 (August/September 1965): 426.

led to the joyful shock of resurrection. The condemned Christ becomes the vindicated Christ. The result? The resurrection is the shocking turn toward Pentecost when it seemed that the cause of Christ had sunk beneath the flames of condemnation and death.

The joyful surprise of the resurrection had Pentecost as its horizon. It also had the implied suffering love of God at the cross as its immediate anchor. Without the resurrection, the baptism in fire would have meant the end, not only for Christ, but also for others. Both Christ and his movement would have come to an abrupt end. Any implication of his identity as the beloved and faithful Son of the Father would have been nullified. There would have been no Pentecost, no church, and no Christian mission. At the crucifixion of Jesus, it did indeed seem as if all was lost for the cause of Christ. Those looking at the turn of events from outside the faith must have been puzzled by the sudden rise of the Christian faith from the ashes of Christ's death.

Near the end of the first century, the Roman senator and historian Tacitus wrote the following about Christ and the sudden and inexplicable rise of the earliest Christian movement:

> Christus, from whom the name [of Christians] had its origin, suffered the extreme penalty during the reign of Tiberius at the hands of one of our procurators, Pontius Pilate, and a deadly superstition, thus checked for the moment, again broke out, not only in Judea, the first source of the evil, but also in the city [of Rome] where all things hideous and shameful from all parts of the world meet and become popular.[51]

What seems striking about this quote is how Tacitus's remarks confirm the accounts of Jesus's crucifixion and resurrection in the New Testament. In both Tacitus and the New Testament, the Jesus movement was suddenly halted, or "checked," at Jesus's crucifixion. But then—just as suddenly—it "broke out" shortly after that event. As Tacitus notes, the Romans regarded the crucifixion as an "extreme penalty," for it was meant to be a public deterrent to illegal resistance to the empire. Crucifixion publicly crushed and discredited a dissident leader and what the movement stood for; there was hence no more effective way of halting a dissident movement than that.

---

51. My translation. Tacitus, *Annuls* 15.44, available in Latin: http://www.perseus.tufts.edu/hopper/text?doc=Perseus%3Atext%3A1999.02.0077&redirect=true.

Especially given the messianic implications of Jesus's claims and the concomitant expectations of his followers, one would think that the Roman strategy would have been quite effective in putting an end to the Jesus movement. And it was. In point of fact, the crucifixion of Jesus did indeed have its intended effect—*at first*. Tacitus admits as much, noting that the public execution of Jesus "checked," or halted, the Jesus "superstition"—"for the moment." The Roman strategy of "extreme punishment" initially seemed to have worked the way it was supposed to. But then something unexpected happened. In Tacitus's words, the Jesus movement "again broke out" and spread, from Judea all the way to Rome. And how does Tacitus explain this surprising development? It was a result of a "deadly superstition" that broke out and spread like a nefarious virus, ending up in Rome, "where all things hideous and shameful from all parts of the world meet and become popular." Tacitus ends up shaking his head and, in the end, blaming Rome. What else could anyone expect but that this city would somehow attract the spread of this rapidly spreading evil so that it would end up reaching this far in its influence?

The New Testament agrees that the Jesus movement was "checked" for the moment in the context of Jesus's gruesome crucifixion, but that it "again broke out," moving from Judea all the way to Rome. But the New Testament has an explanation that Tacitus would not have been prepared to consider. Rather than the Jesus movement breaking out and spreading as a result of some evil virus, it broke out because key members of the movement saw Jesus alive—*raised from the dead.* But there was more. Raised to life, Christ imparted the Spirit of life to them, becoming a "life-giving spirit" (1 Cor. 15:45). He baptized them into the communion and power of the Spirit, which propelled an ever-expanding witness to the reality of the risen Christ in reconciled and reconciling communities that were shaped by the love of God revealed in Christ. The Jesus movement broke out because Jesus turned out to have risen from the dead and poured forth the healing river of the Spirit on all those who called on his name, and was still doing so when the Jesus movement reached Rome and, later, when Tacitus wrote about it. The Christian movement did not ride the wave of an evil virus, but instead the wave of divine healing and restoration.

It is interesting that this "checking," and sudden "breaking out," was just as unexpected among Jesus's following as it was to those who came to observe it from a distance. And both sides came to terms with it in their own way. Tacitus simply included it among other superstitions that had unexpectedly caught fire and spread all the way to Rome, where such phenomena upset the ideal of a uniform and undisturbed *Pax Romana*. The early Christians, who saw these events up close and from the inside, came to understand them fundamentally within their encounter with the risen Christ in the power of Easter life. Seen from either perspective, the rise of the communities of Christ—the rise of the Spirit-baptized life—was a riddle that needed to be explained. Those who began to explain it from an inside perspective did so in a way that was radically different from those who did so from an outside perspective.

The biblical narrative sets up the resurrection of Jesus in a way that highlights the shocking effects of both the crucifixion and resurrection. The crucifixion of Jesus seemed to negate any hope that Jesus was the messianic king and mediator of the Spirit who would redeem Israel and bring to fulfillment the mission to the nations. It is helpful to look at Luke's story of the two travelers on the road to Emmaus shortly after the resurrection of Jesus. These two travelers could never have imagined that the fellow traveler, with whom they walked and chatted about the gruesome crucifixion of Jesus, was Jesus himself, raised from the dead. How could they have known? No one could have expected at that time that Jesus would rise bodily from the dead. One of the two travelers, Cleopas, defined the problem about the crucified Jesus this way:

> The chief priests and our rulers handed him over to be sentenced to death, and they crucified him; but we had hoped that he was the one who was going to redeem Israel. And what is more, it is the third day since all this took place. (Luke 24:20–21)

Cleopas's disappointment is meant in this text to make a point. "We had hoped" speaks of a hope in the past tense, as no longer current, a hope that has in fact been dashed against the rocks of a cruel reality that could not be denied: Jesus was crucified. Jesus was not the first Jewish prophet to be killed, a point that he himself made in his rebuke of Israel (Matt. 23:37). But Jesus was not *only* a prophet, according to the witness of the Gospels. Cleopas makes this much clear: his dashed hopes had to do with expectations that Jesus would "redeem Israel." Such expectations had messianic implications. Prophets might be executed as martyrs by the Romans, but not the Messiah. There is simply no way of reducing the devastating effects of the crucifixion on Jesus's followers by pretending that they could have continued on as his followers by treating him as nothing more than one martyred prophet among others. All four Gospels have John the Baptist announcing the coming one as no *mere* prophet: "But after me comes one who is more powerful than I, whose sandals I am not worthy to carry. He will baptize you with the Holy Spirit and fire" (Matt. 3:11). Christ's crucifixion thoroughly discredited this expectation. To suddenly regard him as merely one prophet among others who had been martyred would have required his followers to simply place him in a league with John the Baptist, and thus to redefine him in total disregard of John's own announcement, as well as key implications of Jesus's life and message. The disciples' loss of hope at the crucifixion is indirect evidence that Jesus made and implied messianic claims.

Cleopas seems to speak for the entire Jesus movement, because a rather dismal situation was apparent among his earliest followers, who were devastated by his crucifixion, so much so that the men among them refused to believe the witness of the women that he had indeed arisen: "Their words seemed to them like nonsense" (Luke 24:11). This inability to accept the first proclamation reflects more than a bias against women (as important as that is for understanding it). The crucifixion caused them to confront a theological contradiction that seemed unresolvable. The leadership of Israel and Rome had just colluded to decisively reject the redemption announced by both John the Baptist and the heavenly Father at the Jordan River, and they had done so in a highly public and shocking display of cruelty and power. It was said that "on those living in the land of the shadow of death a light has dawned" because of Jesus (Matt. 4:16). But how could this be said of him if the shadow of death had swallowed him up without the promised redemption, without the promised flood of the Holy Spirit promised by God?

It is important to note, as we explore this deep disappointment in the Gospel narratives, that we are not simply dealing with the followers' psychological shock at having their cherished leader mocked and unjustly crucified in public. There are deep *theological* reasons for Cleopas's placing any hope concerning Christ in the past tense. Israel had come to expect that God would be present in an unprecedented way through a messianic king who would usher in God's kingdom on earth. As John the Baptist preached, the Spirit would rest uniquely on him and would be poured out richly through him on all who would repent (e.g., Mark 1:8; cf. Joel 2:28–29; Isa. 61:1–3). Christ's crucifixion certainly excluded faith in him as the one who would fulfill such expectations. The idea that the anointed one would fall prey to condemnation and death was unthinkable. So, given the crucifixion, there seemed to be no other options if they were to look elsewhere for the fulfillment of Israel's hopes. John the Baptist's question voiced near the time of his own execution would have become more relevant than ever: "Are you the one who is to come, or should we expect someone else?" (Matt. 11:3). And yet its relevance would have marked the point at which the brilliant light of John's hope was forcibly moved off Jesus and shone in the direction of a yet unknown horizon. No one could have guessed that Christ's resurrection to immortality would suddenly, within three days, change all of that.

But should his followers have been able to anticipate the death and the resurrection of Jesus? Did he not connect his messianic mission to his death and resurrection while teaching them? It is highly significant that the Gospels connect Jesus's predictions of his death to Peter's confession of him as the Messiah. This clarity of insight into Jesus's identity that was already implied by Jesus's Jordan experience would have made the prediction of his death all the more impossible to grasp. The tension between Peter's confession and its seeming contradiction in the coming event of Christ's rejection and death would set the stage for the fulfillment of Christ's role as the Spirit Baptizer who bore for us the baptism in death in order to open up for us a baptism in life. Mark explains the disciples' failure to grasp the significance of the tension as their partial blindness. Mark's account is especially telling: a blind man receives his sight only gradually, just before Peter's confession (Mark 8:22–26). The man sees people "like trees walking around" before he gains the full clarity of his sight (8:24). Then Peter gives a confession that is driven by spiritual insight. Jesus is the Messiah; but he puts the depth of that insight to the test. He immediately says that he must be put to death, but that he would rise again. Peter responds with a stern rebuke (8:31–32). Like the blind man, Peter's insight still lacks depth and clarity. Jesus's path to his glorious reign and to mediating the Spirit of life must proceed through the baptism of his death. Peter could not bear the thought of the rejection and death of Christ. It was a wall beyond which no hope was imaginable. No one besides Jesus could have been expected to imagine it. And yet, until Peter did—until all the disciples did—they could not have grasped the true nature of Jesus's messianic mission. Until they did, they also could not have grasped the nature of their own discipleship, fashioned—as it must become—by the path of self-giving love. Until then, their sight would not be clear.

The blindness of the disciples is how Mark deals with their inability to accept Jesus's prediction of his coming death and the hope of his vindication through resurrection. Luke makes this point especially clear by noting that the disciples simply could not grasp the meaning of such predictions (Luke 9:45; 18:34). Is this explanation convincing as a historical possibility? The issue of the historicity of these accounts of Jesus's prediction of his death has occasioned a lively debate.[52] The specificity of Jesus's predictions of his death and resurrection (e.g., that he will rise in three days) as well as the despair experienced by the disciples during and after the crucifixion imply, for many scholars, that these predictions did not occur or were at least to some degree amplified later by the communities of Jesus. Those who doubt that Jesus made such startling predictions would ask us whether or not it is realistic to assume that it took the angel's reminder at the empty tomb for the disciples to recall that Jesus had predicted his death and resurrection (Luke 24:7–8).

To begin with, it is not far-fetched to imagine that Jesus did come at some point to anticipate an inevitable clash with the Jerusalem leadership, which would lead to his violent death, especially given how the authorities dealt with people accused of blasphemy in those days. It is also arguable that he trusted his Father to vindicate him through resurrection for the sake of his mission.[53] He connected this premonition with the messianic woes he was convinced would occasion the dawn of the kingdom of God, woes that would represent elements of John the Baptist's reference to a coming baptism in fire. Jesus came to believe that he himself would suffer under these woes for the sake of humanity. Why do such assumptions seem plausible? Christ's coming rejection and death on behalf of others and his belief that he would be vindicated just seem too pervasively present in the Jesus traditions to have been simply read into the Jesus story from later sources.[54]

The Gospels convincingly note that the disciples were not able to take in the possibility that their Messiah would redeem Israel and fulfill its witness to the nations by first being handed over by Israel's leadership to death. How could they have taken such a prediction as a literal possibility? Such a thought must have sounded like madness to them. The hope that Christ would yet be vindicated through resurrection would hardly have been sufficient to prevent the disciples from responding with horror and despair at the thought of his being murdered at the hands of pagan Rome and the temple elite in Jerusalem! The Gospels note that this is precisely how the disciples responded. So they reacted in ways we might expect, with deep offense: "'Never, Lord!' Peter said. 'This shall never happen to you!'" (Matt. 16:22).

---

52. A very helpful and thorough guide to the scholarly debate over Jesus's expectation and interpretation of his own death is Scot McKnight, "Jesus and His Death: Some Recent Scholarship," *Currents in Research* 9 (2001): 185–228.

53. I am in agreement here with N. T. Wright, *The Resurrection of the Son of God*, vol. 3 of *Christian Origins and the Question of God* (Minneapolis: Fortress, 2003), 409.

54. See McKnight, "Jesus and His Death," 201–5.

When Jesus persists in predicting, over their protests, his dreadful fate again, "the disciples were filled with grief" (17:23).

Apparently, the hope that he will somehow be raised to life after being put to death by the nation's leadership was of little comfort to the disciples, since on the other side of such a fate, messianic hope must have seemed like an empty promise, false comfort in response to a dark storm that was building its way to an ominous conclusion. Mark makes the case—as does Luke—that the disciples are in a state of denial concerning the possibility of Jesus's dismal fate. Luke says that they had given up trying to understand Jesus's meaning (9:45; 18:34). Jesus often spoke in parables. When something seemed too fantastic to take literally, the disciples would have searched for a hidden meaning; but in this case they simply found it beyond their grasp. It was not until the resurrection that they were able to understand the literal significance of his words.

Peter's taking offense at the prospect that Jesus, as the Messiah, could ultimately be rejected and killed is similar to John the Baptist's protest that Jesus should enter the waters of repentance to receive baptism at John's hands. The two are related. "The baptism of Jesus is, then, the foreshadowing of his death."[55] Jesus's entry into the place of sinners at his baptism is related to his journey to his baptism in fire for the human race. The disciples could have no more grasped the significance of Jesus's baptism in fire than did John the Baptist. To their minds, the Messiah lights the fire on the earth against others and will baptize humanity in the Spirit only if they repent (Luke 9:54). What they could not have anticipated is that Jesus joined his path to ours in death so that he could join his risen life to us as well. His death is seen to be victorious only in the light of the resurrection.

At any rate, after the crucifixion the disciples seem not to have seriously considered resurrection, even in the light of Jesus's expressed confidence that he would be vindicated in this way. Does this reaction seem so unbelievable? After all, resurrection to immortality for the Jews who believed in it was located at the end of the world. Jesus's prediction of vindication in "three days" would have seemed confusing (Mark 8:31). As Jesus lay dead in the tomb, the Temple elite and the Roman emperor still held power. And the disciples could very well be their next victims. Jesus had been crushed, and the world continued on as if nothing had changed. It would be understandable if his prediction of vindication by God did not turn out to have been enough to

---

55. Alan Richardson, *An Introduction to the Theology of the New Testament* (New York: Harper and Row, 1958), 180.

alter the stark reality that they now faced. That Jesus might yet be raised along with the martyrs at the end of time would not have been enough to preserve the messianic hopes of his followers. As I noted above, the Messiah conquers; he is not martyred. It seemed by all accounts that, once Jesus sank beneath the fires of rejection and alienation, any hope that he could be the Baptizer in Spirit and fire sank with him. One would have had to walk in their shoes at that time to understand this.

The resurrection of Jesus in three days was the flame that burst forth from the ashes of despair and allowed Jesus to fulfill his role as Spirit Baptizer in ways that cast John's announcement and the entire witness of the Hebrew Scriptures in a blazingly new light. Messianic hope was only *then* in the present tense. The disciples could finally see clearly all that Jesus had meant. They had to have been surprised by joy. The one who sank beneath the waves of sin and death rose up to be the one who swallows up mortal existence in the limitless ocean of life (2 Cor. 5:4). It took not only resurrection but also Pentecost to fill out the full basis of hope. Through the lens of Pentecost the disciples could see that Jesus, as the risen mediator of the divine Spirit, was Lord, and his reign had relevance not only for humanity but for all of creation. He was the eternal Word destined by the Father to mediate new life to a dying world. The Word of the Father, through whom all things were created and sustained, was now the one who mediated the Spirit of new life to all flesh. All of their preaching and sacraments would occasion his risen and ascended work in the world. This is the theology that grows out of the cross and the resurrection in the light of Pentecost. This is the theology that comes to expression in the New Testament canon and that is to guide Christology today.

The Centrality of Easter to Faith

The witness of the earliest preaching of the apostles was that Christ was raised on the third day, "according to the Scriptures": "For what I received I passed on to you as of first importance: that Christ died for our sins according to the Scriptures, that he was buried, that he was raised on the third day according to the Scriptures" (1 Cor. 15:3-4). This confession was not only Paul's. First Corinthians 15:3-4 seems to be part of a pre-Pauline confessional/kerygmatic statement.[56] This fact undermines the idea that the

---

56. John S. Kloppenberg, "Analysis of the Pre-Pauline Formula 1 Corinthians 15:3b-5

tradition of Christ's bodily resurrection from the tomb is a later mythological development. First Corinthians 15:3–4 contrasts Christ's being "buried" and being "raised," indicating that Christ's resurrection "unearths" him
from burial. There is an empty tomb here in the earliest account available
of Christ's resurrection. An empty tomb implies a bodily resurrection, no
matter how mysterious this body may have been. And this is no later tradition but rather one that Paul himself, as a convert of Jesus, "received" and
"passed on," implying a tradition that goes back to the earliest stage of the
Christian tradition.

So how was this surprisingly new beginning anticipated in Israel? How
is the resurrection of Christ on the third day "according to the Jewish Scriptures"? The texts that speak of the suffering servant are not explicitly connected to a resurrection. Isaiah 53 refers to the fact that the one who has
suffered "will see the light of life and be satisfied" (v. 11); but this is only
vaguely connected to the hope of a resurrection. Even those Old Testament
texts that are quoted in the New Testament in reference to Jesus's resurrection (Ps. 16:8–11; Ps. 110:1; Isa. 55:3) are not obvious allusions to resurrection
if viewed apart from their fulfillment.[57] The Son of man in Daniel 7 ascends
to the throne on a cloud from an earth that is beset with evil powers in implied victory over them, but there is no hint of death or resurrection there.
This text does, however, seem to be thematically connected to the resurrection and a vindication of the faithful in 12:2. It is a connection that will be
explicitly drawn by Christ's followers after his resurrection from the dead.[58]
But the connection would not have otherwise been obvious. Jesus connects
his death and resurrection to that of Jonah's sinking beneath the waves of
despair and his deliverance by God. As Jonah sank beneath the waves of
abandonment and hopelessness—but was raised up in three days—so shall
Christ be raised (Matt. 12:39–40). But Jonah's "resurrection" was most likely
metaphorical. Who would have taken from the story of this disobedient
prophet a prediction of a crucified and risen Messiah had Jesus himself not
applied it to himself in this way?

Not only is a resurrection for God's chosen servant not explicitly foretold; the hope for resurrection in general is only marginally present in the
Old Testament. Daniel 12:2 is an obvious example of such a text. In the Old

---

in the Light of Some Recent Literature," *The Catholic Biblical Quarterly* 40, no. 3 (July
1978): 351.

57. Byron Wheaton, "As It Is Written: Old Testament Foundations for Jesus' Expectation
of Resurrection," *Westminster Theological Journal* 70 (2008): 245.

58. See Wright, *Resurrection of the Son of God*, 114–15.

Testament there were individuals who arrived at the conclusion that God's faithfulness in life would not end at death, but that God would remain faithful even as one descends into *sheol,* where there is no hope: "If I make my bed in the depths you are there" (Ps. 139:8). In spite of these hints, Walther Zimmerli could still make the general claim that hope for life beyond the grave in the Old Testament hardly rates a discussion.[59] The overwhelming hope in the Old Testament was that the nation would as a people multiply and flourish, especially in the sacred land, the city of Jerusalem, and the Temple. Yet the Jewish hopes for national restoration came to be metaphorically described as a "resurrection" by the power of God's prophetic word and the outpoured Spirit (Ezek. 37). The background of this powerful metaphor is God as the one who creates by the divine word and the life-giving Spirit. Echoes of the Genesis creation account are detectable behind texts like Ezekiel 37. Indeed, as N. T. Wright puts it, "It is from the dust that Yahweh creates humans, breathing into them his own breath."[60] Wright is doubtful that the later focus on resurrection in ancient Judaism came from Zoroastrian influence, with its dualistic framework, tracing it rather to the Old Testament belief in creation.[61] The church immediately connected the reality of the resurrection of Jesus to the larger Old Testament reality of God as Creator, who "calls into being things that were not" (Rom. 4:17). Walter Brueggemann points out that "the theological assertion the church has found in the resurrection of Jesus is that here God has powerfully asserted a new governance over the toughest region of creation, namely death."[62] So, though there are no specific verses in the Old Testament that one could point to that explicitly refer to a resurrection of the suffering servant, there is an all-encompassing hope for the Creator's victory over all that opposes the divine purposes for creation through the divine word and the powerful Spirit of life. As Jonah was held under the waves of despair and death, but was raised up by God in three days, so Jesus rose from his baptism of death to the victory of the Spirit of life granted by the Creator, whose power overcomes the deep to make all things new (cf. Matt. 12:40). The difference is that Jonah sank in disobedience to God's cause in the world, while Jesus sank in devotion to it ("something greater than Jonah is here," Luke 11:32). Christ was raised on the

---

59. Walther Zimmerli, *Man and His Hope in the Old Testament* (Naperville, IL: Allenson, 1970); quoted in Wright, *Resurrection of the Son of God*, 99.

60. Wright, *Resurrection of the Son of God*, 122.

61. Wright, *Resurrection of the Son of God*, 122.

62. Walter Brueggemann, "Proclamation of Resurrection in the Old Testament," *Journal for Preachers* (January 1, 1986): 1.

third day, as was Jonah (Jonah 1:17). If we keep Jonah in mind, we can still have a very real sense that Christ was raised on the third day, "according to the scriptures" (1 Cor. 15:4).

There is no doubt that the resurrection of Christ is core to the faith of the New Testament. "If you declare with your mouth, 'Jesus is Lord,' and believe in your heart that God raised him from the dead, you will be saved" (Rom. 10:9). Jesus's atoning death and resurrection were of "first importance" when it came to the early proclamation of the church (1 Cor. 15:3). The church responded to the shocking events of his death and resurrection with a number of interpretive and theological innovations, none of which represented a straight line from the Old Testament to the New, but which are clearly rooted in the Old Testament. I have just mentioned a couple of these innovations, but it would be beneficial, with the help of N. T. Wright, to review them in the context of the others.[63]

First, even where hope in the resurrection was taught in Judaism, it was not generally a major concern. This concern moves in the New Testament from the periphery to the center. The overwhelming presence of resurrection in the gospel of Jesus Christ is enormously difficult to explain without the resurrection of Jesus at the base of it.

Second, there is a spectrum of opinion in ancient Judaism and in sources outside of Judaism concerning life after death. But there is no such spectrum of opinion among the earliest Christians, even though they had come from diverse backgrounds. The unity of view that is reflected in the New Testament is difficult to explain without the role of the resurrection of Jesus as the single source of inspiration.

Third, though not all Jews hoped for a resurrection, the hope for the resurrection that was found, for example, among Pharisees was modified by early Christians in two important ways. The first way represented a mutation of resurrection belief that resulted in a bifurcation between Jesus's resurrection and an analogous resurrection of the faithful at the end. Jewish resurrection belief prior to the time of Jesus located the resurrection at the end time. Jesus's resurrection caused the church to distinguish between Christ as the first fruits of the resurrection and the end time resurrection as the rest of the harvest. The second mutation had to do with the nature of the risen body. Daniel 12:2 states that the risen faithful "will shine like the brightness of the heavens." Not much specificity is offered, but the New Testament draws

---

63. Wright, *Resurrection of the Son of God*, 477–78. The five points discussed here come from Wright.

some startling conclusions about the nature of the risen body. Of course, I am referring here to resurrection in the full sense of that word, namely, final resurrection to immortal existence. The body rises in Jesus's resurrection to immortality and incorruptibility ("you will not allow your holy one to see decay" [Acts 2:27; cf. 1 Cor. 15:53–54]). Christ could pass into the room though the door was locked, and yet he could still be touched (John 20:26–27) or eat fish (John 21:15). Christ's risen body was thus no mere resuscitation of a mortal body back into mortal existence; rather, it was the transformation of a body to the ultimate eschatological—or pneumatological—form of existence. The specificity in the descriptions of what the risen body of Jesus was like makes sense if he had actually encountered his followers.

Fourth, the earliest Christians engaged in innovative interpretations of some Old Testament texts that are not explicitly references to resurrection, using some texts while ignoring others. It looks as though the shocking event of Christ's resurrection had them scrambling to make sense of it in the light of the tradition and, in doing so, they were able to see the tradition in a strikingly new light.

Last, while early Judaism could use resurrection as a metaphor of something detached from its literal meaning (e.g., Ezek. 37), the early Christians spoke of resurrection in specific connection to Jesus's literal rising from the dead.[64] Their metaphorical use of it uniquely covered the entire Christian life; but it had literal resurrection at the horizon. This fact also implies that there is actually a resurrection event behind the early proclamation of Jesus Christ.

The resurrection of Jesus was obviously not simply attached to Jesus by force of argument from Hebrew Scripture. Neither, we might add, could it have been compelled by Jesus's sojourn on earth. There is no doubt that the overall message of the Old Testament concerning the will of the Creator to exercise lordship over all of creation, even in this area of death, definitely points to the resurrection of Jesus as its fulfillment. But that would only have been apparent in the light of Jesus's resurrection itself, especially in the light of Jesus's lordship, expressed not only in his resurrection but in his extending that to creation by imparting the end-time Spirit to all flesh. It is also true that Jesus taught and did a number of things that either implied or explicitly pointed ahead to his resurrection. He made himself indispensable to the reign and purposes of his heavenly Father and to the work of the Spirit in the world, and he spoke with unprecedented authority and finality

---

64. Wright, *Resurrection of the Son of God*, 477–78.

when it came to the law or to the presence and reign of God in the world. He shone with the glory of God at his transfiguration (e.g., Matt. 17:1–8). He defined his entire journey as combining ultimate rejection with hope of vindication (a baptism by fire and the Spirit). But again, only in the light of the resurrection and Pentecost would all of Jesus's followers receive proper verification, confirmation, and illumination.

The resurrection became, without question, the dramatic turning point in the story of Jesus: it represented, together with the crucifixion, the very heart of the Christian faith. Christ's resurrection was, along with the atoning death of Christ, of "first importance" (1 Cor. 15:3). Christ's resurrection was thus the least disputed point in the early preaching of the church. Even skepticism concerning resurrections in general did not lead to a denial of *Christ's* resurrection. Take note of Saint Paul's words:

> But if it is preached that Christ has been raised from the dead, how can some of you say that there is no resurrection of the dead? If there is no resurrection of the dead, then not even Christ has been raised. (15:12–13)

Notice Paul's logic when he reasons with those who were skeptics concerning the possibility of a general resurrection. If there is no resurrection of the saints, then not even *Christ* was raised! The only way that this argument would have carried any weight at all would be if Christ's resurrection were so deeply rooted in the faith and proclamation of the church that even those who were prone to be skeptical about resurrection in general dared not publicly dispute it.

Paul is clear on the point that, without Christ's resurrection, there is no Christian faith: "If Christ has not been raised, our preaching is useless and so is your faith" (1 Cor. 15:14). The possibility that Christ's resurrection could be reduced to a metaphor, such as the one in Ezekiel 37, was unknown to the disciples. One occasionally encounters the idea that the resurrection belief of the earliest Christians was merely due to the lasting power of Jesus's impact on his followers, or to the power of their memory of him or, perhaps, the power and presence of the Spirit of Jesus through the proclaimed word of God. Though all of these facets of Jesus's lasting value and significance are valid points to make, none of them would have endured as significant without the actual resurrection. Such things would not have been adequate to account for how Christ's followers rose up from the ashes of despair to a living hope that burned so brightly they did not even fear their own death in proclaiming Christ. Moreover, the teaching of the New Testament that Jesus has inaugurated the new creation and that the entire creation will be transformed as a result of his destiny with God would be nothing more than wishful thinking—a clear case of fantastic theological overreach—without any literal point of reference like the one granted the people of God through Easter and Pentecost.

The eschatological point of reference of Christ's resurrection is, of course, difficult to grasp, since it refers to a reality beyond the bounds of history. But without a substantive connection between the destiny of Christ and the destiny of the world, one ends up with either a Gnostic gospel (which denies Jesus's bodily death and resurrection) or a modernist reduction of Jesus to one mythological symbol among others, with no actual bearing on the destiny of the cosmos. We learned this much from the limited theology of Rudolf Bultmann. A welcome remedy for such reductionism is the faith of the earliest followers of Jesus, which, in the light of Pentecost, viewed Jesus's resurrection as an event in the Spirit that would eventually lead to the renewal of all things. This cosmic significance connected the resurrection of Jesus to the original act of creation. Abraham is then presented as believing in "the God who gives life to the dead and calls into being things that were not" (Rom. 4:17). Paul thus maintains that "the creation itself will be liberated from its bondage to decay and brought into the freedom and glory of the children of God" (Rom. 8:21). The Christ who was rescued from the decay of death ("you will not let your holy one see decay," Acts 2:27) will rescue all things from the bondage of mortal decay, the judgment against sin that had engulfed all things.

The Spirit who raised Jesus from the dead and who dwells in us (Rom. 8:11) assures us of having a share in the resurrected destiny of Jesus Christ as the one declared to be the faithful Son by the Spirit of holiness (Rom. 1:4). Indeed, the triune God grants us a foretaste of that life in the here and now through the down payment of the Spirit (Eph. 1:13–14; 2 Cor. 5:5). The resurrection is not just an empty wish; it takes hold of us already by the Spirit. The risen Christ, who shares the Spirit of Easter life with others, and with the creation in its totality, grants us full appreciation for the Son's cosmic significance.

The Resurrection as the Overflow of the Spirit

Resurrection existence is filial existence in that it images in flesh the triumph of the Father's love for the world. Resurrection existence is also pneumatic existence, existence completely liberated and permeated by the freedom, holiness, and eschatological reach of the Spirit. The Spirit of holiness that empowered his self-offering on the cross raised him from the dead (Heb. 9:14; Rom. 1:4). Resurrection exceeds the limits of death and overflows it, reaching eschatologically to the renewal of the creation. There is no messianic resurrection without a messianic Pentecost, that is, messianic lordship over the new creation. He is the one whose innermost being will release a river of the Spirit from which others will drink (John 4:14; 7:38-39; 1 Cor. 12:13). He is the Spirit Baptizer as the risen Lord, and he is the risen Lord as the Spirit Baptizer. This is what distinguishes his resurrection from ours, making his alone all-encompassing and all-determinative.

Resurrection existence may be described in language that indicates being swallowed up in the life of God, the ultimate in what we would call a "baptism" in the Spirit, into the faithful life of the Son and the love of the Father. Second Corinthians 5:4-5 is especially noteworthy:

> For while we are in this tent, we groan and are burdened, because we do not wish to be unclothed but to be clothed instead with our heavenly dwelling, so that what is mortal may be swallowed up by life. Now the one who has fashioned us for this very purpose is God, who has given us the Spirit as a deposit, guaranteeing what is to come.

Paul contrasts here the "clothing" of the tent of this mortal body with the clothing of a "heavenly dwelling." He seems to intuit that "clothing" does not quite capture the abundance of life into which the risen body enters, so he shifts metaphors and describes the risen body as a being "swallowed up by life." The risen body is a baptism in life, the life of the Spirit in the image of the victorious Son. The resurrection is the victory of the renewing baptism in the Spirit over the devastating baptism in fire, replacing the latter with a sanctifying force, for the Father raised him "through the Spirit of holiness" (Rom. 1:4). Paul thus refers to the risen body of Christ as a "spiritual body," not in the sense that it is immaterial—for such a thought would not have occurred to Paul—but in the sense that it is fully given over to the liberty of the Spirit (1 Cor. 15:44). A translation better than *spiritual* here might be "pneumatic"—or even "Spiritful"—*body*. Jesus rose up "into the full Spirit-life of the resurrection."[65] "For it pleased God to have all his fullness dwell in him" (Col. 1:19). He was always the radiance of God's glory; his flesh now fully reveals this (Heb. 1:2). The present indwelling of the Spirit and the rich communion with God and others that this occasions thus allow us to already gain a foretaste of resurrection existence in him.

Jesus's faithfulness had the Father's pleasure and the Spirit's anointing all along, making his life "indestructible" (Heb. 7:16), earmarked for resurrection. When Christ rose from the dead, this was the vindication and victory of his entire life, which was dedicated to the will of the Father and given over to the leading of the Spirit. It is the resurrection of Christ's communion with his disciples as well. More expansively, it is the vindication of his connection to all flesh. At his death, Jesus represented all of us in all of our diversity. He made room in himself for us all, earmarked himself for us all as our elder brother and head. In Christ's dying, not only was his isolated life submerged into the abyss of alienation, but his communion with his disciples and the mission he was to share with them as their Lord and elder brother seemed over, as did his communion that was yet to be with all others.

When he was raised from the dead, Christ was installed at the right hand of the Father as the appointed representative to fulfill the promise of this future, which was the Father's promise of the Spirit, the promise of the Messiah's reign over the new creation (Luke 24:49; Acts 2:33–36). When Christ was raised from the dead, the Spirit, who anointed Christ's body, worked through Christ's outpoured life to bless others. By binding us to Christ's life that was given for others, the Spirit seeks to set us apart for Christlike service. Christ's life is characterized by this overflowing, which is a life poured out in the power of the Spirit for our renewal. The Spirit who filled Christ without measure remained with him so as to be the abundant source of new life for all others. The Spirit remained with him all the way to the cross; an event that seemed like the end was actually the event of new beginnings. This is where Christ, empowered by the Spirit, poured out his life to bind himself to us in our pit of despair. In so doing, Christ glorifies the Father by giving himself over to the Father's cause in the world. In resurrection, the Spirit overflows that pit in order to make all things new. The Christ who reconciled all flesh to himself on the cross became the means by which all flesh could drink from the limitless supply of the Spirit in him.

---

65. David Cooke, *The Distancing of God: The Ambiguity of Symbol in History and Theology* (Minneapolis: Fortress, 1990), 366.

In raising Christ by the Spirit, the Father also willed to conform all things to Christ as the icon of the renewed creation. This is why the Spirit would only be given once Christ is glorified (John 7:39). The Spirit glorifies Christ so as to take from him what the Spirit will then grant to creation, namely, the new life promised by the Father. Christ says of the Spirit: "He will glorify me because it is from me that he will receive what he will make known to you" (16:14). New life flows from the Father through Christ and in the Spirit (16:15). The risen Christ is destined at Pentecost not only to bestow gifts on the church but to fill the whole universe (Eph. 4:10). As this culminating act, Pentecost serves in part to explain the eschatological reach and cosmic breadth of the resurrection of this one man. The Word was incarnated in flesh so that out of his fullness we could receive grace (John 1:16); he will be granted authority over the nations at his ascension in order to impart to them new life (17:2); he will be glorified that others will receive the same (16:14); he is sent that they may be sent (17:18); he sanctifies himself in truth that others will be sanctified (17:19); he will be baptized in the Spirit and fire so that others will be baptized in the Spirit. There simply can be nothing that Christ takes on in his Spirit baptism that he does not take on to give to others. So there can be no resurrection without Pentecost, and the Christ cannot be the Christ without this ultimate event of self-giving. When Christ yields to the economy of the Spirit by imparting the Spirit at Pentecost, he is not simply moving from the trajectory of his life mission to something else; instead, this final giving of himself in the Spirit to all flesh is his culminating act, for he spent his life giving himself over to the will of the Father and to the mission of the Spirit in the world.

Conclusion

The atonement is a complex mystery with a simple message. God in Christ, and through the presence of the Spirit, reconciled the world to the divine life, the life freely given, self-offered, and abundantly poured out on all flesh. In the process, God overcame the baptism in fire in order to baptize us in the Spirit. God overcame the darkness of alienation and judgment through suffering love, did not count our sins against us but rather joined us in the midst of our alienation and despair in order to bring us into the divine life. God did this for humanity *representatively* in Christ's crucifixion and resurrection so that God could do this for humanity *actually* through Christ's mediation of the Spirit from the Father on all flesh.

The priority of emphasis in the atonement is to be placed on the divine action, but Christ's fully human participation is important as well. As the Spirit-baptized person, Christ offers himself on our behalf to the Father, "as a fragrant offering and sacrifice to God" (Eph. 5:2). But in doing so, Christ offers himself to the Father's cause in the world, which is the redemption and renewal of humanity. There is no other way than this for Christ, as the bearer of the Spirit, to hallow the Father's name on earth as it is in heaven. In offering himself in this way to the Father, Christ shows himself to be essential to the Father's cause in the world. He shows himself to be one in person with the eternal Son and one in essence with the Father and the Spirit. The cross is actually God removing the sin barrier and meeting us down in the depths of our alienation and despair in order to overcome this through self-giving love. God reconciles humanity to the divine life representatively on the cross and the resurrection so that God could culminate this act at Pentecost.

In anticipation of Pentecost, the atonement is an objectively accomplished event at the cross and the resurrection—*but one that is not closed.* Atonement in the light of Pentecost is an act of communion in which God shares fully in human condemnation and alienation in order for humanity, in all of its God-given diversity, to partake in the divine life and communion. The atonement is covenant-making and is hence open to bearing fruit among reconciled and reconciling communities that are baptized in the Spirit and thus incorporated into the body of Christ. Therefore, the representative act of communion at the cross and the resurrection accomplished by Christ does not annihilate humanity in all of its diversity nor reduce them to a generic mass or an indistinguishable whole. The cross is the basis of a communion in which God creates space in the divine life for a wide diversity of persons, for Christ "purchased for God persons from every tribe and language and people and nation" (Rev. 5:9). The cross cancels all illusions of unjust privilege, for such things are forms of human self-justification and idolatry. But the cross does preserve our God-given diversity; in fact, the cross opens Christ's life to it. Pentecost fulfills it.

On the cross Christ honors the Father and fulfills justice on behalf of humanity by offering himself up to the Father and the Father's cause in the world. There is no other way to hallow the Father's name than to say "your kingdom come, your will be done, on earth as it is in heaven" (Matt. 6:10). What requires satisfaction at the cross is not the Father's self-regard or the Father's anger about being rejected. What requires satisfaction is the Father's love for the world, which the Son gives himself over to without reservation at the cross. This and only this can honor the Father and fulfill justice, a redemptive justice that will be vindicated at the resurrection and offered at Pentecost to a world in dire need of it. Humanity has gone its own way. The cross provides the basis for reconciliation and renewal because the Son has come in our flesh to perfectly go the way of the Father's cause in the world.

The resurrection, in particular, reveals and enacts the victory of Spirit over fire baptism. The shocking and unjust "lynching" of the crucifixion is overturned in the vindication of resurrection (1 Tim. 3:16), revealing in the process that this victory was already implied in the cross itself, for the Spirit bestowed by the Father remained with him even—and especially—*there*. Having descended into the depths of all that contradicts life, Christ rises to bring humanity captive up into the life of the Spirit, the faithful life of the Son, and the love of the Father. The eschatological reach and cosmic breadth of the cross and the resurrection of Jesus are due to their anticipation of Pentecost, the theme of the following and final chapter.

CHAPTER 6

The Christ of Pentecost

"[The Jordan] makes the whole world a sea."
—Origen, *Against Those Who Baptize in a Different Manner*

Christ baptizes others in the Spirit on behalf of the Father and, in so doing, incorporates them into his crucified and risen life. This is the place where we encounter him, the existential beginning of Christology. This is where Christ shows us most clearly the God who overflows outwardly to indwell the other and to incorporate the other into the divine life. This is where he shows us the ideal humanity as entirely given over to this sharing of life. Though Christ's story has its roots in his baptism in the Spirit and fire, Christ is alive and active in the world today as the Spirit Baptizer. His death did not end his story. He rose again and ascended to his throne to impart the Spirit, to reign, to speak, and to intercede as the living Christ. Luke is careful to say that his Gospel only gives us what Christ "*began* to do and to teach" (Acts 1:1). Christ is still living and acting! Chief among his activities is fulfilling the promise of the Father to bestow the Spirit on all flesh (Luke 24:49; Acts 2:33–36). Christ as the last Adam is the "life-giving spirit" (1 Cor. 15:45). In the creation account, the one who bore the designation of "Adam" was on the receiving end of life. He became a living soul by the divine breath. Adam was created to bear the Spirit to the glory of God. It was obviously God who was the life-giver (Gen. 2:7). The power of natural life given by God allowed the original Adam and Eve to pass on their natural image to their offspring (Gen. 5:3). Yet, not even the proliferation of godly seed could fulfill true human destiny as God intended it. Raised from the dust as a living soul, humanity was sadly bound to return to the dust (Gen. 3:19). Surely, Adam's seed was meant for more than this.

An eschatological Adam was destined to come from heaven to bear human flesh anointed by the Spirit so as to hallow the Father's name on earth as it is in heaven. As flesh he was destined to die in solidarity with all flesh. This baptism in fire was important to his glorifying the Father by fulfilling the Father's will and cause in the world. Toward this end, this last Adam would not return to the dust: "You will not abandon me to the realm of the dead, you will not let your holy one see decay" (Acts 2:27). His body will not pass from life with nothing more to his credit than passing on his natural image to his progeny. He will rise and be exalted as Messiah and Lord so as to pass on his immortal image to others by baptizing them in the Spirit of life. The last Adam is the life-giving spirit, the Spirit Baptizer. This is what sets the last Adam apart from the first and makes the last Adam the recapitulation of the human race: "And just as we have borne the image of the earthly man, so shall we bear the image of the heavenly man" (1 Cor. 15:49).[1] This image is not just his exalted image per se, but the faithful image of the Son of the heavenly Father, who has hallowed the Father's name as man of the Spirit and who was vindicated and exalted so as to fulfill the Father's cause in the world, the cause of the triune God, by imparting the Spirit to all flesh. The last Adam, as the life-giving spirit, fulfills his mission for now at Pentecost. His entire sojourn from the moment he came up from Mary's womb to the moment he came up from the grave has led to this climactic moment, where he passes on his image to others by imparting the Spirit to them and incorporating them into his life. Herein he shows his unity with the self-imparting God to creation and the creation renewed within the divine communion. This is the Christ of Pentecost. There is much to discuss in our effort to penetrate this mystery.

The Question of Pentecost

Pentecost is the place where the crucified and risen Christ is revealed as the eschatological man of the Spirit for all of creation. This is because the eschatological last Adam is not only exalted and self-imparting but incorporating of others (1 Cor. 12:13). It is the place where his devotion to the Father's loving cause in the world is realized, glorifying the Father by renewing the creation

---

1. Benjamen L. Gladd, "The Last Adam as the 'Life-Giving Spirit' Revisited: A Possible Old Testament Background of One of Paul's Most Perplexing Phrases," *Westminster Theological Journal* 71 (September 2009): 308.

and fulfilling the Father's promise. Throughout our discussions thus far we have described Spirit baptism as an expansive and eschatological reality. Baptism in the Spirit is indeed an ecclesial reality. It describes one's incorporation into Christ by faith under the sign of water baptism. It also describes as a consequence one's sanctification and empowerment in the Spirit. But it reaches also for eschatological fulfillment, describing our perfect conformity to the image of Christ through resurrection, which is the point when we are fully "swallowed up" or immersed by Christ's immortal life (2 Cor. 5:4) and share ultimately and decisively in his sonship. Paul thus identifies our adoption with our resurrection: "We ourselves, who have the first fruits of the Spirit, groan inwardly as we wait eagerly for our adoption to sonship, the redemption of our bodies" (Rom. 8:23). Our initiation to Christ and his body by faith anticipates this eschatological fulfillment.

The Spirit testifies to our spirits that we are already God's children (Rom. 8:15–16), which is a reality grasped in hope by the Spirit within us. But the reality of our initiation into Christ and into his sonship is not exhausted by ecclesial incorporation, however that may be conceived (evangelically, sacramentally, or charismatically). Spirit baptism is fulfilled eschatologically, when we rise from the dead and are officially Christ's brothers and sisters by sharing fully in his pneumatic existence to the glory of God. This is when mortality is "swallowed up in life" (2 Cor. 5:4). The symbol of water baptism itself points to this fulfillment: "For if we have been united with him in a death like his, we will certainly also be united with him in a resurrection like his" (Rom. 6:5).

Spirit baptism is an eschatological reality. John the Baptist announces Jesus as the Spirit Baptizer in the midst of a discourse on the coming reign of God (Matt. 3:2–3). Jesus does the same (Acts 1:1–5). As I have noted earlier, the account of Jesus's reception of the Spirit has apocalyptic overtones: the heaven opens, the voice of the Father speaks, and the Spirit descends. It is in the last days that the Spirit would arrive, according to Acts 2:17: "In the last days I will pour out my Spirit, says God, on all people." So also the arrival of the Spirit at Pentecost: in the city of Jerusalem, which was associated with the arrival of the kingdom of God, and accompanied by theophanic signs and wonders, such as flames of fire and the sound of a mighty wind (Acts 2:1–4). Pentecost is an end-time event that will lead to final apocalyptic signs of the end, after the witness to the Gentiles has gone forth to the ends of the earth (Acts 1:8; 2:17–20). All of these things are signs of the end. Jesus functions as the Spirit Baptizer within this eschatological framework. Since Spirit baptism is an eschatological reality, it cannot be something administered by the church. The church can only occasion and celebrate *Christ's* ministry as Spirit Baptizer. The church is born in the outpouring of the Spirit, from incorporation into Christ as the mediator of life.

We have up to this point focused on Pentecost as the place and time in which Christ fulfilled the mission that had spanned his entire life. There is no question that we have in part followed Luke in this conviction. Luke clearly distinguishes the events leading up to Pentecost (death, resurrection, ascension) and highlights Pentecost as the climactic moment of Jesus's mission. This is the event that has since impressed itself on the consciousness of the church as that place where one is to celebrate Jesus's impartation of the Spirit on behalf of the heavenly Father, an event of profoundly christological, pneumatological, and ecclesiological significance. We have, however, also implicitly followed John's emphasis on the unity of Jesus's final acts as the Spirit Baptizer. The Evangelist John presents as a "unitary conceptual whole" Christ's acts of dying, arising, ascending, and giving the Spirit.[2] In my view, Luke also does this, even in his effort to more clearly distinguish the various events within this unity (death, resurrection, ascension, and Spirit impartation). Both John and Luke present Christ as imparting the Spirit from the heavenly Father (John 15:26; 20:22; Acts 2:33–36). Paul also assumes that Jesus proves in his resurrection and ascension to be the "life-giving spirit" (1 Cor. 15:45), imparting "gifts to his people" (Eph. 4:8), and baptizing them into the Spirit with the purpose of creating a unified body incorporated into his own risen life and dependent on him for ongoing spiritual sustenance (1 Cor. 12:13). As I have noted above, James Dunn has convincingly made the case that the baptism in the Spirit functions as a kind of root metaphor for New Testament soteriology. It is also a legitimate focus for christological method.

There are, however, a couple of challenges that we need to confront when we focus our Christology on Pentecost. First of all, two of the four Gospels, Matthew and Mark, say nothing about Jesus's impartation or mediation of the Spirit in fulfillment of John the Baptist's announcement concerning the coming Spirit Baptizer. It is interesting that both of these Gospels share with Luke and John the programmatic announcement of John the Baptist that the coming one will baptize in the Holy Spirit and fire. And yet there is no clearly defined event in either Matthew or Mark in which Jesus does this. Of course, Jesus in Matthew brings the kingdom, or reign, of God near to people through Spirit-empowered acts of deliverance from the oppression of the

---

2. James D. G. Dunn, *Baptism in the Holy Spirit*, Studies in Biblical Theology, Second Series 15 (London: SCM Press, 1970), 174.

dark powers: "But if it is by the Spirit of God that I drive out demons, then the kingdom of God has come upon you" (Matt. 12:28); Mark also implies this. And both Gospels share with Luke and John the assumption that Jesus cleansed people and forgave them of their sins (e.g., Matt. 8:3; 11:5; Mark 1:42; 2:5). But, except for Matthew 12:28, none of these possibilities is granted significance as pneumatological events. And none of these texts is granted the climactic significance that John the Baptist's announcement warrants. It would seem that both Matthew and Mark leave the question concerning the fulfillment of Jesus's Spirit-baptizing an open question. Granted, Jesus's cleansing, forgiving, and acts of deliverance are related to his future role as Spirit Baptizer, but these still do not seem adequate as fulfillments of John's announcement, especially in light of its far-reaching *eschatological* implications. Matthew does show Jesus's commissioning of the disciples to make disciples and to baptize them "in the name of the Father, the Son, and the Holy Spirit" (Matt. 28:19); but, unlike John and Luke, this commission is not explicitly connected to a climactic giving of the Spirit. As for the baptism in fire, all three synoptic Gospels share Jesus's prediction of the coming judgment that make up messianic woes (Matt. 24; Mark 13; Luke 21) and Mark joins Luke in including Jesus's reference, in this context, to his death as a baptism (Mark 10:39; Luke 12:50). As a historical issue, it would seem that Matthew's and Mark's intention concerning the ministry of the Spirit Baptizer must remain an open question. Luke and John provide us with the only clear insight that we have into how John the Baptist's announcement was fulfilled.

In both Luke and John, Jesus fulfills his mission as Spirit Baptizer by imparting the Holy Spirit after his resurrection and his glorification from his heavenly Father and in fulfillment of the Father's cause in the world. In John's account, Jesus's act of imparting the Spirit does seem to occur earlier or more closely tied to Jesus's postresurrection appearances than in Luke's account. Like Luke, however, John refers to an impartation of the Spirit after Jesus had been glorified and had gone to be with his Father (John 14:16, 26; 15:26; and 16:7). What, then, is described in John 20:22, where Jesus breathes on the disciples and instructs them to receive the Spirit? Had Jesus already ascended to the Father, so that that verse (20:22) stands as the fulfillment of the predictions of the coming Spirit? Or is 20:22 an actual impartation of the Spirit? Or is it, instead, a case of prophetic drama that foretold of the Spirit, who would be imparted later?[3] Even conceding that there is a difference in

3. Dunn, *Baptism in the Holy Spirit*, 175–77.

timing between the Johannine and Lukan accounts of Spirit impartation, the basic features of the event shared by both accounts allow us to view them as essentially united under the symbol of Pentecost. I agree with Raymond Brown concerning Luke's and John's accounts of Spirit impartation: "We may hold that functionally each is describing the same event."[4] It seems that Paul also holds to a postascension impartation of the Spirit by Christ (Eph. 4:7–8). This functional unity in the witness of the New Testament concerning the impartation of the Spirit should include Paul as well.

Are we justified in discussing this climactic christological event under the banner of Pentecost? Are we justified historically in following the church calendar at this point? A case can be made that we are. In this functional unity of accounts shared by John, Luke, and Paul, Luke's Pentecost account should not be dismissed as merely a theological construction created to give Jerusalem pride of place at the origin of the Spirit's anointing and mission.[5] Dunn makes a convincing case for Jerusalem as the place of the inaugural impartation of the Spirit. First, Paul's defense of his mission in Galatians 1–2 implies that only the Jerusalem church could lay claim to primacy. Though Paul defends his own authority as coming from Christ, he also notes that he went to the leaders of the Jerusalem church to explain his gospel to them in order to make sure that he was not running his race in vain (Gal. 2:2). All indications are that the Jerusalem church exercised wide authority over the Christian mission. Dunn concludes from this that "the Jerusalem Pentecost must have been *the* 'Pentecost' for most of the young church."[6] Second, why were there so many Galileans in leadership and as congregants at the Jerusalem church if this church were not the decisive place where Christianity began (Acts 1:11; 2:7)? Perceiving Jerusalem to have pride of place when it comes to the arrival of the Spirit would explain the movement of so many Galileans to Jerusalem. Dunn concludes from this that "the most important initial experiences of the Spirit happened in Jerusalem" (139). Though the Spirit surely fell in other locations, Dunn holds that a Pentecost event such as the inaugural arrival of the Spirit in Jerusalem makes sense. He concludes that "the Jerusalem Pentecost was determinative for the growth of Christian-

---

4. Raymond E. Brown, *The Gospel according to John XII–XXI*, Word Biblical Commentary 29a (New York: Doubleday, 1970), 1038.

5. As does Ernst Haenchen, *The Acts of the Apostles: A Commentary* (Philadelphia: Westminster, 1971), 172–75.

6. James D. G. Dunn, *Jesus and the Spirit: A Study of the Religious and Charismatic Experience of Jesus and the First Christians as Reflected in the New Testament* (Philadelphia: Westminster, 1975), 138. Hereafter, page references to this work appear in parentheses within the text.

ity as a whole" (139). He also finds it probable that the Day of Pentecost was indeed the time when the Spirit was imparted by Christ. The idea that Luke chose Pentecost merely for its symbolic significance is unlikely, according to Dunn, for "there is no evidence in Acts 2 . . . that Luke was aware of or determined by 'the Jewish Heritage'" in reporting that the Spirit arrived at the Day of Pentecost (140). He concludes that "it is quite probable that Luke dated the events of Acts 2 to Pentecost because that was the date given to him in the earliest accounts of the outpouring of the Spirit—prosaic as such a solution may seem" (141).

Of course, Pentecost as the celebration of the covenant that God made with Israel at Sinai has obvious symbolic significance.[7] The theophany of God that occurs at Sinai (thunder, lightning, and smoke; Exod. 20:18) signals God's holy presence as the Creator and covenant-maker, as does the theophany at Pentecost (sound of a mighty wind, tongues of fire; Acts 2:3–4) that will lead because of Pentecost to the end-time theophany (blood, fire, and billows of smoke; Acts 2:19), as the old creation fully gives way to the new creation through the Messiah and the Spirit of life he imparts. Joel foresaw just such a new creation due to the outpouring of the Spirit on all flesh (Joel 2:28–29; Acts 2:17–18). As I have noted above, Luke is inspired by the hope expressed in Isaiah 40–55 for the restoration of God's people through a new Exodus, except that Luke describes the Promised Land as the life of the Son imparted in the era of the Spirit. Christ journeyed through the fire before us and with us in order to sanctify us as the dwelling place of God. The difference is that at Sinai the law was given as a signpost of the freedom granted at the time of the Exodus, when God raised Israel up from Egypt as a beloved son (Hosea 11:1). Pentecost implicitly celebrated God's raising of Christ as the eschatological Son who fulfills Israel's election and imparts the Spirit so that hearts of stone could turn to hearts of flesh. This humanization by the Spirit begins the fulfillment of the human vocation by joining hearts to the law's witness to the renewal of life and the glorification of the Father before the nations (Ezek. 36:22–27).

There is thus good reason for following the canon in recognizing Pentecost as the pivotal turning point between the witnesses of the Gospels and the rest of the New Testament witness. The effects of that event permeate the New Testament that follows. Pentecost is indeed a symbol of that pivotal shift from the economies of Christ and the Spirit that he bore and then imparted to all flesh. But it is more than a symbol; it is an event that stands with the

---

7. Meredith Kline, "Primal Parousia," *Westminster Theological Journal* 40 (1978): 245–80.

crucifixion and resurrection as part of a seamless narrative of Christ's self-offering on behalf of the Father. He opens his life to the many representatively throughout his story, but also actually at Pentecost. He becomes the sacrament of the Spirit and the Father's love in representation of us so as to transform us into those who can share in this outpouring of his life.

In this Pentecostal event of self-giving, both Christ and the Spirit are mutually determining. Christ becomes, from the incarnation to Pentecost, the icon of the Spirit—so that in imparting the Spirit, Christ ends up imparting his life to us. In this act of impartation, he also reveals himself as our Lord, elder brother, and the head of us (who are his body), the eschatological last Adam. Accordingly, the Spirit remained with Christ in order to be imparted from him, from the embodied manifestation of his faithful sonship that he enjoys in communion with the Father. The Spirit is now the Spirit of that sonship given to many others, opening up to them the *Abba* prayer and the liberated life that glorifies the Father and commits to the Father's cause in the world (Rom. 8:15–16). Not only is Christ the Messiah, or the one anointed by the Spirit; the Spirit is the Spirit of Christ (Acts 2:33; Rom. 8:9). Christ is the elder brother and Lord of the church, and the Spirit is revealed as the ecclesial Spirit of the community of Christ.[8] Christ is the firstborn of the new creation, and the Spirit is the eschatological power of new birth.

Both Christ and the Spirit are shaped by Christ's impartation of the Spirit and the resultant birth of the church. A Christology of Pentecost recognizes that a risen Christ without his church is not the Christ of the New Testament. Note what Paul Tillich has to say on this subject: "The Christ is not the Christ without those who receive him as the Christ."[9] I have been saying all along that, at Pentecost, Christ is revealed as the Spirit Baptizer, the embodiment of the Word and mediator of the Spirit. At Pentecost, "the Spirit makes Christ an eschatological being, the 'last Adam.'" Christ is revealed as a corporate personality, the one who incorporates others into himself and his body, the decisive climax of his journey from the incarnation, through the cross, and at the resurrection.[10]

It is interesting to note that Christopher R. J. Holmes has recently argued that Karl Barth's dynamic, or "actualist," Christology opens up the reality of

---

8. See Simon Chan, "Mother Church: Towards a Pentecostal Ecclesiology," *Pneuma* 22, no. 1 (Fall 2000): 177–208.

9. Paul Tillich, *Systematic Theology*, vol. 3 (Chicago: University of Chicago Press, 1963), 150.

10. John Zizioulas, *Being as Communion* (Crestwood, NY: St. Vladimir's Seminary Press, 1997), 130.

the concrete life of the church as integral to Christ's ongoing identity. Holmes maintains that Barth views Christ as reconstituting Israel as a people around himself as something peculiar to his unique identity. His identity as present to his church incorporates an increasingly expansive and diverse people.[11] Jesus represents all peoples in his own unique Spirit baptism, showing himself to be the ideal person with and for a diversity of others, and, therefore, the eschatological person, the word or sacrament of the Spirit for others. Therefore, at Pentecost he is fittingly revealed as the Spirit Baptizer, the corporate and eschatological personality who incorporates the others into himself. This is chiefly the "why" of Pentecost, when it comes to a Christology of Pentecost: the Spirit-baptized becomes the Spirit Baptizer. Even the Christ who returns will bring to full public disclosure this Christ, who became a communal person by imparting the Spirit to all flesh. This is his identity forever.

Christ as Lord

How high did Jesus rise? He rose to the throne to reign as the Lord of life, to impart the Spirit to all flesh so that all flesh might be freed to confess him as Lord (1 Cor. 12:3). The ascension is an important link between the resurrection and Pentecost. The one who descended to death on the cross as a servant ascended to the throne of God as Lord:

> Therefore God exalted him to the highest place
> and gave him the name that is above every name,
> that at the name of Jesus every knee should bow,
> in heaven and on earth and under the earth, and every tongue
> acknowledge that Jesus Christ is Lord,
> to the glory of God the Father. (Phil. 2:9–11)

It is noteworthy that, though there is no explicit reference to resurrection in the above text, the ascension implies it. The ascension is Christ's rising to the throne to reign. Edward Schillebeeckx concludes that "the ascension is indeed the resurrection in its fullness."[12] Alan Richardson observes: "It would

---

11. Christopher R. J. Holmes, "The Church as the Presence of Christ: Defending Actualist Ecclesiology," *Pro Ecclesia* 21, no. 3 (2012): 268–80.

12. Edward Schillebeeckx, *Christ the Sacrament of the Encounter with God* (Kansas City, MO: Sheed and Ward, 1987), 26–27.

appear that the primitive apostolic teaching did not separate the ascension from the resurrection of Christ."[13] In Daniel 7, the Son of man "approaches" the throne of the Ancient of Days on the clouds of heaven (7:13). He ascends from the beasts of the earth as if victorious over them. As I noted above, there is an implied connection with Daniel 12:2, which speaks of the vindication of the faithful by way of resurrection. The ascension of one such as the Son of man on clouds of heaven in Daniel 7:13 may lie behind Luke's point that a cloud hid Jesus from the disciples' sight when he finally ascended to heaven (Acts 1:9). Luke makes a point of concluding Christ's resurrection with his ascension to heaven (Luke 24:49-53), as does John (e.g., John 14:1-4; 20:17); and the Apocalypse does also (Rev. 5:13). Paul, too, speaks of the ascension as encapsulating in itself the full victory of Christ's resurrection (Rom. 10:5-7; Eph. 1:20; 4:8). So also Hebrews: "After he had provided purification for sins, he sat down at the right hand of the Majesty in heaven" (Heb. 1:3).

There is strong language used in the New Testament about the finality of the resurrection, ascension, and enthronement in establishing Christ's reign as something once and for all. One may especially notice Luke's emphasis on the ascension of Christ because of Acts' strategic location in the biblical canon, between the Gospels and the letters in the New Testament. Eric Franklin suggests that Luke did not wish to eclipse the importance of eschatological hope for the Second Coming of Christ—only to understand it in reference to Christ's ascension. It is the ascension that leads to the final victory of the *parousia*. For Luke, "the Ascension is the ultimate event which controls his thought upon the *Parousia*."[14] The *parousia* (Christ's future coming) will not be the point at which Christ is first glorified over the nations but is rather the disclosure of a lordship that is already "an established fact."[15] Note Acts 2:34-35:

> "The Lord said to my Lord:
>   'Sit at my right hand
> until I make your enemies
>   a footstool for your feet.'"

Luke's quoting from Psalm 110:1 here looks forward to the ultimate victory, but from the established fact of Christ's enthronement. Equally strong lan-

---

13. Alan Richardson, *An Introduction to the Theology of the New Testament* (New York: Harper and Row, 1958), 198.

14. Eric Franklin, "The Ascension and the Eschatology of Luke-Acts," *Scottish Journal of Theology* 23 (1970): 192.

15. Franklin, "The Ascension and the Eschatology," 193-94.

guage can be found in Paul, where Christ is said to have ascended to his reign "far above all rule and authority, power and dominion, and every name that is invoked, not only in the present age but also in the one to come" (Eph. 1:21). Notice the finality of the victory of Christ's ascension and enthrone-ment that establishes his rule "not only in the present age but also in the one to come." Notice, especially, Jesus's past tense (in John 17:2) concerning his ascension: "For you granted him authority over all people." The risen Christ says this of himself in Matthew as well: "All authority in heaven and on earth has been given to me." Already!

The once-and-for-all or established nature of the ascension is equally strong in the book of Revelation. Christ has the keys of death and hades already (Rev. 1:18). Even more striking is 5:13, which is sung as a result of the exalted Christ even before the final conflict is described:

Then I heard every creature in heaven and on earth and under the earth and on the sea, and all that is in them, saying:

"To him who sits on the throne and to the Lamb
be praise and honor and glory and power,
for ever and ever!"

Every creature in all of creation already praising the exalted Lamb! Christ is the "man child" who will "rule the nations with a rod of iron," and for this reason he "was snatched up to God and to his throne" (Rev. 12:5). None of this is to deny the significance of Christ's future coming in actualizing his liberating reign throughout creation. One is not to downplay the need to struggle to bear witness in the world and to overcome. Revelation places a lot of emphasis on overcoming the beast through the self-sacrificial path of following the Lamb: "They triumphed over him by the blood of the Lamb and by the word of their testimony" (12:11). But there is no question that Christ ascends to the throne to reign and that this reign has final and per-manent validity.

The Christ of Pentecost reigns. His ascension involves his enthronement so that he would be Lord over *all nations* and not just Israel. He ascends to the throne of the Ancient of Days as one like the Son of man and is given "authority, glory, and sovereign power; all nations and peoples of every lan-guage worshiped him. His dominion is an everlasting dominion that will not pass away, and his kingdom is one that will never be destroyed" (Dan. 7:14). Jesus preferred the title Son of man, as the Gospels make abundantly clear. Mark alone has Jesus using it of himself seventeen times. He gives it a novel interpretation, characterizing his path to ascendance as the path of suffering love and service to others: "For even the Son of Man did not come to be served, but to serve, and to give his life as a ransom for many" (Mark 10:45). It is divine love that reigns in Christ's ascension, which is why Christ's reign is liberating and knows no boundaries. Christ accepts the title Son of David (e.g., Mark 10:47–48; 12:35), though the Gospels do not have him using this title of himself, perhaps because of its nationalist overtones. Christ is indeed the Messiah of Israel, but his destiny is to be the Spirit Baptizer who fulfills Israel's witness by opening the life of the Spirit to the nations. "For you granted him authority over all people that he might give eternal life to all those you have given him" (John 17:2). The Christ of the Gospels thus prefers a title that has more global and eschatological implications, the reigning Son of man as described for us in Daniel 7:14: "All nations and peoples of every language worshiped him." As Son of man, he is the representative human. But he is also described as divine. He rides upon the clouds, as was said uniquely of God (Ps. 18:10–13; 68:33; 104:3; Isa. 19:1; Nah. 1:3), and all peoples worship him (only God is worshiped).[16]

Christ reigns over the nations as the Lord of life, right in the midst of this dying world. John the Revealer saw a vision of the exalted Christ this way:

> I turned around to see the voice that was speaking to me. And when I turned I saw seven golden lampstands, and among the lampstands was someone like a son of man, dressed in a robe reaching down to his feet and with a golden sash around his chest. The hair on his head was white like wool, as white as snow, and his eyes were like blazing fire. His feet were like bronze glowing in a furnace, and his voice was like the sound of rushing waters. In his right hand he held seven stars, and coming out of his mouth was a sharp, double-edged sword. His face was like the sun shining in all its brilliance. (Rev. 1:12–16)

Christ appears in the above text with descriptions appropriate to both the reigning Son of man and the Ancient of Days in Daniel 7:9–14 (depictions that are human and divine). He had the light of God shining forth from him (the "radiance of God's glory"; Heb. 1:3). Christ stood in the midst of

---

16. See Tremper Longman III, "The Messiah: Explorations in the Law and the Writings," in *The Messiah in the Old and New Testaments*, ed. Stanley E. Porter (Grand Rapids: Eerdmans, 1997), 27.

the lampstands of the churches that were to reflect his light to the world. However, this exalted Christ not only shows forth the light of God, he possesses the keys of death and Hades, for he has already conquered and is the Lord of life! John continues from the above text to describe his prophetic commissioning:

> When I saw him, I fell at his feet as though dead. Then he placed his right hand on me and said: "Do not be afraid. I am the First and the Last. I am the Living One; I was dead, and now look, I am alive for ever and ever! And I hold the keys of death and Hades. (Rev. 1:17–18)

John rightly falls prostrate in an act of worship before him. The vision he saw of Christ implied a divine presence. That Christ is the first and the last, a designation that belongs to God alone (Isa. 44:6), confirmed this. The witness of the church for the coming kingdom may lead to death. But fear not! Christ has conquered. He already has the keys to death and Hades. He has already taken sovereignty over them, for he is the Lord of life. The one who descended into death and Hades on our behalf rose again in sovereignty over them. He has the power to deliver us from the hold of death and Hades. He is the living one who can now grant life to others. Saying of Christ, "He reigns!" is a battle cry to pray and bear witness in anticipation of the day when death and Hades are vanquished in the flames of divine judgment. "Then death and Hades will be thrown into the lake of fire" (Rev. 20:14). To say "Christ reigns!" is also a great comfort—that, even now, death has no ultimate power over us.

Christ's ascension and enthronement are thus connected to his impartation of the Spirit. As I noted earlier, though Christ is the king, the Spirit is the kingdom. The salvation he imparts in his liberating reign comes in the presence and power of the Spirit. Such was foreshadowed in his life ministry (Matt. 12:28). This divine reign is actualized now among those who drink of the Spirit from him, for the kingdom of God is not a matter of food laws, of material eating and drinking, "but of righteousness, peace and joy in the Holy Spirit" (Rom. 14:17). His first and most important kingly act, therefore, is to *impart the Spirit* (Acts 2:33–36). It is from this lordship that he mediates the Holy Spirit and his risen life to all flesh, for only the Lord can impart the Spirit of life. Only the Lord can conquer death, show that death and despair do not reign, but that life and hope do reign: "I will put breath in you, and you will come to life. Then you will know that I am the Lord" (Ezek. 37:6). The Spirit's role is thus to bear witness to Christ's liberating lordship in all circumstances and to bring creation into his liberating reign (1 Cor. 12:3). Christ was destined in the Spirit to be the Lord of the kingdom Christ himself proclaimed. All are to be brought under Christ's lordship in order to seek first the kingdom of God and its righteousness and to hallow the Father's name on earth as it is in heaven, as an invitation for the Father's kingdom to come (Matt. 6:9–10, 33).

The Spirit of Christ is substantive to a biblical understanding of Christ's reign. The Father's promise of the Spirit is the promise of the kingdom of God on earth. The kingdom of God comes with the presence of God to overthrow the dark powers so as to inaugurate the reign of life (Matt. 12:28). Proposed here is the idea that opening God's reign to others by imparting the Spirit is the goal of the messianic king, just as transforming all things so that they bear the Son's image in glory to the Father is the goal of the Spirit's sovereign witness. Both imparting the Spirit and the image of the faithful Son are the goal of the kingdom, for this is how God has determined to reign from all eternity. The Father has always meant to include the many in the liberating reign enacted in the Son and by the Spirit. The *Abba* prayer of the coming kingdom is meant to have broad boundaries. The reign of the triune God is meant to be a liberating and incorporating force that extends to all times and places—and beyond.

God's lordship and reign, therefore, are not decisively disclosed this side of history until the resurrection, exaltation, and Pentecost. The phrase "God reigns" means that God the Creator alone is the life-giver, and will raise the dead and make all things new. This is God's purview as Creator, the chief characteristic of the divine authority and reign: "Then you, my people, will know that I am the Lord, when I open your graves and bring you up from them. I will put my Spirit in you and you will live" (Ezek. 37:13–14). Though the establishment of divine lordship is metaphorical in this text, it will take on a literal meaning later—upon the resurrection of Christ and Pentecost. Christ proves lordship and his kingly authority by showing that he—and not the powers of darkness and death—reigns. He will not relinquish the kingdoms of this world to the power of darkness, sin, and death. Christ will not relinquish lordship over creation to the devil. The risen and exalted Christ of Pentecost reigns as the Lord of life: "I am alive for ever and ever! And I hold the keys of death and Hades" (Rev. 1:18). Therefore, at his ascension, he pours forth the Spirit to reclaim the creation for his lordship—for the reign of life. He will put his Spirit in us and will one day raise the dead and make all things new. Then all will know what the church knows already, namely, that he is indeed the Lord who reigns.

Christ's reign as the Lord of life, of the new creation, is not visibly disclosed until final eschatological fulfillment, when the Father's cause in the world is fulfilled, the cause for which Christ gave himself throughout his life. This is the cause that will be fulfilled when the Father declares, "I am making everything new" (Rev. 21:5). We do not have access to this fulfillment except through the dim glasses of faith. Until the Lord returns, we know of Christ's lordship only through the Spirit of life, incorporated into Christ, communing with him, and encountering him in core practices, such as the preaching of the word, the sacraments, and acts of love and justice. Another way of saying this is that Jesus's Spirit-baptized existence is fulfilled when he acts at Pentecost as Lord, or as the Spirit Baptizer and ongoing source of life. He is baptized in the Spirit leading up to his resurrection so that he could be the one through whom the Spirit overflows to others from the Father (John 7:38). We encounter him as Spirit Baptizer both as divine and as human, or as the Lord who imparts the Spirit and as the embodied medium in the image of whom the Spirit-baptized creation will be shaped. This medium is the faithful Son who becomes the mediator of the Spirit by yielding in all things to the Father's reign.

As the ascension fulfills the resurrection, so the outpouring of the Spirit fulfills the resurrection/ascension, for the Spirit overflows Jesus's exaltation in order to incorporate the many into Christ. Isn't this the goal and fulfillment of Christ's baptism in the Spirit? Wasn't it that all along? Christ is anointed of the Spirit to be the Spirit Baptizer. His baptism in fire plays a crucial role here as well, for Christ representatively bound himself to us in our captivity to sin and death in order to bring us into his spiritual liberty, his spiritual fullness. At the resurrection/ascension, his liberty and fullness in the Spirit that had already been representatively earmarked for us is abundantly offered to us as a source of liberty, life, and hope. His exaltation was not just for himself but for us. It was not just representative, but was a gift poured out and offered, reaching out to us and seeking to draw us in.

The connection between Christ's ascension to lordship and mediation of the Spirit of life implies that Pentecost is a unique event. Though Christ's mediation of the Spirit at Pentecost is an ever-expanding and diversifying event in the life of the church and the lives of individuals, the Pentecost event itself is still unique. The Pentecost event is a turning point in Christ's work, bringing the thrust of the resurrection and ascension to fulfillment. Christ rises all the way to the throne to reign precisely as the Lord of life, the mediator of the Spirit to all flesh. The initial outpouring of the Spirit is part of Christ's enthronement as Lord of the church and of history (Acts 2:33–

36). The bestowal of the Spirit at Pentecost is inseparable from the lordship revealed at the resurrection/ascension, for this bestowal "is Christ's actual exercise of lordship," making the resurrection itself "an eternally enduring act of salvation."[17] He is enthroned as Lord precisely to be the Lord of life for his people. The confession at the base of the church and its birth in the world is solidified there, for it is only by the Spirit that we can confess him as Lord (1 Cor. 12:3). Schillebeeckx notes that the ascension "is the prelude to the giving of the Spirit."[18] It is from here that the Spirit is imparted. Indeed, the ascension shows that the resurrection is a rising to lordship, to the impartation of the Spirit, to reclaiming the dying creation for the Lord of life.

The worship of Christ as Lord and mediator of life is ancient, arguably the initial response of the Jesus movement to their encounter with Christ (John 20:28; Phil. 2:9–11; Rev. 5).[19] The implication of confessing Jesus as Lord in the ancient hymn of Philippians 2 is one indication of this fact. The Father is glorified in glorifying Christ—and through him renewing creation for this glory—as the Son is glorified in glorifying the Father (and taking creation up into this glorification). The practice of confessing Jesus as Lord in a way that glorifies the Father affirms the full deity of the Son (against subordinationism or a dyohypostatic Christology), since Jesus is confessed as *Lord.* The distinction of the Son from the Father is also affirmed (against modalism), since Christ is confessed as Lord to the glory of the *Father* (implying a relationship of persons). That the Son mediates the Spirit from the Father is no denigration of his deity, for the only way *to* God is *through* God. God is self-mediating. Christ mediates from within the divine self-impartation (as the miahypostatic Christology affirmed). The emphasis on the worship of Christ in the Apocalypse accents his mediation as integral to the divine self-disclosure, which is why Christ is worshiped, but the angelic messenger who shows John the visions is not (19:10). This worship of Christ that begins in 1:17 ("I fell at his feet as dead") fully supports the deity of the Son, for he receives the same praise as that granted to the Father:

> "To him who sits on the throne and to the Lamb
> be praise and honor and glory and power,
> for ever and ever!" (Rev. 5:13)

17. Schillebeeckx, *Christ the Sacrament*, 22.
18. Schillebeeckx, *Christ the Sacrament*, 23-24.
19. Important here is Larry Hurtado's masterful *Lord Jesus Christ: Devotion to Jesus in Earliest Christianity* (Grand Rapids: Eerdmans, 2005).

This worship of Christ in the Apocalypse indicates that this practice would not have seemed strange to the churches of Asia Minor late in the first century. Indications are that hymns continued to be sung in worship to Christ throughout the early centuries of the church.[20] This issue becomes important near the time of Nicaea, since the Arians continued to worship Christ even though they lacked an adequate theological reason for doing so, a point that Athanasius did not overlook.[21]

As the Lord, Christ is the one through and in whom the church has its life as one body in the Spirit. Through the Spirit Baptizer, the church came into being as a communion of saints receiving the Spirit from him. We continue to be dependent on him as the Lord and mediator of life. Thus Paul describes the ecclesial outcome of Spirit baptism this way:

> Just as a body, though one, has many parts, but all its many parts form one body, so it is with Christ. For we were all baptized by one Spirit so as to form one body—whether Jews or Gentiles, slave or free—and we were all given the one Spirit to drink. (1 Cor. 12:12–13)

The above text could be translated to say "in one Spirit we were all baptized unto one body," with Christ implied as the Spirit Baptizer. The meaning, as Robertson and Plummer noted, is as follows: "The Spirit is the element in (*en*) which the baptism takes place, and the one body is the end (*eis*) to which the act is directed."[22] Thayer also maintains that the *eis* of this text indicates an effect, namely, "we were all baptized in one Spirit with the effect of participating fully in one body."[23] I agree with Ralph Del Colle when he says, "The church exists in the outpouring of the Holy Spirit."[24] More pre-

20. Josef A. Jungmann, *The Place of Christ in Liturgical Prayer*, 2nd ed. (London: Geoffrey Chapman, 1989).

21. Jaroslav Pelikan, *The Christian Tradition: A History of the Development of Doctrine*, vol. 1: *The Emergence of the Catholic Tradition* (Chicago: University of Chicago Press, 1971), 1:199.

22. A. T. Robertson and Alfred Plummer, *A Critical and Exegetical Commentary on the First Epistle of St. Paul to the Corinthians*, 2nd ed. by Samuel Rolles Driver, Alfred Plummer, and Charles Augustus Briggs, International Critical Commentary (Edinburgh: T & T Clark, 1963), 272.

23. J. H. Thayer, *A Greek-English Lexicon of the New Testament* (New York: American Book Co., 1889), 94.

24. Ralph Del Colle, "The Outpouring of the Holy Spirit: Implications for the Church and Ecumenism," in *The Holy Spirit, the Church, and Christian Unity: Proceedings of the Consultation Held at the Monastery at Bose, Italy, 14–20 October, 2002*, ed. D. Donnelly, A. Denaux, and J. Fameree (Leuven: Leuven University Press, 2005), 249.

cisely, the church is born and exists in the self-giving of the Spirit Baptizer. It is from and in him that we drink of the Spirit. It is in his image that this drinking shapes us.

Revering Christ as Lord calls into question all unjust use of privilege, all claims to lordship over one another. We submit to one another out of reverence to Christ (Eph. 5:21). Take a look at what Galatians 3:26–28 says:

> So in Christ Jesus you are all children of God through faith, for all of you who were baptized into Christ have clothed yourselves with Christ. There is neither Jew nor Gentile, neither slave nor free, nor is there male and female, for you are all one in Christ Jesus.

Ben Witherington has made the case that this text undermines all unjust hierarchies based on privilege.[25] Markers that justified privilege—male over female, Jew over Greek, free over bond—are discarded, and all are granted equal dignity because they all put on Christ, they all bear his Spirit, and they are all equal siblings under his lordship alone. Christ as Lord creates a community in which all idolatrous forms of lordship are repudiated. Paul reminds masters that they share a brotherhood with their servants under Christ's lordship under which there is no favoritism (Eph. 6:9; cf. Phil. 1:16). Christ as elder brother creates a community in which all have equal dignity as his siblings. Christ as Spirit Baptizer creates a community in which all equally bear the Spirit in fulfillment of whatever unique gifting they may have from God. The Spirit-anointed Messiah imparts the Spirit to create a community that bears witness to God's compassionate justice not only in word but in their common life.

Luke also makes a point of the fact that the Spirit-baptized community crosses concrete and specific boundaries in order to bring about a just community that lives in service to Christ's lordship. Sons and daughters, young and old, and Jew and Gentile equally bear the Spirit in witness to Christ (Acts 2:17–18; 10). They shared resources with the poor (2:45), and they heard and acted on complaints of neglect by Hellenistic Jews (6:1). The Gentiles and followers of John the Baptist are granted the Spirit and incorporated into the messianic community through faith in Christ alone. No other requirement is needed (Acts 10; 19). The entire journey of the church in the Spirit in Acts is a journey from and toward the Christ, who bound himself to all flesh at

---

25. Ben Witherington III, "Rite and Rights for Women—Galatians 3:28," *New Testament Studies* 27, no. 5 (1981): 593.

the incarnation and at the cross in order to bless all flesh with the renewing power of the Spirit. All illusions of privilege based on self-serving agendas must fall to the agenda of the just reign of the Lord, who imparts the Spirit.

All members submit to one another out of reverence to Christ as Lord (Eph. 5:21) and in solidarity with him as elder brother (Rom. 8:29). The clergy who exercise oversight are not the only ones who stand *in persona Christi* (in the person of Christ, or representing Christ). All congregants speak the truth of Christ in love to one another in the Spirit of Christ (Eph. 4:15). All members are gifts to one another, including those who uniquely exercise the ministry of oversight. Hans Küng popularized the notion of the "charismatic structure of the church" in his classic book *The Church*, where he made it the overall context in which the church's gifts of oversight are to be discussed.[26] Juridical thinking tended to be mistrustful of movements of the free Spirit of God for fear of a non-regimented enthusiasm. The tendency has been to "sacramentalize or make uniform the charism, and hence the workings of the Spirit" (184). The result was a clericalism in which the notion of ministry is initially and enduringly discussed in the context of the clergy. Neglected are the richness, variety, and exuberance of spiritual gifts as pictured in such texts as 1 Corinthians chapters 12–14 and exercised throughout the lives of "ordinary" Christians in witness to Christ. Christ is the Lord and elder brother for all Christians.

Küng wished to reverse the historical trend toward clericalism. Rather than subsume charism under church office, Küng wished to do the opposite, namely, subsume office beneath charism (187). Since spiritual gifts are universally exercised by all as everyone in the church is called and commissioned to serve as bearers of the Spirit in witness to Christ, they are not peripheral but are instead central to the church. Küng concludes that the charismatic structure of the church "includes but goes far beyond the hierarchical structure of the church" (188). Küng does not deny the unique role played by those who exercise the ministry of oversight. After all, the church is founded on the prophets of old and the apostolic witness, with Christ as the chief cornerstone (Eph. 2:20). Those blessed with the ministry of oversight will bear the primary (though not exclusive) responsibility

26. Hans Küng, *The Church* (New York: Sheed and Ward, 1967), 150–90. Hereafter, page references to this work appear in parentheses within the text. This concept is also developed by Miroslav Volf in *After Our Likeness: The Church as the Image of the Trinity* (Grand Rapids: Eerdmans, 1997), esp. 231. See also Veli-Matti Kärkkäinen, "Pentecostalism and the Claim for Apostolicity: An Essay in Ecumenical Ecclesiology," *Ecumenical Review of Theology* 25 (2001): 323–26.

of continuously placing the unfinished business of the apostolic witness to Christ before the church. But this responsibility is still shared by all. Küng thus places both gifts of oversight and other giftings within an overarching concept of the church as a fellowship of faith in which all members (including ordained clergy) as bearers of the Spirit are gifted to bless one another. For Küng, "the church must be seen first as a fellowship of faith and only in this light can ecclesiastical office be properly understood" (363).

All believers receive the Spirit through and in Christ (they are not dependent on the clergy for this); all believers bear the Spirit; all have the privilege in Christ of praying, of bearing witness, of ministering, of joining the messianic mission. Christ has bound himself to each one of us. His body is a diverse communion in which the least honorable members by external reckoning receive more honor, and those who suffer are upheld and strengthened (1 Cor. 12:21-26). The Christ who identifies himself with everyone shapes them by the Spirit into his image so that these members identify with one another out of reverence to him and in glory to the Father. The whole is absolutely dependent on him as are the branches to a vine for nourishment, growth, and sanctified purpose (John 15:1-17). In imparting the Spirit, Christ imparts himself in a way that opens his spiritual fullness as Lord and elder brother to all of his members. Hebrews 2:11 says this about Christ: "Both the one who makes people holy and those who are made holy are of the same family. So Jesus is not ashamed to call them brothers and sisters."

We learn from the crucified and risen Christ that God's reign does not conquer and oppress but rather invites and liberates. We learn that humans may, in him, approximate Christ's "Pentecostal" humanity by opening their lives in communion with God in a way that is also open to others, engaging in acts of communal worship, mission, justice, and ministry. Christ's Pentecostal humanity is an ecclesial humanity that reaches out to the world. Those who cling to their own self-centered ways or who prefer isolation in service to these ways cannot know the riches of the kingdom of God. "For whoever wants to save his life will lose it, but whoever loses his life for me will save it" (Luke 9:24). Christ pours out his life at the cross to bind himself to the many in the midst of their fallenness and their unfulfilled yearning for God. He rises in order to provide a way for them to be free. As the Lord, he pours out the Spirit in order to take them into union with himself. He is the Lord of the new creation as the Lord of the church. We are his body, and we seek to be the church for others as he has acted toward the world in fulfillment of the Father's love.

Christ as Prophet

The Christ who reigns mediates the Spirit of life as the Word of the Father. Christ not only *spoke* the word of God; he *was* the Word embodied. That made him a prophet in a way that was unique. He is indispensable to the word of the gospel, to the good news of God's self-impartation to the world. This is why he alone has the authority to break the seals of the scroll and disclose its content. As the one who redeemed us, he is worthy to open the scroll that bears witness to him:

> "You are worthy to take the scroll
> > and to open its seals,
> because you were slain,
> > and with your blood you purchased for God
> > persons from every tribe and language and people and nation."
> > > > > (Rev. 5:9)

He is thus the one who addresses us in the gospel today. Rudolf Bultmann famously declared that Jesus Christ rose from the dead into the kerygma.[27] And there is definitely a sense in which he was right. There is no question that the Christ incarnated in flesh in Mary's womb now speaks to us through the words of the gospel—which he wears as the cloak through which he addresses us. This is surely Bultmann's central concern, and it is one that must be taken seriously. Contrary to Bultmann, however, one cannot collapse the resurrection of Jesus and his self-giving at Pentecost into the proclamation of the church. It is for this reason that we must also read with considerable ambivalence Bultmann's proposition that "belief in the resurrection and the faith that Christ Himself, yes God himself, speaks in the proclaimed word (2 Cor. 5:20) are identical."[28] The bodily resurrection and Christ's presence in the kerygma are indeed identical only in the sense that the same Christ is present in both. But they are not identical in the sense that the fundamental declaration of the incarnate Word through the bodily resurrection and self-impartation at Pentecost has no reality aside from the proclamation of the church.

---

27. Rudolf Bultmann, *Das Verhältnis der urchristlichen Christusgebotschaft der historischen Jesus* (Heidelberg: C. Winter, 1960), 27.

28. Rudolf Bultmann, *Theology of the New Testament*, trans. Kendrick Grobel (New York: Charles Scribner's Sons, 1951), 1:305.

The Word was made flesh as the Word's self-declaration. Christ is exalted to be the fitting means through which the living Word addresses us and makes us new. The Spirit will be given according to John only *once Jesus was glorified* (John 7:39). The Word made flesh that is destined to self-impart to creation by imparting the Spirit must first overcome our baptism in fire and fulfill his baptism in Spirit within *his own embodied existence*. The Word of the Father self-imparts only through the embodied mediation of his risen and exalted humanity, for the goal of that impartation is to be the liberation of creation by the Spirit. The original "proclamation" of God's self-giving love is thus the risen and ascended Christ of Pentecost. This is the Word that the Spirit first proclaims and that bears the theological weight of all future proclamation. The eternal Word is self-declared by the Spirit in Jesus's embodied life, a declaration that is decisively disclosed at his resurrection and Pentecostal self-impartation (Rom. 1:4; 1 Cor. 15:45). Christ will bear the cloak of the church's Scripture and proclamation, but only in witness to this self-declaration as the embodied icon of the Spirit, the embodiment of self-giving love for the redemption and renewal of the world. The proclamation of the church cannot take the place of this, cannot by itself bear this kind of theological weight.

The Spirit imparted from Christ as the Word of the Father thus grants us discernment to hear his voice in the proclamation or witness of the church. The Lamb's discerning eyes are the sevenfold Spirit that "God sent out into all the earth," a cryptic reference to Christ's self-impartation by imparting the Spirit at Pentecost (Rev. 5:6). There are various reasons that one is to see these seven eyes of the Lamb as the Spirit of God rather than, say, as seven angels. First, John is clear that no creature in heaven or on earth can look upon the scroll (5:3–4). Angels in the Apocalypse hardly qualify as an exception to this rule, for they are part of creation (cf. 22:8–9). If Christ is an exception due to his divine status, so also must be his eyes (the seven spirits) that behold the scroll. That the seven eyes of the Lamb can behold the scroll places them on the divine side of the divine-creature divide. The same is true of the worship of the Lamb. As the Lamb receives worship from the angelic hosts (in fact, from all creatures), his eyes are inseparable from him—on the receiving end of this praise. Note also that the seven spirits occupy the part of the triadic greeting in Revelation 1:4–5, where one would expect the *Holy Spirit* to be:

> John,
>
>   To the seven churches in the province of Asia:
>   Grace and peace to you from him who is, and who was, and who

is to come, and from the seven spirits before his throne, and from Jesus Christ, who is the faithful witness, the firstborn from the dead, and the ruler of the kings of the earth.

The number seven not only alludes to the churches addressed in the book but also to fullness or perfection. The seven spirits could thus be viewed as the Spirit in the fullness of the Spirit's discernment offered to the churches.

It is by the Spirit of discernment that the words of Jesus will be heard and appropriately lived: "Whoever has ears, let them hear what the Spirit says to the churches" (Rev. 2:29), "for it is the Spirit of prophecy that bears testimony to Jesus" (Rev. 19:10). Jesus Christ is the way, the truth, and the life (John 14:6). The truth of the church's proclamation is the truth of Christ incarnated, anointed, crucified, and risen to offer new life. The church lives from the Spirit of prophecy in testimony to Jesus and in praising him to the ultimate glory of the Father.

It is from the seed of the proclaimed word that the light of Christ dawns and grows in our lives: "We also have the prophetic message as something completely reliable, and you will do well to pay attention to it, as to a light shining in a dark place, until the day dawns and the morning star rises in your hearts" (2 Pet. 1:19). The light of Christ reflected by Scripture and the proclaimed word gets inside of us via the Spirit and transforms us into witnesses to Christ. "And we all, who with unveiled faces contemplate the Lord's glory, are being transformed into his image with ever-increasing glory" (2 Cor. 3:18). Believers will shine like the stars in their risen bodies, according to Daniel 12:3. The word of God causes that light to dawn in our hearts already, a foretaste through the down payment of the Spirit of the risen life yet to come, which will bring to us the fullness of Christ's sonship in relation to the Father. It is indeed from the seed of the word that the life of the Spirit in Christ sprouts and is continually guided: "For you have been born again, not of perishable seed, but of imperishable, through the living and enduring word of God" (1 Pet. 1:23). We are born anew in Christ by this word: "He chose to give us birth through the word of truth, that we might be a kind of first fruits of all he created" (James 1:18). The proclaimed word of God is the means by which Christ speaks to us and draws us to himself. It is the means by which he joins us to himself and through this to his cause in the world and to the path that he took toward fulfilling it. He baptizes us in the Spirit by means of this word and continues to fill us as we commit our lives to following it in his likeness.

The proclamation of the church was not historically left only to an orally transmitted tradition. We have the Old Testament Scripture, which grants us access to those texts through which the earliest Christians beheld Jesus. In the New Testament canon we have before us valuable access to the original narrative of Christ's sojourn on earth, to the ways he taught us or otherwise acted to redeem us. We have access to the original proclamation that was so vital to Christ's address to and through the church as it was birthed and spread in the world. The church now has an enduring and objective guide to the proclamation that occasions Christ's continued address to us as the people of God. The Christ who imparted the Spirit did so in a way that inspired precisely this scriptural medium that Christ would wear down through history to speak to us and through which the Spirit would grant us discernment of Christ's voice. The words of the prophets that are contained in Scripture are thus inspired in their continued witness: "Prophets, though human, spoke from God as they were carried along by the Holy Spirit" (2 Pet. 1:21).

The same may be said of the apostolic witness at the core of the New Testament (1 Cor. 2:13). By way of the Spirit, we catch a glimpse of what these New Testament witnesses heard in the Spirit when they wrote. We are bound to them and to their witness by the Spirit in Christ. Every time we gather around Scripture, we ask Christ to speak to us as he spoke to them when they wrote. This is what binds us to them and to their mission, and ultimately to the Christ who bound himself to us all. Paul explains that the Spirit is granted to us for the sake of discerning what we may call the benefits of Christ, to understand the riches of life freely given to us in him. For this reason the Spirit inspires the proclamation that we now know to be present in Scripture:

> What we have received is not the spirit of the world, but the Spirit who is from God, so that we may understand what God has freely given us. This is what we speak, not in words taught us by human wisdom but in words taught by the Spirit, explaining spiritual realities with Spirit-taught words. (1 Cor. 2:12–13)

The implication in all of this is that Scripture has primacy of place in Christ's address to the church and the granting of discernment in the Spirit. In fact, Scripture in the hands of the Spirit Baptizer and the Spirit he imparts is relevant for all times and places. As the Spirit Baptizer, Christ imparts to all flesh the eschatological Spirit of truth, which grants this scriptural witness vast global and far-reaching eschatological significance. That scriptural witness will thus not be fulfilled until heaven and earth pass away and the new creation arrives in Christ's image:

Do not think that I have come to abolish the Law or the Prophets;
I have not come to abolish them but to fulfill them. For truly I tell
you, until heaven and earth disappear, not the smallest letter, not the
least stroke of a pen, will by any means disappear from the Law until
everything is accomplished. (Matt. 5:17–18)

Note that Scripture cannot pass away until "everything is accomplished" or
fulfilled. Scripture has an eschatological reach in the direction of ultimate
fulfillment. The above text from Matthew is thus to be understood in the
light of the Great Commission, which concludes that Gospel. The disciples
are to make disciples of all nations in witness to the Lord Jesus Christ and in
fulfillment of the Scripture that is fulfilled in him. Christ will be with them
"to the very end of the age" toward the fulfillment of this scriptural witness:

Then Jesus came to them and said, "All authority in heaven and on
earth has been given to me. Therefore go and make disciples of all
nations, baptizing them in the name of the Father and of the Son
and of the Holy Spirit, and teaching them to obey everything I have
commanded you. And surely I am with you always, to the very end
of the age." (Matt. 28:18–20)

Christ is present with them in their journey toward the climax of the scriptural witness precisely as they proclaim the word and baptize those who
believe and are united to Christ by the Spirit of life.

Though the Spirit-baptized church of Christ has prophets, they do not
bear the same authority as Old Testament Scripture or the apostolic witness
that has its origin in the risen and exalted Christ. Paul thus corrects the
Corinthian prophets:

Or did the word of God originate with you? Or are you the only
people it has reached? If anyone thinks he is a prophet or otherwise
gifted by the Spirit, let him acknowledge that what I am writing to
you is the Lord's command. But if anyone ignores this, he will himself
be ignored. (1 Cor. 14:36–38)

First Corinthians 14:3 notes that the prophets are valuable in admonishing
and encouraging the people of God through their discernment in the Spirit.
All believers participate to some degree in prophetic gifts, in the discernment
of the Spirit (Rev. 2:29; 19:10). But the text quoted above (from the same

chapter in 1 Corinthians) makes it clear that their voice is not the same as the apostolic witness. The voice of the prophets in the churches is derivative and not original. Along with multiple other gifts from the Spirit, they are to be devoted to the primary witness that guided the reception of Christ by faith and continues to guide it down through history. In an obvious reference to the Spirit of truth, Paul says that Scripture is "God-breathed" in granting the wisdom that leads to faith in Christ and following in the way of Christ (2 Tim. 3:15–16). Timothy felt beleaguered in the ministry, so Paul encouraged him to lean on the witness of Scripture in his service to Christ, which would be useful for every aspect of his ministry as a leader.

The scriptural witness to Christ is not only to be understood, but also embodied, in the shared life of the Spirit-baptized community. We are living letters from Christ, "written not with ink but with the Spirit of the living God, not on tablets of stone but on tablets of human hearts" (2 Cor. 3:3). Christ writes his witness on our lives by the Spirit he imparts to us. The glory of the risen and ascended Lord that shines through the "old covenant" Scripture when it is read in faith ends up, through the Spirit, shining forth through our lives in relationship to one another (3:14–18). This glory is not some mystical aura but rather the glory of self-giving love. This glory now shines through lives liberated by the Spirit and lived in witness to Christ's self-giving at the cross and at Pentecost. "Where the Spirit of the Lord is, there is freedom" (3:17). The body of Christ is diversely contextualized and gifted to bear a colorfully diverse witness to the liberating life of Jesus. The self-giving Christ comes to us in the scriptural witness in a way that addresses and changes us, draws us into the way of his faithful witness by incorporating us into him and his body: "I have been crucified with Christ and I no longer live, but Christ lives in me. The life I now live in the body, I live by faith in the Son of God, who loved me and gave himself for me" (Gal. 2:20). Our shared life together in Christ is fashioned by the Spirit in Christ's image: *Christ is formed in us* (Gal. 4:19). Scripture inspired by the Spirit functions as the living witness to the church's conformity to Christ in all things.

The central place of Christ in the church's reading of Scripture must not be underestimated. As the Spirit Baptizer, Christ imparts the Spirit of truth that bears witness to him. Scripture has its core in Jesus, for the Hebrew Scripture looks forward to him, and the New Testament witness looks back to him and forward to him as the fulfillment, in memory, hope, and current communion with and in him. As I have observed above, Jesus claimed that the law and the prophets are fulfilled in him (Matt. 5:17). Christ says to his Father as he comes into the world, "It is written about me in the scroll" (Heb.

10:7). Indeed, Scripture grants wisdom unto salvation through faith in him (2 Tim. 3:15). He is the eternal Word of the Father made flesh (John 1:14), the one whose word comes to us in these last days to bring all things to fulfillment (Heb. 1:1). Christ is the Word heard in all inspired words.

In offering Christ to the readers, Scripture thus provides them with its own standard of interpretation. I speak here not only of hearing Christ speak to us in the words of Scripture but also to what the biblical narrative tells us of what he meant to history from the context of his historic mission. God was fully and decisively revealed precisely in that mission that was lived out from the incarnation to Pentecost. The church has indeed been commissioned to faithfully witness to the overall message of Scripture (its general sense) down through history; and it has at times done that admirably, but only when that witness to Scripture was faithful to the way of Christ. Christ is sufficient to guide the church's reading and embodiment of Scripture. Paul lived the crucified and risen life by living according to the Son, "who loved me and gave himself for me" (Gal. 2:20). The christological orientation of Scripture in the context of the self-giving of the triune God does not require a completion of its witness through a mediation imported from outside its pages. The leadership of the clergy and the guidance of the postbiblical tradition help us by pointing us to the Christ of Scripture as the hermeneutical key to the faithful interpretation of the whole of scriptural revelation. But any interpretation of Scripture that is not faithful to Christ is not faithful to the church either. Regarding the christological focus of Scripture, Heinrich Ott declares that "the word does not need mediation, insofar as it unlocks itself."[29] It does just that in its witness to Christ.

The proclamation of Scripture that is birthed and heard in the Spirit will thus bear witness centrally to Christ. Christ is the Lord of Scripture, for he imparts the Spirit to inspire Scripture and turn it into a witness to himself. Christ is thus the chief subject matter of Scripture, for he—and not Scripture—is essential or indispensable to God's self-disclosure. God was revealed in various ways and contexts through the voices of the prophets, but only Christ as the favored Son is "the radiance of God's glory and the exact representation of his being" (Heb. 1:3). Christ imparts the Spirit of truth by which all witnesses gain their relevance. All Scripture is to be interpreted in a way that is faithful to his liberating story as the Redeemer who imparts the Spirit of truth upon all flesh. Luther states this principle quite boldly:

29. Heinrich Ott, "Protestant Reflections on the Nature of the Church," in Evin Valyi Nagy and Heinrich Ott, *Church as Dialogue* (Philadelphia: Pilgrim Press, 1969), 78.

And the scriptures must be understood for Christ, not against him. Therefore a passage of scripture must relate to him or it cannot be regarded as true scripture. If, therefore, our adversaries should use scripture against Christ, we shall use Christ against the scripture.[30]

Luther uses such shocking rhetoric to make a point. For the biblical text to function as Holy Scripture, it will function by the power of the Spirit to bear authoritative witness to the eternal Word of the Father made flesh. The church must seek to interpret the text in harmony with that witness that was embodied among us in Christ's sojourn on earth to the cross and beyond.

Of course, Scripture joins with other core practices as the means by which the Spirit guides the church's discernment and faithful witness to Christ. But Scripture has pride of place. Kevin Vanhoozer has helpfully responded critically to the failure of postliberal theology adequately to account for the role of Scripture as the measure of the church's core practices. Vanhoozer uses a theatrical model to make the case for Scripture's privileged place among the core practices. As the written script governs a creative performance, so also the Holy Scripture's witness to Christ should govern the direction of the church's creative "performance," or the living witness to Christ in the world through various core practices (proclamation, sacrament, discipleship, mission, etc.).[31] But this is not to deny that Christ is present and discerned through all of the church's core practices. But Scripture, heard and lived in a way that is faithful to Christ, offers us the privileged voice of the Spirit in the churches for discerning Christ among us all.

Christ as High Priest

We cry out for God in the Spirit with sighs too deep for words (Rom. 8:26). We do so from the depth of human need for God. How do we know that we are not crying out into thin air? How do we know we are not abandoned and alone? We need to connect our cry to Christ's crying out to God from the cross, from the depth of hopelessness and abandonment (Mark 15:34). He bound himself to us—crying out, as our representative, to God. The fact that his heavenly Father heard him and did not abandon him offers hope

30. Quoted in Ott, "Protestant Reflections," 83.

31. Kevin Vanhoozer, *The Drama of Doctrine: A Canonical Linguistic Approach to Christian Doctrine* (Philadelphia: Westminster John Knox, 2005).

to us all. The fact is that the Father sent him there for that purpose, and the Spirit was poured out to draw us into the Son's crucified and risen life. This is the gospel.

Christ as our great high priest continues to function as our mediator to the Father, a mediation of which we are able by the Spirit to partake. We come first with the desire to glorify God and to petition for God's kingdom in our lives and in the world. The first petition thus joins us to the divine cause in the world. But we also pray for our own needs, for how can we comfort others if we have never known that comfort for ourselves (2 Cor. 1:4). Our petitions before the great high priest have as their ultimate goal our taking on Christ's image so that we may offer ourselves in the Spirit as living sacrifices for God and God's purposes in the world (Rom. 12:1).

Hebrews accents the "once and for all" nature of Christ's sacrifice on the cross. It is the Son of God and not mere animals that is sacrificed; he offers up by the Spirit a faithful and indestructible life to the Father on our behalf (Heb. 7:16; 9:14). He perfectly fulfills the Father's will on behalf of humanity. "And by that will, we have been made holy through the sacrifice of the body of Jesus Christ once for all" (10:10). As a result, "he has appeared once for all at the culmination of the ages to do away with sin by the sacrifice of himself" (9:26). Yet there is also a sense in the book of Hebrews in which Christ's sufficient mediation between God and humanity is continuous, not in the sense that Christ's act of self-sacrifice is repeated, but in the sense that his self-sacrifice is ongoing in its application and effects. Christ is throughout history the great high priest who empathizes with our weaknesses and trials and intercedes for us. Hebrews notes that Christ's intercession is not only all-sufficient to remove sin and reconcile us to God, but Christ's role as intercessor never ends. His faithfulness as the Son of the Father needs nothing to complete it, for it is a perfect sacrifice, setting aside the temple cult (10:5–14). The Father's intention was always that the faithful Son would come to "set aside" the sacrificial system so as to establish the new covenant whereby humanity is made holy through the sacrifice of Christ's embodied self-offering, given "once and for all." The Spirit showed "that the way into the Most Holy Place had not yet been disclosed as long as the first tabernacle was still functioning" (9:8). After fulfilling the Father's intention and in following the lead of the Spirit, Christ did away with the barriers of sin and death in order to make way for the Spirit and to open his life to others. Christ's ongoing intercession then flows from the sufficiency of his original act of self-giving.

Though Hebrews does not highlight Christ's outpouring of the Spirit in fulfillment of his role as the intercessor, the implication is there. Hebrews refers to those who leave Christ as those who "have tasted the heavenly gift, who have shared in the Holy Spirit, who have tasted the goodness of the word of God and the powers of the coming age" (6:4–5). Regardless of how one interprets this passage—and the falling away described in the next verse—the point remains that the gift of the Spirit can be viewed as the focus of the verse and thus of the life that Christ opens up to us as intercessor. In other words, Christ's role as intercessor involves the transformative work of the Spirit, a life awakened to Christ by the Spirit and reaching for God through Christ's intercession.

All of this provides Hebrews with the necessary background for understanding Christ's ongoing high-priestly ministry. Though Christ provided sanctification once and for all through his atonement as the bearer of the Spirit, we may be said to continually have access to him as an ongoing source of grace to help us in times of trial and need. He binds us to him by the Spirit. Thus, his exaltation does not remove him from us, for Christ remains empathetic with our needs and is faithful to help us through the trials of life. The Christ who learned faithfulness through suffering was "made perfect" so as to grant salvation to all (Heb. 5:9). He is now prepared as high priest to grant us grace as we follow in his path of learning faithfulness through our trials. He remains personally involved in people's lives: receiving petitions, sustaining, strengthening, and comforting by way of "grace" that he bestows on us (4:14–16).

Christ's high-priestly ministry has its basis in his embodied mediation of the Spirit. Through this embodied act of self-giving he became the sacrament of the new creation. The fact that Christ was divine *and* human explains how he was able to become the sacrament of the Spirit. Note what Schillebeeckx says: "Because the saving acts of the man Jesus are performed by a divine person, they have divine power to save, but because this divine power to save appears to us in visible form, the saving activity of Jesus is *sacramental*." For Schillebeeckx, Christ is the "primordial sacrament," "the only way to the actuality of redemption."[32] The fullness of grace belonging to Christ as the God-man "was intended by God to be a source of grace for others." The Spirit of life joins us to his exalted body so that we could enjoy communion with God and be shaped in Christ's image, thus participating in his mission in the world. The cross and the resurrection reveal the overcoming love of God for humanity. In the end, "Christ's love for man thus manifests God's love for men by actually be-

---

32. Schillebeeckx, *Christ the Sacrament*, 14–15 (italics in original); see also 26–27.

stowing it."[33] This is the meaning of Pentecost, the decisive culmination of Christ's messianic mission to extend God's transformative love to creation. Schillebeeckx concludes that the bestowal of the Spirit through the Son is "the climax of his work of salvation that links the ascension with the Parousia."[34]

The Spirit binds us to Christ not only through the proclamation of the gospel but also through signs of water baptism and the Lord's Supper, where Christ is committed to being present and active as the mediator of new life. Christ as the primordial sacrament of the Spirit is celebrated and proclaimed through the sacraments of baptism and the Lord's Supper. The church of the Apocalypse not only lives from the word of prophecy shared among all of its members, but they also wear the white robes washed clean that are indicative of baptismal gowns (Rev. 7:14), and they sup with the Lord at his invitation (Rev. 3:20). In Luke's Gospel, the two travelers on the road to Emmaus recognized the risen Christ in the breaking of the bread (Luke 24:30–32). This account is significant for signaling a church that would recognize Jesus as present in the ongoing breaking of the bread. After Pentecost, the church of Acts also engages in proclamation, water baptism, and the breaking of bread (Acts 2:38–44). The church did not create these practices; Christ gave them to the church. These are core practices that the church "bears" in Christ so as to "put on Christ" and to function as the dwelling place of the Spirit.[35]

The evangelical tradition can take note of the fact that John Calvin emphasized the importance of the sacraments in the church's life, even in one place noting an advantage to them over the proclaimed word: "The sacraments bring with them the clearest promises, and, when compared with the word, have this peculiarity that they represent promises to the life, as if painted in a picture." Calvin noted that, in the sacraments, "the Spirit performs what is promised."[36] One could say that, for Calvin, the Spirit's performance involves our performance in faith, which is important to the meaning of the sacrament. One should not denigrate the value of what the sacramental sign means to the church. Tom Driver points out that there is actually a deep human longing for ritual performance that exists at the very core of our life together. This fact tends to be overlooked in Western culture. Indeed, sacraments point to an

---

33. Schillebeeckx, *Christ the Sacrament*, 17.

34. Schillebeeckx, *Christ the Sacrament*, 21.

35. See Reinhard Hütter, *Suffering Divine Things: Theology as Church Practice* (Grand Rapids: Eerdmans, 1999).

36. John Calvin, *The Institutes of the Christian Religion*, 4.14.1, trans. Henry Beveridge, vol. 2 (Grand Rapids: Eerdmans, 1979).

"alternate world," and they nourish an "imaginative vision" of God's goal and cause for the world. This cause is the coming kingdom, where, nourished by the Spirit, we image Christ in loving and just communities to the glory of the Father. The Father's name is to be hallowed throughout the earth as it is now in heaven. We celebrate and affirm this vision in the Spirit as more real than the material world perceived with the empirical senses. This alternate world subverts the external world and calls us toward action to change it.

There is a special relationship between water baptism and the baptism in the Holy Spirit. "Repent and be baptized, every one of you, in the name of Jesus Christ for the forgiveness of your sins. And you will receive the gift of the Holy Spirit" (Acts 2:38). Christ's death was like a new Exodus to the Promised Land of the Spirit. In baptism, we ritualize our journey with him (buried and raised with him) into new life. The Christ, who received the Spirit after his baptism, then commissioned his disciples to engage in their mission among all nations, to disciple others, and to baptize them "in the name of the Father, the Son, and the Holy Spirit" (Matt. 28:19). The Pentecost event hovers in the background of this charge, for water baptism as practiced throughout the church's Spirit-empowered mission was also to bear the name of that very same Spirit that rested on Christ. We are baptized in the name of the Father, who sent the Son and promised the Spirit. We are baptized in the name of the Son, who was sent by the Father and who incorporates us into himself by baptizing us in the Spirit. We are baptized in the name of the Spirit, who bears witness to the Son and shapes us into the image of the Son so that we can hallow the Father's name—on earth as it is in heaven.

Jesus's baptism of repentance and hope was connected to his reception of the Spirit in that he would be led of the Spirit to take on our baptism in fire in order to overcome it in his baptism in the Spirit. We were careful not to make Christ's baptism the key element of the story of his reception of the Spirit; we resisted formalizing this experience in John's water rite. Yet a theological connection between the rite and the reception of the Spirit cannot be denied, since Jesus received the Spirit at the Jordan River under the sign of this water rite, just as Jesus was conceived by the Spirit in Mary's womb under the sign of the virginal conception. And so our own baptism in the Spirit (into Christ) occurs under the sign of our *water baptism*. The idea that Jesus's water baptism, connected as it was to his reception of the Spirit, was paradigmatic for Christian baptism has been held not only by theologians from sacramental traditions but also by some leading free-church theologians.[37]

---

37. See Geoffrey Wainwright, *Christian Initiation* (Philadelphia: John Knox, 1969), 50–51.

There is indeed a sense in which there is but one baptism—in water and Spirit (Eph. 4:5). In baptism we are buried with Christ in order to rise to newness of life (Rom. 6:1–5). This passage from death to life affirms the baptism in the Holy Spirit, whereby we join Christ in his passage through the fire of death to the sanctifying baptism in the Spirit that culminates at his resurrection and exaltation. Though this passage is fundamentally by faith in the gospel, one cannot reduce water baptism to an empty symbol. We are buried and raised in the Spirit with Christ "through baptism" (Rom. 6:4; Col. 2:12), implying a deeper relationship between baptism in water and Spirit, in which the spiritual passage is confirmed and deepened by the water rite. The Christ that we join in the passage from death to life poured out his life in communion with others at Pentecost. Likewise, we lay down our lives in faith and water baptism only to receive them back again as ecclesial personalities lived out in communion with others. We extend the hospitality of our fellowship to the world as Christ did. So we now live in newness of life, in service to righteousness (Rom. 6).[38]

The sign of water baptism provides the church with the ritual context in which Spirit baptism can be celebrated and confirmed throughout the churches both globally and historically, but also in a way that has far-reaching eschatological implications.[39] Indeed, in water baptism we ritually die and rise with Christ in a way that not only points to the basis of our baptism in the Spirit but ahead to its horizon, our resurrection from the dead, at which time our mortal existence will be "swallowed up by life" (2 Cor. 5:4). "For if we have been united with him in a death like his, we will certainly also be united with him in a resurrection like his" (Rom. 6:5). Water baptism is the sign of Christ's share in our death so that we can have a share in his life. He is the life-giving spirit (1 Cor. 15:45). The alternate world we inhabit through the water rite of baptism allows us to catch a glimpse of that day, currently staggering to the imagination, when "the earth will be filled with the knowledge of the glory of the Lord as the waters cover the sea" (Hab. 2:14). In baptism, we embrace not only our personal passage into such waters of life and hope, but we begin to yearn, pray, and work for the day when countless others can be submerged in the liberty and purity of life in the Spirit. In the

38. See my earlier discussion of this issue in Frank D. Macchia, *Baptized in the Spirit: A Global Pentecostal Theology* (Grand Rapids: Zondervan, 2006), 72–73.

39. I agree with Donald Gelpi: "The Christian encounters his God not simply by delving into his own human psyche but by acknowledging God's saving presence in the historical Christian community of which he is a member." Gelpi, *Pentecostalism: A Theological Viewpoint* (New York: Paulist Press, 1971), 145.

context of Scripture and our performance of the sacraments, we cultivate such a vision, such a life.

The Spirit Baptizer not only incorporates us into his life by faith and water baptism, he also invites us to dine with him in the breaking of the bread and the drinking of the cup. Christ offered up his body to be broken so that we could eat the bread as a sign of healing in him. And he drank the bitter cup of wrath or alienation so that in him we could drink from the cup as a sign of justification and communion. The meal is possible because of the Holy Spirit's incorporation of us into Christ, and the ongoing work of sanctifying, nourishing, and elevating us in union with him.

Christ's act of incorporating us into his body is thus the framework for connecting the sign of the sacred meal to the sign of water baptism: "For by one Spirit we were all baptized into one body, whether Jews or Greeks, whether slaves or free, and we were all made to drink of one Spirit" (1 Cor. 12:13). This reference to drinking together (in 1 Cor. 12) from one Spirit cannot be separated from what Paul says in 1 Corinthians 10 about how the Israelites ate spiritual food and drank spiritual drink from Christ, the rock in the desert (10:3–4), which Paul connects later in the chapter with the "cup of thanksgiving" that gives us a share in the blood of Christ and the "bread that we break" that gives us a share in Christ's body (10:16). Paul is even careful to note how the bread broken in many pieces symbolizes many members in Christ being nourished together from spiritual food (10:17). The drinking together from one Spirit among those who have been baptized in the Spirit and incorporated into Christ in 12:13 should also be viewed in the context of Paul's teachings about the Lord's Supper in 1 Corinthians 10 and 11. Just as we are incorporated into Christ by faith under the sign of water baptism, so are we diversely nourished, sanctified, and empowered by the Spirit in Christ under the sign of the sacred meal. Both water baptism and the Lord's Supper are rituals that occasion the blessings of life in the Spirit in union with the Spirit Baptizer.

This insight contributes to the growing awareness of the Spirit's role in the shared meal in the ecumenical movement. Michael Welker notes that the "ecumenical discourse in the last decades of the twentieth century on a world level has led to a growing awareness that the Lord's Supper is—among many of its other dimensions—an impressive mirror that allows for a nuanced appreciation of the working of the Holy Spirit."[40] Welker sees the Lord's Supper as the place where the Spirit's work is dramatically symbolized, affirmed, and

40. Michael Welker, "Holy Spirit and Holy Communion," *Word and World* 23, no. 2 (Spring 2003): 154.

received. He says specifically that the Lord's Supper reveals the fact that the "Holy Spirit keeps, saves, and elevates us, making us one while preserving essential and legitimate differences."[41] The Christ who made space in himself on the cross for many diverse members now invites them all to partake of him together in unity by the Spirit he imparts.

As I have noted earlier, Christ's Last Supper referred to his death as a covenant-making event that is to be signified among his followers through a shared meal. As the first Exodus led to the covenant of Sinai, so the new Exodus to the promised Spirit leads to the new covenant of Christ's self-sacrifice. Christ knew during the Last Supper that his followers would fall and be scattered at his death (Mark 14:27). But he also knew that they would sup with him again when God's reign would be fulfilled on the earth (14:24–25). In anticipation of that day, Christ brought this covenant community and meal into being at Pentecost by bestowing the Spirit onto all flesh and incorporating others into himself to drink of his Spirit. The Lord's Supper thus involves *epiclesis,* or invocation of the Spirit, for it is Christ as the source of spiritual life and communion who makes the sacred meal an occasion of communion with our Lord. Note how the Faith and Order paper entitled *Baptism, Eucharist, and Ministry* links the real presence of Christ in the meal with the work of the Spirit.

> Being assured by Jesus' promise in the words of institution that it will be answered, the Church prays to the Father for the gift of the Holy Spirit in order that the eucharistic event may be a reality: the real presence of the crucified and risen Christ giving his life for all humanity. (Eucharist II.C.14)

The *epiclesis* of the Spirit during the Lord's Supper is significant here, because this invocation points to the fact that the sacred meal comes into being at Pentecost as the ritual means by which Christ is now present to nourish us by the Spirit and to draw us into communion (1 Cor. 12:13). The meal is sanctified as the occasion in which we are further sanctified. The meal does not just signify Christ's presence; it also signifies our presence in him, seeking spiritual nourishment in faith and committed in the unity of fellowship to being an instrument of blessing to others.[42] John McKenna

---

41. Welker, "Holy Spirit and Holy Communion," 154.

42. John H. McKenna, "Eucharistic Epiclesis: Myopia or Microcosm," *Theological Studies* 36, no. 2 (June 1975): 268–78.

concludes rightly that the *epiclesis* "gives voice to the Spirit's role in the accomplishment of Christ's life-giving function in the Eucharist."[43]

As a pneumatological reality, Christ's presence experienced in the Lord's Supper is dynamic and inviting, a presence freely given as a constant source of new life. Karl Rahner's understanding of the Lord's Supper as a "sign" of the Lord's presence can help us conceptually grasp this point. Rahner did not regard sacramental efficacy as reducible to some kind of material causation that was explicable metaphysically. Rather, he understood sacramental efficacy in the context of a dynamic sign that occasions personal encounter. Rahner contrasts the sign value of the sacrament with a simplistic understanding of "sign" as an intellectual reference to some other reality. For Rahner, in the process of sacramental signification the reality signified becomes present or is experienced through the visible sign. The reality signified is actually present in the process of signification, in a way analogous to how we as "souls" are present as "bodies." Through sacramental signification, the eschatological presence of God is experienced among believers through the visible sign.[44] One is also reminded here of Tillich's view of the Lord's Supper as participating "in the power of what it symbolizes, and, therefore, it can be a medium of the Spirit."[45] The free presence of the Spirit brings us into communion with the Christ who has incorporated us into himself.

The Lord's Supper as an event in the Spirit has a transcendent point of reference, for it connects us to Christ's ongoing high priestly ministry at the throne of grace. *Baptism, Eucharist, and Ministry* appropriately makes this connection: "The eucharist is the sacrament of the unique sacrifice of Christ, who ever lives to make intercession for us" (Eucharist II.B.8). Of course, Christ's sacrifice on the cross for us is "once for all" (Heb. 9:26). But the Christ of Pentecost continues to nourish and sanctify us in the victory of that sacrifice. Baptized into Christ by the Spirit, we receive grace in time of need as we commune with our High Priest and intercessor (Heb. 4:14-16). He is the living sacrament of the Holy Spirit, the very Spirit by whom our groaning for the liberty of God's kingdom reaches Christ and through him the heavenly Father (Rom. 8:26). This connection to Christ's ongoing intercession raises the question as to whether in the meal Christ is present to us,

---

43. McKenna, "Eucharistic Epiclesis," 279.

44. See Karl Rahner, "The Theology of the Symbol," 221-52; "The Word and the Eucharist," 253-86; and "The Presence of Christ in the Sacrament of the Lord's Supper," 287-311, in Rahner, *Theological Investigations*, vol. 4 (New York: Seabury, 1982).

45. Tillich, *Systematic Theology*, 3:123.

or we are elevated to the place of Christ's reign and high-priestly ministry so as to be present to him. At the very least, one must say that the two are functionally one in the presence of the Spirit!

We should also add that *epiclesis* is connected to *anamnesis* (remembrance). Our remembrance in the Spirit connects our encounter with Christ in the meal to Christ's sojourn to the cross, to the place where Christ opened his life to us in all of our particularity and at the point of our greatest need. The Christ who is present to us in the meal was that Christ and still is. Indeed, Christ intercedes for us as the crucified Christ who bore our wounds so that we may be healed. We do not "remember" him in the meal as a mere mental exercise; but it is also a deep experience of his binding himself to us on the cross in love, at the point of our greatest hopelessness and desperation. Such remembrance is vital to our communion with Christ as our high priest: "Do this in remembrance of me" (1 Cor. 11:24). And while connecting in the meal to Christ's intercession for us, we are also reminded of his intercession for the world. So we dedicate ourselves as we participate in his broken body and spilled blood in communion to follow him and his path of self-sacrificial love. Lastly, the meal points ahead to the eschatological fulfillment of the kingdom of God on earth when the creation is renewed in order to become the dwelling place of God, and all are called to drink from the waters of life.[46] "Come! Let the one who is thirsty come; and let the one who wishes take the free gift of the water of life" (Rev. 22:17). The high-priestly ministry of the Spirit Baptizer who gives himself for the sake of the world can help us appreciate various accents that have historically been raised concerning the Lord's Supper.

Remembrance is inseparable from hope in our experience of Christ in the meal. His presence with us on the cross at the point of deepest hopelessness shows us that no matter how deep the pit is into which we descend, he is with us there. "If I make my bed in the depths, you are there" (Ps. 139:8). In a sense, the Spirit Baptizer takes us into himself throughout his life on earth, from the incarnation to the cross. In communion with Christ by the Spirit, he reminds us that he has taken us through the fire and into his love, and there remains nothing that can henceforth separate us from that love, no matter how dark. Our shared remembrance thus opens up future hope for the day when Christ will come again (1 Cor. 11:23–26). *Baptism, Eucharist, and Ministry* speaks of the *anamnesis* of the Lord in the Lord's Supper in this way:

---

46. See Geoffrey Wainwright, *Eucharist and Eschatology* (London: Epworth Press, 1971).

Christ himself with all that he has accomplished for us and for all creation (in his incarnation, servant-hood, ministry, teaching, suffering, sacrifice, resurrection, ascension and sending of the Spirit) is present in this *anamnesis*, granting us communion with himself. The eucharist is also the foretaste of his *parousia* and of the final kingdom. (Eucharist II.B.6)

Christ's ongoing ministry as high priest and primal sacrament of the Spirit allows us to speak of this sacred meal as opening up participation in Christ as the living Lord (1 Cor. 10:16). As participation in Christ as mediator of the Spirit, the Lord's Supper also involves a living participation in Christ's cause, or self-giving for the world, which is also the Father's and the Spirit's cause. Pentecost implies a reconciled and reconciling people. Look at another passage from *Baptism, Eucharist, and Ministry*:

In Christ we offer ourselves as a living and holy sacrifice in our daily lives (Rom. 12:1; I Pet. 2:5); this spiritual worship, acceptable to God, is nourished in the eucharist, in which we are sanctified and reconciled in love, in order to be servants of reconciliation in the world. (Eucharist II.B.10)

Communion and participation in Christ involves self-giving in relation to one another. The Lord's Supper is a meal of unity in which the large diversity of members are like pieces of that one loaf of bread that is Christ: "Because there is one loaf, we, who are many, are one body, for we all share the one loaf" (1 Cor. 10:17). The alternate world envisioned in the Lord's Supper is one in which the new humanity will never feel spiritually barren again but will be filled to overflowing by the waters of life (Rev. 22:17; John 4:13–14). Dressed in robes of righteousness, they will all dine with their Lord and elder brother with the joy and extravagance of a wedding celebration (Rev. 19:6–9). As we take the sacred meal, we commune with our Lord in remembrance, thanksgiving, and hope, reaching for that day of fulfillment and vowing to pray and work toward occasioning signs of it, not only among ourselves but also in a barren and hungry world.

The Christ Who Sends

When Christ appeared to his disciples, as told in the opening verses of Acts 1, he had just been raised from the dead, an end-time event. Jesus discussed the kingdom of God with them, also of final significance to history. He then told the disciples that they would be baptized in the Holy Spirit very soon, another end-time event. It would occur in the city of Jerusalem, the key location historically for the arrival of the end-time kingdom of God (Acts 1:1–5). John the Baptist's announcement was about to be fulfilled, and the disciples understood the eschatological significance of this entire moment. The new Exodus to the restoration of the people of God was about to be fulfilled. So their question to Jesus at this point was quite understandable: "Lord, are you at this time going to restore the kingdom to Israel?" (1:6). The baptism in the Spirit was to accomplish precisely this goal. The judgment would remove all of the sinful and destructive barriers to the fulfillment of God's kingdom on earth. Those who repented and hoped for the redemption of Israel would be swept up into the renewing power of the Spirit. Wasn't it time to restore the kingdom to Israel?

Jesus's answer to their question is telling. Not only was it not for them to know the times and seasons of history (Acts 1:7), but the great outpouring of the Spirit would not end the age—not right away. God's promise to Abraham to bless the nations had to be fulfilled *first*. Israel's renewal would be inseparably tied to that.

> May God be gracious to us and bless us
> > and make his face shine on us—
> so that your ways may be known on earth,
> > your salvation among all nations. (Ps. 67:1–2)

So the disciples were to wait for the Spirit, who would fall on them in order to make them living witnesses to Christ to the ends of the earth (Acts 1:8). Robert Jenson proposes that the Father delayed the Second Coming of Christ and the fulfillment of the kingdom in order to make room for the church and its mission: "When the Spirit descends eschatologically yet without raising all the dead and ending this age, the time for the church is opened."[47] This delay makes the mission of the church to the nations enormously important

---

47. Robert W. Jenson, *Systematic Theology*, vol. 2: *The Works of God* (New York: Oxford University Press, 1999), 2:172–73.

to the nature and purpose of the kingdom of God, the nature and purpose of the church! One could also say that, on Pentecost, Christ opened up the era of his own body on earth and his journey with them toward the fulfillment of their witness and their hallowing of the Father's name in history: "And surely I am with you always, to the very end of the age" (Matt. 28:20). The fact that the Spirit Baptizer delayed the conclusion of history for the sake of the church's mission—the mission of the triune God—makes that mission crucial to the church, to history itself.

As the one who imparts the Spirit, the risen Christ is granted authority over all people (John 17:2). After announcing that "all authority" had been given to him, Christ thus commissioned his disciples to make disciples of all nations, "baptizing them in the name of the Father and of the Son and of the Holy Spirit" (Matt. 28:19). Mission leads to the sign of baptism, for the faith in the risen Christ involves baptism in the Holy Spirit, incorpo-ration into Christ as the ongoing source of life (cf. 1 Cor. 12:13). Mission involves incorporation into an increasingly and expansively diverse body of Christ on earth. By commissioning the mission, Christ yields himself to the eschatological freedom and reach of the Spirit, to his own becoming an increasingly expansive and diverse existence in and beyond the world. The Christ of global mission is the multicontextual Christ "on the way" toward ultimate and final self-disclosure.

Christ came to seek and to save the lost (Luke 19:10). Can his body on earth do any less? As the Father sent the Son, so Christ sends the Spirit and, with the Spirit, the anointed people of God. Our identification with Christ involves our bearing the cross in self-sacrificial love for humanity and knowing in that love the power of Easter life (Gal. 2:20). It involves the recognition of ourselves as sent, as Jesus was sent by the Father. We bear the Spirit from Jesus for this purpose. As the prelude to breathing the Spirit upon the disciples, Jesus said, "Peace be with you! As the Father has sent me, I am sending you" (John 20:21). Christ is active at the forefront of the church's mission, for it is primarily his mission—and the mission of his Father and the Spirit. Later, Christ takes an active role by speaking to Peter about the Gentile mission. The Lord's voice tells Peter to eat ani-mals traditionally regarded as unclean. When Peter protests, the Lord tells him what should be obvious: "Do not call anything impure that God has made clean" (Acts: 10:15). This experience not only prepared Peter to bear witness in the home of the Gentile Cornelius; it also prepared him to bear important witness at the Jerusalem Council of the fact that God cleansed the Gentiles' hearts by faith when they received the Holy Spirit from the

Lord (15:9), just as the Jews had received the Spirit in Acts 2. Not only did Christ act throughout the expanding mission of the church through the Spirit, but he appeared and spoke dramatically to direct that mission at crucial points.

Christ also blocked Paul's path when he was hunting down those who fled from Palestine to Syria to escape persecution. Christ appeared to him and asked, "Saul, Saul, why do you persecute me?" (Acts 9:4). Christ self-identified that intimately with his church! Saul was literally blinded by the encounter, but Christ met him in that dramatic way to call him to do an about-face in his life so that Paul could serve the Christ he had persecuted by persecuting Christ's body, the church. Ironically, Paul would have much to suffer himself thereafter in furthering the mission of the church that he had caused to suffer so much. The one who has been blinded by the blazing light of Christ's appearance now had to share that light of Christ with others— that they may see. Christ then spoke to the prophet Ananias, asking him to minister to Paul in his time of need. He informed Ananias: "This man is my chosen instrument to proclaim my name to the Gentiles and their kings and to the people of Israel. I will show him how much he must suffer for my name" (Acts 9:15–16). Ananias called him "brother Saul" and laid his hands on him to pray for the very man who had been up to that moment the chief enemy of the church. Christ was directly involved at the cutting edge of the church's expanding mission as a reconciled and reconciling community of love, repentance, and redemptive justice.

One more example of Christ's involvement in the expanding global mission of the church may be found in the book of Revelation. Christ is the Lamb that takes the scroll containing the good news of God's victory over sin and death so that he can open its seal and reveal its content. Since the chief subject matter of the scroll is his death and resurrection, he alone is worthy to look on the scroll and to reveal its contents (Rev. 5:1–5). Later in the book, John takes this scroll and eats it. It is sweet to the taste but bitter to the stomach, for John must also suffer for the expanding mission of the church. He must join with the Lamb, who was crucified for the world, and he must be willing to suffer in bearing witness on the world's behalf. This is John's prophetic and missionary commissioning. He writes: "Then I was told, 'You must prophesy again about many peoples, nations, languages and kings'" (10:11). The Christ who "purchased for God persons from every tribe and language and people and nation" (5:9) then imparts the Spirit (the sevenfold Spirit) "into all the earth" (5:6). The purpose of this is for John and many others to bring the gospel to "many peoples, nations, languages and kings," so that they too may by the Spirit join themselves to Christ's expanding mission in the world.

Christ poured forth the Spirit on all flesh (Acts 2:17), which resulted in a missionary movement that was to encompass all of humanity, for he is not only the Lamb born from Israel but the Son of man, who is to be worshiped by "all nations and peoples" (Dan. 7:14; cf. Rev. 7:9–10). Israel is called to bear witness to the nations of the marvelous things that God has done (Ps. 9:11; 67:2; Isa. 12:4) or to glorify God in the midst of the nations (Ps. 18:49). The purpose of this witness is that the nations might bring God glory (Ps. 45:17). "May the nations be glad and sing for joy, for you rule the peoples with equity and guide the nations of the earth" (Ps. 67:4); "Be still, and know that I am God; I will be exalted among the nations, I will be exalted in the earth" (Ps. 46:10). Indeed, "may all kings bow down to him and all nations serve him" (Ps. 72:11), a hope that awaits future fulfillment (Ps. 86:9). All nations are meant to be blessed through this (Ps. 72:17). Israel will receive the Spirit so as to glorify God before the nations by keeping God's law (Ezek. 36:22–27). Also implied is that God will accomplish all of this through the arrival of an anointed servant. God will pour out the Spirit upon his servant, and he will bring justice to the nations (Isa. 42:1). Christ is indeed this servant; he will bear the Spirit so as to hallow the Father's name on earth as it is in heaven. He is the seed by which the nations will be blessed (Gal. 3:16). The mandate to witness to the nations is indeed handed down from the risen Christ to the church (Matt. 28:19), for the end will not come until this task is fulfilled (Matt. 24:14). The Spirit will come upon the people of God to empower their witness to Christ so that their witness will reach the ends of the earth (Acts 1:8).

In the mission of the church, the church should never fail to heed the direction of Christ's inaugural address, which showed a preferential option for the poor and the oppressed, those who suffer the most from the oppression of sin in the world. The Christ who bears the suffering of humanity is especially directed to them and is especially present in acts of mercy and justice on their behalf. These are the least among Christ's brothers and sisters, who, he reminds us, are to be especially favored, for the goodness shared on their behalf is shared with Christ: "Whatever you did for one of the least of these brothers and sisters of mine, you did for me" (Matt. 25:40). We speak not only of the poor and oppressed among the Christian communities of faith, but also of those to whom the good news goes out, for all humans live and move and have their being in God. Humans are to be viewed as God's offspring, having within the realm of God's created order a sibling relationship with the Word who created them and earmarked them for redemption and renewal in the Spirit of life (Acts 17:28).

The more deeply the church delves into Christ, the more deeply will its members extend themselves to those who are oppressed, and the more extensive their reach toward them is, the more deeply they encounter Christ. As the Christ of Pentecost, he is the Christ for others, as Bonhoeffer famously reminded us. The Christ is *himself* by constantly reaching out *beyond himself* in the love of the Father and the eschatological freedom of the Spirit. So we also become ourselves in Christ by reaching out beyond ourselves to bless others in the image of Christ and by the power of the Spirit.

The Coming Christ

Christ is yet to come, which is why we can only behold him through Scripture and the witness of others—as though we are looking at a dim mirror image (1 Cor. 13:12). Since we can only dimly see his glory, our own destiny in him is thus unclear to us. He has bound us to himself by the Spirit. Our destiny is now linked to his. We have in him, as the Spirit Baptizer, passed from death to life, but the richness of that life is not yet fully in our grasp. "For you died, and your life is now hidden with Christ in God" (Col. 3:3). We do not yet see who we are destined to be, because we do not yet fully see him. Indeed, "now we are children of God" but "what we will be has not yet been made known." Yet "we know that when Christ appears, we shall be like him, for we shall see him as he is" (1 John 3:2). In the Spirit, our lives are so inextricably tied to his that we will only be revealed in glory once he is revealed at his coming. And all of creation implicitly yearns for that revelation so that it too might be revealed in all of its God-intended glory as the temple of the Spirit in reflection of the glory of Christ. "For the creation waits in eager expectation for the children of God to be revealed" (Rom. 8:19).

Baptized in the Spirit, we do not yet drink from the Spirit's fullness; incorporated into Christ, we do not yet fully know his sonship nor his communion with his heavenly Father; being in Christ's image, we are not yet fully free to give of ourselves as he did. We are the children of God, and yet we continue to await our adoption as children, which Paul defines as "the redemption of our bodies" (Rom. 8:23). Our baptism in the Spirit has not yet reached its eschatological embodiment and liberty in the Spirit, and in the image of Christ. Our mortal existence has not yet been "swallowed up by life" (2 Cor. 5:4). How we yearn to behold the face of Christ, for we will only grasp our true destiny in the Spirit when we grasp his. "For now we see only a reflection as in a mirror; then we shall see face to face" (1 Cor. 13:12). He will at that time see his reflection in us, and we will then see who we were always meant to be in him, a diverse reflection of his image as vessels of his Spirit: the One in the diverse many and the diverse many in the One. This is the Christ as the Spirit Baptizer in eternal relationship to his body. This is the Christ of the *parousia* (future coming) as seen through the lens of Pentecost: the *parousia* of Christ is the fulfillment of Pentecost.

The coming of Christ is of cosmic significance. The event of Pentecost reaches for cosmic renewal. The reign of Christ established now once and for all is then to be fully revealed and actualized throughout creation. The theophany of Pentecost (tongues of fire, the sound of a mighty wind) implies a new creation motif. Christ has defeated sin and death and has taken his throne at the right hand of his Father, and God's Holy Spirit has arrived to begin renewing the creation in Christ's image. The end will come through cosmic upheaval and renewal, as symbolized through a theophany of blood, fire, and billows of smoke, as well as the sun turning dark and the moon turning to blood (Acts 2:19–20). Paul grants us a more richly theological picture of Christ's ultimate defeat of death and renewal of creation. If Christ was indeed raised by the Spirit, then so will humanity be raised by the same Spirit. Paul's assumption is that there is an *inseparable union* between redeemed humanity and Christ in the Spirit. For Paul, Christ is the one who bestowed the Spirit through his risen life so as to incorporate the new humanity into himself (1 Cor. 12:13). The result is that those who bear the Spirit in him share in his destiny. "And if the Spirit of him who raised Jesus from the dead is living in you, he who raised Christ from the dead will also give life to your mortal bodies because of his Spirit who lives in you" (Rom. 8:11).

That is Paul's logic in 1 Corinthians 15, which becomes clear in verses 22–26:

> For as in Adam all die, so in Christ all will be made alive. But each in turn: Christ, the firstfruits; then, when he comes, those who belong to him. Then the end will come, when he hands over the kingdom to God the Father after he has destroyed all dominion, authority and power. For he must reign until he has put all his enemies under his feet. The last enemy to be destroyed is death.

As Christ died and was raised by the Spirit in offering to the Father on our behalf, so the creation is brought from death to life in the end, and is offered to the Father in the image of the exalted Christ. This is the reign of Christ established at Pentecost and the outpouring of the Spirit fulfilled throughout the creation. Paul drives home the connection that he has assumed throughout the chapter on the resurrection. How can someone say that the dead are not raised, for "if there is no resurrection of the dead, then not even Christ has been raised" (1 Cor. 15:13). That consequence alone should be enough to make anyone among the Corinthian believers think twice. Who among believers can deny that Christ was raised? That denial would completely nullify the faith of the church (15:14)! But why does Paul assume that Christ's resurrection is so inextricably tied to ours? The answer is in the above text: just as we are bound to Adam in our death, so we are bound to Christ by the Holy Spirit in resurrection.[48] As all die in Adam, so all are made alive in the last Adam—"when he comes" (15:23). At that time Christ will offer up the creation that is renewed in his image to the heavenly Father. This was Christ's goal as Spirit Baptizer all along, namely, to join the creation to himself so that his self-giving to the Father's glory could by means of the Spirit include the sanctified creation. Pentecost has the *parousia* as its *telos,* and the *parousia* has Pentecost as its basis.

Why do we not reflect on Christ from the vantage point of the *parousia*? When it happens, we will! Until then, we are privileged to have the Christ of Pentecost, the narrative that leads up to it, and the horizon that it points us to in hope. Pentecost, our experience of Christ as the "life-giving spirit" (1 Cor. 15:45), grants us a guarantee and foretaste of that horizon. This foretaste is "Christ in us" by way of the Spirit. Paul wrote to his audience that Christ present in us as the guarantee of our future transformation in Christ's image is the core of the mystery of the Gospel: "God has chosen to make known among the Gentiles the glorious riches of this mystery, which is Christ in you, the hope of glory" (Col. 1:27). Christ dwells in our hearts by faith that we may be rooted and established in love and gain a foretaste in communion with God's people of its height, breadth, and depth (Eph. 3:17–18). Christ is "formed" in us (Gal. 4:19) that we may live for him as he has lived for us as our crucified and risen Savior (Gal. 2:20). Christ in us is thus not confined to the inner recesses of private piety. By indwelling us, Christ also incorporates us into himself, into his larger life for others: "If you remain in me and I in you, you will bear much fruit" (John 15:5). The

---

48. William Dykstra, "1 Corinthians 15:20–28: An Essential Part of Paul's Argument against Those Who Deny the Resurrection," *Calvin Theological Journal* 4, no. 2 (November 1969): 203–9.

Christ in us and we in Christ thrives necessarily as both an individual and a corporate experience. Driven by the Spirit of the crucified and risen Christ, this sharing of life grows deeper as it expands outward. It is ever expanding, enriching, and challenging. It overcomes barriers and opens up many different possibilities of compassionate and just reconciliation.

After Christ returns, our intimate union with him continues. He remains the temple in which we dwell by the Spirit. Notice this brilliant portrayal of Christ in the heavenly city at the end of time:

> I did not see a temple in the city, because the Lord God Almighty and the Lamb are its temple. The city does not need the sun or the moon to shine on it, for the glory of God gives it light, and the Lamb is its lamp. The nations will walk by its light, and the kings of the earth will bring their splendor into it. On no day will its gates ever be shut, for there will be no night there. The glory and honor of the nations will be brought into it. (Rev. 21:22–26)

Notice how Christ is the temple and its light, the heart of God's dwelling in the new creation and the source of our ongoing communion in and with God. John's blazing vision of the exalted Christ in the first chapter of the Apocalypse is brilliant—but not yet fully disclosed. This Christ stands among the lampstands, which are the churches, and addresses them with words of admonition and rebuke. But in the above text, Christ is the temple of the heavenly city containing the pure and holy people of God. The vision of the first chapter occurred in the midst of a world still dominated by sin and darkness, in the midst of nations still angry in their response to God. The flames of God's baptism in fire borne by Christ for the sake of the world were coming upon the world to stop the destruction and begin the renewal (11:18). But the Christ in the text quoted above welcomes the kings of the nations and incorporates their splendor into the light of his glory. There are indeed flames of judgment outside the gates of the end-time heavenly city, according to John (22:15), but the gates of the divine hospitality that characterizes the temple never close (21:25). Those who wash their robes may enter the gates of the city (22:14).

In reading the book of Revelation, we might wonder why the fire of judgment is still allowed to flood the earth near the end if Christ has already borne it for creation. Christ noted that a fire would be kindled on the earth, though he also noted that he must bear it for creation through the baptism of his death to provide a path to renewal (Luke 12:49–50). To some, the role

346

of Christ in imparting wrath (the "wrath of the Lamb") is most troubling (Rev. 6:16). This issue is made even more troubling by the way the Apocalypse uses "holy war" rhetoric when it speaks of Christ. Upon his return, people mourn (1:7), and those who oppose God's purposes will seek to hide themselves from his wrath (6:16). He comes on a conquering steed for war and judgment (19:11). He will strike down the nations and rule over them with an iron scepter (19:15). There is no question that Jesus is the victor here in a way that seems to cast an ominous shadow on those who oppose the truth and grace of God. How is this the Christ who bears humanity's baptism in fire in order to baptize all in the Spirit? He baptizes in the Spirit and fire. But what does this mean?

We need to make a few points here. First, the role of Christ as final judge is important to define in order to preserve the truth and justice of God's redemptive action on behalf of the world. It is true that, when Christ is exalted as judge in the book of Acts, his first act is to turn with grace to those who opposed him by bestowing the Spirit and granting in his words and very person the good news to be proclaimed. But the deceit and darkness that are held up in opposition to God's cause in the world must be exposed and overcome. As final judge, Christ is vital to the point that deception will not have the final word in history. When he comes, "he will bring to light what is hidden in darkness" (1 Cor. 4:5).

Second, the Apocalypse tells us in effect that even the worst imaginable flood of evil on the earth cannot overwhelm the renewing power that comes forth from the crucified and risen Christ. Christ's wrath in the world is thus *for the sake* of the world. He strikes out against evil, not for the sake of furthering the violence of the end time, but for the sake of putting an end to it ("destroying those who destroy the earth"; Rev. 11:18). Of course, he prefers their repentance and renewal. But he also wishes to save the earth from their destruction. The tribulation begins with the wrath of the nations against God, bringing war, famine, and death to the earth (6:1–8). When the innocents who are unjustly slain cry out for justice, Christ gets involved (6:9–10). He strikes out against the seats of power in order to put an end to the violence, and to bring justice and peace to the earth.

Third, though the Apocalypse uses holy war rhetoric to describe Christ's involvement in the end-time renewal, what he does is anything but using "war" as we understand that term. Notice that the sword that strikes down the nations is not a material sword. His followers do not form armies with material weapons to conquer the earth. They overcome by the blood of the Lamb (Rev. 12:11). The sword that strikes down the nations proceeds from the *mouth* of Christ: it is the word of truth. "Coming out of his mouth is a sharp sword with which to strike down the nations. He will rule them with an iron scepter" (19:15). And striking down the nations cannot mean *annihilating* them. If it were to mean that, how could he be said to rule over them? Striking down the nations means humbling them with the truth, removing them from power toward the goal of their humility and repentance. This is why they are found in Christ's reign of peace in the very next chapter (chap. 20) of Revelation. Christ must be the final judge, for grace must conquer by the truth of the Word of God made flesh. But God's will is that grace overflow all boundaries to draw all flesh into life. Mark Bredin suggests that the rhetoric of holy war is transformed in Revelation into a struggle for the ascendance of self-sacrificial love and truth over violent hate and deception. The result is a presentation of Jesus "as a non-violent, faithful witness whose message is for all nations."[49]

Fourth, in the pages of the Apocalypse the thousand-year reign of peace towers over the time of judgment in length of time. The time of trial lasts only three and a half years (seven by some estimates), while the time of peace is a thousand years! Even allowing for symbolism here, the clear impact of this difference conveys a sense of extravagance of the time of peace that overwhelms the time of wrath. Indeed, Christ reveals for all time that, where sin increases, grace increases all the more (Rom. 5:20). Such is the consistency with the extravagance and eschatological reach of the Spirit and of the Spirit Baptizer. The fire of judgment borne by Christ is overwhelmed by the baptism in the Spirit that he opens up to us in its place—indeed, that he opens up to the entire world. The messianic woes of judgment upon the earth are thus overwhelmed by the grace offered in the time of peace, for Jesus overcame the baptism in fire to baptize in the Spirit. In the Apocalypse there is a rainbow by the throne at the beginning of the prophecies, pointing to the Creator's covenant commitment to all living things (Rev. 4:3). The creation that is wounded by sin and death will rise again in the glorious image of Christ, in a state far higher than the depths of evil into which it was plunged. The Apocalypse concludes appropriately with this: "The Spirit and the bride say, 'Come!' And let the one who hears say, 'Come!' Let the one who is thirsty come; and let the one who wishes take the free gift of the water of life" (22:17). Christ never ceases to be the one through whom the fountain of the Spirit of life flows. The Spirit-baptized church seeks to work

---

49. Mark Bredin, *Jesus, Revolutionary of Peace: A Non-violent Christology in the Book of Revelation*, Paternoster Biblical Monographs (Waynesboro, GA: Paternoster, 2003), 215.

with others to overcome evil with good in the here and now in order to create signs of the final renewal in the here and now. The Apocalypse reminds us that the one who baptizes in the Spirit and fire causes the arc of history to bend toward justice and peace, no matter what.

Conclusion

As the last Adam, Christ is representatively baptized in the Holy Spirit and fire so that, as the divine Lord, he could impart the Spirit through the sacrament of his vindicated and exalted humanity. The exalted Christ of Pentecost incorporates creation into his life and the life of the triune God. He reveals the self-imparting and incorporating God and the indwelt and incorporated man. But he does so in a way that opens God to humanity in all of its diversity. The Christ of Pentecost is present in and among us, expansively so, throughout the increasingly diverse body incorporated into him through baptism in the Holy Spirit. As the Christ of Pentecost, he is indeed the multicontextual Christ "on the way" to final disclosure at the *parousia*. He reigns as the one who imparts new life. He is the Lord of life over his community of diversely gifted members. He is the Word that mediates the Spirit, and he speaks to us in Scripture, in proclamation, and in testimony—so as to bear the weight of proclamation. He mediates the Spirit as the sacrament at the core of all our sacramental practices. He also intercedes for us as the great high priest. He is the one sent from the Father to save the lost and liberate the oppressed as he leads in the missionary life of the church. He is coming again as the one who will be fully disclosed by the Spirit. His final self-disclosure discloses us in him. On the road to Pentecost, Christ offered himself up to the Father and to the Father's cause in creation. At the end, he offers himself again, but this time he is wearing the cloak of the renewed creation, anointed of the Spirit. Faith will be turned to sight, and our communion with him—and, in him, with one another—will have a directness that is currently unimaginable. Christ will be the final judge, for the grace of Christ must conquer in the service of divine truth. The abundance of grace in the Spirit he imparts will overwhelm the forces of sin and death in the direction of life. That is consistent with the work of the Spirit Baptizer. Where dehumanization and death abound, the work of the Spirit Baptizer abounds all the more! Our loyalty to the Spirit Baptizer will accept this truth as both a challenge and a comfort.

Bibliography

Anselm. *Cur Deus Homo*. In *St. Anselm: Basic Writings*. Translated by S. N. Deane. La Salle, IL: Open Court, 1968.

Apollinaris of Laodicea. *On the Union in Christ of the Body with the Godhead*. In *The Christological Controversy*. Translated and edited by Richard A. Norris Jr. Sources of Early Christian Thought. Philadelphia: Fortress, 1980.

Arius. *Arius' Letter to Alexander of Alexandria*. In *The Trinitarian Controversy*. Translated and edited by William C. Rusch. Philadelphia: Fortress, 1980.

———. *Arius' Letter to Eusebius of Nicomedia*. In *The Trinitarian Controversy*. Translated and edited by William C. Rusch. Philadelphia: Fortress, 1980.

Athanasius. *Four Discourses against the Arians*. Translated by John Henry Newman and Archibald Robertson. In Nicene and Post-Nicene Fathers, Second Series, vol. 4. Edited by Philip Schaff and Henry Wace. Buffalo, NY: Christian Literature Publishing, 1892.

———. *On the Incarnation*. Translated by Archibald Robertson. In *Christology of the Later Fathers*. Edited by Edward R. Hardy. Louisville: Westminster John Knox, 2006.

———. *Orations against the Arians*. In *The Christological Controversy*. Translated and edited by Richard A. Norris Jr. Sources of Early Christian Thought. Philadelphia: Fortress, 1980.

Augustine. *De Trinitate*. Translated by Edmund Hill. Hyde Park, NY: New City Press, 1991.

Aulen, Gustaf. *Christus Victor: An Historical Study of the Three Main Types of the Idea of Atonement*. New York: Macmillan, 1969.

Ayres, Lewis. *Nicaea and Its Legacy: An Approach to Fourth Century Trinitarian Theology*. New York: Oxford University Press, 2004.

Baillie, D. M. *God Was in Christ*. London: Faber and Faber, 1948.

Balthasar, Hans Urs von. *Mysterium Paschale*. Grand Rapids: Eerdmans, 1990.

Barnes, Michel Rene. *The Power of God: Dynamis in Gregory of Nyssa's Trinitarian Theology*. Washington, DC: Catholic University of America Press, 2016.

Barth, Karl. *Action in Waiting for the Kingdom of God*. Rifton, NY: Plough, 1969.

———. *Church Dogmatics*. I/1: *The Doctrine of the Word of God*. Translated by G. W. Bromiley. Edinburgh: T & T Clark, 1975.

————. *Church Dogmatics. I/2: The Doctrine of the Word of God.* Translated by G. W. Bromiley et al. Edinburgh: T & T Clark, 1978.

————. *Church Dogmatics. II/1: The Doctrine of God.* Translated by T. H. L. Parker et al. Edinburgh: T & T Clark, 1957.

————. *Church Dogmatics. II/2: The Doctrine of God.* Translated by G. W. Bromiley et al. Edinburgh: T & T Clark, 1978.

————. *Church Dogmatics. III/2: The Doctrine of Creation.* Translated by H. Knight et al. Edinburgh: T & T Clark, 1960.

————. *Church Dogmatics. IV/1: The Doctrine of Reconciliation.* Translated by G. W. Bromiley. Edinburgh: T & T Clark, 1956.

————. *Church Dogmatics. IV/2: The Doctrine of Reconciliation.* Translated by G. W. Bromiley. Edinburgh: T & T Clark, 1958.

————. *Church Dogmatics. IV/4: The Doctrine of Reconciliation.* Translated by G. W. Bromiley. Edinburgh: T & T Clark, 1969.

————. *Christ and Adam: Man and Humanity in Romans 5.* New York: Collier Books, 1957.

————. *Dogmatics in Outline.* London: SCM Press, 1955.

————. *Evangelical Theology: An Introduction.* Grand Rapids: Eerdmans, 1992.

————. "Rudolf Bultmann—An Attempt to Understand Him." In *Kerygma and Myth: A Theological Debate.* Edited by Hans-Werner Bartsch. London: SPCK, 1962.

Barth, Markus. *Acquittal by Resurrection.* New York: Holt, Reinhart, and Winston, 1964.

Beasley-Murray, G. R. "Jesus and the Spirit." In *Mélanges Bibliques.* Edited by A. Descamps and R. P. A. Halleaux. Gembloux: Duculot, 1970.

Becker, Joachim. *Messianic Expectation in the Old Testament.* Philadelphia: Fortress, 1980.

Bird, Michael F. *Are You the One Who Is to Come? The Historical Jesus and the Messianic Question.* Grand Rapids: Baker Academic, 2009.

Bonhoeffer, Dietrich. *Act and Being.* New York: Harper and Row, 1962.

————. *Christology.* London: Collins, 1978.

————. *Communion of Saints: A Dogmatic Inquiry into the Sociology of the Church.* New York: Harper and Row, 1963.

Boyarin, Daniel. *Border Lines: The Partition of Judeo-Christianity.* Philadelphia: University of Pennsylvania Press, 2006.

Bredin, Mark. *Jesus, Revolutionary of Peace: A Non-violent Christology in the Book of Revelation.* Paternoster Biblical Monographs. Waynesboro, GA: Paternoster, 2003.

Brown, Colin. "Ernst Lohmeyer's Kyrios Jesus." In *Where Christology Began: Essays on Philippians 2.* Edited by Ralph P. Martin and Brian J. Dodd. Louisville: Westminster John Knox, 1998.

————. "What Was John the Baptist Doing?" *Bulletin for Biblical Research* 7 (1997): 37–50.

Brown, Joan Carlson, and Rebecca Parker. "For God So Loved the World?" In *Christianity, Patriarchy, and Abuse: A Feminist Critique.* Edited by Joan Carlson Brown and Carol R. Bohn. New York: Pilgrim Press, 1989.

Brown, Raymond. *The Birth of the Messiah: A Commentary on the Infancy Narratives of Matthew and Luke.* New Haven, CT: Yale University Press, 1999.

————. *The Death of the Messiah: From Gethsemane to the Grave.* 2 vols. New Haven, CT: Anchor Bible Edition, 1994.

————. "Does the New Testament Call Jesus God?" *Theological Studies* 26 (1965): 545–73.

————. *The Gospel according to John XII–XXI.* Word Biblical Commentary 29a. New York: Doubleday, 1970.

————. *Jesus—God and Man.* New York: Macmillan, 1967.

————. "Three Quotations from John the Baptist in the Gospel of John." *The Catholic Biblical Quarterly* 22, no. 3 (July 1960): 292–98.

————. *The Virginal Conception and Bodily Resurrection of Jesus.* New York: Paulist Press, 1973.

Brueggemann, Walter. "Proclamation of Resurrection in the Old Testament." *Journal for Preachers* 9, no. 3 (January 1986): 2–9.

————. *Theology of the Old Testament: Testimony, Dispute, Advocacy.* Minneapolis: Fortress, 2005.

Bultmann, Rudolf. *Faith and Understanding.* Vol. 1. New York: Harper and Row, 1966.

————. *History and Eschatology.* Edinburgh: University Press, 1957.

————. *Jesus Christ and Mythology.* London: SCM Press, 2012.

————. "The New Testament and Mythology." In *Kerygma and Myth.* Edited by Hans-Werner Bartsch. New York: Harper and Row, 1961.

Calvin, John. *Institutes of the Christian Religion.* 2 vols. Translated by Henry Beveridge. Grand Rapids: Eerdmans, 1979.

Castelo, Daniel. *The Apathetic God: Exploring the Contemporary Relevance of Divine Impassibility.* Paternoster Theological Monographs. Eugene, OR: Wipf and Stock, 2009.

Chalamet, Christophe. "No Timelessness in God: On Differing Interpretations of Karl Barth's Theology of Eternity, Time and Election." *Zeitschrift für dialektische Theologie,* Supplement Series 4 (January 1, 2010): 21–37.

Chamblin, Knox. "John the Baptist and the Kingdom of God." *Tyndale House Bulletin* 13 (October 1963): 7–15.

Chan, Simon. "Mother Church: Towards a Pentecostal Ecclesiology." *Pneuma* 22, no. 1 (Fall 2000): 177–208.

Coakley, Sarah. "What Does Chalcedon Solve and What Does It Not? Some Reflections on the Status and Meaning of the Chalcedonian 'Definition.'" In *The Incarnation.* Edited by Stephen T. Davis et al. Oxford: Oxford University Press, 2002.

Cockerbill, Gareth Lee. "Structure and Interpretation in Hebrews 8:1–10:18: A Symphony in Three Movements." *Bulletin for Biblical Research* 11, no. 2 (2001): 179–201.

Coffey, David. "The Theandric Nature of Christ." *Theological Studies* 60 (1999): 405–31.

Cone, James H. *The Spirituals and the Blues.* Maryknoll, NY: Orbis Books, 1982.

Cooke, David. *The Distancing of God: The Ambiguity of Symbol in History and Theology.* Minneapolis: Fortress, 1990.

Crisp, Oliver. *God Incarnate: Explorations in Christology.* London: T & T Clark, 2009.

Cyril of Alexandria. *Commentary on John.* Vol. 1. Translated by P. E. Pusey. Oxford: James Packer and Co., 1874.

————. *Cyril's Letter to Eulogius.* In *Saint Cyril of Alexandria and the Christological Controversy.* Translated and edited by John McGuckin. Crestwood, NY: St. Vladimir's Seminary Press, 2004.

————. *Homily Given at Ephesus on St. John's Day, in the Church of St. John.* In *Saint Cyril of Alexandria and the Christological Controversy.* Translated by John McGuckin. Crestwood, NY: St. Vladimir's Seminary Press, 2004.

————. *Scolia on the Incarnation.* In *Saint Cyril of Alexandria and the Christological Controversy.* Translated by John McGuckin. Crestwood, NY: St. Vladimir's Seminary Press, 2004.

————. *Second Letter of Cyril to Succensus.* In *Saint Cyril of Alexandria and the Christological Controversy.* Translated by John McGuckin. Crestwood, NY: St. Vladimir's Seminary Press, 2004.

————. *The Third Letter of Cyril to Nestorius.* In *Saint Cyril of Alexandria and the Christological Controversy.* Translated by John McGuckin. Crestwood, NY: St. Vladimir's Seminary Press, 2004.

Dabney, Lyle. "The Justification by the Spirit: Soteriological Reflections." *International Journal of Systematic Theology* 3, no. 1 (March 2001): 46–68.

————. "Naming the Spirit: Towards a Pneumatology of the Cross." In *Starting with the Spirit.* Task of Theology 2. Edited by Stephen Pickard and Gordon Preece. Hindmarsh, AU: Australian Theological Forum, 2001.

Dantine, Wilhelm. *Justification of the Ungodly.* St. Louis: Concordia, 1968.

Davidson, Ivor J. "Pondering the Sinlessness of Jesus Christ: Moral Christologies and the Witness of Scripture." *International Journal of Systematic Theology* 10, no. 4 (October 2008): 372–98.

Del Colle, Ralph. *Christ and the Spirit: Spirit-Christology in Trinitarian Perspective.* New York: Oxford University Press, 1994.

————. "The Outpouring of the Holy Spirit: Implications for the Church and Ecumenism." In *The Holy Spirit, the Church, and Christian Unity: Proceedings of the Consultation Held at the Monastery at Bose, Italy, 14–20 October, 2002.* Edited by D. Donnelly, A. Denaux, and J. Famerée. Leuven: Leuven University Press, 2005.

Descartes, René. *Meditations on First Philosophy: With Selections from the Objections and Replies.* Translated by John Cottingham. Cambridge, UK: Cambridge University Press, 1986.

Dunn, James D. G. *Baptism in the Holy Spirit.* Studies in Biblical Theology, Second Series 15. London: SCM Press, 1970.

————. *Christianity in the Making.* Vol. 3: *Neither Jew nor Greek: A Contested Identity.* Grand Rapids: Eerdmans, 2015.

————. *Christology in the Making: A New Testament Inquiry into the Origins of the Doctrine of the Incarnation.* Grand Rapids: Eerdmans, 1996.

————. *Jesus and the Spirit: A Study of the Religious and Charismatic Experience of Jesus and the First Christians as Reflected in the New Testament.* Philadelphia: Westminster, 1975.

Dykstra, William. "1 Corinthians 15:20–28: An Essential Part of Paul's Argument against Those Who Deny the Resurrection." *Calvin Theological Journal* 4, no. 2 (November 1969): 195–211.

Ehrman, Bart. *How Jesus Became God: The Exaltation of a Jewish Preacher from Galilee.* New York: HarperOne, 2014.

Eusebius. *Eusebius of Caesarea's Letter to His Church concerning the Synod at Nicea*. In *The Trinitarian Controversy*. Translated and edited by William C. Rusch. Philadelphia: Fortress, 1980.

Evans, Craig A. "Jesus' Self-Designation 'The Son of Man' and the Recognition of His Divinity." In *Oxford Readings in Philosophical Theology*. Vol. 1: *Trinity, Incarnation, Atonement*. Edited by Michael Rea. New York: Oxford University Press, 2009.

————. "The Messiah in the Old and New Testaments: A Response." In *The Messiah in the Old and New Testaments*. Edited by Stanley E. Porter. Grand Rapids: Eerdmans, 2007.

Fairbairn, Douglas. *Grace and Christology in the Early Church*. Oxford Early Christian Studies. Oxford: Oxford University Press, 2003.

Feuerbach, Ludwig. *The Essence of Christianity*. 2nd edition. New York: Calvin Blanchard, 1855.

Franklin, Eric. "The Ascension and the Eschatology of Luke-Acts." *Scottish Journal of Theology* 23 (1970): 191–200.

Gathercole, Simon J. *The Pre-existent Son: Recovering the Christologies of Matthew, Mark, and Luke*. Grand Rapids: Eerdmans, 2006.

Gavrilyuk, Paul L. *The Suffering of the Impassible God: The Dialectics of Patristic Thought*. Oxford Early Christian Studies. New York: Oxford University Press, 2004.

Gelpi, Donald L. *Pentecostalism: A Theological Viewpoint*. New York: Paulist Press, 1971.

Gibson, David. *Reading the Decree: Exegesis, Election, and Christology in Calvin and Barth*. London: Bloomsbury/T & T Clark, 2012.

Gladd, Benjamen L. "The Last Adam as the 'Life-Giving Spirit' Revisited: A Possible Old Testament Background of One of Paul's Most Perplexing Phrases." *Westminster Theological Journal* 71 (September 2009): 297–309.

Gorman, Michael J. *The Death of the Messiah and the Birth of the New Covenant: A (Not So) New Model of the Atonement*. Eugene, OR: Cascade Books, 2004.

Gregory of Nazianzus. *Theological Orations*. Translated by Charles Gordon Brown and James Edward Swallow. In *Christology of the Later Fathers*. Edited by Edward R. Hardy. Louisville: Westminster John Knox, 2006.

Gunton, Colin. "The Spirit Moved over the Face of the Waters: The Holy Spirit and the Created Order." *International Journal of Systematic Theology* 4, no. 2 (July 2002): 190–204.

Habets, Myk. *The Anointed Son: A Trinitarian Spirit Christology*. Princeton Theological Monograph Series. Eugene, OR: Wipf and Stock, 2010.

Haenchen, Ernst. *The Acts of the Apostles: A Commentary*. Philadelphia: Westminster, 1971.

Hagner, Donald. *Matthew 1–13*. Word Biblical Commentary 33A. Dallas: Word, 1993.

Hanby, Michael. *Augustine and Modernity*. Radical Orthodoxy Series. Florence, KY: Routledge, 2003.

Hanson, R. P. C. *The Search for the Christian Doctrine of God: The Arian Controversy, 318–321*. Grand Rapids: Baker Academic, 1988.

Harrison, Everett. *Romans*. Expositor's Bible Commentary. Grand Rapids: Zondervan, 1976.

Hay, Andrew R. "The Heart of Wrath: Calvin, Barth, and Reformed Theories of Atonement." *Neue Zeitschrift für Systematische Theologie und Religionsphilosophie* 55, no. 3 (2013): 361–78.

Hengel, Martin. *The Atonement: The Origins of the Doctrine in the New Testament*. Translated by John Bowden. Philadelphia: Fortress, 1981.

Hick, John. *The Metaphor of God Incarnate: Christology in a Pluralistic Age*. Louisville: Westminster John Knox, 1993.

Hooker, Morna. *The Gospel according to St. Mark*. Black's NT Commentaries. Peabody, MA: Hendrickson, 1991.

Hurtado, Larry W. *Lord Jesus Christ: Devotion to Jesus in Earliest Christianity*. Grand Rapids: Eerdmans, 2003.

Hütter, Reinhard. *Bound to Be Free: Evangelical Catholic Engagements in Ecclesiology, Ethics, and Ecumenism*. Grand Rapids: Eerdmans, 2004.

———. *Suffering Divine Things: Theology as Church Practice*. Grand Rapids: Eerdmans, 1999.

Irenaeus. *Against Heresies*. In *The Apostolic Fathers: Justin Martyr and Irenaeus*. Ante-Nicene Fathers. Vol. 1. Edited by Alexander Roberts and James Donaldson. Translated by A. Cleveland Cox. Reprint: Peabody, MA: Hendrickson, 1994.

Jenson, Robert W. "Identity, Jesus, and Exegesis." In *Seeking the Identity of Jesus: A Pilgrimage*. Edited by Beverly Roberts Gaventa and Richard B. Hays. Grand Rapids: Eerdmans, 2006.

———. *Systematic Theology*. Vol. 1: *The Triune God*. New York: Oxford University Press, 1997.

———. *Systematic Theology*. Vol. 2: *The Works of God*. New York: Oxford University Press, 1999.

Johnson, Luke Timothy. *Living Jesus: Learning the Heart of the Gospel*. New York: HarperCollins, 1999.

Jüngel, Eberhard. *God's Being Is in Becoming: The Trinitarian Being of God in the Theology of Karl Barth*. Grand Rapids: Eerdmans, 2001.

Jungmann, Joseph A. *The Place of Christ in Liturgical Prayer*. 2nd edition. London: Geoffrey Chapman, 1989.

Kärkkäinen, Veli-Matti. *Christ and Reconciliation*. Vol. 1 of *A Constructive Christian Theology for the Pluralistic World*. Grand Rapids: Eerdmans, 2013.

———. *One with God: Salvation as Deification and Justification*. Collegeville, MN: Liturgical Press, 2004.

———. "Pentecostalism and the Claim for Apostolicity: An Essay in Ecumenical Ecclesiology." *Ecumenical Review of Theology* 25 (2001): 323–26.

———. *Trinity and Revelation*. Vol. 2 of *A Constructive Christian Theology for the Pluralistic World*. Grand Rapids: Eerdmans, 2014.

Käsemann, Ernst. *Perspectives on Paul*. Mifflintown, PA: Sigler Press, 1996.

Kasper, Walter. *Jesus the Christ*. Kent, UK: Burns and Oates, 1976.

Kay, James F. *Christus Praesens: A Reconsideration of Rudolf Bultmann's Christology*. Grand Rapids: Eerdmans, 1994.

Killgallen, John Jay. "A Rhetorical and Source-Traditions Study of Acts 2.33." *Biblica* (January 1996): 178–96.

Kitamori, Kazoh. *Theology of the Pain of God*. Eugene, OR: Wipf and Stock, 2005.

Kleinknecht, H. "B. The Logos in the Greek and Hellenistic World." *Theological Dictionary of the New Testament*, vol. 4. Edited by Gerhard Kittel. Grand Rapids: Eerdmans, 1967.

Kline, Meredith. "Primal Parousia." *Westminster Theological Journal* 40 (1978): 245–80.

Kloppenberg, John S. "Analysis of the Pre-Pauline Formula of 1 Corinthians 15:3b–5 in the Light of Some Recent Literature." *The Catholic Biblical Quarterly* 40, no. 3 (July 1978): 351–67.

Küng, Hans. *The Church*. New York: Sheed and Ward, 1967.

Ladd, George Eldon. *The Gospel of the Kingdom*. Grand Rapids: Eerdmans, 1959.

Lamm, Julia A. *The Living God: Schleiermacher's Appropriation of Spinoza*. University Park, PA: Pennsylvania State University Press, 1996.

Lienhard, Joseph T. *Contra Marcellum: Marcellus of Ancyra and Fourth Century Theology*. Washington, DC: Catholic University of America, 1999.

Lochman, Jan M. *Reconciliation and Liberation: Challenging a One-Dimensional View of Salvation*. Philadelphia: Fortress, 1980.

Longman, Tremper, III. "The Messiah: Explorations in the Law and the Writings." In *The Messiah in the Old and New Testaments*. Edited by Stanley E. Porter. Grand Rapids: Eerdmans, 2007.

Lossky, Vladimir. *The Mystical Theology of the Eastern Church*. Crestwood, NY: St. Vladimir's Seminary Press, 1976.

Luther, Martin. *Lectures on Galatians 1519*. In *Luther's Works*. Edited by Jaroslav Pelikan. St. Louis: Concordia, 1963.

Lyons, J. A. *The Cosmic Christ in Origen and Teilhard de Chardin: A Comparative Study*. Oxford Theological Monographs. Oxford: Oxford University Press, 1982.

Macchia, Frank D. *Baptized in the Spirit: A Global Pentecostal Theology*. Grand Rapids: Zondervan, 2006.

———. *Justified in the Spirit: Creation, Redemption, and the Triune God*. Grand Rapids: Eerdmans, 2010.

Mallia, Paul. "Baptized into Death and Life." *Worship* 39, no. 7 (August/September 1965): 425–30.

Mannermaa, Tuomo. *Christ Present in Faith: Luther's View of Justification*. Minneapolis: Augsburg/Fortress, 2005.

Marcus, Joel. "Rivers of Living Water from Jesus' Belly." *Journal of Biblical Literature* 117, no. 2 (Summer 1998): 328–30.

Marxsen, W. *Der Evangelist Markus*. Göttingen: Vandenhoeck and Ruprecht, 1956.

McCormack, Bruce. "Grace and Being: The Role of God's Gracious Election in Karl Barth's Theological Ontology." In *The Cambridge Companion to Karl Barth*. Edited by John Webster. Cambridge, UK: Cambridge University Press, 2000.

McDermott, Brian O. "Roman Catholic Christology: Two Recurrent Themes." *Theological Studies* 41, no. 2 (June 1980): 339–37.

McDonnell, Kilian. *The Baptism of Jesus in the Jordan*. Collegeville, MN: Liturgical Press, 1996.

McGuckin, J. A. "The Strategic Adaptation of Deification." In *Partakers of the Divine Na-*

ture: The History and Development of Deification in the Christian Traditions. Edited by Michael J. Christensen and Jeffrey A. Wittung. Grand Rapids: Baker Academic, 2006.

McKenna, John H. "Eucharistic Epiclesis: Myopia or Microcosm." *Theological Studies* 36, no. 2 (June 1975): 265–84.

Menzies, Glen. "Pre-Lukan Occurrences of the Phrase 'Tongues of Fire.'" *Pneuma* 22, no. 1 (Spring 2000): 27–60.

Meyendorff, John. *Christ in Eastern Christian Thought.* Washington, DC: Corpus Books, 1969.

Moltmann, Jürgen. "Die Rechtfertigung Gottes." *Stimmen der Zeit* 7 (July 2001): 435–42.

———. *The Spirit of Life: A Universal Affirmation.* Minneapolis: Fortress, 1992.

———. *The Trinity and the Kingdom.* New York: Harper and Row, 1981.

Morris, Thomas V. "The Metaphysics of God Incarnate." In *Oxford Readings in Philosophical Theology.* Vol. 1: *Trinity, Incarnation, Atonement.* Edited by Michael Rea. New York: Oxford University Press, 2009.

Nestorius. *Nestorius' First Sermon against the Theotokos.* In *The Christological Controversy.* Translated and edited by Richard A. Norris Jr. Sources of Early Christian Thought. Philadelphia: Fortress, 1980.

———. *Nestorius' Second Letter to Cyril.* In *The Christological Controversy.* Translated and edited by Richard A. Norris Jr. Sources of Early Christian Thought. Philadelphia: Fortress, 1980.

Niebuhr, Richard H. *The Kingdom of God in America.* New York: Harper and Row, 1937.

Nolland, John. *Luke 1–9:20.* Word Biblical Commentary 35A. Dallas: Word, 1989.

Norris, Richard A., Jr. "Introduction." In *The Christological Controversy.* Sources of Early Christian Thought. Philadelphia: Fortress, 1980.

Oglevie, Heather. "Entire Sanctification and the Atonement: A Wesleyan Demonstration." *Wesleyan Theological Journal* 50, no. 1 (Spring 2015): 38–52.

Olson, Roger. "The Self-Realization of God: Hegelian Elements in Pannenberg's Christology." *Perspectives in Religious Studies* 13, no. 3 (Fall 1986): 207–33.

Origen. *On First Principles.* In *The Christological Controversy.* Translated and edited by Richard A. Norris Jr. Sources of Early Christian Thought. Philadelphia: Fortress, 1980.

Ott, Heinrich. "Protestant Reflections on the Nature of the Church." In *Church as Dialogue.* Edited by Evin Valyi Nagy and Heinrich Ott. Philadelphia: Pilgrim Press, 1969.

Pannenberg, Wolfhart. *Jesus—God and Man.* Philadelphia: Westminster, 1978.

———. *Systematic Theology.* 3 vols. Grand Rapids: Eerdmans, 1991–98.

———. *Theology and the Kingdom of God.* Philadelphia: Westminster, 1969.

Pao, David W. *Acts and the Isaianic New Exodus.* Eugene, OR: Wipf and Stock, 2016.

Pelikan, Jaroslav. *The Emergence of the Catholic Tradition.* Vol. 1: *The Christian Tradition: A History of the Development of Doctrine.* Chicago: University of Chicago Press, 1971.

Pinnock, Clark. *Flame of Love: A Theology of the Holy Spirit.* Glen Ellyn, IL: InterVarsity, 1999.

Rahner, Karl. *Theological Investigations.* Vol. 4. Translated by Kevin Smyth. New York: Seabury, 1982.

Richardson, Alan. *An Introduction to the Theology of the New Testament.* New York: Harper and Row, 1958.

Ritschl, Dietrich. *Memory and Hope: An Inquiry Concerning the Presence of Christ.* New York: Macmillan, 1967.

Robertson, A. T., and Alfred Plummer. *A Critical and Exegetical Commentary on the First Epistle of St. Paul to the Corinthians.* Edited by Samuel Rolles Driver, Alfred Plummer, and Charles Augustus Briggs. International Critical Commentary. Edinburgh: T & T Clark, 1963.

Rogers, Eugene. *After the Spirit: A Constructive Pneumatology from Resources outside the West.* Grand Rapids: Eerdmans, 2005.

Sanchez, Leopoldo A. *Receiver, Bearer, and Giver of God's Spirit: Jesus' Life in the Spirit as a Lens for Theology and Life.* Eugene, OR: Pickwick, 2015.

Scheck, Thomas P. *Origen and the History of Justification: The Legacy of Origen's Commentary on Romans.* Notre Dame, IN: University of Notre Dame Press, 2008.

Schillebeeckx, Edward. *Christ the Sacrament of the Encounter with God.* Kansas City, MO: Sheed and Ward, 1963.

Schleiermacher, Friedrich. *The Christian Faith.* Philadelphia: Fortress, 1976.

Schweitzer, Albert. *The Quest of the Historical Jesus.* Minneapolis: Fortress, 2001.

Segundo, Juan Luis. *The Historical Jesus of the Synoptics.* Maryknoll, NY: Orbis Books, 1985.

Smeaton, George. *The Doctrine of the Holy Spirit.* London: Banner of Truth Trust, 1958.

Sobrino, Jon, SJ. *Christology at the Crossroads.* Maryknoll, NY: Orbis Books, 1978.

Soelle, Dorothée. *Christ the Representative: An Essay in Theology after the Death of God.* Philadelphia: Fortress, 1967.

———. *Political Theology.* Philadelphia: Fortress, 1974.

Staniloae, Dimitru. "Trinitarian Relations and the Life of the Church." In *Theology and the Church.* Crestwood, NY: St. Vladimir's Seminary Press, 1980.

Sumner, Darren O. "The Two-fold Life of the Word: Karl Barth's Critical Reception of the *Extra Calvinisticum.*" *International Journal of Systematic Theology* 15, no. 1 (January 2013): 42–57.

Thayer, J. H. *A Greek-English Lexicon of the New Testament.* New York: American Book Co., 1889.

Tillich, Paul. *Systematic Theology.* Vol. 2. Chicago: University of Chicago Press, 1957.

———. *Systematic Theology.* Vol. 3. Chicago: University of Chicago Press, 1976.

Torrance, Thomas F. *The Doctrine of Grace in the Apostolic Fathers.* Grand Rapids: Eerdmans, 1959.

———. *Incarnation: The Person and Life of Christ.* Downers Grove, IL: InterVarsity, 2008.

Twombly, Charles C. *Perichoresis and Personhood: God, Christ, and Salvation in John of Damascus.* Princeton Theological Monograph. Eugene, OR: Pickwick, 2015.

Vanhoozer, Kevin J. "The Atonement in Postmodernity: Guilt, Goats, and Gifts." In *The Glory of the Atonement: Biblical, Historical, and Practical Perspectives.* Edited by Charles E. Hill and Frank A. James III. Downers Grove, IL: InterVarsity, 2004.

———. *The Drama of Doctrine: A Canonical Linguistic Approach to Christian Doctrine.* Louisville: Westminster John Knox, 2005.

Vermes, Geza. *Jesus the Jew: A Historian's Reading of the Gospels*. Philadelphia: Fortress, 1981.

Volf, Miroslav. *After Our Likeness: The Church as the Image of the Trinity*. Grand Rapids: Eerdmans, 1997.

———. *Exclusion and Embrace: A Theological Exploration of Identity, Otherness, and Reconciliation*. Nashville: Abingdon, 1996.

Von Rad, Gerhard. *Theology of the Old Testament*. Vol. 1: *The Theology of Israel's Historical Traditions*. Translated by D. M. G. Stalker. New York: Harper and Row, 1962.

Wainwright, Geoffrey. *Christian Initiation*. Philadelphia: John Knox, 1969.

———. *Eucharist and Eschatology*. London: Epworth Press, 1971.

Weinandy, Thomas. *The Father's Spirit of Sonship: Reconceiving the Trinity*. Eugene, OR: Wipf and Stock, 2011.

Welker, Michael. *God the Revealed: Christology*. Grand Rapids: Eerdmans, 2013.

———. *God the Spirit*. Minneapolis: Fortress, 1994.

———. "Holy Spirit and Holy Communion." *Word and World* 23, no. 2 (Spring 2003): 154–59.

———. "The Holy Spirit." *Theology Today* 46, no. 1 (April 1989): 5–20.

Wheaton, Byron. "As It Is Written: Old Testament Foundations for Jesus' Expectation of Resurrection." *Westminster Theological Journal* 70 (2008): 245–53.

Williams, Rowan D. "Jesus Christ." In *Dictionary of Ecumenical Movements*. Edited by Nicholas Lossky et al. Grand Rapids: Eerdmans, 1992.

Witherington, Ben, III. "Rite and Rights for Women—Galatians 3:28." *New Testament Studies* 27, no. 5 (1981): 593–604.

Wright, N. T. *How God Became King: The Forgotten Story of the Gospels*. New York: HarperOne, 2016.

———. *Jesus and the Victory of God*. Vol. 2 of *Christian Origins and the Question of God*. Minneapolis: Fortress, 1997.

———. *The Resurrection of the Son of God*. Vol. 3 of *Christian Origins and the Question of God*. Minneapolis: Fortress, 2003.

Yong, Amos. *Beyond the Impasse: Toward a Pneumatological Theology of Religion*. Grand Rapids: Baker Academic, 2003.

———. *Hospitality of the Other: Pentecost, Christian Practices, and the Neighbor*. Maryknoll, NY: Orbis, 2008.

Ziesler, J. A. *The Meaning of Righteousness in Paul: A Linguistic and Theological Inquiry*. Cambridge, UK: Cambridge University Press, 1972.

Zimmerli, Walther. *Man and His Hope in the Old Testament*. Naperville, IL: Allenson, 1970.

Zinzendorf, Nicholas Ludwig, Count von. *Ein und Zwanzig Discurse über die Augsburgische Konfession: 1748, Der achte Discurs. Hauptschriften*, vol. 6. Hildesheim, 1963.

Zizioulas, John D. *Being as Communion*. Crestwood, NY: St. Vladimir's Seminary Press, 1997.

Index of Names

Abelard, 273
Alexander of Alexandria, 145
Anselm, 266–74
Apollinaris of Laodicea, 14, 171, 178–79
Arius, 13, 145–53
Athanasius, 77, 90, 93, 124, 135, 139–40,
    145–52
Augustine, 1–4, 28
Aulen, Gustaf, 267–68, 271–72
Ayres, Lewis, 73n6, 80n26, 81n29, 81n30

Baillie, D. M., 75–76
Balthasar, Hans Urs von, 34, 35, 229–30,
    247
Barnes, Michael Rene, 73
Barth, Karl: analogy of love, 86, 101;
    anhypostasis/enhypostasis, 180;
    atonement, 260–62; baptism in Spirit
    and fire, 194, 232–34; christological
    method, 12, 20, 37–39, 41, 45, 52,
    243; Christ's sinlessness, 169; divine
    freedom, 85, 131; election, 132–34; *extra
    calvinisticum*, 76–78; Jewish identity
    of Christ, 195, 198; paradox of grace,
    82–84; virginal conception, 61, 86, 131,
    159–64, 240
Beasley-Murray, G. R., 202
Bonhoeffer, Dietrich, 59, 66, 85, 165,
    179–80, 343
Bousset, Wilhelm, 35–36
Boyarin, Daniel, 80n24
Bredin, Mark, 348
Brown, Joan Carlson, 279

Brown, Raymond E., 18–19, 92, 135, 159,
    196, 306
Brueggemann, Walter, 268–70
Bultmann, Rudolf, 17–18, 45, 106–7, 119,
    295, 321

Cabasilas, Nicholas, 188
Calvin, John, 48–49, 261, 331
Chamblin, Knox, 193
Coakley, Sarah, 178n116, 179n120, 179n121
Coffey, David, 157n60, 181n128, 187
Cone, James H., 251
Crisp, Oliver, 161n69, 163–64
Cyril of Alexandria, 75, 92, 125, 150, 156,
    164, 174–79, 186

Dabney, Lyle, 156n59, 233n67
Dantine, Wilhelm, 47
Davidson, Ivor, 166, 168
Del Colle, Ralph, 39, 317
Descartes, René, 102–3
Driver, Tom, 331–32
Dunn, James D. G.: *Abba* prayer of
    Christ, 208–9; baptism in Spirit and
    fire, 18, 38, 184; deity of Christ, 89, 91;
    John the Baptist, 193–94; Logos doc-
    trine, 79, 96–97; Pentecost, historicity
    of, 304–8

Edwards, Jonathan, 274, 278
Ephrem the Syrian, 205
Eusebius of Caesarea, 152–53

360

Index of Subjects

Index of Scripture References